*Oxford Studies in Social History*
*General Editor: Keith Thomas*

# Sleepless Souls

# Sleepless Souls

*Suicide in Early Modern England*

MICHAEL MACDONALD
TERENCE R. MURPHY

CLARENDON PRESS · OXFORD

*Oxford University Press, Walton Street, Oxford* OX2 6DP

*Oxford New York Toronto*
*Delhi Bombay Calcutta Madras Karachi*
*Kuala Lumpur Singapore Hong Kong Tokyo*
*Nairobi Dar es Salaam Cape Town*
*Melbourne Auckland Madrid*
*and associated companies in*
*Berlin Ibadan*

*Oxford is a trade mark of Oxford University Press*

*Published in the United States by*
*Oxford University Press Inc., New York*



*First issued as paperback 1993*



*British Library Cataloguing in Publication Data*
*MacDonald, Michael, 1945–*
*Sleepless souls: suicide in early modern England—*
*(Oxford studies in social history).*
*1. Great Britain. Suicide, history*
*I. Title II. Murphy, Terence R.*
*362.28*

*ISBN 0–19–822919–4*
*ISBN 0–19–820450–7 (Pbk)*

*Library of Congress Cataloging in Publication Data*
*MacDonald, Michael, 1945–*
*Sleepless souls: suicide in early modern England/Michael*
*MacDonald, Terence R. Murphy*
*p. cm.—. (Oxford studies in social history)*
*Includes bibliographical references.*
*1. Suicide— England—History. 2. England—Social conditions.*
*I. Murphy, Terence R. II. Title. III. Series.*
*HV6548.G8F55 1990*
*362.2'8'0941—dc20*
*90.33323*

*ISBN 0–19–822919–4*
*ISBN 0–19–820450–7 (Pbk)*

1 3 5 7 9 10 8 6 4 2

*Printed in Great Britain*
*on acid-free paper by*
*The Alden Press, Oxford*

That for seven lusters I did never come
To do the rites to thy religious tomb,
That neither hair was cut or true tears shed
By me o'er thee as justments to the dead,
Forgive, forgive me, since I did not know
Whether thy bones had here their rest or no.

Robert Herrick, 'To the Reverend Shade of His Religious Father' (1648)

# PREFACE

THIS is a work of social and cultural history, and it has an argument, which is spelled out in the Introduction. It is comprehensive in the sense that it attempts to analyse suicide at all levels of society and from many different perspectives, but it is not intended as a definitive history of self-destruction in the early modern centuries. It focuses on the rise and fall of hostility to suicide and savage punishment of it in the centuries between 1500 and 1800. Many topics that are not germane to the central themes of the book have been ignored; many suicides, including some by notable figures, have not been mentioned. Some of the issues passed over here in silence are missing because little information survives about them in the records. We do not know much about how people who attempted suicide and failed were treated in Tudor and Stuart England, for instance, except that they were often given medical treatment and kept guarded by their families (for reasons which will be obvious in light of the penalties discussed in Chapter 1). Our own keenest regret in this regard, however, is that so few accounts have survived of the personal reactions of family members to suicides and of their feelings and experiences afterwards. A few vivid and moving testimonies, such as Robert Herrick's poem to his father, quoted as the epigraph to the book, still exist, but they are too few and too sparsely scattered over the centuries to serve as the basis for generalizations. We could find even fewer accounts of how survivors were subsequently treated by their neighbours.

We do not, of course, claim to have examined every possible source. The evidence about suicide in early modern England is vast in scope, and it is exceedingly diverse and dispersed in many archives, buried as small nuggets in mountains of words that have nothing to do with self-killing. That is the main reason why this book is a team effort. Originally we were both working on the history of suicide in the Tudor and Stuart period, and I had developed an interest in the eighteenth century as well.

In 1983, we decided to pool our research so that we could cover the whole period from 1500 to 1800. In that same year, Professor Murphy suffered a serious illness from which he has slowly recovered. Our initial plan to write separate drafts, covering the period up to 1660 and from 1660 to 1800, had therefore to be modified. The division of labour that we eventually worked out has been as follows. Professor Murphy searched the records of the central courts of King's Bench, the Palatinate of Lancaster, and High Court of Admiralty between 1485 and 1714 for suicide inquisitions and for suicides noted in the controlment rolls. I scoured local record offices and the records in the Public Record Office for inquisitions from the period 1660 to 1799. I also examined the other sources for the whole period and analysed the inquisition data that both of us had collected statistically. I wrote the text of the book, and Professor Murphy reviewed it, suggesting revisions which have been included in the final version.

Various parts of this book have appeared as articles elsewhere, although the arguments and evidence presented in them have been revised, rearranged, and greatly expanded here. For allowing me to reprint material in those which I wrote I am grateful to the editors of *Past and Present, Representations, Psychological Medicine*, the *Shakespeare Quarterly*, and the *Milbank Quarterly*. Professor Murphy acknowledges the permission of the *Sixteenth Century Journal* to use parts of his article on child suicide, and I thank Routledge for permitting me to republish large chunks of prose from my Introduction to their new edition of John Sym's *Lifes Preservative Against Self-Killing*.

In the course of my research and writing, I have been assisted by many institutions and people. The archivists who helped me to locate documents and permitted me to consult them deserve thanks first, for without them I could not have discovered much of the evidence I have used. I am especially grateful to the late N. H. MacMichael and the staff of the Westminister Abbey Library and Muniments Room, who not only made their vast collections of coroners' records available but also extended an enormous kindness to my family. They brightened my mother-in-law's last visit to England, at a time when the future seemed bleakest, by showing her parts of the Abbey that are seldom visited by tourists and giving her a unique view of the opening of parliament. She cherished the memory of that day for the remaining months of her life. Among the other archivists who were particularly helpful, I would like especially to single out the staffs of the record offices of Cumbria (Carlisle), Dorset, the Corporation of London, and Greater London.

The librarians and curators of manuscripts at the Guildhall Library, the Bodleian Library, and the British Library rivalled one another with knowledgeable assistance.

My research in these and other archives would have been impossible without generous financial support, and I am grateful to the National Endowment for the Humanities and the University of Wisconsin for funds to do research abroad in 1982–3. The Wellcome Unit for the History of Medicine at Oxford, then directed by Charles Webster, provided me and my wife with places to work and intellectual support during that year. A fellowship from the John Simon Guggenheim foundation and further support from the University of Wisconsin, and the American University enabled me to complete the statistical analysis of the inquisition data and begin writing in 1984–5. Thanks to this support, analysing the statistical data was not a solo effort. Julia Adams coded much of them, read them into the computer, and did the preliminary computer runs. She was ably assisted by Marie LaBerge. I was very fortunate that Ms Adams decided to take a break from sociology to work for me. A Romnes Fellowship from the Graduate School of the University of Wisconsin funded a return trip to do research in the Public Record Office in the summer of 1986 and enabled me to hire Genie Brown to do some essential counting and checking. Finally, after my move to the University of Michigan in 1988, the University and the History Department provided the computer, supplies, and postage that I needed to finish the book.

My friends, acquintances, and family have volunteered their help in various ways. Ian Archer, Thomas G. Barnes, Jonathan Barry, Robert Bucholz, Elizabeth Gilliam, David Harley, Cynthia Herrup, R. F. Hunnisett, Alexander Murray, Gary Owens, Margaret Pelling, and John Walsh all gave me references and advice. This does not exhaust the list: others who helped with specific points are mentioned in the notes. Alan Macfarlane has probably forgotten by now that he lent me over a hundred references to suicides when I first expressed interest in the subject as a raw graduate student in 1971. I can no longer remember which were his originally: they have become my own. We cultural historians call this sort of theft by amnesia appropriation; it is a kind of identification that is based on a strong admiration. For comments on papers previewing parts of the argument or drafts of chapters I am especially beholden to Steven Feierman, Alexander Murray, Lawrence Stone, Paul Seaver, Keith Thomas, Kirk Willis, and the members of Keith Thomas's seminar in early modern history at Oxford, who suffered through an inchoate attempt to explain what this book would be about and offered very helpful suggestions early in my research for it. Jonathan Barry and Blair Worden were particularly generous. Wallace T. MacCaffrey waded through a draft of the whole book and made helpful suggestions. The joy and encouragement that the Love Prize of the North American Conference on British Studies brought me was wonderful, and I am thankful to Paul Slack and to David Cressy and his committee for nominating and selecting an article that epitomizes the second part of this book for it. I am grateful as well to the critics of that article, especially Donna T. Andrew, whose objections forced me to rethink a number of points and investigate them and others in more depth. I made my disagreements with Professor Andrew plain in a response to her Comment on my article; here I wish to emphasize our points of agreement and how much I have profited from our exchange.

To the extent that I have learned how to respond positively to scholarly criticism, I have done so by following the example of Lawrence Stone, whose writings have provided models for me and whose enthusiasm has encouraged me to tackle large problems and propose bold solutions for them. Paul Seaver has read virtually everything that I have written, accepting with forbearance the role of mentor and supervisor that I shall not let him relinquish. Specialists in British history will recognize instantly that this book, like my last, takes as its starting-point issues that derive from Keith Thomas's great *Religion and the Decline of Magic*. Once more I owe much to his scholarship and his generosity. As the editor of this series, he read the entire manuscript and saved me from many foolish and careless errors. I also benefited greatly from the detailed and insightful comments of Oxford University Press's anonymous reviewer. Throughout the project, Martha Murphy has done everything in her power to ensure its completion. I am very grateful to her. Of all the people who have helped me, however, Carol Dickerman has been the most unstinting. She set aside her own work in African history to copy records with me as my time in England was running out in 1983, and she has helped me in many ways, large and small, since then. These debts I can perhaps partially repay; but there are others I shall never be able to discharge. She has endured my obsession with a lugubrious topic during a time we have had to assume a crushing domestic responsibility that sometimes blighted her personal triumphs, often disrupted our work, and frequently forced us to make considerable unplanned-for sacrifices, which I have seldom borne cheerfully. I wonder at her patience and am amazed each day by her love and my luck.

Were this my book alone, and I could dedicate it to anyone I chose, I would give it to her.

M.M.
*Ann Arbor, Michigan*

# CONTENTS

# LIST OF FIGURES

# LIST OF TABLES

# ABBREVIATIONS

| | |
|---|---|
| Adams, *Essay Concerning Self-Murther* | J. Adams, *An Essay Concerning Self-Murther* (London, 1700) |
| Anderson, *Suicide in England* | O. Anderson, *Suicide in Victorian and Edwardian England* (Oxford, 1987) |
| Bodl. | Bodleian Library, Oxford |
| BL | British Library, London |
| *Complete Peerage* | G. E. C[ockayne], *The Complete Peerage*, 13 vols. (London, 1910–59). |
| CRO | County Record Office |
| *CSPD* | *Calendar of State Papers, Domestic* |
| *DNB* | *Dictionary of National Biography* |
| HMC | Historical Manuscripts Commission |
| London Inquisitions | Corporation of London Record Office, Coroners' Inquisitions, 1785–1800 |
| MacDonald, *Mystical Bedlam* | M. MacDonald, *Mystical Bedlam: Madness, Anxiety and Healing in Seventeenth-Century England* (Cambridge, 1981) |
| Moore, *Full Inquiry into Suicide* | C. Moore, *A Full Inquiry into the Subject of Suicide*, 2 vols. (London, 1790) |
| Norwich Inquisitions | Norfolk and Norwich Record Office, Coroners' Inquisitions, 1669–1799 |

| | |
|---|---|
| PRO | Public Record Office |
| RO | Record Office |
| Sym, *Lifes Preservative* | J. Sym, *Lifes Preservative Against Self-Killing*, ed. M. MacDonald (1637; repr. London, 1988) |
| Thomas, *Religion and Magic* | K. Thomas, *Religion and the Decline of Magic* (New York, 1971) |
| Umfreville, *Lex coronatoria* | E. Umfreville, *Lex coronatoria; or, The Office and Duty of Coroners*. (1761; repr. Bristol, 1806) |
| Westminster Inquisitions | Westminster Abbey Library and Muniment Room, Coroners' Inquisitions, 1760–99 |
| Wymer, *Suicide and Despair* | R. Wymer, *Suicide and Despair in Jacobean Drama* (London, 1986) |

# *Introduction*

DEATH has a history. The ways people die have changed over the centuries; beliefs about death and burial customs have changed even more profoundly. Massive epidemics and periodic famines have disappeared from the western world; they have been replaced by the slaughter of world war and by genocide. Individuals seldom die in the prime of their lives, struck down by fevers and infections; most of us perish in old age, succumbing to diseases of the heart. That is why the killers that do not respect age, cancer and AIDS, are so terrifying. When mortality rates were very high, in the medieval and early modern period, death was accepted as a part of life—'Tame Death', Philippe Ariès called it. The dying tried to end their lives well, observing customary rituals; the survivors played their parts, too, as participants in the rites of dying and later in the rites of burial. Dying was an art. During the seventeenth and eighteenth centuries, less and less emphasis was placed on the hour of death. The art of dying became more dependent on the art of living, living as a good Christian. The notion that there were good and bad ways to die nevertheless survived and flourished; in the nineteenth century death was sentimentalized, particularly in Victorian England. Finally in the twentieth century, when mortality rates are lower than ever before, we have come to fear death, to put it out of our minds. We have forgotten how to die, and the dying have to struggle as best they can to invent death.[1] There are no handbooks any more. Funerals have become perfunctory, embarrassed gatherings; their rituals are malleable. Social critics mock attempts to elaborate them as tasteless. Mourning is a

[1] The literature on the history of death is huge and growing fast. Fundamental texts are P. Ariès, *Western Attitudes Toward Death From the Middle Ages to the Present*, trans. P. M. Ranum (Baltimore, 1974); id., *The Hour of Our Death*, trans. H. Weaver (New York, 1981); M. Vovelle, *La Mort en l'occident de 1300 à nos jours* (Paris, 1983); D. E. Stannard, *The Puritan Way of Death* (New York, 1977); J. McManners, *Death and the Enlightenment* (Oxford, 1981); R. Favre, *La Mort dans la littérature et la pensée françaises au siècle des lumières* (Lyons, 1978).

private, even secret business. Who would now wear black, proclaim his grief, maintain a liminal aloofness amid the business of living?

Suicide has always been a very special way of dying. It, too, has a history. In most places and in most eras of western history, suicide has been the very negation of the good death. But bad death has altered no less than good death. The methods by which people take their own lives have changed as more lethal and less painful instruments have been invented. As social, economic, and cultural changes have reshaped the circumstances of individual lives and our criteria for happiness and misery, the motives for suicide have changed as well. But the greatest changes have been in attitudes and responses to suicide, which have shifted strikingly from tolerance to severity and back again to tolerance over the last two thousand years. Ancient philosophies that condoned and in some circumstances celebrated suicide gave way in the Middle Ages to theological condemnations and folkloric abhorrence. The Reformation intensified religious hostility to self-murder in England and some other European countries. Finally, in the eighteenth century, Enlightenment philosophy and the secularization of the world-view of European élites prompted writers to depict suicide as the consequence of mental illness or of a rational choice, and these concepts still dominate discussions of self-destruction today. Responses to actual suicides have changed no less dramatically, although not simply because of these shifts in religious and philosophical fashion. Classical philosophy was tolerant toward suicide, but the law punished certain sorts of self-killing, even in ancient Rome. Secular and religious punishments grew more savage in the Middle Ages, but they were seldom enforced. The law was much more strictly applied in the early modern period in England and in some other countries as well. Finally, after 1700, the customs that disgraced suicides and penalized their families were gradually abandoned and repealed all over Europe.

The dramatic changes in attitudes and responses to suicide make it an historically interesting subject. It is also an important one, because those changes were the product of a complex interplay of broad historical forces. The study of suicide permits one to trace the trajectory of social and cultural change from a perspective that makes those forces visible. Describing them and tracing their origins in the political events, religious changes, social transformations, and intellectual developments of the early modern centuries is the main concern of this book. This approach is different from the one that has been favoured by most students of the history of suicide. They have either been content to trace its intellectual and legal history, or they have tried to reconstruct the suicide rate and to use it as an index of the health of the social organism, adopting the basic hypothesis and some of the methods of study that Emile Durkheim expounded in *Suicide* almost a century ago.[2]

Easily the most sophisticated example of historical Durkheimianism is Olive Anderson's magisterial *Suicide in Victorian and Edwardian England.* Anderson is a realist, aware of the faults implicit in official statistics on suicide but convinced that the faults are not so great as to invalidate them altogether. Analysing contemporary statistics with caution and sensitivity, Anderson is able to show that there were important regional, gender, and occupational differences in the suicide rate and that these altered over time. Her main achievement as a historical sociologist is the discovery that suicide had a different history for men and women in modern Britain. The suicide rate among young and old men gradually increased in the growing cities and towns; it decreased among young and old women. 'A complex network of changes in health, psychological environment and general prospects', she argues, made life easier for young and old women and harder for old men.[3] Anderson's study is, however, not merely statistical. She employs coroners' papers and a wide range of printed sources to recreate both what she calls the 'experience' of suicide and to trace changes and variations in attitudes and responses to suicidal death. Perhaps the most impressive aspect of this part of her book is her persuasive contention that 'Dying by suicide was . . . an experience deeply affected by its specific historical context'. The circumstances and precipitating causes of suicide differed in London from those in rural east Sussex, and they changed over time. Mid-Victorian Londoners died squalid, drunken, impulsive deaths; their rural counterparts took their lives to free themselves from pain or depression; Edwardian suicides were prompted by mental agony.[4]

This book is very different from Olive Anderson's. Most obviously, it is based far less on suicide statistics. Like other early modern legal records, coroners' inquisitions do not readily lend themselves to statisti-

[2] E. Durkheim, *Suicide: A Study in Sociology*, trans. J. A. Spaulding and G. Simpson (London, 1970).

[3] Anderson, *Suicide in England*, 418. Other recent, important statistical studies, which treat the early modern period, are M. Zell, 'Suicide in Pre-Industrial England', *Social History*, xi (1986), 303–17; S. J. Stevenson, 'The Rise of Suicide Verdicts in South-East England, 1530–1590: The Legal Process', *Continuity and Change*, ii (1987), 37–75; id., 'Social and Economic Contributions to the Pattern of "Suicide" in South-East England, 1530–1590', ibid. 225–62.

[4] Anderson, *Suicide in England*, 420.

cal generalization. Many records have been lost; others—including those from the most important jurisdiction of all, London—were never returned to the central courts and have vanished. Moreover, we were able to find few of the dramatic statistical variations among regions and groups or over time that Anderson identified. This is most likely to be due to the inadequacies of the records, rather than to the uniformity of suicide rates. It has, in any case, severely limited the conclusions that can be drawn from inquisition data.[5] A different kind of approach to the subject has therefore been necessary. We have largely rejected the Durkheimian fixation with the suicide rate in favour of focusing on the meaning of suicide. This is not in itself a novel departure. Sociologists opposed to the 'positivism' of Durkheim and his students have long insisted that official statistics are bogus because the classification of suicidal deaths is a complex social process that results in verdicts more dependent on the attitudes of officials and procedures that they use than on what really happened. They have called for the study of the 'social meanings' of suicide—how it is defined and identified, and how it is understood by suicides themselves, by their survivors, and by society at large.[6]

Much of this recent trend in the sociology of suicide has been grounded in European philosophical traditions that are hostile to empiricism. It is broadly consistent with similiar movements in anthropology and literary theory, which also stress the elusiveness of reality and emphasize the importance of decoding the meanings implicit in social actions and in texts. While we do not entirely endorse the rejection of statistics and of attempts to discover what 'really' causes suicides, we believe that treating suicide as a cultural phenomenon is the best course for the historian of early modern England. The documents that we use are the records of what people thought about suicide and how they reacted to suicidal deaths. The attitudes of the people who created them changed greatly over time. Any attempt to minimize or ignore the effect that those changes had on the classification of deaths—and hence of what we know about the rate of suicide—would be folly. On the other

[5] The problems that confront the historian using these data are discussed in Appendix 2.

[6] J. D. Douglas, *The Social Meanings of Suicide* (Princeton, 1967); H. Garfinkel, *Studies in Ethnomethodology* (Englewood Cliffs, NJ, 1967); J. M. Atkinson, *Discovering Suicide* (London, 1978); S. Taylor, *Durkheim and the Study of Suicide* (London, 1982). For more traditional sociological approaches, see S. Perlin (ed.), *A Handbook for the Study of Suicide* (New York, 1975); E. Stengel, *Suicide and Attempted Suicide*, rev. edn. (Harmondsworth, 1969); A. Giddens (ed.), *The Sociology of Suicide* (London, 1971).

hand, by making the meaning of suicide the central theme of the study, we can examine the records for what is actually in them—the beliefs of people who responded to suicides and the attitudes of different groups to suicide itself. Occasionally, as we shall see, it is possible to make inferences about what drove people to kill themselves and even about the thoughts and feelings of some men and women who took their own lives. Such inferences are possible only after one has grasped what contemporaries thought about suicide and how their beliefs changed. Historians are doomed to try to view the past through a veil of language, woven on a loom of convention. What we see of the events behind the veil will always be partial and uncertain. But if we focus our attention first on the production of meaning and how it changed, we shall be able to reduce the distorting effects of contemporary beliefs and conventions and to illuminate the process of cultural change as well.

The thesis that we argue below can be stated briefly. During the early modern period attitudes and responses to suicide first hardened and then grew more tolerant and sympathetic. The intensification of hostility to self-killing in the sixteenth and early seventeenth centuries was the result of the Tudor revolutions in government and religion—the rise of the modern state and the Protestant reformation. The decline in severity to suicide after 1660 had more complex causes. They included local hostility to the forfeiture of self-murderers' goods, the abolition of the prerogative courts during the English revolution, the governing élite's intensified reverence for private property, the reaction against religious enthusiasm, the rise of the new science, Enlightenment philosophy, the increase in literacy among the middling classes, the vast expansion of the periodical press, and the gradual absorption of empirical epistemology into the mentality of the upper and middle classes. Relatively straightforward as the rise and fall of hostility to suicide was, it was neither inevitable nor unopposed. The intensification of severity was largely the by-product of political and religious change. The spread of tolerance was the consequence more of the effects that the revolution had on legal institutions and local government and of broad cultural developments than any concerted campaign to reform the treatment of suicides. The rise of severity was opposed by some humanists and physicians; its decline was denounced by clerical conservatives, Methodists, and evangelicals. This complex interplay of opposing opinions and influences was characteristic of cultural change in early modern England. A highly stratified nation, the country grew increasingly diverse as the period progressed. It would be difficult indeed to discover any issue on which there was a nation-wide consensus among all classes.

The middle section of this book describes the declining severity to self-killing as the secularization of suicide. The word 'secularization' is liable to misunderstanding, and needs precise definition. We mean by it the rejection of belief in the frequent and potent intervention of the supernatural in the natural world.[7] English society was secularized in the late seventeenth and eighteenth centuries to the extent that its governing classes repudiated religious enthusiasm and refused institutional sanction to beliefs in magic, witchcraft, diabolical possession, healing miracles, and other related phenomena. We do not mean to imply that religion became unimportant in English society nor that suicide was no longer viewed as a sin after about 1700. But self-killing lost its supernatural character—at least in the eyes of the upper and middling classes—and that change was one aspect of a wider growth of scepticism about the supernatural. It would perhaps have been more exact to describe this process as the demystification or disenchantment of suicide. But both of these words have misleading connotations as well, and secularization is used in the sense we employ it here by other writers who discuss the decline of religious enthusiasm and of magic.[8]

Élites all over Europe rejected religious zeal and abandoned magical beliefs in the eighteenth century. And elsewhere as in England attitudes to suicide generally became more secularized and more tolerant. But the

[7] For a succinct and insightful critique of the way in which historians have used and misused the term, including objections to the way the present authors use it, see T. Kselman, 'Funeral Conflicts in Nineteenth-Century France', *Comparative Studies in Society and History*, xxx (1988), 238–31.

[8] In our discussion of 'secularization', we frequently resort to two other terms misused much more often than secularization: 'popular culture' and 'élite culture'. We understand popular culture in two senses: the first, equivalent to 'plebeian culture', connotes beliefs and practices that were mainly confined to the lower strata of society; the second, frequently used by historians but seldom clarified, connotes beliefs and practices that were common to *all* social strata. In this sense, the phrase distinguishes popular culture, in which the élite might participate, from learned subcultures, in which *only* the élite might participate. Thus witchcraft beliefs were a part of Tudor popular culture; humanism was not. Both senses of the phrase are useful in understanding different phenomena. We have not tried to make a pedantic distinction between them, always using 'plebeian' when we meant subaltern; we trust that the sense we intend will be plain in context. 'Élite culture' is not without its complications as well. We use it to indicate the values and beliefs of the governing classes and the educated élite—the gentry, the merchant grandees, and lay and ecclesiastical intellectuals: the group that was called polite society in the later 17th and 18th centuries. We are well aware of the crudity of these distinctions and the ways in which intellectual and social change altered their terms and the composition of the groups to whom they are applied between 1500 and 1800. We think that they are nevertheless valuable in understanding the broad sweep of change over the three centuries we examine.

pace of change varied greatly from country to country, region to region, and the fragmentary scholarship that now exists suggests that the dynamics of change were also quite various. In some places—France and Geneva, for example—legal officials took the lead in decriminalizing self-killing. In others—Zurich, for instance—enforcement of the law actually increased in the late seventeenth and eighteenth centuries, although the punishments it imposed grew less severe.[9] In England, as we shall see, it was men of middling status, serving as coroners' jurors, who took the first steps toward suspending the law of suicide and who were mainly responsible for the change. Before we finally understand the history of suicide in Europe we shall have to know much more about its history in each of the major cultures on the continent. That is one reason why this book focuses on England. Except for a few references we have even avoided using evidence from the rest of Britain. There is reason to believe that folk beliefs about self-murder may have been distinctive in Wales and Scotland and stronger than those in England. They certainly endured longer. Moreover, the Scottish authorities had a completely different system for prosecuting self-killing, about which nothing has been published.

One compensation for the geographical narrowness of this book is its very long temporal span. This is a study modelled on what the French would describe as the serial history of *mentalité*, a partially quantitative analysis of attitudes and behaviour in the *longue durée*.[10] The advantage of this very long perspective is that both large-scale changes and perdurable continuities are more easily identified than they would be in a briefer period. From a survey of several centuries in the history of suicide in England, one conclusion seems inescapable: that history is only comprehensible if one acknowledges that big events and profound changes occurred during the early modern period. Attitudes and responses to suicide were strongly influenced by all of the 'revolutions' of the centuries between 1500 and 1800—the Tudor revolutions in government and religion, the English Revolution of 1640–60 and the Revolution of 1688, the Enlightenment revolt against religious zeal, and the rise of the popular press, the last and most influential stage of the print revolution. To call all of these events revolutions is to choose a metaphor that emphasizes that they produced profound and far-reaching changes.

[9] A. Bayet, *Le Suicide et la morale* (Paris, 1922). L. Haeberli, 'Le Suicide à Genève au XVIIIe siècle', in *Pour une histoire qualitative* (Geneva, 1975); M. Schär, *Seelennöte der Untertanen: Selbstmord, Melancholie und Religion im Alten Zürich, 1500–1800* (Zurich, 1985).

[10] We have in mind, e.g., M. Vovelle, *Piété baroque et déchristianisation* (Paris, 1973).

This is an old-fashioned interpretation of English history. Revisionist historians, reacting against the teleology implicit in 'whig' history, have rightly attacked the insidious tendency to depict momentous events as inevitable. They have shown that the Protestant Reformation was neither inevitable nor widely welcomed, that the English Revolution was neither inevitable nor desired, and that the Enlightenment did not diminish greatly the role of religion in English life. But they have also minimized the importance of those events and ignored their profound and unintended consequences. The social historians who have joined their ranks have similarly overemphasized the virtual immobility of early modern society. It is true that the structure of some basic institutions and cultural values attached to them did not alter greatly among the mass of the people between the Black Death and the Industrial Revolution. The family is the most conspicuous example. We shall see that this accounts for enduring similarities in the motives to which many suicides were attributed. On the other hand, there were very significant changes in popular beliefs, in legal institutions, in the mode of communication, and in the economy that changed attitudes and responses to suicide radically.

It is one of the aims of this book, therefore, to advance what might be called light-heartedly a 'neotraditional' view of English cultural and social history, using the history of suicide as a case-study. It attempts to study suicide on all levels of historical analysis, and argues that changes on each of the levels of social life, from the village community to the whole country, were interrelated. The beliefs that individuals held about suicide and how they behaved when a suicide occurred both reflected broad cultural and social trends and also helped to alter those trends over time. We shall see that changes in ordinary people's view of suicide were not simply the consequence of shifting opinion among the educated élite. Nor were alterations in the treatment of suicide simply the consequence of decisions taken by legal and religious authorities. Change was generated both by pressure from below—from village communities and from the middling sort of men who sat on coroners' juries—as well as from above—from the courts and from the church.

The plan of the book is simple. The first two of its three parts are devoted to the rise and fall of severe attitudes to and punishments for suicide. Each of them comprises three chapters, the first of which traces the course of change in the way suicides were treated, the second of which describes the main currents of opinion about self-killing, and the third of which assesses views that dissented from the prevailing trends. The advantage of this rather arbitrary organizational plan is that it enables us to juxtapose and link evidence about behaviour (mostly drawn from coroners' inquisitions and papers) and attitudes (drawn from a very wide range of sources). It also captures some of the complexity of social change and cultural change. A key metaphor in this work —clichéd though it might be—is oceanographic. The tides of change in attitudes to suicide flowed first in one direction, toward greater severity, then gradually ebbed and flowed in the other, toward greater tolerance. In each era in this long tidal cycle, however, the main current of opinion was accompanied by an undertow of opposition and eddies of ambivalence. This image is far from perfect, but it does convey our conviction that attitudes are fluid and shifting, that they set up their own oppositions, and that while the direction of their main flow may be relatively obvious, establishing with precision their force, their timing, and their extent is much harder.

The first two parts of the book are thus a sort of story, with a coherent narrative pattern of rise and fall. The last part of the book, also comprising three chapters, looks at the history of suicide differently. It abandons the perspective of the historical oceanographer, charting the tides of change, and adopts instead the viewpoint of contemporaries, the men and women who encountered actual suicides, learned about them from the press or took their own lives. These chapters are concerned with how suicides were identified and how people understood them. They examine the institutions that distinguished suicide from other sorts of sudden death and the folk beliefs about the states of mind and social situations that drove people to take their own lives. They try, in so far as it is possible, to discover the folk psychology and folk sociology of suicide, and to show how beliefs about the motives for suicide were articulated to fundamental social institutions and to codes of conduct that were class- and gender-specific. This last part of the book also traces a significant change that occurred in the way that people learned about suicide, a movement away from ritual identification and condemnation and toward reading and writing. We argue that there was a transformation in the mode of communication in the seventeenth and eighteenth centuries.[11] Older, ritual kinds of communication based on the local community were gradually eclipsed by new forms of print media, notably newspapers and magazines, that spread news throughout the whole nation. We examine the style of printed reports of suicides in the

[11] We have borrowed the phrase 'mode of communication' from P. Burke, *The Historical Anthropology of Early Modern Italy* (Cambridge, 1987), although we use it in a more restricted sense.

eighteenth century and argue that they promoted the secularization of attitudes to suicide and taught potential suicides themselves conventions that they employed in suicide notes as they attempted to determine the meaning of their own deaths.

Finally, the book ends with some reflections on the patterns of continuity and change that we have discovered, and with a brief foray into the decades after 1800, when the law of suicide was at last reformed by stages. The Epilogue is intended both to restate the main features of our argument in terms that highlight its implications for the study of social and cultural change and to bridge the gap between the stopping-point we chose, 1800, and the starting-points of Anderson's book, which opens around 1850, and of the more recent work by Barbara Gates, which begins in 1822.[12] Because we hope that this book will make a contribution to early modern European history, and not merely to the history of suicide, we have tried to generalize our findings in terms that will be meaningful to historians interested in the interrelationship of social, cultural, and political change. In our attempt to integrate those domains of history—too often treated in isolation—we have followed the lead of David Sabean, whose brilliant *Power in the Blood* seems to us to be the most successful attempt so far to solve the problem.[13] But we have also ventured beyond Sabean's terms, raising issues that he does not stress, but which are particularly significant in terms of the historiography of early modern England.

The Envoi, with which the Epilogue ends, is frankly an afterthought, and our reflections on the early decades of the nineteenth century are highly provisional. They erect a hastily built and temporary span over a crucial period about which a great deal more needs to be learned. As historians trained in the Tudor and Stuart period, we were struck initially by the profound changes in attitudes and practices that occurred during the course of the eighteenth century. The trend toward leniency that we detected was mostly complete as a social phenomenon by 1800, and we found that we learned little that was new by studying inquisitions from the last decade or so of the eighteenth century. It was only after we began closely to examine the course of legal reform that we realized how many important problems were raised by the lag between the rise of

[12] B. T. Gates, *Victorian Suicide: Mad Crimes and Sad Histories* (Princeton, 1988). The research for this book and the first draft of its text had been completed when Anderson's book appeared late in 1987; it had been submitted for publication when Gates's monograph was published late in 1988.

[13] D. W. Sabean, *Power in the Blood: Popular Culture and Village Discourse in Early Modern Germany* (Cambridge, 1984).

lenient practices and the repeal of the penalties for self-murder. By then limitations of time and money made it unfeasible to do more than to work with the materials available to us in the United States, mostly parliamentary debates and readily available printed sources. We are sure that in future other researchers will replace our ramshackle work with a stronger edifice traversing the void between the end of the early modern period and the Victorian age.

# I

# THE ERA OF SEVERITY

The Divil he said did tempt him long,
  Any many times before,
For all he did resist him strong,
  He nere would give him ore,
Thus have you heard the doleful end,
  of *Gibbs*, which is too true.

Charles Hammond, 'The Devils
Cruelty to Mankind' (1663)

# 1

# *The Crime of Self-Murder*

SUICIDE was a terrible crime in Tudor and early Stuart England. Self-killing was a species of murder, a felony in criminal law and a desperate sin in the eyes of the church. 'For the heinousnesse thereof', observed Michael Dalton, 'it is an offence against God, against the king, and against Nature.'[1] Suicides were tried posthumously by a coroner's jury, and if they were convicted as self-murderers, they and their heirs were savagely punished. Their moveable goods, including tools, household items, money, debts owed to them, and even leases on the land that they had worked were forfeited to the crown or to the holder of a royal patent who possessed the right to such windfalls in a particular place. The suicide of an adult male could reduce his survivors to pauperism. Self-murderers were denied Christian burials; their bodies were interred profanely, with a macabre ceremony prescribed by popular custom. The night following the inquest, officials of the parish, the churchwardens and their helpers, carried the corpse to a crossroads and threw it naked into a pit. A wooden stake was hammered through the body, pinioning it in the grave, and the hole was filled in. No prayers for the dead were repeated; the minister did not attend. These rituals were occasionally modified or suspended, but some form of profane burial was routinely ordered in cases of self-murder.[2]

The state of mind of self-killers at the time that they committed their fatal deed was crucial. To be a self-murderer, to be judged guilty of felonious suicide, one had to be sane. Men and women who slew themselves when they were mad or otherwise mentally incompetent

[1] M. Dalton, *The Countrey Justice*, 3rd edn. (London, 1626), 234.

[2] For the fullest description of an inquest and burial, including a rare example of a coroner's order describing the rites of desecration, see T. R. Forbes, *Chronicle from Aldgate* (New Haven, 1971), 164–5; id., 'London Coroners' Inquests for 1590', *Journal of the History of Medicine and Allied Sciences*, xxviii (1973), 382.

were not convicted for their crime. Juries chose between two verdicts to distinguish the guilty from the innocent. A suicide whom they deemed sane was returned a *felo de se*, a felon of himself; one who was insane was proclaimed *non compos mentis*, not of sound mind. Edmund Wingate explained concisely that a guilty self-murderer had to have been capable of premeditating his crime: 'He is *felo de se* that doth destroy himself out of premeditated hatred against his own life.' Idiots and lunatics were spared both the secular and religious penalties.[3]

The law against self-murder was rigorously enforced in the sixteenth and early seventeenth centuries. Suicides were very seldom spared punishment for their crime. Over 95 per cent of the men and women who killed themselves between 1485 and 1660 were convicted as *felones de se*; fewer than 2 per cent were excused as persons *non compos mentis*.[4] The rigour with which the law against suicide was enforced in the sixteenth and early seventeenth centuries distinguishes this period from the centuries before and afterwards. Prior to about 1500, suicide was seldom punished; after about 1660, it was gradually secularized and decriminalized. In this chapter and the next we shall explore the reasons why attitudes and responses to self-killing grew harsher in the sixteenth and early seventeenth centuries. Our argument will be that the virtually universal condemnation of self-murder in this period was the product of an array of political, religious, and intellectual changes that were aspects of much broader transformations. Moreover, behind the apparent unity of response to suicide lay differences of outlook that varied between social classes. One of our aims is to capture something of the dynamic quality of cultural change. At each stage in the evolution of beliefs about suicide we shall therefore try to identify the historical forces and varying perspectives that produced the prevailing attitudes and practices and then led to their dissolution.

## SUICIDE IN THE MIDDLE AGES

The penalties for suicide used in England were very old by 1500. Their precedents had originated in the ancient world and evolved gradually

[3] E. Wingate, *Justice Revived: Being the Whole Office of a County Justice of the Peace* (London, 1661), 61, 88. For good brief descriptions of the law of suicide, see J. Cowell, *Institutiones juris anglicani ad methodum et seriem institutionum imperialum compositae et digestae* (London, 1605), 249; Dalton, *Countrey Justice*, 234–5; M. Hale, *Historia Placitorum Coronae: The History of Pleas of the Crown*, ed. S. Emlyn, new edn. (London, 1800), ii. 411–18; Moore, *Full Inquiry into Suicide*, ii. 305–22; J. Stephen, *A History of the Criminal Law of England* (London, 1883), iii. 104–5.

[4] PRO, KB 9, 10, 11, 140; PL 26; HCA 1.

into their early modern forms; similar laws and customs existed in many parts of Europe. Greek and Roman attitudes to suicide had been generally tolerant, although not so tolerant as is widely believed. Some philosophers condemned self-destruction as an act of desertion that defied the gods and deprived the state of a citizen. Pythagoras, in a simile that survived for more than a thousand years, compared suicides with soldiers who deserted their posts. Socrates agreed that men could not legitimately kill themselves without divine permission. Aristotle stressed that a man owed obligations to the state that he could not cancel by his own unilateral action. Stoic and Epicurean philosophers, on the other hand, taught that suicide could be justified. It was a legitimate way to end a life of unremitting pain and it might be an act of nobility, an expression of political or philosophical principle. These views gained their greatest currency in Rome. The deaths of Lucretia and Cato were honoured as blows against tyranny that marked the beginning and the end of the Republic, and the philosopher Seneca—the chief exponent of the nobility of suicide—killed himself on Nero's orders. Still, the combination of religious beliefs, philosophical scruples, and practical considerations led the ancients to punish some sorts of suicides by forfeiture of property, profane burial, or mutilation. Theban suicides were left unburied, and Athenians who killed themselves had the hand that took their lives struck off. Roman custom and law condemned all suicides who hanged themselves and others whose deaths were deemed criminal or harmful. Because of a powerful taboo against hanging, those who used that method to kill themselves were left unburied. Criminals, soldiers, and slaves were punished by forfeiture of their goods or the dishonourable disposal of their corpses. The suicides of these classes of men defied the obligations that they owed to the state or to their masters. Broad exemptions were allowed for those who took their lives out of *taedium vitae* or to escape a painful illness, rather than to shirk their duty.[5]

[5] The fullest discussion of suicide in the ancient world is R. Hirzel, 'Der Selbstmord', *Archiv für Religionwissenschaft*, xi (1908), 75–104, 243–84. Still useful, despite its age, is Moore, *Full Inquiry into Suicide*, i, chs. 3–7. Good brief surveys in English also include W. E. H. Lecky, *History of European Morals From Augustus to Charlemagne* (New York, 1869), i. 223–35, ii. 46–65; E. Westermarck, *The Origin and Development of the Moral Ideas*, 2nd edn. (London, 1926), ii. 246–51; H. R. Fedden, *Suicide: A Social and Historical Study* (New York, 1972), ch. 4. For discussions of Roman ideas and law, which differ on some key issues, see Y. Grisé, *Le Suicide dans la Rome antique* (Paris and Montreal, 1982), 247–81; M. Griffin, 'Philosophy, Cato, and Roman Suicide', *Greece and Rome*, xxxiii (1986), 64–77, 192–202; J. M. Rist, *Stoic Philosophy* (Cambridge, 1969), ch. 13; A. Vandenbossche, 'Recherches sur le suicide en droit romain', in *Mélanges Henri Grégoire, Annuaire de l'Institut de philologie et d'histoire orientales et slaves*, xii (Brussels, 1953), 470–516; J. -C. Genin, 'Réflexions sur l'originalité juridique de la répression du suicide en droit romain', *Melanges offerts au professeur Louis Faletti*, Annales de la Faculté de droit et des sciences économiques de Lyon (Paris, 1971), 233–93.

During the Middle Ages attitudes and responses to suicide gradually hardened. The generally permissive practices of classical Rome gave way in the fifth and sixth centuries to broader condemnations and punishments. St Augustine roundly denounced philosophical defences of self-destruction and even condemned the actions of Lucretia and Cato. He believed that Christians could only commit suicide legitimately when they were commanded by God to do so, as he maintained biblical self-killers such as Samson must have been.[6] The early councils of the church imposed rather mild sanctions for suicide, forbidding the usual rites of Christian burial and prayers for the dead.[7] Theological and legal severity increased in the high Middle Ages. St Thomas Aquinas extended Augustine's arguments against suicide, elaborating some of the Greek objections to it and adding the new claim that it was a violation of natural law.[8] Most western European governments promulgated laws requiring the forfeiture of some part of a suicide's property, and many regions adopted rituals for desecrating their corpses.[9]

The rituals for punishing suicide were born of demotic belief and custom. They all embodied the notion that suicide was abhorrent and polluting. They ostracized the self-killer symbolically from the community of the living and the dead. At Metz and Strasburg, for example, the corpses of self-murderers were placed in tuns and set adrift on a river, a physical recreation of the eternal wandering to which suicides' souls were widely supposed to be condemned. But there were very striking variations in ritual symbolism from place to place. In parts of France and Germany suicides were dragged on hurdles to a place of execution, where they were hanged in chains and left to rot. In medieval Zurich,

6 Augustine, *Concerning the City of God*, trans. H. Bettenson (Harmondsworth, 1972), 26–39.

7 The legislation is conveniently summarized in C. A. Kerin, *The Privation of Christian Burial: An Historical Synopsis and Commentary*, Catholic University of America Canon Law Studies, No. 136 (Washington, DC, 1941), 14–16, 18, 51–2.

8 T. Aquinas, *Summa Theologiae* (New York, 1975) xxxviii. 2a, 2ae, Q. 64, 5 (pp. 31–7).

9 At least two important studies of suicide in the Middle Ages are under way, a book by Alexander Murray and a doctoral dissertation by Abigail Freedman. In the mean time, see F. Bourquelot, 'Recherches sur les opinions et la législation en matière de mort volontaire pendant le moyen âge', *Bibliotheque de l'École des chartes*, iii (1841–2), 539–60, and iv (1842–3), 242–66; J. -C. Schmitt, 'Le Suicide au moyen âge', *Annales, E.S.C.*, xxxi (1976), 3–28; A. Bayet, *Le Suicide et la morale* (Paris, 1922). Bayet's insistence on the moderation of the church and the savagery of popular superstitions is overdone, but it certainly contains an element of truth. For the relationship between religion and folklore in the early Middle Ages, see J. Le Goff, *Time, Work and Culture in the Middle Ages*, trans. A. Goldhammer (Chicago, 1980), 153–8. J. Donne, *Biathanatos*, ed. M. Rudick and M. P. Battin (New York, 1982), and Moore, *Full Inquiry into Suicide*, i. 286–305, are still useful.

retributions were prescribed that were Dantesque, inverting symbolically the methods that suicides used to end their lives. Those who jumped to their deaths, for example, were interred beneath a mountain; those who drowned were buried in sand. Elsewhere, including England, suicides were buried in a highway, often at a crossroads, pinioned in their graves with a wooden stake. These local variations in ritual detail are striking and plainly meaningful. They were almost certainly the residue of regional differences in religious belief and practice that were pre-Christian or that had developed over the centuries out of the dialectic between folk culture and Christianity.[10] Moreover, although at some point in the late Middle Ages civil lawyers added to the *Corpus juris civilis* a gloss stipulating the use of the punishments practised in northern France, this does not seem to have resulted in any uniformity of practice prior to the sixteenth century.[11]

In England the Council of Hertford adopted a canon denying suicides normal funerals and burials in 672, and a canon traditionally attributed to King Edgar reiterated the prohibition and exempted madmen soon after the year 1000. The latter read in part: 'It is neither lawful to celebrate mass for one who, by any diabolical instigation hath voluntarily committed murder on himself, nor to commit his body to the ground with hymns and psalmody or any rites of honourable sepulture.'[12] After that, the English church was silent on the subject of suicide until 1662, when a rubric forbidding ministers to read the burial service over 'such as have laid violent hands upon themselves' was at last inserted in the Book of Common Prayer.[13] No ecclesiastical legislation

[10] Fedden, *Suicide*, 140; Bayet, *Le Suicide et la morale*, 441; J. Delumeau, *La Peur en occident (XIV$^e$–XVIII$^e$ siècles)* (Paris, 1978), 84–7.

[11] For references to this gloss, see W. Fulbeck, *A Parallel or Conference of the Civill Law, the Canon Law, and the Common Law of this Realme of England* (London, 1601), 89–90; J. Domat, *The Civil Law in Its Natural Order: Together with the Publick Law*, trans. W. Strahan (London, 1712), ii. 640. We owe a considerable debt to Richard M. Fraher, who kindly outlined for us the possible origins of this prohibition in a personal communication, 17 Mar. 1987.

[12] Moore, *Full Inquiry into Suicide*, i. 307–9, provides what is still the best history of early ecclesiastical legislation in England, although it is inaccurate in some of its details. The Council of Hertford's adoption of earlier prohibitions against normal funerals was implicit in its agreement to a compendium of earlier canons. Suicide was, however, discussed explicitly in Theodore's penitential, which was contemporaneous: A. W. Haddan and W. Stubbs (eds.), *Councils and Ecclesiastical Documents Relating to Great Britain and Ireland* (Oxford, 1871), iii. 197–8. For the Anglo-Saxon original of Edgar's canon and a Latin translation, see B. Thorpe (ed.), *Ancient Laws and Institutes of England* ([London], 1840), 406. This canon is no longer attributed to Edgar himself, and it has been redated; it is still generally referred to as 'Edgar's canon'.

[13] F. Procter and W. H. Frere, *A New History of the Book of Common Prayer* (London, 1902), 636.

—in England or elsewhere—stipulated the forms of burial to be used to punish self-murderers. The rites of desecration were genuine popular customs, accepted by the church and the state as an essential part of punishing suicide but not enjoined by either institution. Precisely when they came into use is mysterious. Edgar's canon excludes self-murderers from consecrated ground, but it was apparently unique in referring to their interment.[14] All of the other early sources merely forbade the normal Christian ceremonies. Perhaps the popular customs of burial were already more or less fixed by the end of the tenth century.

The rites of desecration expressed a profound conviction that self-murder was a supernaturally evil act. The same message was repeated by the clergy, more and more insistently as the Middle Ages progressed. Churchmen since the time of Theodore had attributed wilful suicide to the incitement of Satan. The penitential traditionally ascribed to Egbert, written in the middle of the eighth century, blamed self-murder on 'the instigation of the devil', a phrase that was repeated and elaborated throughout the Middle Ages.[15] It appears that there was a growing insistence on the sinfulness and diabolical causes of suicide. Early penitentials, such as Theodore's, carefully qualified their condemnation of self-killers. Provided that they had previously been pious, Theodore exempted from any penalty people who were 'vexed by the devil', so that they acted unwittingly. He thought that those who killed themselves out of desperation or fear should be left to the judgement of God. Only when people took their lives wilfully was it manifestly illicit to celebrate mass for them.[16] By the fourteenth century, however, theologians and didactic writers had developed a conventional religious psychology of suicide that stressed the sinfulness of the act, rather than the situations that mitigated it.[17]

Sermons, religious literature, and visual depictions of self-murder ascribed it to the sin of despair, the gravest temptation the devil inflicted on Christian souls. The fourteenth-century mystical reverie *The Cloud of Unknowing*, for example, warned believers against the temptation to

[14] Thorpe, *Ancient Laws and Institutes*, 406.

[15] Moore, *Full Inquiry into Suicide*, i. 307.

[16] Haddan and Stubbs, *Councils and Ecclesiastical Documents*, iii. 197–8.

[17] S. Snyder, 'The Left Hand of God: Despair in Medieval and Renaissance Tradition', *Studies in the Renaissance*, vii (1965), 18–59. Various aspects of the theology of suicide and its complex relationship with despair and *acedia* in medieval thought and art are illuminated by S. Wenzel, '"Acedia" 700–1200', *Traditio*, xxii (1966), 73–102; S. Wenzel, *the Sin of Sloth: Acedia in Medieval Thought and Literature* (Chapel Hill, 1967); A. Sachs, 'Religious Despair in Medieval Literature and Art', *Mediaeval Studies*, xxvi (1964), 231–56.

'unbe' that was the form of madness the devil inspired in gloomy minds.[18] Allegory enabled medieval artists and writers to integrate theology and psychology. Because of successive waves of iconoclasm during the Reformation and the English Revolution, few examples of visual representations of despair survive in England. In France and Italy the sin was often depicted as a suicide, sometimes together with a tempting demon. The most famous example is Giotto's *Desperatio* in the Arena Chapel at Padua.[19] Middle English religious literature, however, supplies many allegorical depictions of the temptation to self-murder. The Kentish poem *Ayenbite of Inwit*, for example, warned that the devil cast man into 'wan-hope' (despair) and 'therefore he porchaceth his dyath | and him-zelve | slayth'.[20] In *Piers Plowman* Avarice is saved from hanging himself by Repentance after he has fallen into despair.[21] These allegorical conventions were developed still more vividly in popular religious drama, where the instruments of suicide frequently served as the attributes of Despair. The crucial moment in the moralities is when the figure representing mankind despairs and is tempted to kill himself. A late example is John Skelton's *Magnyfycence*, whose central character is persuaded by Despair that his sins are so grievous that God will not forgive them. Echoing Magnificence's own words, wishing that he were dead, Despair urges him, 'ryd thy selfe rather than this lyfe for to lede'. Suddenly, Mischief appears and offers to Magnificence the instruments of self-murder: 'Lo, here is thy knyfe and a halter, and or were go ferther, | Spare not thy selfe, but boldly the[e] murder.' He chooses to stab himself and is only prevented from carrying out his resolution by Good Hope, who enters suddenly, crying to him not to slay himself 'agaynst Nature and Kynde'.[22]

The common law condemned suicide as self-murder by the time of Bracton, in the mid-thirteenth century. Bracton himself spelled out the concept of *felo de se* in his great treatise on the English law and twice reiterated the exemption for persons *non compos mentis*. But Bracton also

18 Snyder, 'Left Hand of God', 23.

19 Sachs, 'Religious Despair', 239–41; J. Stubblebine, *Giotto: The Arena Chapel Frescoes* (New York, 1969), pl. 57. The same picture programme shows Judas, a suicide, hanging in Hell: ibid., 186–7, pl. 76.

20 Quoted in Sachs, 'Religious Despair', 243–4.

21 William Langland, *Piers Plowman*, ed. G. Kane and E. T. Donaldson (London, 1960), B text, Passus v, ll. 279–95; Wymer, *Suicide and Despair*, 167, n. 3.

22 J. Skelton, *Magnyfycence*, in *Four Morality Plays*, ed. P. Happé (Harmondsworth, 1979), ll. 2284–2344. For discussions of this theme and other examples, see R. Potter, *The English Morality Play* (London, 1975). 47–8; Wymer, *Suicide and Despair*, 59.

insisted that when felons slew themselves to escape the consequences of their actions, their lands as well as their goods were forfeit, and he included sheer weariness with life among the mental defects that excused self-slaying.[23] Noting that Bracton is ambiguous about the application of the law of self-murder and its penalties, the pre-eminent authorities on the history of medieval English law, Sir Frederick Pollock and Frederic William Maitland, suggest that the *felo de se* verdict was used at first only to punish criminals, as it had been in Roman law, and that its scope was gradually broadened after Bracton's time to include ordinary suicides.[24] This hypothesis probably gets the trajectory of change right, for it parallels the general development of the law of suicide elsewhere in Europe, but its chronology seems wrong. The crown had already begun to punish self-murder itself, confiscating the goods of sane suicides, in the 1230s and 1240s.[25] Royal interest in *felo de se* deepened in the fourteenth century, when the crown realized that it could yield windfalls that were an attractive kind of patronage. Richard II gave part of the property of a number of suicides to courtiers, and like other medieval monarchs he also granted away the rights to the goods of felons of themselves to noblemen and lesser landlords.[26]

By the high Middle Ages, therefore, suicide was condemned by religion, folk belief, and the common law. The crown had a financial incentive to enforce the law of *felo de se*, and the church had begun to espouse a consistently harsh interpretation of suicide that reinforced popular religious beliefs. And yet juries very seldom returned verdicts of *felo de se* prior to 1500. This has prompted some historians to leap to the conclusion that suicide was very rare.[27] Village solidarity and

[23] H. de Bracton, *Bracton on the Laws and Customs of England*, ed. and trans. S. E. Thorne (Cambridge, Mass., 1968), ii. 323, 423–4. Bracton was, of course, the compiler and not the author of this book, although it is customary to write as if he were.

[24] F. Pollock and F. W. Maitland, *The History of the English Law Before the Time of Edward I*, 2nd edn. (Cambridge, 1968), ii. 488; A. Harding, *A Social History of English Law* (Harmondsworth, 1966), 64.

[25] C. F. A. Meekings and D. Crook (eds.), *The 1235 Surrey Eyre*, Surrey Record Society, 32–3 (Guildford, 1979–83), i. 109–10, ii. 387; H. M. Chew and M. Weinbaum (eds.), *The London Eyre of 1244*, London Record Society, vi (London, 1970), 16, 49, 55; M. T. Clanchy (ed.), *Civil Pleas of the Wiltshire Eyre, 1249*, Wiltshire Records Society, xxvi, 1970 (Devizes, 1971), no. 183; R. F. Hunnisett, *The Medieval Coroner* (Cambridge, 1961), 30 n. 4.

[26] *Calendar of the Patent Rolls, 1381–1385*, 339; *CPR, 1391–1396*, 239, 266; *CPR, 1396–1399*, 184, 291, 326, 459. We have been unable to tell from the calendared rolls precisely when this practice began. We would hesitate to attribute it to Richard.

[27] See, for example, P. E. H. Hair, 'A Note on the Incidence of Tudor Suicide', *Local Population Studies*, no. 5 (1970), 36–43; id., 'Deaths from Violence in Britain: A Tentative Secular Survey', *Population Studies*, xxv (1971), 5–24.

Catholic doctrine have both been credited with the allegedly low rate of self-destruction. Although the possibility that suicide was indeed much less common than it was in later centuries cannot be ruled out, there is a more plausible explanation for the rarity of *felo de se* on medieval coroners' rolls. Barbara Hanawalt has argued convincingly that many suicides were concealed as accidents. 'Community feeling', she observes, 'would [have been] with the surviving family.'[28] Moreover, as both the evidence she has assembled and that from other printed and unpublished sources suggests, medieval juries were less hesitant to bring in *non compos mentis* than their Tudor and Stuart successors.[29] There can be little doubt that Hanawalt is right. To take but one example, the crown later proved that a Bedfordshire man who drowned in a well in April 1278 had killed himself. But the jury, which comprised as usual men from the four surrounding townships, had returned a verdict of misadventure on his body, probably because he had been ill when he died. They also allegedly concealed his goods from royal officials.[30] The crown successfully challenged the verdicts of coroners from time to time, but its supervision of this aspect of their duties was rather lax. Coroners were unpaid and easily corruptible.[31] Even when verdicts that were unfavourable to the deceased were returned, medieval juries seem often to have undervalued the goods of self-murderers, as they did those of other felons.[32] Enforcement of the law was thus left largely in the hands of a local official and a jury of local men. However much they may have abhorred suicide itself, they usually preferred to acquit self-killers, rather than to deprive their heirs, possibly impoverishing a family. It would not, we think, be going too far to say that the law of self-murder was only enforced when it was unavoidable to do so.

28 B. A. Hanawalt, *Crime and Conflict in English Communities, 1300–1348* (Cambridge, Mass., 1979), 101–4.

29 B. A. Hanawalt, *Crime in East Anglia in the Fourteenth Century: Norfolk Gaol Delivery Rolls, 1307–1316*, Norfolk Record Society, xl (Norwich, 1976), Just 3/48, mm. 20, 22d. William Schara, who is writing a dissertation about insanity in medieval England, reports that his research in criminal records confirms Hanawalt's arguments about the concealment of suicide as misadventure and the use of the *non compos mentis*: personal communication, 27 May 1986. See also Hunnisett, *Medieval Coroner*, 21. Juries seem to have been uncharacteristically severe when they met in conjunction with an eyre: *The Eyre of Northamptonshire*, ed. D. W. Sutherland, Selden Society, xlvii–xlviii (London, 1983), 153, 183, 188, 193, 196.

30 R. F. Hunnisett (ed.), *Bedfordshire Coroners: Rolls*, Publications of the Bedfordshire Historical Record Society, xli (Streatley, 1961), no. 197.

31 Hunnisett, *Medieval Coroner*, ch. 7.

32 Ibid. 108, 122, 130.

## THE TUDOR REFORMS

All that changed in the sixteenth century. The Tudor revolutions in government and religion greatly increased both the rigour with which the law of suicide was enforced and popular hostility to self-murder. Large ideas have become unfashionable in English history, and none more so than the concept of 'the Tudor revolution in government'. Even Sir Geoffrey Elton's own students have begun to turn on him, hacking the idea that made him famous into disjointed bits.[33] But in at least one obscure sinew of the body politic, the law of suicide, there was indeed something very like a Tudor revolution in government, even if it started earlier and took a bit longer to complete than Sir Geoffrey would have insisted in his youth. A new law regulating the pay and performance of coroners was passed in 1487 that made them responsible for holding inquests on every violent or suspicious death that occurred in their jurisdictions. This statute was fine-tuned by a writ in 1509 and a second statute in 1510, and a regular procedure for returning inquisitions to the court of King's Bench and recording their verdicts was established.[34] Coroners were henceforth paid one mark (13*s.* 4*d.*) for every homicide verdict (including verdicts of *felo de se*) that they returned, the fee to be deducted from the forfeited property of the guilty person. To ensure compliance with the law, they were required to return copies of their inquisitions at the semi-annual meetings of the assizes in their counties. The clerk of the assize subsequently forwarded them to the court of King's Bench, where they were reviewed and enrolled.[35]

The motive behind these reforms was a blend of public spirit and governmental greed typical of Henry Tudor. They were part of a series of measures designed both to improve the detection of homicide and also to ensure that the crown collected all of the profits of justice to which

[33] G. R. Elton, *The Tudor Revolution in Government* (1953; repr. Cambridge, 1966); C. Coleman and D. Starkey (eds.), *Revolution Reassessed: Revision in the History of Tudor Government and Administration* (Oxford, 1986).

[34] 3 Henry VII, c. 1; 1 Henry VIII, c. 7; R. F. Hunnisett, *Calendar of Nottinghamshire Coroners' Inquests, 1485–1558*, Thoroton Society, xxv (Nottingham, 1969), pp. xviii–xix; id. *Sussex Coroners' Inquests, 1485–1558*, Sussex Record Society, lxxiv (Lewes, 1985), pp. xiii–xiv.

[35] The steps that preceded the filing of an inquisition in King's Bench are neatly summarized in S. J. Stevenson, 'The Rise of Suicide Verdicts in South-East England, 1530–1590: The Legal Process', *Continuity and Change*, ii (1987) 43–4 and Fig. 2.

it was entitled.[36] The crown was equally concerned with suppressing the violence that had become endemic in the fifteenth century and with gaining as much as it could from its rights to the goods of felons and to deodands. The chattels of suicides, including not merely moveable property but also leases and debts owed to the deceased, were forfeited to the king's almoner, purportedly for charitable purposes. About the almoners little is known. They were invariably churchmen, usually highly favoured bishops or royal servants. Charity began at home. Although almoners were supposed to treat the survivors of suicides and the forfeiters of deodands mercifully, the office apparently yielded significant profits. It is difficult to explain why it was such a plum appointment otherwise. Occasionally, when a windfall was especially rich, the crown ordered the almoner to share the booty with other courtiers. The almoner, or more commonly his deputy, normally compounded with the survivor for a portion of the value of the self-murderer's goods. Almoners seem to have had several deputies active in the counties and also to have been notified of potential forfeitures by King's Bench. Few flagrant suicides by men or women who possessed any goods worth the taking were likely to escape notice.[37]

The key to the Tudor system of enforcing the law of suicide was the Court of Star Chamber. The King's council sitting in judicial session, the Court of Star Chamber was politically intimidating and legally nimble. Its members were the most prestigious politicians in the realm; its procedures were swift and efficient. The almoners established their right to sue in Star Chamber to recover the goods of suicides late in the 1530s

36 The most innovative aspect of this set of reforms was the creation in 1508 of the office of surveyor of the king's prerogative. The surveyor's main responsibilities were to survey and seize the forfeited property of 'persons convicted, attainted, outlawed or waived for felony, murder or the like offence'. Whether the surveyor's charge extended to the goods of suicides and deodands is not clear. The office was abolished in 1513: C. H. Williams (ed.), *English Historical Documents, 1485–1558* (London, 1967), 500; W. C. Richardson, 'The Surveyor of the King's Prerogative', *English Historical Review*, lv (1941), 52–75; id., *Tudor Chamber Administration* (Baton Rouge, La., 1952), 195.

37 It is not precisely clear how the procedures for payment normally worked. Many Star Chamber cases make it plain that deputy almoners compounded directly with the families of suicides, taking a portion of the value of the goods. The deputy then reported to King's Bench that the almoner was satisfied, and proceedings to surrender the goods were halted. If the amounts the almoner took were recorded, as some contemporary remarks suggest they must have been, we have been unable to find a listing of them in the surviving records of King's Bench and Exchequer. For some clues about what was supposed to happen (but often did not), see M. Dalton, *Officium vicecomitum: The Office and Authoritie of Sherifs* (London, 1623), 33, 186–7.

or early in the 1540s.[38] The leading figure in this development was almost certainly one of Thomas Cromwell's protégés, Nicholas Heath.[39] The resort to Star Chamber as an alternative to King's Bench was characteristic of Henrician law reform, which championed the equity and conciliar courts at the expense of the ancient common-law courts.[40] In this case, however, instead of competing with King's Bench, Star Chamber complemented it. King's Bench monitored the activities of coroners on a routine basis, reviewing inquisitions, challenging obviously suspicious returns, amercing townships for failing to report deaths, and ordering officials to appear and surrender confiscated goods.[41] Star Chamber meanwhile served as the ultimate deterrent to evasion and fraud, a blunderbuss the almoner could point in the direction of anyone bold enough or clever enough to defy King's Bench.

Star Chamber was a large weapon to use against delinquents in cases where the financial stakes were often trivial. Many suicides forfeited nothing at all. Just over half of the *felo de se* inquisitions mentioning property declared that the deceased possessed no goods; many others said that his goods were worth nothing or valued them at very small sums. The crown did not normally pursue the matter further unless there

38 Because of the loss of records from this period, there is inevitably some doubt about just when and by whom the right of almoners to sue was won. J. A. Guy, who has examined the uncalendared and inaccessible records of the court and is its foremost historian for the Tudor period, dates it from the 1530s. The calendared examples he cites, however, seem all to be from the next decade: *The Court of Star Chamber and its Records to the Reign of Elizabeth I*, Public Record Office Handbooks, No. 21 (London, 1985), 37. The language of the bills from the 1540s and the answers given to the charges in them strongly hints that the jurisdiction of Star Chamber had not yet been firmly established: PRO, STAC 2/1/101–8, 110–12. The best guess, based on Dr Guy's opinion and our own less complete and expert reading of the evidence, would be a date late in the 1530s, perhaps 1538 or 1539.

39 Heath was almoner 1539–47. The practice of suing in Star Chamber may have originated with Heath's predecessor Edward Foxe (almoner 1532–8), who was even more closely allied with Cromwell. Just one of Foxe's cases regarding suicide, initiated by his executors after his death, survives: STAC 2/6/75–7. For the relationship of Heath and Foxe to Cromwell, see e.g. G. R. Elton, *Reform and Reformation: England 1509–1558* (London, 1977), 184–5.

40 J. A. Guy, *The Cardinal's Court* (Hassocks, 1977); id., *Court of Star Chamber and its Records*; id., *The Public Career of Sir Thomas More* (Brighton, 1980), 39–40; M. Blatcher, *The Court of King's Bench* (London, 1978); J. H. Baker, 'Introduction', *The Reports of Sir John Spelman*, 2, ed. J. H. Baker, Selden Society, xciv, 1977 (London, 1978), ch. 2, are the chief sources for the development of the two courts in this period.

41 The activities and routines of King's Bench are vividly depicted in Hunnisett, *Sussex Coroners' Inquests*, pp. xlvi–xlvii and cases cited in the index, s.v. 'suicide, forfeiture for'. The court's vigilance in seeking forfeitures is illustrated on every controlment roll for the period: see e.g. PRO, KB 29/209 [1574], mm. $1^r$–$6^r$, esp. $3^r$ (a village amerced 10*s.* for withholding goods) and $3^v$ (an answer that the deceased was *non compos mentis*).

was some reason to suspect fraud. Over one-third of reported self-murderers were women, at least half of whom were wives whose husbands would legally possess their goods. Another large class of *felones de se* were labourers, servants, soldiers, paupers, and other riff-raff, who were inherently unlikely to have valuable property. Moreover, as we shall see in a later chapter, financial ruin and destitution were commonly mentioned motives for suicide throughout the early modern period. The abnormally high number of reported suicides in a few years of bad harvests and high prices also suggests that many suicides were poor. It is not surprising, then, that two-thirds of the forfeitures mentioned in surviving inquests were valued at less than five pounds. On the other hand, really rich men—usually merchants—were occasionally convicted of self-murder. Between 1570 and 1600, for instance, the crown learned of ten persons whose confiscated goods were worth over £100, including a tanner who forfeited £730. The largest haul reported to the crown during the whole Tudor and Stuart era seems to have been the £8,875 that a squire named William Toomes left in 1655; five other men and a woman left goods valued at £500 or more.[42] Had all the forfeitures listed on inquests been collected in full, the crown would have realized a yearly income between 1540 and 1640 of several hundred pounds a year (rising from a low of about £225 to a high of about £540). Unfortunately, it is impossible to know how much the almoner actually collected from the survivors of self-murderers.

Despite the relatively limited financial gains to be had, the almoners sued in Star Chamber and sued often. Hundreds of cases survive in the extant records of the court charging families, neighbours, coroners, and juries with concealing the property of suicides. The almoner was a privileged prosecutor in the court and so it cost him only half the normal fees to sue there, even if he lost and had to pay costs. More important, perhaps, was the matter of principle. Evasion of the king's right to the goods of suicides and deodands flouted the royal prerogative—as Star Chamber bills routinely pointed out—and the king's council was naturally concerned to see that the privilege was not eroded. The councils of Protestant Edward and Catholic Mary were equally willing to hear suits

[42] For the tanner, see KB 9/647/2, mm. 166–7 (James Morsse). For the other very high valuations mentioned, see KB 9/866/2, mm. 141–3 (William Toomes); KB 9/561, mm. 4–5 (William Gonson); KB 9/725/4, m. 580 (John Brande); KB 9/793/1, mm. 63–4 (Robert Burges); KB 9/889/2, m. 111 (Elizabeth Gould); KB 11/6/1, m. 1 (John Grange); KB 11/9/2 (John Robens). The loss of almost all of the London inquisitions has doubtless destroyed records of many more substantial forfeitures, for the property of merchants was all vulnerable to confiscation.

brought by the almoner, and there was no slackening in the number of cases concerning suicides' goods in the Elizabethan Star Chamber.[43] The great seventeenth-century expert on the court, William Hudson, stressed the importance of suing delinquents even when little money was involved. Indeed, the almoner's freedom to use the power and prestige of the court was essential to enforcing the law, Hudson remarked, for suicides normally killed themselves secretly, 'soe that if there bee not a strict meanes to sifte the same out when he is dead, it will hardly bee discouered'.[44] After about 1540, therefore, the two most prestigious tribunals in the land were working in tandem and with unprecedented efficiency to ensure that the law of self-murder was enforced.

The results of the government's reforms are reflected in the dramatic increase in suicides reported to King's Bench. The average number of suicide inquisitions rose rapidly after 1500, far exceeding the rate of growth in the population, until the rate of reported suicide reached a sort of jagged plateau between about 1560 and 1630. The vast majority of these suicides was judged guilty of self-murder. (See Table 1.1 and Figure 1.1.) It is unlikely that the take-off between 1500 and 1560 was simply or even mainly the result of an increasing suicide rate, for a very similar pattern may be detected in the reporting of accidents and natural deaths during that period.[45]

## THE REFORMATION OF SUICIDE

The Tudor revolution in religion, like the reforms in government, fostered intolerance of suicide. Like the reforms in government, the reformation was a slower and less thorough revolution than we once believed it to have been. The reformers swept away many of the rituals

[43] The continued influence of Nicholas Heath may have encouraged this continuity of effort. A moderate reformer in the 1530s, Heath grew more conservative in later years, and he served on the council in Mary's reign, when he took an active part in reorganizing the business of Star Chamber: Guy, *Court of Star Chamber*, 10; *DNB*, s.v. 'Heath, Nicholas'. The activities of the almoners in Star Chamber may be traced in cases listed under the names of individual almoners and, occasionally, their deputies in PRO, STAC 2, 3, 4, 5, 7, and 8.

[44] Huntington Library, MS EL 7921, fos. $38^v$–$40^r$, $105^v$–$106^r$. We are grateful to Thomas G. Barnes for information on the almoner in Star Chamber.

[45] A rise in the real rate of suicide cannot, of course, be ruled out. Administrative reform may well have coincided with a growth in the numbers of suicides per capita. For the rise in reporting accidents and natural deaths, see Hunnisett, *Sussex Coroner's Inquests*, pp. xvii–xx; id. *Calendar of Nottinghamshire Coroners' Inquests*, pp. xviii–xix.

Table 1.1. *Suicide Verdicts Returned to King's Bench, 1485–1659*

| Years | *Felo de se* | *Non compos mentis* | Mixed | Ambiguous | % *Felo de se* |
|---|---|---|---|---|---|
| 1485–99 | 6 | | | | 100 |
| 1500–9 | 61 | 1 | | | 98.4 |
| 1510–19 | 108 | 1 | 5 | | 94.7 |
| 1520–9 | 216 | 10 | 1 | | 95.2 |
| 1530–9 | 343 | 18 | 11 | 11 | 89.6 |
| 1540–9 | 499 | 15 | 14 | 5 | 93.6 |
| 1550–9 | 714 | 7 | 10 | 1 | 97.5 |
| 1560–9 | 798 | 14 | 4 | 1 | 97.7 |
| 1570–9 | 940 | 15 | 4 | | 98.0 |
| 1580–9 | 909 | 5 | 8 | 1 | 98.5 |
| 1590–9 | 797 | 5 | 9 | | 98.3 |
| 1600–9 | 873 | 7 | 14 | | 97.7 |
| 1610–19 | 967 | 1 | 8 | | 99.1 |
| 1620–9 | 751 | 17 | 12 | | 96.3 |
| 1630–9 | 503 | 12 | 9 | | 96.0 |
| 1640–9 | 328 | 22 | 6 | | 92.1 |
| 1650–9 | 654 | 6 | 60 | | 90.8 |
| TOTALS | 9,467 | 156 | 175 | 19 | 96.4 |

*Source*: PRO, KB 9, 10, 11, 140; PL 26; HCA 1.

and symbols of the old religion. Priests lost many of the sacred and magical powers popularly attributed to them in the Middle Ages. The sacraments were demystified, exorcism was effectively abolished, funerals were gradually simplified, and prayers for the souls of the dead were forbidden. Auricular confession gave way to 'practical divinity'—an active sort of pastoral care. Churches were stripped of much of the ornamentation that was the essential equipment of medieval piety. Changing the minds of the laity was more difficult than reforming doctrine. The new clergy had to rely mainly on preaching and catechism to teach the doctrines of the faith to a populace that was on the whole unreceptive. Progress was slow, and it was not until the end of Elizabeth's reign that the majority of the people had been won over to Protestantism. In some counties conversion had still not proceeded very far by 1600, and a good many men and women of humble social standing probably remained ignorant of essential Protestant doctrines throughout the sixteenth and seventeenth centuries. Theirs was a faith that was infused with Christian symbolism and grounded on social virtue: it

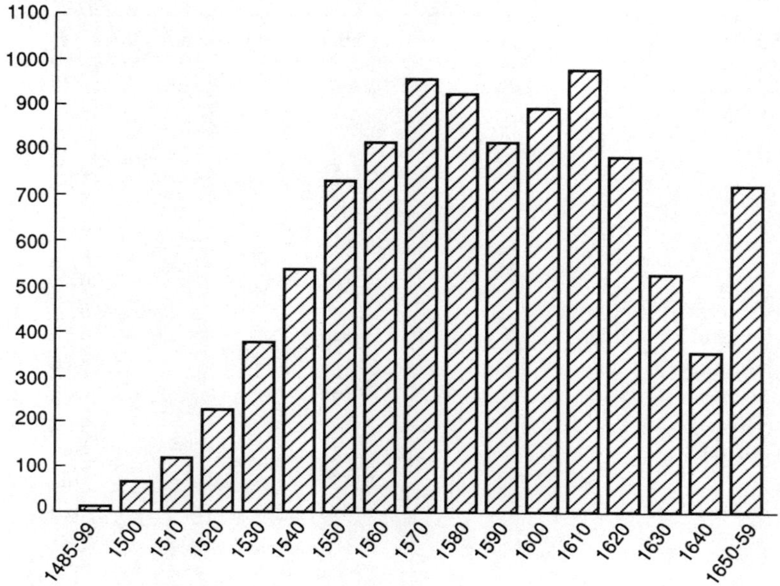


FIG. 1.1. Reported suicides, 1485–1659
*Source*: PRO, KB 9, 10, 11, 140; PL 26; HCA 1.

lapsed easily into an outlook that seemed to the godly to be an unwitting compound of the old heresies of dualism and Pelagianism. 'The progressive internalization of the Protestant Reformation', Patrick Collinson points out, 'was making a religious divide', a divide that was both geographical and social, separating conservative counties such as Lancashire from radical ones such as Essex and widening the cultural gap between the educated élite and the illiterate poor.[46]

Historians have recently depicted the reformation as a campaign against popular culture. And no one can doubt that Puritan zealots were determined to create a godly Zion that was free from the superstition, idolatry, and immorality that they believed typified the beliefs and customs of the common people. From their point of view, the English

[46] P. Collinson, 'The Elizabethan Church and the New Religion', in C. Haigh (ed.), *The Reign of Elizabeth I* (London, 1984), 174. See also, P. Collinson, *The Religion of Protestants* (Oxford, 1982); K. Wrightson, *English Society, 1580–1680* (London, 1982), ch. 7; C. Haigh (ed.), *The English Reformation Revised* (Cambridge, 1987); and, most importantly, Thomas, *Religion and Magic*.

were only partially Christianized at best, and to a certain extent they were right. But in some ways Protestant reformers actually intensified traditional beliefs and practices. They certainly heightened popular fear of demons and witches, for example, reinterpreting old ideas about mystical harm in new and more sophisticated ways. In a similar fashion, they adopted medieval and demotic beliefs about the supernatural causes and consequences of suicide and placed them in a Protestant theological context. The aim of Protestant divines was to win souls, and they fashioned a religious psychology that was a powerful evangelical weapon. The 'rhetoric of the spirit', as William Haller once called it, employed many of the figures and tropes used in the religious art and literature of the past.[47] The preachers insisted, as their medieval forebears had, that suicide was a diabolical crime, a terrible sin instigated by Satan, in whose malevolent powers everyone believed. Moreover, although the reformers attacked a very wide array of traditional religious rituals on the grounds that they were relics of the pagan past, the Protestant clergy fully endorsed the rites of desecration. Not one word of protest seems to have been raised against them, even by the most radical puritans, and they were practised far more frequently than ever before.

Protestant divines depicted self-murder as an expression of despair, the very antithesis of Christian hope. The future archbishop of Canterbury, George Abbot, summed up clerical opinion when he declared that suicide was 'a sin so grieuous that scant any is more hainous unto the Lord'.[48] The absolute unlawfulness of suicide was stressed in sermons, devotional works, treatises, and didactic literature by writers of every hue in the Protestant theological spectrum. Abbot, for example, was a Calvinist; his anti-Calvinist friend Lancelot Andrewes was equally vehement on the heinousness of self-killing: 'It is worse than beastly to kill or drown or make away with ourselves; for... the very swine would

[47] W. Haller, *The Rise of Puritanism* (New York, 1957), 33–4, 155. See also, P. Collinson, *The Birthpangs of Protestant England* (London, 1988), ch. 4.

[48] G. Abbot, *An Exposition Upon the Prophet Jonah* (London, 1600), 132. See also, A. Anderson, *The Shield of our Saftie* (London, 1581), sigs. K–M; S. Bird, *The Lectures of Samuel Bird of Ipswidge Upon the 11. Chapter of the Epistles Unto the Hebrewes* (Cambridge, 1598), 98–102; C. Sutton, *Disce Mori: Learn to Die* (London, 1600), 288–90; J. Dodd, *A Treatise or Exposition Upon the Ten Commandments* (London, 1603), pt. ii, fos. $43^{v}$–$44^{r}$; W. Vaughan, *The Golden Grove*, 2nd edn. (London, 1608), chs. 19, 29–34; T. Cartwright, *Christian Religion* (London, 1611), 105–6; G. Strode, *The Anatomie of Mortalitie* (London, 1632), 282; W. Ames, *Conscience with the Power of Cases Thereof* (n.pl., 1639), 186; J. Taylor, *Ductor Dubitantium*, in his *The Whole Works*, ed. A. Taylor and P. Eden (Edinburgh, 1852), 96–7. R. L. Greaves, *Society and Religion in Elizabethan England* (Minneapolis, Minn., 1981), 533, 845–6 discusses these and other clerical statements deploring suicide.

not have run into the sea but that they were carried by the devil.'[49] Following the example of Augustine, Protestant writers repeatedly declared that self-murder was contrary to divine law. The fact that both the Bible and the early church afforded them few proofs of this conviction only deepened the clergy's determination to popularize Augustine's insistence that suicide was forbidden by the Sixth Commandment and that the early martyrs who killed themselves were not examples for ordinary Christians to emulate.[50] These arguments were not very convincing, as John Donne made devastatingly plain in *Biathanatos*, but they were often repeated and widely believed. They provided the theological basis for the Protestant preachers' assertion that self-murder was spiritually significant.[51]

The clergy taught that self-murder might come directly from God, in retribution for some grievous sin, or indirectly, through Satan's temptations. Medieval preachers had interpreted suicide as proof that the Lord intervened in this world to punish the wicked and reward the faithful. John Mirk in his *Festial*, for instance, stressed that several of the persecutors of Jesus and the early church—notably, Herod, Judas, and Pilate—had killed themselves.[52] Mirk's sixteenth- and seventeenth-century counterparts used the same examples and cited new ones to demonstrate that theirs was the true church and to confirm the doctrine of providence. John Foxe's stories of Catholic persecutors of English Protestants who subsequently fell mad or killed themselves were the most widely read collection of judgements against sinners in the Elizabethan age. (They will be described in a later discussion of the use of suicide in sectarian propaganda.) Foxe's *Acts and Monuments*, familiarly known as the Book of Martyrs, was almost as widely read as the Bible; together with the scriptures and the Book of Common Prayer, it was

[49] L. Andrewes, *The Works* (Oxford, 1854), vi. 219. See also, Taylor, *Ductor Dubitantium*, 93.

[50] See, for example, J. King, *Lectures Upon Jonah, Delivered at Yorke in... 1594*, 6th edn. (London, 1618), 184–90; Abbot, *Exposition Upon Jonah*, 125–35; Vaughan, *Golden Grove*, chs. 15–29.

[51] The only point on which clerical writers moderated their condemnation of suicide was in their discussions of the fate of self-murderers' souls. Some of them thought, as Luther had, that suicides might repent between their sinful act and their death, and so cautioned against assuming that all suicides were damned. See, for instance, Vaughan, *Golden Grove*, ch. 29. Abbot's opinion, once more, seems representative. He argues that although God might sometimes pardon self-murderers, it would be 'monstrous' to presume that he does so in particular cases: *Exposition Upon Jonah*, 132. See also, S. E. Sprott, *The English Debate on Suicide* (La Salle, Ill., 1961), 13.

[52] P. B. R. Doob, *Nebuchadnezzar's Children: Madness in Middle English Literature* (New Haven, 1974), 131–2.

kept in parish churches all over England. The lurid violence of its descriptions of the sufferings of many Protestant martyrs attracted readers with magnetic force.[53]

It also encouraged imitators: the Book of Martyrs generated a whole genre of judgement books.[54] One of the most popular was Thomas Beard's *Theatre of God's Judgements*, which went through numerous editions, expansions, and redactions in the seventeenth century. It was pirated and plagiarized. Beard devoted a whole chapter to sinners who had murdered themselves. He repeated all of Foxe's stories and briefly mentioned others, including two or three men whom he knew personally who had, he claimed, been struck down by God in retribution for their avarice.[55] Although scholars declare that Beard departed from Calvinist orthodoxy, he was not by any means unusual in his conviction that almost any sin might bring divine retribution down on the offender.[56] Edmund Bicknoll, for instance, told of two recent suicides in his diatribe against swearing. One of them, a Londoner almost eighty years old, disembowelled himself in 1577 because of his remorse over tricking a man out of some money many years earlier. In this story, like many others, Satan is the sword of God's wrath, playing on the man's guilt and luring him to his death.[57] In his standard guide for pious diarists, John Beadle urged the godly to record judgements on notorious sinners who committed suicide.[58] The London turner Nehemiah Wallington not only noted suicides in his journals but also kept a special manuscript that included 'A Memorial of those that laid violent hands on themselves'.[59] Even at the end of the Stuart period, when the doctrine of particular providences had begun to fall into disfavour, pious writers continued to

[53] J. Foxe, *The Acts and Monuments*, ed. J. Pratt, 4th edn. (London, n.d. [1877]), viii. 646. See also, i. 89, 91–3; viii. 634, 635, 642, 646, 648–9.

[54] Thomas, *Religion and Magic*, ch. 4.

[55] T. Beard, *The Theatre of God's Judgements*, 3rd edn. (London, 1631), 30, 65, 75, 215–16, 306–17.

[56] For Beard's heterodoxy, see P. S. Seaver, *Wallington's World: A Puritan Artisan in Seventeenth-Century London* (Stanford, 1985), 45–8, 219–20 n. 1.

[57] E. Bicknoll, *A Svvoord against Swearing* (London, 1579), fos. $34^{v}$, $37^{r}$–$38^{v}$. See also, A. Gibson, *The Lands Mourning for Vaine Swearing* (London, 1613), 51, cited in Sprott, *English Debate*, 34.

[58] J. Beadle, *The Journal or Diary of a Thankful Christian* (London, 1656), 23–4.

[59] Seaver, *Wallington's World*, 31, 60, 204; BL, Sloane MS 1457, fos. $6^{r}$–$8^{r}$. For examples of other diaries that relate suicides as examples of God's judgements, see Thomas, *Religion and Magic*, 93; E. Burghall, 'Providence Improved', in T. W. Barlow, *Cheshire: Its Historical and Literary Associations* (Manchester, 1855), 154, 156. The witch-hunter John Stearne concluded that the death in gaol of a man accused of making a covenant with the devil and who had attempted suicide was 'a just judgement of God': C. L'E. Ewen, *Witchcraft and Demonianism* (London, 1933), 307.

attribute suicides to divine punishment. Among the 'remarkable providences' recorded by William Turner in his immense 1697 collection, for instance, were several suicides, including that of a sectarian preacher who ran mad and killed himself, a punishment for living adulterously with another man's wife.[60]

Popular though books of judgements were, suicide was interpreted far more often as the result of diabolical temptation than divine retribution. Just as they emphasized the power of God more vehemently than medieval Catholics had, so the reformers stressed the potency and dangerousness of the devil. Satan was above all the Tempter, injecting ungodly urges into people's minds and luring them on to despair and self-destruction.[61] At the very beginning of the Reformation, Hugh Latimer warned that some men are so vexed by the assaults and temptations of the Devil that 'they rid themselves out of this life'.[62] The great Elizabethan Puritan divine, Richard Greenham worried that 'Satan doth make many now adaies' end their lives.[63] George Abbot thought that suicide itself was such a grievous sin that it proved Satan's power to gain possession of a man.[64] Among the principal causes of self-murder, declared John Sym in the first treatise entirely devoted to the subject, are 'the strong impulse, powerfull motions, and command of the Devill'.[65] Easily the most elaborate discussion of the ways in which Satan enticed men and women to kill themselves was included in Richard Gilpin's 1677 treatise on the devil's wiles. 'Satan seeks the ruin of our Bodies, as well as of our Souls, and tempts Men often to Self-Murther,' Gilpin began his remarks on suicide. He then proceeded to list no fewer than eight ways in which the Tempter fostered suicidal thoughts.[66] The devil

60 W. Turner, *A Compleat History of the Most Remarkable Providences* (London, 1697), pt. 1, ch. 138, 65 (irregular pagination). See also, ibid., pt. 1, 17, 136–7.

61 Thomas, *Religion and Magic*, 472–6 is the best discussion of the symbolism and psychology of temptation by the devil.

62 H. Latimer, *The Works of Hugh Latimer*, ed. G. E. Corrie, Parker Society (Cambridge, 1844–5), i. 435.

63 R. Greenham, *The Works of the Reverend and Faithfull Servant of Jesus Christ M. Richard Greenham* (London, 1599), 239.

64 Abbot, *Exposition Upon Jonah*, 125.

65 Sym, *Lifes Preservative*, 246–7.

66 R. Gilpin, *Daemonologia sacra; or, a Treatise on Satan's Temptations* (London, 1677), part 3, 108–16. For other examples of sermons and tracts acknowledging Satan's role in suicide, see King, *Lectures upon Jonas*, 189; W. Willymat, *Physicke, To Cvre the Most Dangerous Disease of Desperation* (London, 1607), 7, 12–16, 24–34, 70–1; Sutton, *Disce Mori*, 289–90; Strode, *Anatomie of Mortalitie*, 271; T. Brookes, *The Select Works of the Rev. Thomas Brookes* (London, 1824), ii. 440–1; S. Ward, *Sermons and Treatises*, ed. J. C. Ryle (Edinburgh, 1862), 58–9; R. Capel, *Tentations*, 4th edn. (London, 1650), 192–4; W. Denny, *Pelecanicidum; or the Christian Advisor Against Self-Murder* (London, 1653), 29; Greaves, *Society and Religion*, 532, 533; J. O. King III, *The Iron of Melancholy* (Middletown, Conn., 1983), 51–2.

was a literal symbol of suicidal despair—a real being who also signified the spiritual and emotional state of the desperate sinner.

The figure of the devil as a tempter had played a part in popular religion for centuries. The imagery of the moralities, in which actors personified supernatural beings who in turn personified states of mind and grace, had become fundamental to lay piety and psychology. Instead of rejecting this old habit of thought, Protestant divines appropriated it and used it to depict suicide in ways that both preserved the continuity of popular beliefs about the act and placed them in a new theological context. Like medieval preachers before them, they used personification and allegory to categorize behaviour and dramatize the spiritual significance of emotions. When they spoke of the devil tempting people to despair and suicide, they were personifying suicidal urges and classifying them as the antithesis of the godly state of mind.[67] Their goal was to persuade down-hearted sinners that the way to happiness as well as salvation was through conversion. The abolition of the confessional and the necessity of converting the populance to a new and intellectually demanding religion required new strategies of pastoral care and conversion. These were developed quite self-consciously. Leaders of the church urged ministers to be attentive to the spiritual needs of their flocks and to pay particular attention to those of their parishioners who were ill or disturbed. They were to take every opportunity to explain to afflicted people the religious significance of their misfortunes and urge them to adopt a more godly course of life. To communicate effectively and persuasively with the unregenerate, ministers therefore adopted some of the key figures in the traditional language of popular religion. They embraced the imagery of the morality play, the psychomachy, and incorporated it into a distinctively Protestant psychology of sin and redemption.

Puritan writers, the most avid exponents of 'practical divinity', published tract after tract, sermon after sermon, identifying suicidal despair as the work of the devil and offering the promise of greater strength to resist such feelings. Richard Sibbes, for example, observed that carnal men sank deeper and deeper into despair until at last they killed themselves. But godly men could recover themselves, for 'there is an art or skill of bearing troubles, if we could learn it,... as in bearing of a burden there is a way so to poise it that it weigheth not over heavy'.[68] This was

[67] Haller, *The Rise of Puritanism*, esp. chs. 1 and 4, is still the most persuasive account of Puritan rhetoric. See also, J. S. McGee, *The Godly Man in Stuart England* (New Haven, 1976), ch. 2.

[68] R. Sibbes, *The Complete Works*, ed. A. B. Grosart (Edinburgh, 1862–4), i. 148; see also i. 319.

a theme reiterated by dozens of divines: by famous men such as Richard Greenham, William Perkins, Robert Bolton, and Richard Baxter; by obscure sermonizers such as Robert Yarrow, Samuel Hoard, and Richard Capel.[69] Again and again in these and other discussions of the religious significance of suicide, divines depicted hapless sinners as souls poised between saving grace offered by God and his good angels and self-murdering despair inspired by the devil and his demons, just as the medieval moralities had. They stressed above all that the cosmic struggle between God and Satan, the angels and the demons, the saints and the unregenerate, was replicated in the mind and heart of every person. The spiritual warfare took place on every plane of existence; human emotions had their counterparts in the unseen world of the supernatural. The Fiend exploits the guilty conscience of reprobates, asserted William Willymat in a typical passage, so that 'at last they fall too, and lyeelde [*sic*: yield]... to dispatch themselves with their own hands,... so giving themselves over to the Devill'. Speedy repentance, he went on to warn, is the only possible remedy for Satan's dreadful promptings. Christ is the pattern for resisting his temptations.[70] Baxter stated the antithesis between the powers of good and evil: 'We feel that the Devil is present with us, by his Temptations continually, in all our Duties mollesting or hindering us: And are the Angels less intent upon their Work?'[71] The literal allegory that linked events on the supernatural plane with human emotions and actions formed the common ground between the preaching of the divines and the religion of the common people. For the latter were notoriously prone to interpret events in almost manichaean terms, as the outcome of a struggle between good and evil spirits.

The same symbolism may be found in lay religious literature and popular drama, although it was not, of course, always used with the same evangelical purpose. A well-known example is the Despair canto of the *Faerie Queene*, which identifies suicidal feelings as a 'devilish thought' and

[69] See e.g. Greenham, *The Works*, esp. 217–79; W. Perkins, *The Workes of that Famous and Worthy Minister of Christ in the University of Cambridge, Mr. William Perkins*, (London, 1626), i. 55–6, 87, 375–6; R. Bolton, *Instructions for a Right Comforting of Afflicted Consciences*, 2nd edn. (London, 1635); R. Baxter, *The Practical Works*, ed. W. Orme (London, 1830), xvii. 236–85; id., *The Signs and Causes of Melancholy*, ed. S. Clifford (London, 1716); R. Yarrow, *Sovereign Comforts for a Troubled Conscience* (London, 1634); S. Hoard, *The Soules Miserie and Recoverie* (London, 1636); Capel, *Tentations*; T. Wilson, *Saints by Calling* (London, 1620); and, above all, Sym, *Lifes Preservative*.

[70] Willymat, *Physicke*, 70–1 and *passim*.

[71] R. Baxter, *The Certainty of the World of Spirits* (London, 1691), 234.

personifies despair as the bearer of the instruments of death, just as medieval preachers and playwrights had. Persuaded that he has committed unforgivable sins, the Redcrosse Knight is presented by Despair with the means to kill himself:

> Than gan the villein him to oucercraw,
> And brought vnto him swords, ropes, poison, fire,
> And all that might him to perdition draw;
> And bad him choose, what death he would desire.[72]

Just as the knight has taken up a knife and raised his hand, Una, the embodiment of hope, snatches it out of his hand:

> Come, come away, fraile, feeble, fleshy wight,
> Ne let vaine words bewitch thy manly hart,
> Ne diuelish thoughts dismay thy constant spright.
> In heauenly mercies hast thou not a part?[73]

Spenser's subtle presentation of the conflict between suicidal desperation and Christian hope was imitated by many lesser poets, seldom read today, for the rest of the sixteenth and seventeenth centuries.[74] Although he was probably not among those directly influenced by Spenser, John Bunyan perpetuated the allegorical tradition in *The Pilgrim's Progress*, a book that shaped the thoughts of generations of readers, many of them men and women of very humble rank and limited learning, for a century and more after its publication in 1678. Languishing in the dungeon of Doubting Castle, Christian and Hopeful are tempted by Giant Despair to kill themselves: 'He told them that since they were never like to come out of that place, their only way would be, forthwith to make an end of themselves, either with Knife, Halter or Poison: For why, said he,

[72] E. Spenser, *The Faerie Queene*, I. ix. 50, cited from *The Works of Edmund Spenser, A Variorum Edition*, ed. E. Greenlaw, C. G. Osgood, and F. M. Padelford, i (Baltimore, 1932).

[73] Ibid. I. ix. 53.

[74] F. I. Carpenter, 'Spenser's Cave of Despair: An Essay in Literary Comparison', *Modern Language Notes*, xii (1897), 129–37; *Works of Edmund Spenser*, i. 270–81 reviews many of the sources, analogues, and works influenced by this passage. For suggestive readings of it, see H. Skilsky, 'Spenser's Despair Episode and the Theology of Doubt', *Modern Philology*, lxxviii (1980–1), 227–42; K. Williams, *Spenser's World of Glass* (Berkeley, 1966), 25–8; J. Nohrnberg, *The Analogy of the Faerie Queene* (Princeton, 1976), 152–5; and especially P. Alpers, *The Poetry of the Faerie Queene* (1967; repr. Columbia, Mo., 1982), 352–61.

should you chuse life, seeing it is attended with so much bitterness?'[75] It would not be hard to find close parallels to these lines in any number of spiritual autobiographies. Allegory was not necessarily an obstacle to psychological insight.

In *Doctor Faustus* Christopher Marlowe makes the role of the devil in instigating suicide more explicit than it is in the allegories of Spenser and Bunyan. Urged by a good angel to repent and by a bad one to despair, Faustus cries 'My heart is hardened: I cannot repent.' Immediately he hears a devilish voice:

> 'Faustus, thou art damn'd'; Then guns and knives,
> Swords, poison, halters, and envenom'd steel
> Are laid before me to dispatch myself.

When Faustus again yields to despair later in the play, Mephistophilis offers him a dagger and Faustus exclaims: 'Damn'd art thou, Faustus, damn'd; despair and die!' At this moment the Old Man, like the allegorical virtues in medieval drama, intervenes and stays Faustus's hand.[76] Elizabethan and Jacobean dramatists often alluded to the old notion that suicidal despair was a temptation implanted by Satan or some monstrous demon, even in plays set in pre-Christian times. Standing at the bottom of the cliffs of Dover, Edgar explains to the blind Gloucester that it was a fiend that led him to the precipice off which he imagines he flung himself:

> Methought his eyes
> Were two full moons, he had a thousand noses,
> Horns whelked and waved like the enridgèd sea.

'I took it for a man', the blind old man replies, 'Often 'twould say "the fiend, the fiend". He led me to that place.'[77] Both the traditional interpretation of suicidal emotions as diabolical temptations and the symbolic dichotomy between despair and comfort, damnation and salvation, were kept alive even as the stage became increasingly secular. 'The particular climactic image of the older drama—mankind poised between comfort

75. J. Bunyan, *Grace Abounding for the Chief of Sinners and The Pilgrim's Progress*, ed. R. Sharrock (London, 1966), 232. For sources and analogues that provide more examples of the linkage of the devil, despair, and suicide in literature and sermons, see H. Golder, 'Bunyan's Giant Despair', *Journal of English and Germanic Philology*, xxx (1931), 368–70.

76. C. Marlowe, *Doctor Faustus*, in *The Complete Plays of Christopher Marlowe*, ed. I. Ribner (New York, 1963), II. ii. 18–25; V. i. 55–64; Wymer, *Suicide and Despair*, 23.

77 W. Shakespeare, *King Lear*, in his *Complete Works*, ed. G. B. Harrison (New York, 1952), IV. vi. 69–79.

and despair—had a secure niche in the Jacobean imagination,' remarks Rowland Wymer.[78]

One play that has not survived in the literary canon deserves special emphasis because of the enduring popularity of the story it told. Nathaniel Woodes's *The Conflict of Conscience* was a late morality, dramatizing the life and death of Francesco Spiera—known to the English as Francis Spira. Spira was an Italian Protestant who recanted his religion and subsequently died of guilt and despair. His story was ready-made for the playwright. After his recantation Spira refused to eat. He languished for many days, racked by despair, lamenting his apostasy. He was tormented sometimes by devilish presences. As he lay dying, he was attended by a group of sympathetic clergymen, who endeavoured to reassure him of God's mercy and who recorded his lengthy speeches. The scene was the psychomachy personified, and after Spira's death it was seized upon not merely by the clerical participants, who published their eyewitness accounts, and by Woodes, but also by writers all over Protestant Europe. There were Latin, French, German, and English versions of the story. The first English rendition appeared in 1550, a translation of one of the eyewitness accounts, and Spira's tale was retold in Foxe's Book of Martyrs. He quickly became famous—he was referred to by Latimer, Reynolds, Bradford, Sandys, and other sixteenth-century English Protestants. Woodes's play, which was published in 1581, appeared in two versions. One has a happy ending: Spira repents at the moment of his deepest despair. In the other, he hangs himself at the instigation of the devil.[79]

Woodes's play has been claimed as one of the sources for *Doctor Faustus*.[80] The case for direct influence is difficult to establish because of the absence of parallels in the language of the two works. But their affinities go deeper than verbal borrowing. Most important in this context, both moralities borrow the structure of the psychomachy and establish links between apostasy, despair, and suicide. Renunciation of religious truth in favour of false doctrine leads to diabolical temptations to despair and self-murder. *Doctor Faustus* was played and replayed throughout the seventeenth and eighteenth centuries—it is the show

78 Wymer, *Suicide and Despair*, 60 and ch. 3 generally.

79 N. Woodes, *The Conflict of Conscience: 1581*, ed. H. Davis and F. P. Wilson (Oxford, 1952); L. B. Campbell, '*Doctor Faustus*: A Case of Conscience', *PMLA* lxvii (1952), 219–39; C. Wine, 'Nathaniel Wood's *Conflict of Conscience*'. *PMLA* l (1935), 661–78; L. M. Oliver, 'John Foxe and *The Conflict of Conscience*', *Review of English Studies*, xxv (1949), 1–9.

80 Campbell, '*Doctor Faustus*: A Case of Conscience'.

being staged in Hogarth's panorama of the chaos at Southwark Fair. *The Conflict of Conscience* quickly vanished from the boards—if it was ever played at all. But Spira's story endured and became a Protestant *topos*, a warning against the perils of apostasy and the single most influential depiction of religious despair, at least before Bunyan's *Grace Abounding*. A new English version of the story was written by Nathaniel Bacon and published in 1637 or 1638.[81] The manuscript of Bacon's book circulated clandestinely among Puritans before it was published: Nehemiah Wallington copied out the whole text in 1635. Thomas Beard included a brief retelling of the story in his book of judgements. Every Protestant evangelical of the seventeenth and eighteenth centuries referred to Spira —Perkins, Bolton, Wesley, and a host of others.[82] The precise method of Spira's death was left unclear in many versions. But invariably he is at the very least tempted to kill himself. Bacon's treatment of the theme is almost comic in its earnestness. Seeking to refute Spira's conviction that his despair cannot be relieved and that he is possessed by the devil himself, his clerical friends challenge him—if his situation is really so desperate, then why has he not yet tried to kill himself? 'You say you are desperate, O Spira!... Why then do you not strive with some weapon or other, violently to make an end of your life, as desperate men use to do?' He calls for a sword.[83] The symbolic association of Satan, apostasy, despair, and suicide was implanted in the Protestant mind, and the Spira story was its most popular and enduring presentation. The last edition of Bacon's *Fearfull Estate* was issued in 1845.

Satan was also cast as the tempter in ballads and broadsheets reporting actual suicides. For example, one of the several pamphlets that recounted the sensational crime of Sir John Fites (or Fitz) in 1605 conjectured that he had been tempted by Satan to kill his neighbour, servant, and wife, and that afterwards, tormented by 'the threatenings of Sathan, who visibly (it may be) appeared unto him, menacing him with eternal

[81] N. Bacon, *A Relation of the Fearefull Estate of Francis Spira in the Year 1548* (London, 1638). Citations are of the 1657 edition.

[82] Seaver, *Wallington's World*, 202; Beard, *Theatre of Gods Judgements*, 73–4. For discussion of the Spira story and later references to it, see B. Opie, 'Beyond Ideology: Apostasy and the Horrors of Selfhood in Some Renaissance Texts', *Mentalités/Mentalities*, ii (1984), 21—33; id., 'Nathaniel Bacon and Francis Spira: The Presbyterian and the Apostate', *Turnbull Library Record,* xviii (1985), 33–49; M. MacDonald, '*The Fearefull Estate of Francis Spira*: An Essay in Historical Psychology', forthcoming.

[83] Bacon, *Fearfull Relation*, 75–6.

damnation', he fell on his sword.[84] In Charles Hammond's ballad, 'The Devil's Cruelty to Mankind', a vivid description of the suicide in 1663 of George Gibbs, Gibbs himself blames Satan for his gristly end. Having risen from his bed, slashed open his belly, and pulled out his bowels, he lay dying for eight hours, telling of the many previous temptations he had endured before he finally succumbed to the devil:

> The Divil he said did tempt him long,
> and many times before,
> For all he did resist him strong,
> he nere would give him ore.[85]

The mixture of moralizing supernaturalism and vivid reportage, which seems almost surreal today, persisted in the journalistic reports of several self-murders in the 1680s. The most elaborate of them, an account of the death in Newgate of Robert Long, a rebel convicted for his part in Monmouth's Rebellion, turns into a kind of broadside sermon. Self-murderers, its author declares, cast the 'Talent of Life in the Face of their Creator'. Failing to consider their fate after death, they are easy prey for 'the Enemy of Mankind', who 'takes the advantage to push them into Ruin, and heighten the Sence of their Guilt into that of a desperate Despair'.[86] Such warnings were not merely tropes; they invoked a danger that was widely held to be terrifyingly real.

84 *The Bloudy Booke; or, The Tragicall and Desperate End of Sir John Fites (alias) Fitz* (London, 1605), sig. D3$^{r-v}$. See also, J. H. Marshburn, *Murder and Witchcraft in England, 1550–1640* (Norman, Okla., 1971), 113–19.

85 H. E. Rollins, (ed.), *The Pack of Autolycus* (Cambridge, Mass., 1927), 125. See also, *A New Ballad, Shewing the Great Misery Sustained by a Poore Man in Essex*, 2 parts (London, 1630), pt. 2.

86 *A Sad and Dreadful Account of the Self-Murther of Robert Long, alias Baker* (London, 1685). See also *The Sad and Dreadful Relation of a Bloody and Cruel Murther Committed by Mr. Thomas Law, a Minister in Heart-Street, Covent-Garden, Upon his own Person* (London, 1684); *Sad and Dreadful News from Kings-Street in Westminster, A Most Lamentable Relation of the Untimely End of the Lady Phillips* (London, 1684); *Account of a Most Strange and Barbarous Action: How a Prisoner's Wife of Ludgate Threw Her Self from the Leeds into Black Fryers* (London, 1685); *Sad and Dreadful News from Dukes-place near Aldgate; or, a True Account of a Barbarous and Unnatural Self-murther Committed by Dorcas Pinkney* (London, 1686), 1; M. Spufford, *Small Books and Pleasant Histories* (London, 1981), 210.

## 2

# *The Instigation of the Devil*

THE increasing rigour with which the law was enforced and the growing emphasis on the spiritual significance of the crime intensified both the folkloric and religious bases for popular horror of suicide. The coroner's inquest and burial of the corpse were rituals of interpretation. They identified a death as a suicide and dramatized the jury's verdict to the whole neighbourhood. The rites of desecration were collective expressions of the community's conviction that self-murder was a heinous crime. Their ritual symbolism branded suicides as pariahs, excluding them from the churchyard, and condemning them to an eternal journey that had no destination. Historians and anthropologists have in recent years taught us to be sensitive to symbolic actions like the ritual burials of suicides. For they are keys to understanding how men and women in the past understood the social and metaphysical basis of the world in which they lived. From this perspective, it is plain that although ordinary people accepted the clerical élite's view that self-murder was a satanic sin, they also retained other, older beliefs about its supernatural significance. For the rites of desecration focused on the spiritual consequences of suicide. They treated the suicide's corpse as a polluted being, and they sought to counteract the malevolence of his ghost. The status of ghost beliefs in Protestant theology was uncertain. Some reformers maintained that they were illusions of the devil or mere supersititions; others accepted their existence, and the ranks of the anti-sceptics grew in the later seventeenth century, as the clergy rallied to combat the advancing trend toward scepticism.[1] But no religious authority explicitly sanctioned the rites of desecration or endorsed the notion that suicides' ghosts were dangerous and must be laid.

[1] Thomas, *Religion and Magic*, 587–93.

The rites of desecration thus complemented the prevailing theology of suicide, but they did not grow out of it. There was an overlap between the learned and the demotic understanding of self-murder, and so everyone, including the clergy, accepted the rituals of burial as legitimate, as necessary as the ceremonies of Christian burial. A similar sort of complementarity, but not identity, may be seen in élite and plebeian beliefs about the supernatural causes of self-murder. Ordinary men and women accepted the clerical teaching that the devil instigated self-murder. Accounts of diabolical temptations were common among people who experienced suicidal despair or tried to kill themselves. The language of popular religious psychology stressed Satan's power to drive ordinary men and women to commit suicide, and it may be found even in legal documents, where one would least expect it. But the ordinary layman's devil had greater autonomy than the theologians' Satan. His temptations were less trials of faith than all-out assaults on one's sanity. The impulses he implanted were almost irresistible, alien to the normal personality of the individual. They were to be combated by any means that worked, by magic and physic as well as by prayer and repentance. Moreover, the common people attributed suicidal urges to witches as well as to Satan, and those malevolent figures caused suicidal despair for their own reasons. They certainly did not serve as the instruments of God to punish sin or test one's strength. The common people's response to suicide, and their explanations for it, thus interpreted its significance in somewhat different terms from those preached by the clergy. Clerical ideas were reinterpreted in terms of lay religious beliefs that stressed the immanence of a wide range of spiritual powers not clearly under the control of God or his church.

The clergy used the notion that suicide was a diabolical temptation for their own purposes as well. So long as self-murder was universally condemned as a heinous sin, it was an effective weapon in the arsenal of sectarian polemicists. Both Protestant and Catholic writers capitalized on the suicides of prominent members of the opposite confession. And as English Protestantism became increasingly fragmented, rival groups within the church and among the dissenters also strove to prove that the creeds they hated were doctrines of desperation. The symbolism of this propaganda was on one level simple: the antagonistic faith drove its members to a state of despair, the psychological equivalent of apostasy, and to suicide, the gravest sin a Christian could commit. But a subtler message was conveyed in some polemics on sectarian suicides. They depicted religious suicides as new Spiras and taught that self-murder was the inevitable consequence of capitulation to pressure from the ecclesiastical authorities. The belief that suicide was a desperate sin was therefore a means at once of discrediting rival sects and of strengthening the resolve of the members of one's own with a dreadful warning.

## POPULAR BELIEFS ABOUT SUICIDE

The most dramatic expression of popular hostility to suicide was the rites of desecration. A genuine demotic custom, performed by laymen without clerical participation, they were an expression of a deeply held conviction that self-murder was supernaturally evil. The church's acceptance of their legitimacy is surprising from one perspective. Protestant reformers were determined to rid the church of ritual that embodied medieval Catholic and pagan elements. The ritual burial of suicides contained both. But just as the church adopted and transformed the medieval symbolism of the psychomachy in order to emphasize the religious significance of suicide, so it also decided informally to sanction the rites of desecration. Since the Protestant clergy stressed the supernatural causes of self-murder, they had either to replace or to tolerate the popular religious practices that dealt with its supernatural consequences. They chose to tolerate them. This was an easy enough compromise to make. Suicide was not a very frequent occurrence, compared with the other ways that people died. Moreover, the church had stopped short of eliminating many other folkloric customs surrounding mourning and burial—a fact Puritans descried—and so a concession of this sort was not unique.

The derivations of the rituals are obscure. Some of their details inverted Christian mortuary customs; others were plainly pagan in origin. Suicides, for example, were sometimes placed face down or buried in graves dug north and south. The bodies of the dead were normally placed face up in a grave that was oriented east and west, so that they could rest in a sleeping position, ready to rise up and face the Lord on the day of judgement. But the most distinctive features of profane burial, siting the grave in a highway or crossroads and driving a stake through the body, almost certainly originated in pagan religion, although the stake may have come in time to serve as a means of preventing the resurrection of the suicide's body at the Last Judgement.[2]

By purloining some ideas from anthropology, it is possible partially to unriddle the rituals' symbolism. Mortuary rites all over the world characteristically proceed through three phases: separation, transition, and integration.[3] During the period of separation, the person prepares for death; during the period of transition, or liminality as the anthropologists call it, he is mourned and ritually removed from the world and set on his journey to the afterlife; during the period of integration, he is reincorporated into a new community, the community of the dead. Normal English customs of death and burial embodied these three phases. Strict rituals of forgiveness and repentance were supposed to precede death, which normally took place in the company of family and friends, from whom one took one's leave as one died. After these rites of separation, there was a liminal phase of mourning and interment. During the prescribed period of mourning, when the loss of the deceased was shared by family and neighbours, the survivors donned special mourning clothing to symbolize their bereavement and customary rites, such as bell-ringing, were performed. The most charming of the latter was the practice of 'telling the bees', notifying the dead person's hive of the loss of their 'king' and the succession of a new master. The transition from the community of the living to that of the dead was dramatized in the funeral rites. Full Christian burial began with the transportation of the corpse to the grave, borne along above the ground, on the shoulders of the deceased's friends or hired paupers. The black symbols of oblivion

[2] For descriptions of profane burial, see e.g. T. R. Forbes, *Chronicle from Aldgate* (New Haven, 1971), 164–70; D. Hey, *An English Rural Community: Myddle under the Tudors and the Stuarts* (Leicester, 1974), 46; J. C. Cox, *The Parish Registers of England* (London, 1910), 114–16; C. Gittings, *Death, Burial and the Individual in Early Modern England* (London, 1984), 72–3; E. Ettlinger, 'Folklore in Oxfordshire Churches', *Folklore*, lxxiii (1962), 175; W. Rendle, 'A Suicide's Burial [temp. Jas. II]', *Notes and Queries*, 7th ser., iii (1887), 359. For some (rather dubious) discussion of these customs see R. M. Dorson, *Peasant Customs and Savage Myths: Selections from the British Folklorists* (London, 1968), i. 324–5; and M. Puhvel, 'The Mystery of the Cross-Roads', *Folklore*, lxxxvii (1976), 167–77. Jean Delumeau argues that the French rituals for burying suicides are instances of the Christianization of pre- or at least non-Christian customs: *La Peur en occident (XIV^e–XVIII^e siècles)* (Paris, 1978), 84–5.

[3] The classic statement of this pattern is A. Van Gennep, *The Rites of Passage*, trans. M. B. Vizedom and G. L. Caffee (Chicago, 1960), esp. ch. 8. Important recent works on mortuary ritual include R. Huntington and P. Metcalf, *Celebrations of Death* (Cambridge, 1979); S. C. Humphreys and H. King (eds.), *Mortality and Immortality* (New York, 1981); M. Bloch and J. Parry, *Death and the Regeneration of Life* (Cambridge, 1982).

were offset with flowers and garlands, placed on the coffin and later on the grave, green symbols of rebirth. Finally, at the churchyard the burial office was said, and the corpse was buried in the ground or in the church. The grave was dug in a manner that symbolized the hope of the resurrection, as we have already seen. Its placement in the churchyard or the church was also significant, for the Reformation had in this instance failed to achieve the Protestant goal of demystifying space—some parts of the burial ground were held to be more holy than others, notably the south and east sides. The north was dreaded. Moreover, graves were usually located in family groups. The burial thus implanted the deceased among the community of the dead (who were, of course, also the community's dead), and did so in a manner that preserved the position he had occupied during his lifetime in the social and family structure of the parish.[4]

Suicide has always been regarded, among a great many cultures, as the quintessential 'bad death'. It may be extenuated, excused, or glorified in certain circumstances, but deliberate self-killing is very widely condemned. In many places, as Arnold Van Gennep long ago pointed out, suicides were believed 'to wander between the world of the dead and that of the living'. Like unbaptized babies, who have not yet been incorporated into the world of the living, they cannot fully enter the realm of the dead, since they did not await Death's summons. The unbaptized and suicides are, Van Gennep stresses, the most dangerous of the dead. Excluded from the society of the departed, they wish to return to that of the living, and as they cannot, 'they behave like hostile strangers to it'.[5] Their ghosts are dangerous and intrusive. The suicide, in other words, never escapes the liminal stage between death and arrival in the land of the dead. Liminality, as Victor Turner explains, is a state in which 'the characteristics of the ritual subject (the "passenger") are ambiguous; he passes through a cultural realm that has few or none of the attributes of the coming state'.[6] It was the very ambiguity of the state of eternal transition that made it most terrifying. 'The unclear is the unclean',

[4] For these customs, see Gittings, *Death, Burial and the Individual*, 139; J. Brand, *Observations on Popular Antiquities*, ed. H. Ellis (London, 1813), iii. 292–7; A. Wood, *The Life and Times of Anthony Wood*, ed. A. Clark, Oxford Historical Society, 19, 21, 26, 30, 40 (Oxford, 1891–1900), i. 276; and, most illuminating of all, D. Cressy, 'Death and the Social Order in Elizabethan Essex', unpublished typescript, 1987 (abstract in *Social History Society Newsletter*, xii [Spring 1987], 8).

[5] Van Gennep, *Rites of Passage*, 160–1.

[6] V. Turner, *The Ritual Process* (Ithaca, 1969), 94. See also, id., *The Forest of Symbols* (Ithaca, 1967), ch. 4.

Turner has remarked, acknowledging his debt to Mary Douglas, 'transitional beings are particularly polluting, since they are neither one thing nor another'.[7]

It is liminality that the rites of desecration practised in medieval and early modern England expressed above all. Suicides were denied the usual rites of mourning. Their bodies were interred in the dark, without a coffin and the garlands that might have adorned it. They were buried in a roadway, sometimes at a crossroads, rather than in the churchyard in the place where they 'belonged'. Folklorists and historians have exercised considerable ingenuity in explaining the preference for highways and crossroads. Some suggest that it was a ploy to baffle the suicide's ghost, for he would not know which road to follow. At the very least the choice plainly symbolizes the fact that suicides, unlike other kinds of dead people, never complete their transition to the afterlife. They were excluded from the communities of living and dead and set on an eternally unfinished journey. The ghosts of suicides were believed to be restless and malevolent; the stake driven through the suicide's body was supposed to fix his spirit in its grave. In William Sampson's play, *The Vow Breaker*, a faithless young woman whose lover kills himself after she has married another man remarks spitefully:

> My best counsell is that you bury him as the custome of the Country is, and drive a stacke through him; so perhaps I that had no quietness with him, whilst he liv'd, may sleepe in peace now he's dead.[8]

This passage recites a genuine popular belief. *The Vow Breaker* was based on an actual incident that became the most famous ghost story about a suicide in early modern England. A gentleman's son living in Nottingham, James Bateman, fell in love with a farmer's daughter. The young couple's blissful courtship was spoiled by the intervention of her parents, who persuaded her to renounce her troth and marry a rich old man named German instead. In a fit of despondent malice, Bateman hanged himself in her home on the day of her wedding. To compound his revenge, he reappeared as a ghost, tormenting her and, finally, causing her to vanish. Bateman's story was retold in dozens of contemporary ballads and pamphlets, as well as in Sampson's play. It survived as a folk-tale, known variously as *Young Bateman's Ghost* or *The Fair*

[7] Turner, *Forest of Symbols*, 97.

[8] Quoted in Wymer, *Suicide and Despair*, 118; W. Sampson, *The Vow Breaker*, ed. H. Wallrath, Materialien zur Kunde des älteren Englischen Dramas, No. 42 (Louvain, 1914), II. iv. 123–6.

*Maid of Clifton*, until modern times.[9] Stories of Bateman's ghost were popular partly because so many people believed that the spirits of suicides actually did haunt the living. Keith Thomas relates the Jonsonian tale of a conjurer named Robert Tooley—a character straight out of the *Alchemist*—who gulled a client into believing that he was plagued by the ghost of a neighbour who had killed himself, then charged him 20*s*. to banish it.[10]

The road and the stake served another purpose as well. Self-murderers, explained John Weever, were buried in a highway 'with a stake thrust through their bodies, to terrifie all passengers, by that so infamous and reproachfull a buriall, not to make such their finall passage out of this world'.[11] From the point of view of the authorities, profane burial was an effective deterrent to suicide as well as a customary ritual. In 1590 the coroner of the city of London ordered that the end of the stake driven through Amy Stokes's corpse should be left exposed, 'as a memoryall' to discourage others from following her example.[12] A later coroner contrived an especially elaborate variation on this theme for the burial of the traitor Miles Sindercombe in 1657. Sindercombe's corpse was dragged to the grave behind a horse (an inversion of the practice of carrying the body aloft), with his 'head forward', and buried beneath a scaffold. 'He was turned in stark naked, and a stake, spiked with Iron, was driven through him into the earth; that part of the Stake that remained above ground being all plated with Iron, which may stand as an example of terror to all Traytors for the time to come.'[13]

Variations were sometimes made in the basic elements of the ritual. Suicides were occasionally buried in open fields instead of in a roadway.[14] A few were also placed in the north side of the churchyard, together with

[9] J. H. Marshburn, *Murder and Witchcraft in England, 1550–1640* (Norman, Okla., 1971), 88–90; K. Briggs, *Dictionary of Folk-Tales*, 2 pts. in 4 vols. (Bloomington, Ind., 1971), pt. B, i. 449–50; *Bateman's Tragedy* (London, n.d. [*c.* 1720?]), reprints several of the earlier versions of the tale.

[10] Thomas, *Religion and Magic*, 594–5. See also, D. Jones-Barker, *The Folklore of Hertfordshire* (London, 1977), 82–3; R. L. Tongue, *Somerset Folklore*, ed. K. M. Briggs (London, 1965), 104; W. Sikes, *British Goblins* (Boston, 1881), 330–1 [Wales]; Briggs, *Dictionary of Folk-Tales*, pt. B, i. 424–5, 442, 451, 587. An illuminating discussion of popular beliefs about the soul and mortuary rituals is R. Richardson, *Death, Dissection and the Destitute* (London, 1987), esp. ch. 1.

[11] J. Weever, *Ancient Funerall Monuments* (London, 1631), 22.

[12] Forbes, *Chronicle from Aldgate*, 165.

[13] *The Whole Business of Sindercome* (London, 1657), 16.

[14] H. Fishwick, 'Suicides Buried in the Open Fields', *Notes and Queries*, 10th ser., iv (1905), 346; Yorkshire Archaeological Society, *Parish Registers*, vol. cxlvi (1983), Register of Birstall, 175.

unchristened infants and excommunicates, other eternally liminal souls. This practice became very widespread in the eighteenth century, when the transition to the *non compos mentis* verdict meant that more and more churches were obliged to bury suicides in the churchyard. In the sixteenth and seventeenth centuries, it was probably a compassionate concession to the family or, perhaps, a way of registering dissent from the coroner's verdict.[15] Whatever variations may have been occasionally made in the ritual performance, the rites themselves plainly signified that self-murder was a spiritually dangerous, polluting act that condemned the soul to eternal wandering and imperilled the community.[16]

The clergy tolerated the rites of desecretation as an additional punishment for the heinous sin of self-murder, an elaboration of the church's own penalties, the denial of funeral services and exclusion from hallowed ground.[17] As Christian evangelists, however, their main concern was with its supernatural causes and eschatological implications. By the reign of Elizabeth, if not earlier, they had persuaded men and women of every

[15] For the burials in the north side of the churchyard (prior to 1700), see Cox, *Parish Registers of England*, 115; Wood, *Life and Times*, ii. 354, 503–4; P. Laslett, *The World We Have Lost Further Explored*, 3rd edn. (New York, 1984), 175; Yorkshire Archaeological Society, *Parish Registers*, cxxv, Register of Drypool (1961), 17. Henry Machyn reported that several clergy attended the burial of a London woman in 1562, including 'Veron the Frenchman', who preached a sermon and would not allow her body to be brought into the church. Possibly she had been judged *non compos mentis* and like the churlish priest in *Hamlet* 'Veron' would only allow 'maimed rites': *The Diary of Henry Machyn*, ed. J. G. Nichols, Camden Society, os, xlii (London, 1848), 284. For an apparently similar case, see *The Registers of St. Mary le Bowe, Cheapside, All Hallows, Honey Lane, and of St. Pancras, Soper Lane, London*, ed. W. Bruce Bannerman, Harleian Society Pubs., Register Section, xliv (London, 1914), 292.

[16] A fuller discussion of profane burials is unfortunately impossible here. Very few records describing them were kept, and the most promising source of evidence, parish registers, proved uninformative or misleading. Because self-murderers would normally have been buried outside the churchyard, priests were not obligated to record their deaths, and a great many suicides pass unnoticed in the appropriate registers. Those who are noticed are usually described simply as persons who killed themselves, with no mention of where or how they were buried. Others were obviously exceptional cases—persons *non compos mentis*, suicides buried on the north side of the chruch for some reason or, in at least one instance, a person who repented before dying. For examples of registers recording burials outside the chruchyard in highways or fields, see Yorkshire Archaeological Society, *Parish Registers*, xlii, Register of Thirsk (1911), 55; ibid., cxii, Register of Cantbey (1941), 87; cxlvi, Register of Birstall (1983), 175; *The Registers of St. Olave, Hart Street, London, 1563–1700*, ed. W. Bruce Bannerman, Harleian Society Pubs., Register Section, xlvi (London, 1916), 169, 172; *The Register of St. Mary Somerset, London*. Pt. ii: *Burials, 1557–1853*, ed. W. Bruce Bannerman, Harleian Society Pubs., Register Section, lx (London, 1930), 35. For the apparently unique case of repentance, followed by burial in the churchyard, see Yorkshire Archaeological Society, *Parish Registers*, cxl, Register of Almondbury, vol. 1, pt. 2 (1975), 55.

[17] Sym, *Lifes Preservative*, 277–8.

rank and calling that suicide was instigated by the devil. Because of their piety and their preoccupation with their spiritual state, Puritans and sectarians were especially likely to interpret suicidal impulses as satanic temptations. Many of them told of encounters with the devil when they were depressed or unsure of God's grace. The youthful Puritan Nehemiah Wallington, for example, was provoked by the devil into eleven suicide attempts. Satan manifested himself to Wallington as a crow, as his sister, as a minister, and, more conventionally, as a disembodied voice. His conviction that God and the devil are palpable presences, pulling him this way and that, implanting the urge to die and strengthening his will to live, recapitulates the ancient pattern of the moralities:

> Then Satan temted me againe and I resisted him again. Then he temted me a third time, and I yielded unto him and I pulled out my knife and put it neere my throte. Then God of his goodness caused me to consider what would follow if I should do so. . . . With that I felle out a weaping and I flong away my knife.[18]

Edward Burghall, a Cheshire Puritan, noted in his diary that a woman of Aston-Green had drowned herself 'by the instigation of the devil' in 1636.[19] Several of the humble men and women who were members of Henry Walker's Baptist congregation told stories of satanic temptations to self-murder in the autobiographies they dictated to him. After the death of her husband, a woman whom Walker identifies only as D.M. was enticed by the devil to go to a pond and drown herself and her baby. Only God's providence, intensifying her love for her child, saved her.[20] John Gilpin, an ex-Quaker, claimed that he was tempted and even possessed by Satan when he was a member of the sect. One night he began to wonder if the power he felt within him was divine or diabolical: 'And my hand was carried to take up a Knife which lay upon the Table; . . . [then] my hand was carried with it towards my throat, and the voice said to me, *open a hole there, and I will give thee the words of eternall life.*'[21] Pious men and women continued to attribute suicidal urges to the devil's wiles throughout the seventeenth century. Like their Puritan forebears, the Nonconformist faithful related close encounters with the Fiend at

[18] Guildhall Library MS 204, 1–10 (we are grateful to Paul Seaver for giving us a transcript of these pages); P. S. Seaver, *Wallington's World* (Stanford, 1985), 22, 31, 69.

[19] E. Burghall, 'Providence Improved', in T. Worthington Barlow, *Cheshire: Its Historical and Literary Associations* (Manchester, 1855), 156.

[20] H. Walker, *Spirituall Experiences of Sundry Beleevers* (London, 1652), 35–6; see also 6, 26, 358–9. This book is sometimes attributed to Vavasour Powell.

[21] J. Gilpin, *The Quakers Shaken* (London, 1653), 8.

length in their autobiographies. Hannah Allan's *Satan His Methods and Malice Baffled*, for example, is a long and vivid description of 'the great Advantage the Devil made of her deep Melancholy', tempting her to apostasy and suicide.[22]

It was not just religious zealots who believed that the devil was the author of self-destruction. The great Elizabethan magus John Dee noted that three people he knew killed themselves 'by the fende his instigation'.[23] One of Dee's most ardent admirers, the astrological physician Richard Napier, wrote down the symptoms of 139 men and women who were 'tempted' to kill themselves between 1597 and 1634. Some of them actually saw or heard the Tempter or one of his demons; many more believed that unnamed spirits or witches had implanted their suicidal urges in their minds. Elizabeth Hayford, for instance, saw the devil, who told her that she could never be saved, and Robert Toe believed that the 'black boy' from whom he had bought a knife was Satan himself. The anguished Richard Lea told Napier that a malevolent spirit 'will speak often to him and appear in the likeness of a man, and to kill him, and would draw him away'.[24] Napier's clients were mostly humble folk: farmers and artisans of middling rank, their wives and servants, occasional cottagers and labourers, and some outright paupers. From the opposite end of the social ladder, Queen Elizabeth's godson, John Harington—a libertine famous to posterity for his poem celebrating the water-closet—repeated the conventional belief in the devil's powers in his otherwise decidedly unconventional dialogue on the legitimacy of suicide: 'SATAN is not only dampned, but a Suggester, a mover, and perswader, readie to entice, willing to betraye, earnest to bewitche, strong to envince [*sic*], . . . to bring to desperacion.'[25]

22 H. Allan, *Satan His Methods and Malice Baffled . . . Reciting the Great Advantage the Devil Made of Her Deep Melancholy; and the Triumphant Victories, Rich and Sovereign Graces God Gave Her Over All His Strategems and Devices* (London, 1683). For other examples, see R. Baxter, *The Certainty of the World of Spirits* (London, 1691), 38, 40, 96–7; O. Heywood, *Oliver Heywood: His Autobiography, Diaries, Anecdote and Event Books*, ed. J. Horsfall Turner (Brighouse and Bingley, 1882–5), ii. 299, iii. 95, 191–2; J. King, *The Iron of Melancholy* (Middletown, Conn., 1983), 49–54; W. Haller, *Rise of Puritanism* (New York, 1957), 113.

23 J. Dee, *The Private Diary of Dr. John Dee*, ed. J. O. Halliwell, Camden Society, os, xix (London, 1842), 3, 35–6, 40, 43. For Dee's attempt to exorcise a suicidal woman see ibid. 35–6, and below.

24 Bodl., Ashmole MSS 217, fo. 67$^r$ (Hayford); 414, fo. 194$^v$ (Toe); 199, fos. 11$^r$, 28$^r$ (Toe); 215, fo. 298$^v$ (Lea). See also, Ashm. 404, fo. 289$^v$ (Morton); 227, fos. 57$^r$ (Neale), 94$^v$ (Chalice); 409, fo. 83$^v$ (Payne); 218, fo. 42$^v$ (Southan). For other examples of satanic temptation to self-murder, see Thomas, *Religion and Magic*, 474–5, 521; Essex County RO, D/P 27/1/2, 9; C.H. L'E. Ewen, *Witchcraft and Demonianism* (London, 1933), 294, 298. For parallels in colonial Massachusetts, see H. I. Kushner, *Self-Destruction in the Promised Land* (New Brunswick, NJ, 1989), 21–7.

25 BL, Add. MS 27632, fo. 122$^v$.

Popular belief in the devil's role in driving people to self-murder persisted throughout the seventeenth century and into the eighteenth. Asked why he had cast himself into a pond in 1677, Anthony Joyce replied that he had been 'led by the Devil', and went on to declare that his reason for trying to kill himself was that he had 'forgot to serve God as he ought'. His kinsman Samuel Pepys, who recorded his explanation, was inclined to believe that his business failures were the real reason for his desperation.[26] An eleven-year-old girl told a constable who was examining her in 1690 that the day before her mother committed suicide she was visited by 'a strange man in black'. The girl overheard her mother say to the stranger that she was worried what would become of her children, and he answered that she should have no care for them because they would be provided for. A gentleman who heard the story commented cautiously: 'It's a wicked age, and what this black man was, God knows.' The constable, 'a respectable citizen', certainly thought he knew, or else he would not have believed and spread the little girl's tale.[27] As we shall see in a later chapter, these notions survived in the next century, conspicuously in the sermons of Nonconformist divines and the writings of Methodist preachers, less conspicuously in ballads, broadsheets, folklore, and, most importantly, the minds of ordinary men and women: suicides, attempted suicides, and witnesses who appeared before inquests.

The conviction that suicide had supernatural causes was not simply derived from Protestant preaching. It had been incorporated into popular religion. Most English men and women identified with the Church of England, and 'popular Anglicanism', as it has recently begun to be called, was certainly the dominant current of religious belief in the seventeenth and eighteenth centuries.[28] But the Anglicanism of the ministers was not necessarily the same as the Anglicanism of their flocks. Some have depicted it, and not without good reason, as a kind of magical Pelagianism allied with a vague allegiance to Protestantism.[29] While there was a good deal of popular Protestant piety, the consequence in part of the rhetorical stratagems and flexibility about aspects of traditional belief to which we have alluded, there were nevertheless areas of

[26] S. Pepys, *The Diary of Samuel Pepys*, ed. R. Latham and W. Matthews (London, 1970–83), ix. 32.

[27] HMC, Report 5, *Pine Coffin*, 380.

[28] For this view, see P. Collinson's magisterial *The Religion of Protestants* (Oxford, 1982), ch. 5.

[29] For this view, see Thomas, *Religion and Magic*, another magisterial work.

disagreement between the clerical establishment and the 'multitude'. Preachers complained incessantly that the common people exaggerated the power of witches and spirits, and while sensitive historians have taught us to be wary of such pronouncements, this refrain was sounded so often, and is so plausible, that it seems to us to be mulish to doubt it. Laymen certainly attributed suicidal temptations to a wider range of evil powers that the clergy did, and they often sought magical means to combat them. Many believed, for instance, that witches could plunge their victims into suicidal gloom. Agnes Buttres, a young woman whom Richard Napier treated in 1618, blamed her attempted suicide on a witch's 'bad tongue' and 'praised God that she had escaped' death. Her mother agreed and told the astrologer that her daughter had been 'tempted to drown herself but that God stopped her'.[30] Christopher Monke of Swythland in Leicestershire, testifying before Leicester authorities in 1620, accused the Reverend Gilbert Smyth of bewitching his wife and son, causing the boy to cut his own throat.[31] In a deposition justifying her allegation that Margaret Francis had bewitched her, Joan Harvye wrote that in her fits she had seen 'a little black boy with glistering eyes tempting her, and speaking to her, and she to it; and she was tempted also to drown herself'.[32] Richard Bovet retold a story about a Somerset lad of about eighteen who had been bewitched into repeated suicide attempts in his 1684 collection of proofs of the existence of spirits and witches.[33] Jane Wenham, the last woman convicted of witchcraft in England, in 1712, was accused by her neighbours of causing preternaturally two girls to try to drown themselves.[34]

Orthodox clergymen taught that because the devil could tempt people to kill themselves only with God's permission, the best remedies for suicidal feelings were prayer and conversion to a godly life. But many victims of desperation sought illicit remedies for their anguish. Some resorted to exorcists. Jesuit priests, for example, claimed that they had

[30] Bodl., Ashmole MS 201, fos. $133^{r}$, $142^{r}$ (Buttres, Buttiresse). See also Ashmole MSS 193, fo. $278^{r}$ (Chaukly); 198, fo. $103^{v}$ (Carter); 220, fos. $21^{v}$ (Franklin), $29^{v}$–$30^{r}$ (Holder); 235, fo. $28^{r}$ and 217, fo. $4^{r}$ (Cox); 200, fo. $223^{v}$ (Haddon); 202, fo. $187^{v}$ (Morgan); 404, fo. $289^{v}$ (Morton); 193, fo. $208^{v}$ (Frone); 239, fo. $31^{r}$ (Pattifort); 409, fo. $60^{v}$, 408, fo. $46^{v}$ (Payne); fo. $53^{v}$ (Perrot); 413, fo. $181^{r}$ (Russe); 193, fo. $119^{r}$ (Sanford); 201, fo. $53^{v}$ (Tims); 227, fos. $180^{v}$–$181^{r}$ (Turnell); 215, fos. $141^{v}$, $169^{v}$ (Worlye); 402, fos. $120^{v}$, $144^{r}$, $159^{v}$ and 217, fo. $141^{r}$ (Toms); 407, fo. $176^{r}$ and 194, fo. $40^{r}$ (Richards).

[31] Ewen, *Witchcraft and Demonianism*, 425.

[32] Ibid. 192; for other examples, see 190, 210.

[33] R. Bovet, *Pandaemonium*, ed. M. Summers (Aldington, Kent, 1951), 116.

[34] Ewen, *Witchcraft and Demonianism*, 385, 389. See also, J. Raine (ed.), *Depositions from the Castle of York*, Surtees Society, xl (Durham, 1861), 112, 209.

A PERFORMER OF MIRACLES OR MAGIC FEATS



relieved the torment of a man who supposedly 'under the influence of witchcraft' had tried to throw himself in a river.[35] The papists were widely believed to be the most successful exorcists, even after the Reformation. To counter the evangelistic advantage that the papists gained from dispossessions, the Puritans and later the Nonconformists also catered to popular fear of the devil and evil spirits. Using rituals of prayer and fasting they battled with the supernatural powers who urged men and women to despair and kill themselves. In a famous case in 1574 that set the precedent for later Protestant exorcisms, John Foxe organized a session of turbulent prayer to dispossess a law student whose afflictions had begun with several suicide attempts.[36] One of the patients dispossessed by John Darrell, the controversial Puritan thaumaturgist, was also an attempted suicide.[37] In their anxiety to discredit Darrell and the Puritans, the ecclesiastical authorities banned healing fasts in 1604, but some ministers nevertheless persisted in casting spirits out of despairing men and women.[38] And in the later seventeenth century, a circle of Nonconformist divines in the north of England held fasts for a number of melancholy and suicidal people. The most eminent among them, Richard Gilpin, strongly endorsed the practice. 'The Temptation [to commit suicide] must also be opposed with *Fasting and Prayer*.'[39]

Other suicidal men and women resorted to still more unorthodox means to combat the assaults of the supernatural. John Dee anointed his servant Anne Frank with holy oil. She had long been tempted by 'a wycked spirit' to kill herself, and at her request, Dee prayed 'for vertue and powr and Christ his blessing of the oyle to the expulsion of the wycked; and then twyse anoynted [her]. The wycked one did resist a while.' Dee's magic was to no avail. Satan prevailed over the power of prayer and holy oil, and after one more suicide attempt she slashed her throat fatally.[40] Simon Forman, Dee's rather disreputable contemporary,

35 H. Foley, *Records of the English Province of the Society of Jesus* (London, 1877–83), vii. 1145.

36 Thomas, *Religion and Magic*, 482–3.

37 J. Darrell, *A True Narration of the Strange and Grevous Vexation by the Devil of 7 Persons in Lancashire, and William Somers of Nottingham* (n.pl., 1600), 16–17.

38 Thomas, *Religion and Magic*, 483–7.

39 R. Gilpin, *Daemonologia Sacra*, pt. 3, 116. See also, Heywood, *Autobiography*, ii. 280–1, iii. 125, 163; Thomas, *Religion and Magic*, 487; M. MacDonald, 'Religion, Social Change and Psychological Healing in England, 1600–1800', in W. J. Sheils (ed.), *The Church and Healing*, Studies in Church History, xix (Oxford, 1982), 101–25; D. Harley, 'Mental Illness, Magical Medicine and the Devil in the North of England, 1650–1700', unpublished paper, Wellcome Unit for the History of Medicine, Oxford, 1987.

40 Dee, *Private Diary*, 35–6.

gave an astrological amulet to the young William Lilly's master to ward off suicidal temptations by a 'haunting spirit'.[41] This kind of amulet, called a sigil, seems to have been in demand by melancholy folk. Richard Napier, Forman's highly reputable protégé, gave them to at least one-fifth of his suicidal clients.[42] Ann Cox, for instance, returned repeatedly to Napier over a half-dozen years, complaining that she 'heareth voices tempting her to despair and to make herself away'. At various times she feared she was 'haunted', that 'the Devil was within', and she suspected that one Goody Shelton had bewitched her. The treatment that had afforded her the most lasting relief was an amulet. In 1625 Napier wrote in his practice book that she had 'had a sig[il] and was well three years, now of late ill with much evil motions'. He gave her another.[43] Village wizards, 'cunning' or 'wise' men and women as they were often called, also treated the whole range of mental afflictions, employing a large and miscellaneous repertoire of magical rites. Given the vast numbers of troubled folk whom famous astrologers like Forman and Napier treated, it is certain that many suicidal people must have resorted to their humbler, cheaper competitors. An Essex clergyman remarked in the early seventeenth century that cunning men and women 'helpe ignorant and unsetled persons, in cases of distraction' and other calamities.[44]

The belief that suicide was ungodly and diabolical may be found even in the language of legal documents and witnesses' testimony. Coroners' inquests on the bodies of self-murderers, like other felony indictments, alleged that a self-murderer committed his crime, 'not having the Fear of God before his Eyes but moved and seduced by the Instigation of the Devil'.[45] The coroner of the liberty of Writtle in Essex departed from the usual litany when he stated in his inquisition that the shockingly violent

41 W. Lilly, *History of His Life and Times* (1715; repr. London, 1822), 33.

42 This may well be a substantial underestimate of the demand for sigils. Napier was inconsistent in recording the remedies he prescribed and almost certainly dispensed more sigils than his notes indicate. He also did not learn to make them until he had been practising for some years: MacDonald, *Mystical Bedlam*, 294 n. 198. Sir Richard Napier noted that a sigil cast in 1604 (probably by Forman) caused the wearer to be merry and was good against witchcraft and evil spirits but another cast in 1611 (by the elder Napier) was effective against 'diseases of deep desperation and melancholy diseases': Bodl., Ashmole MS 1453, fos. 241, 247.

43 Bodl., Ashmole MSS 235, fos. 28$^r$, 76$^v$; 217, fo. 4$^r$ (Cox).

44 Quoted in A. Macfarlane, *Witchcraft in Tudor and Stuart England* (New York, 1970), 121.

45 For printed examples of the formula see, R. F. Hunnisett, *Calendar of Nottinghamshire Coroners' Inquests, 1485–1558*, Thoroton Society, xxv (Nottingham, 1969), p. xxv; Umfreville, *Lex coronatoria*, 358. Coroners and juries occasionally departed from the formula and described the Devil's temptations in their own words: see, e.g., Essex County RO, D/DP/M 607/12; PRO, KB 9/696, m. 341.

suicide of Thomas Graves had been precipitated 'by the mocyon of the wycked Spirite'.[46] Several witnesses in the contentious inquest into the suicide of John Atkinson in Cumberland in 1696 testified that he had spoken before his death of 'Hell and all [the] devell['s] Spiritts'. When one of his relatives, William Atkinson, sensing that he was melancholy, asked him how he was, he replied 'never worse, and said that God had forsaken him and the devill had gotten holden of him'. William grabbed John and demanded what made him talk like that: 'the devill,' he answered.[47] Evidence of godliness was naturally a strong reason to believe that doubtful deaths were not self-murders. Accused of misrepresenting Richard Gylderall's suicide as an accident, a group of his Yorkshire neighbours responded in Star Chamber by inverting the formula. Gylderall, they swore, 'was a man of good name and fame, creditt and estimacon, and one who was thought [to have] had the fear of god before his eyes'.[48] The bill that the almoner entered in Star Chamber against Ellen Johnson described her husband Lancelot's state of mind before his drowning as 'ungodly'. Denying that he had committed suicide, she insisted in her answer that her husband had 'carried himself in an exceeding honest upright godly and religious fashion' and lived in good repute among his neighbours. He had gone through every office in the parish and died a churchwarden; he had never been given 'to any ungodly or unreligious course' and had not uttered 'desperate or ungodly speeches'.[49] The coroner immortalized in the law reports on Barclay's Case in 1658 had wrongly refused to consider several affidavits declaring a putative suicide to have been a pious man for it was his duty to hear all the evidence as to the deceased's guilt or innocence.[50] In his charge to a jury in 1716, the mayor and coroner of Folkestone explained that a person who is *felo de se* is 'a Man [who] hangs or kills himselfe for want of Grace'.[51]

The combination of government pressure and religious change

[46] Essex County RO, D/DP/M 607/12.

[47] Cumbria RO, D/Lec/CR I, 5/3.

[48] PRO, STAC 5/A22/1.

[49] PRO, STAC 8/3/10. See also J. Miller and K. H. Rogers, 'The Strange Death of Edward Langford', *Wiltshire Archaeological and Natural History Magazine*, lxii (1967), 108. Stevenson rightly remarks that evidence about the godliness of the deceased figured largely in Star Chamber cases in which the manner of death was disputed: S. J. Stevenson, 'Social and Economic Contributions to the Pattern of "Suicide" in South-East England, 1530–1590', *Continuity and Change*, ii (1987), 232–3.

[50] Barclay's Case, *English Reports*, lxxii. 1273. 'Barclee fuit pious home et cy mult tender le preservation de son vie come ascune home.'

[51] Kent AO, U 279/O4/1–3.

explains why the law of suicide was so rigorously enforced in the sixteenth and early seventeenth centuries. Neither factor by itself accounts for the intensified severity of this period. The crown disciplined coroners and juries who blatantly defied the law, and coroners were probably especially anxious to avoid prosecution. And yet the behaviour of coroners' juries went beyond mere compliance. They often returned verdicts of *felo de se* when it was impossible to prove with certainty that a suicide had occurred. Over one-third of all the deaths that were classified as self-murders were drownings. Frequently there was no physical evidence (an eyewitness, a note, or a pile of folded clothes, for instance) to prove that a death had been a suicide; sometimes there was not even any circumstantial evidence (when a drowned person had been a total stranger, for example). One authority has suggested that up to one half of all the suicides by drowning could just as plausibly have been returned as accidents.[52] There was plenty of scope for mercy, had juries been inclined to construe the evidence narrowly. An exception will prove the rule. An Elizabethan jury haled into Star Chamber for returning a verdict of misadventure in the drowning of Elinor Johnson stuck by their story that there was nothing to prove that she had killed herself. The almoner lamely demanded to know what evidence there was that she had *not* killed herself; why else would she have gone to the pond at night? The defendants answered only that there was no evidence that she had been suicidal, and it had been a tempestuous night, so her death must have been accidental.[53]

There was another way in which juries could have behaved more mercifully, had they wished to do so. Fewer than 2 per cent of suicides were found to have been insane when they killed themselves, as we have already seen. This is an unbelievably low figure, even given a very rigorous definition of insane behaviour.[54] An example will show just how resistant to bringing in *non compos mentis* verdicts juries could be. After the suicide in 1560 of Thomas Spryngold of King's Lynn, a coroner's jury found him *felo de se* and his goods were confiscated.

[52] For examples of ambiguous cases, see Hunnisett, *Nottinghamshire Coroners' Inquests*, nos. 292, 294, 304. S. J. Stevenson, 'The Rise of Suicide Verdicts in South-East England: The Legal Process', *Continuity and Change*, ii (1987), 63–5 is the source of the high estimate of the prevalence of such cases.

[53] PRO, STAC 5/A43/1. See also, STAC 8/2/42.

[54] For what it is worth—and given the vast differences in attitudes to suicide and certification procedures, it is not worth very much—about 60% of suicides today are psychiatrically ill: D. Lester, *Why People Kill Themselves: A 1980's Summary of Research Findings on Suicidal Behaviour*, 2nd edn. (Springfield, Ill., 1983), 106.

Complaining that his property should have been used to relieve his 'poor infant children', Spryngold's family sued the town officials, who had the right to the goods, on the grounds that the suicide had been 'madd and frantyke' when he killed himself. They produced no fewer than ten witnesses, including the local minister, all of whom swore that Spryngold had long been insane. When asked questions, said one neighbour, 'he answered Lyke A mad old fole, as he was wont to doe'. And when the parson tried to persuade him to forsake his mad fancies, he 'toke up a pype and pyped, nothing regarding his instrucion and good Counsell'. None of this testimony inclined the jury to mercy.[55] Sussex juries brought in verdicts of *felo de se* on Thomas Wood and Richard Hartlye in spite of the fact that both of them were described as insane in the very inquisitions they returned. They even admitted that Hartlye had been 'made [mad] about xii yeres paste before his deathe'.[56]

We should not assume that juries returned *felo de se* verdicts in such cases merely because they were overawed by the coroner or royal officials. Juries could and did act independently and even defiantly when they were persuaded that they were right. The jury who investigated the death of the prosperous clothier Edward Langford, for example, stuck to their story that he had been murdered by some unknown person in spite of the almoner's charge that they were guilty of 'open and manifest perjury'. The almoner guessed the value of Langford's goods at £1,000, and he pursued them vigorously. Unsatisfied with the jury's answer to his bill, Star Chamber administered a probing set of interrogatories to them. Explanations were demanded for incidents in Langford's past that might have been suicide attempts. The almoner battered at the jury's stubborn insistence that the death had been a homicide with a series of leading questions: why had two persons been named arbitrarily as suspects in the case; why had the hue and cry not been raised if the death had really been a murder; what exactly had Langford said about the dreams he had had the night before he died; had the place he was found

[55] PRO, REQ 2/84/12.

[56] Wood died in 1535, Hartlye in 1554; R. F. Hunnisett, *Sussex Coroners' Inquests: 1485–1558*, Sussex Record Society, lxxiv (Lewes, 1985), nos. 83, 178. See also, Stevenson, 'Rise of Suicide Verdicts', p. 63; Hunnisett, *Sussex Inquests*, nos. 99, 212; PRO, KB 9/706, m. 255 (Arthur Symons, 1600); KB 9/594/1, m. 74 (Robert Gervis); KB 9/728/3, m. 204 (Richard Deering, 1609); KB 9/747/2, m. 143 (Richard Bell, 1614); KB 9/769/3, m. 223 (John Nethersole, 1622); KB 9/780/2, mm. 147, 148 (Robert Fry, 1622); KB 9/845/2, m. 264 (Henry James, 1649); KB 9/845/3, m. 325 (Matthew Peckover, 1649); KB 9/852/1, m. 48 (Nicholas Hardie, 1651); KB 9/852/1 (John Gaston, 1651); KB 9/872/2, m. 109 (Sydney Montague, 1656); KB 9/879/1, m. 8 (Roger Oakes, 1658). PRO, STAC 5/A5/12; STAC 5/A24/24; STAC 8/1/6; STAC 8/3/14 are also pertinent.

showed signs of a struggle; had they been bribed? They denied every allegation he implied. It was a vigorous defence, and the fact that his widow quickly remarried another clothier suggests that it was a successful one. If she retained her husband's goods, which included obviously valuable stock, she would have been an attractive match to a man in the same trade.[57] The exception once more proves the rule. The high percentage of doubtful cases that were classified as self-murders and the low percentage of cases that were excused on account of insanity indicate that the humble men who served on coroners' juries were willing participants in the reign of severity.

The conviction that self-murder was a diabolical deed was what set it apart from most other crimes. Every crime could be viewed as a sin, and hence an ungodly act inspired by Satan, but only a few offences, notably self-murder and witchcraft, were regarded as primarily supernatural.[58] And yet it would not do to leave the impression that suicides were always and only understood in supernatural terms. The belief that the devil was the first cause of self-destruction coexisted with other beliefs about its causes that were social and psychological. As we shall see later in this book, ordinary men and women routinely explained suicide as the consequence of distressing events and emotional tribulations, describing the personal misfortunes or mental and physical illnesses that had motivated people to take their own lives.[59] The supernatural and natural explanations for self-murders were not antithetical. Instead, they complemented one another, and they may be found in sources such as the legal documents we have just discussed, side by side without any hint of contradiction.

The coexistence of spiritual and secular causes was not unique to suicide; it was a characteristic of both plebeian and élite thinking about a range of mental and physical events. Responding to a rare sceptical assertion that illnesses could not have both supernatural and natural causes, the physician Stephen Bradwell described the logic of dual causation with unusual clarity: 'The Divell maie be found, to have his hand in sundry bodely afflictions, which have no supernaturall symptomes to discover them. ... For naturall and supernaturall causes maie Concur, ... and are not contraries that expell on[e] another.'[60] Like the

57 Miller and Rogers, 'Strange Death of Edward Langford'. See also PRO, STAC 8/2/42.

58 C. B. Herrup, 'Law and Morality in Seventeenth Century England', *Past and Present*, no. 106 (1985), 102–23.

59 Chapter 8. Cf. Stevenson, 'Social and Economic Contributions to Suicide', 234.

60 S. Bradwell, 'Mary Glovers Late Woefull Case,' BL Sloane MS 831, fo. 74$^{v}$.

effects of witchcraft and diabolical possession, self-murder could be thought of as a natural calamity and a supernatural event. The cause that any witness or writer adduced depended on many factors, most of which cannot even be guessed at from the surviving documents. The circumstances in which he spoke or wrote, the audience he addressed, his mood at the moment, the method of the suicide, and the observer's relationship to the dead person all seem to have played their parts in various accounts. The complexity of the possible responses to a suicide and of the explanations available for it explains why diarists and other writers seldom depicted suicides uniformly either as provoked by Satan or prompted by natural causes. For instance, as several writers have observed, Ralph Josselin attributes only one of the seven suicides and two threatened suicides that he recorded explicitly to diabolical causes. That does not mean, however, that he believed that one was attributable to Satan whereas the others were due to mundane causes. He was invoking different levels of causation in different cases.[61] There were almost certainly some plebeian sceptics, who disbelieved that the devil had a hand in self-murder as some others disbelieved the powers popularly attributed to witches, but we have encountered no clear evidence of such sentiments among the common people. Despite these qualifications, the essential point remains that the role of the devil in popular interpretations of suicide became more conspicuous in the sixteenth and early seventeenth centuries.

## SECTARIANISM AND SELF-MURDER

The horror that suicide aroused inevitably made it the subject of sectarian controversy. The rivalries that accompanied the Reformation and persisted throughout the sixteenth and seventeenth centuries created opportunities to exploit such deaths to gain a propaganda advantage. There was scriptural authority for interpreting self-murder as an indication of divine displeasure with rival confessions. Glossing the suicide of Ahithophel, the Geneva Bible observed that 'Gods just vengeance even in this life is powered on them, which are enemies, traitours, or persecu-

[61] Cf. the discussions in M. Zell, 'Suicide in Pre-Industrial England', *Social History*, xi (1986), 316; A. Macfarlane, *The Family Life of Ralph Josselin* (Cambridge, 1970), 169–70; *The Diary of Ralph Josselin, 1616–1683*, ed. A. Macfarlane (Oxford, 1976), 18. Elsewhere, Josselin attributes a suicide to 'sad sins, judgements ... [and] feare of want': ibid. 362.

tors of his Church'.[62] It was a lesson early Protestants took to heart. John Foxe included stories of papists and apostates who slew themselves in his *Acts and Monuments*. Their suicides were signs of the special favour Foxe believed God bestowed on the English church, and he compared them with the deaths of Biblical figures—Pontius Pilate, Saul, Ahithophel, and Judas. His examples were drawn mainly from the reigns of Edward and Mary, but he told of some who died as he was writing. These included Henry Smith, a lawyer who hanged himself in 1559 after renouncing Protestantism. He died, Foxe claimed, with his agnus dei and other 'idolatrous trash' beside him.[63] Popery provided no consolation to save apostates who fell into despair. 'No man', on the other hand, 'is able to bring forth any one example . . . of any . . . true gospeller, that either killed himself or showed forth any signification or appearance of despair.'[64]

The controversy over the death of Sir James Hales, of which he was well aware, may have encouraged Foxe to compile his list of Catholic self-murderers for *Acts and Monuments*. A distinguished jurist and dedicated Protestant, Hales had assisted the government of Edward VI to impose the new religion on the nation. One of the victims of his efforts had been Stephen Gardiner, the conservative bishop of Winchester. The accession in 1553 of the Catholic Queen Mary led inevitably to Hales's ruin. Gardiner became the lord chancellor in the new regime, and he swiftly revenged himself by depriving Hales of his judgeship and imprisoning him. As he lay in Fleet prison, he was harried by Gardiner's agents, whose imprecations and threats drove him to recant his religion. In despair over his apostasy and his peril, he tried unsuccessfully to kill himself with a penknife. Gardiner seized the opportunity to proclaim publicly in Star Chamber that Hales's suicide attempt showed that Protestantism was a 'doctrine of desperation'.[65] To Hales's beleaguered co-religionists, his deed was a calamity. Awaiting his own trial and execution for heresy, Bishop John Hooper reacted by writing a short treatise that attempted to place the blame on the Catholics. As long as Hales had remained steadfast in his faith, Hooper argued, he had been able to withstand imprisonment and harsh treatment. But when

[62] *The Geneva Bible: A Facsimile of the 1560 Edition*, ed. L. E. Berry (Madison, 1969), 2 Sam. 17: 23.

[63] J. Foxe, *The Acts and Monuments*, ed. J. Pratt, 4th edn. (London, n.d. [1877]), viii. 646. See also, i. 89, 91–3, viii. 634, 635, 642, 646, 648–9.

[64] Ibid. viii. 642, 648–9, 668, 670.

[65] Ibid. vi. 715.

Gardiner and his men persuaded him to recant, he lay down his defences against Satan. Is it any wonder, Hooper asks sarcastically, that the devil entered into a man who had credited a false Christ made of bread? 'No, doubtless; for his new-made Christ is not able to keep the devil away.' Popish doctrine thus opened the way for evil spirits and self-murder.[66] Hooper's pamphlet was not published in full until the nineteenth century; it was obsolete before it could have been put in a printer's hands. For as soon as he had recovered from his wounds, Hales was released on Gardiner's orders, and returning to his estate in Kent, he immediately drowned himself.

The propaganda disaster suffered by the Protestants was enormous. Everyone knew what had happened. Hales's widow added to the public fame of the event by suing the government for seizing her husband's property illegally. The case turned on a technicality, but it excited enough interest to merit a report by the distinguished jurist Edmund Plowden. Plowden's account of the case, which was published in 1571, was read by every aspiring lawyer in the land and by many laymen as well, including perhaps William Shakespeare.[67] Even before Plowden's report appeared, Protestant spokesmen had begun trying to rehabilitate Hales's reputation. The task was a delicate one, for they disapproved of suicide at least as violently as their Catholic opponents, perhaps more so. Hooper's manuscript found its way into the hands of John Foxe, who printed part of it and added his own praise of Hales's character. Foxe also attempted rather diffidently to depict Hales as a Protestant martyr, assailing the 'cruel handling of the malignant papists' and comparing him to the virgins of the early church who drowned themselves rather than submit to ravishment and idolatry. 'Who can tell', Foxe asks rhetorically, 'whether master Hales meaning to avoid the pollution of the mass, did likewise choose the same kind of death, to keep his faith undefiled?' And yet Foxe was uncomfortable with the logic of his own arguments, fearing that they might seem to condone self-murder. He is not, he assures the reader, attempting to excuse the heinous fact of Hales's death, which he wishes were drowned in oblivion. Hales was, he

[66] J. Hooper, 'A Brief Treatise Respecting Judge Hales', in his *The Later Writings of John Hooper*, ed. C. Nevinson, Parker Society (Cambridge, 1852), 374–80.

[67] *Hales* v. *Petit*, *English Reports*, lxxv. 387–405; William Shakespeare, *Hamlet*, ed. H. Jenkins (London, 1982), v. i. 10 20; *DNB*, s.v. 'Hales, James'; R. M. Frye, *The Renaissance Hamlet* (Princeton, 1984), 363 n. 15, cites the relevant scholarship. The echo of Plowden's Law French in Shakespeare's verse sounds very faint to our ears. Although Plowden was a Catholic, his report concerns legal matters exclusively and does not reflect his personal religious views.

concludes, neither to be accounted among the martyrs nor, on the other hand, to be reckoned among the damned.[68]

Other writers had fewer scruples about presenting Hales simply as the heroic victim of papist tyranny. The story of his life and death was recounted briefly by Raphael Holinshed, whose history was the secular counterpart of Foxe's Book of Martyrs. Together they presented the authorized version of history for Elizabeth's subjects. Holinshed described Hales as a 'man wise, vertuous, and learned in the lawes of the realme', who found himself in trouble because of his religious views, like many others at the time, and who was confused and terrified by his gaoler. His death, Holinshed declares, 'was much lamented'.[69] The story was revived by Gilbert Burnet and John Strype in their histories of the Reformation. At the time they were writing, in the late seventeenth and early eighteenth centuries, royal Catholics seemed once again to threaten English Protestantism, and Strype thought it fitting to paraphrase the substance of Hooper's treatise, 'wherein the blame of this action was retorted upon the papists themselves'.[70] Strype also plundered Foxe's manuscripts for instances to add to his list of men whom popery drove to self-destruction or to attempt suicide.[71] Burnet's version of Hales's story was modernized slightly to conform with contemporary thinking about suicide: he ignored the supernatural implications of the judge's despair and self-murder and stated simply that hard treatment at the hands of the Catholic gaolers had 'turned his brain'.[72]

Elizabethan Protestants had their best opportunity to link Catholicism with treason and suicidal desperation in 1585. Accused of plotting to free Mary Queen of Scots and achieve toleration for English Catholics, Henry Percy, eighth earl of Northumberland, was committed to the Tower of London, where he languished for six months and finally shot himself to death. Catholic propagandists immediately issued a pamphlet in Cologne, charging that Northumberland had been murdered on the order of the vice-chancellor, Sir Christopher Hatton. The government's agents responded with *A True and Summarie Reporte* of the earl's treasons and suicide. The pamphlet purported to be a transcript of a hearing held

68 Foxe, *Acts and Monuments*, vi. 710–17.

69 R. Holinshed, *Holinshed's Chronicles of England, Scotland, and Ireland* (London, 1807–8), iv. 8–9.

70 J. Strype, *Ecclesiastical Memorials*, vol. iii, part 1 (Oxford, 1822), 274–6; G. Burnet, *The History of the Reformation*, ed. E. Nares (New York, 1842), ii. 383–4.

71 Strype, *Ecclesiastical Memorials*, vol. iii, pt. 1, 276–9.

72 Burnet, *History of the Reformation*, ii. 384.

in Star Chamber three days after Northumberland's death. It included testimony from the politicians and officials of the Tower who were directly concerned and an account of the earl's last days by a servant who swore that he had seen a pistol smuggled into Northumberland's cell. Fearing that his master might kill himself, he warned him that 'the Deuill was great', but he 'could by no means prevaile with the Earle in that behalfe'. The pamphlet concluded that Northumberland had been struck down by God as a punishment for his treasons: 'God by his judgement had for his sinnes and ingratitude taken from him his Spirit of grace and deliuered him ouer to the enemie of his soule, who brought him to that most dreadful and horrible end whereunto he is come.'[73] Holinshed reprinted the whole text of this pamphlet in his *Chronicles*. Stressing that the earl killed himself out of 'his owne diuelish intent', Holinshed also printed an English translation of the coroner's inquisition, an unusually full and wide-ranging document that rehearsed the government's version of how Northumberland had prepared for his suicide as well as the facts of his death.[74]

As the Reformation progressed the struggle between Protestant and Catholic developed into a more complex and volatile rivalry. The Church of England split into Puritan and Anti-Puritan factions, and so the religious politics of self-murder came increasingly to focus on the pernicious effects of predestinarian doctrines. Anti-Calvinist writers both in the church and among the recusant community charged that the Puritans' excessive emphasis on the certainty that many would be damned and the uncertainty over who would be saved drove pious men and women to despair and self-destruction. Robert Burton invented a new name for pathological doubt about one's spiritual state, religious melancholy, and he charged that the Puritans were tearing and wounding people's consciences, so that they were almost mad with fear and sorrow. But 'the greatest harm of all proceeds from those thundering ministers', whose preaching was 'a most frequent cause' of despair, whose prognostic was self-murder.[75] Puritans were vulnerable on this

73 *A True and Summarie Reporte of the Declaration of Some Part of the Earl of Northumberelands Treasons . . . Together with the Examinations & Depositions of Sundrie Persons Touching the Maner of His Most Wicked & Violent Murder Committed upon Himselfe with his Owne Hand, in the Towre of London, the 20. Day of Iune, 1585* [London, 1585], 17, 22. For a suit over money forfeited when the earl was convicted as a *felo de se*, see PRO, STAC 5/A3/7.

74 Holinshed, *Chronicles*, iv. 602–15.

75 R. Burton, *Anatomy of Melancholy*, ed. H. Jackson (London, 1978), iii. 398–404, 408. See also, J. Taylor, *The Whole Works*, ed. A. Taylor and P. Eden (Edinburgh, 1852), ix. 272; J. F. Sena, 'Melancholic Madness and the Puritans', *Harvard Theological Review*, lxvi (1973), 294–309; L. Babb, *The Elizabethan Malady* (East Lansing, Mich., 1951), 47–54.

point, for their willlingness to exploit the terrifying drama of the psychomachy and stress on the perils of damnation did influence a good many neurotic and depressive men and women. Puritan preachers were themselves given to melancholia, and some declared that the godly were more often the target of Satan's temptations than the unregenerate. Among 'the tentations to murther, which follow many of the people of God', warned Richard Capel, 'are to murther ones self, or ones nearest friends, as parents, wife, children'.[76]

It is difficult to determine just how widespread religious melancholy may have been among the godly. By the turn of the sixteenth century, Calvinist divines had incorporated suicidal crises into a typological scheme of conversion and redemption. Young men and women in the throes of guilt over their past sins were supposed to experience profound remorse, even to the point of despair. The godly life was a difficult one, and extreme turmoil sometimes accompanied the decision to separate oneself from the ordinary world, with all its sensual and social comforts, and to pursue an austere and often ridiculed lifestyle. Recognizing this, the preachers stressed the spiritual significance of that turmoil and emphasized in contrast the comparative peace of mind conversion brought with it. Thus Nehemiah Wallington's morbid preoccupation with his sinfulness and his repeated attempts at suicide when he was twenty and twenty-one years old recapitulated an ideal pattern of religious experience.[77] So did George Trosse's tormented descent into suicidal despair and madness after he realized how sinful his life had been. The voyage from a seafaring life to a presbyterian ministry led through the slough of despond.[78] John Bunyan described the same journey, with all its extremes of anguish and diabolical temptation, in *Grace Abounding*, a book that did more to publicize the pattern than any other.[79] The Puritans thus, in effect, institutionalized suicidal moods, presenting them as the emotional symbol of the liminal stage between the sinful life and regeneration. For this reason some converts may

[76] R. Capel, *Tentations*, 4th edn. (London, 1650), 192. See also, T. Wilson, *Saints by Calling* (London, 1620), 30, 111–12, 142, 145–6; G. Trosse, *The Life of the Reverend Mr. George Trosse*, ed. A. W. Brink (Montreal, 1974), 20–31; W. Hunt, *The Puritan Moment* (Cambridge, Mass., 1983), 119–22.

[77] Seaver, *Wallington's World*, ch. 2, is a vivid depiction of Wallington's spiritual crises and their meaning; parallels are cited on pp. 213, 214. See also, C. Hill, *A Tinker and a Poor Man* (New York, 1989), 184–7.

[78] Trosse, *Life*, e.g. 89.

[79] J. Bunyan, *Grace Abounding to the Chief of Sinners and Pilgrim's Progress*, ed. R. Sharrock (London, 1966). For an excellent discussion of the pattern of affliction and redemption in Puritan works, see O. C. Watkins, *The Puritan Experience* (Oxford, 1972).

actually have exaggerated their torment in their autobiographies. On the other hand, many of the godly were never tempted to murder themselves, and the clergy deeply resented the accusation that Puritans were especially morbid. 'The world's objection is that of all kind of men in the world, those that profess religion are the most melancholy', fumed Richard Sibbes. 'But if that be so, it is because they are not religious enough. . . . The true character of a Christian is to be cheerful and none else can be truly cheerful and joyous.'[80]

Suicides by Puritans were certainly less frequent than their enemies implied, but there was at least one memorable example that seemed to prove the perils of Calvinism. In 1600, William Doddington, a rich Puritan merchant and an intimate of leading figures in the government, flung himself to his death from the steeple of St Sepulchre's in London. A pamphlet announcing his suicide appeared immediately and was quickly suppressed by the privy council.[81] How widely it may have circulated or what its message may have been is impossible to know, since no copies survive, but the regime may have been concerned that Catholics would exploit the suicide for propaganda purposes. News of Doddington's death certainly travelled quickly through the recusant underground. Father John Gerard, living disguised as a layman in the house of Lady Agnes Wenman, exploited his knowledge of what had happened to make a fool of George Abbot. A strong Calvinist, Abbot was already a considerable personage, and although he had attacked Gerard fiercely in print, he had no idea that the gentleman he met at Lady Agnes's home was his adversary. Realizing that Abbot did not yet know of Doddington's suicide note, in which he expressed his hope for God's mercy, Gerard drew Abbot into a conversation about the Puritan's fate in the next world. 'Poor fellow', Gerard began, 'What could have induced him to destroy his body and soul in one fell act?' Abbot protested that it was not for mortals to pass judgement on Doddington. Gerard granted that he might indeed have repented while he was falling

[80] R. Sibbes, *The Complete Works*, ed. A. B. Grosart (Edinburgh, 1862–4), ii. 456, vii. 212. See also Wilson, *Saints by Calling*, 142; R. Bolton, *Instructions for a Right Comforting [of] Afflicted Consciences*, 2nd edn. (London, 1626), 204–12; R. Yarrow, *Soveraigne Comforts for a Troubled Conscience* (London, 1634), 15–16.

[81] Norfolk and Norwich RO, Knyvett Papers, KNY 743, is the fullest explanation of the story. We are grateful to Gary Owens for sharing with us his transcript of this document. Doddington was the brother-in-law of Sir Francis Walsingham and an official of the royal mint: C. Read, *Mr Secretary Walsingham and the Policy of Queen Elizabeth* (n.pl., 1967), iii. 426; S. E. Lehmberg, *Sir Walter Mildmay and Tudor Government* (Austin, Tex., 1964), 306. See also, G. B. Harrison, *The Elizabethan Journals* (Garden City, NY, 1965), ii. 149; *Acts of the Privy Council, 1599–1600*, NS xxx (London, 1905), 286.

to his death, but the last act he had committed was a mortal sin. Abbot responded that it was not clear that Doddington's deed was a mortal sin, which afforded Gerard an opportunity to assert that suicide was against the law of God. 'He forbids us under pain of hell to kill anyone, and particularly ourselves, for charity begins at home.' Gerard had no doubt he had won the argument: 'The good doctor was caught.' He and Lady Agnes were vastly amused when Abbot declined to discuss theology further.[82] Abbot's discomfort was certainly genuine, for he shared Gerard's conviction that suicide was in general a damnable crime.[83]

Sectarianism sustained the old controversy over which faith was the doctrine of desperation into the late seventeenth and early eighteenth centuries. The suicide of John Child in 1684 sparked a controversy among dissenters that lasted for almost a century. Child had been a leading Baptist preacher and had distinguished himself by defending his sect against the Quakers. In 1682, motivated it is said by fear of persecution and eagerness to advance himself in the world, he renounced his faith and published a book calling upon all dissenters to reconcile themselves to the Church of England.[84] But instead of prosperity and happiness, Child's apostasy brought him only guilt and melancholy. After one futile attempt to hang himself, he succeeded in committing suicide in October 1684. Two broadsheets describing his death appeared immediately. One recounted his past career without mentioning his apostasy, blaming his self-murder on his inability to withstand Satan's temptations. This squib seems to have been intended to link Child's despair with his sectarianism.[85] A rival broadsheet, wonderfully illustrated, was also issued at about the same time. Viewing the suicide from the Baptist perspective, *A Warning from God to all Apostates* compared Child's fate with Francis Spira's. Persons who forsake the church, it argues, exhibit the worst vices. They commit the sin of the fallen angels, and it is no wonder that 'Satan takes full Possession of them, and leads them into pernicious Error of Delusion'.[86]

82 J. Gerard, *The Autobiography of a Hunted Priest*, trans. P. Caraman (New York, 1952), 170–1. Doddington is called Dorrington in some sources; his suicide note is signed with the former name: BL, Lansdowne MS 99, no. 32, fos. $88^r$–$89^v$.

83 G. Abbot, *An Exposition upon Jonah* (London, 1600), 133.

84 *DNB*, s.v. 'Child, John'.

85 *Sad and Lamentable News from Brick-lane in the Hamlet of Spittle-Fields, or a Dreadful Warning to Such as Give Way to the Temptations of the Devil, in the Deplorable Example of Mr. John Child Once Famous Anabaptist Teacher Who Falling into Despair Committed a Barbarous and Unnatural Murther Upon his Own Person* (London, 1684).

86 *A Warning from God to All Apostates . . . Wherein the Fearful States of Francis Spira and John Child Are Compared* (London, 1684).

The parallel between Spira and Child was developed much more effectively by two Baptist ministers, Thomas Plant and Benjamin Dennis, who published in 1688 a fifty-page pamphlet entitled *The Mischief of Persecution Exemplified*. Plant and Dennis write as if they were among the clergy who prayed with Child in his last days. They recount his conversations with the people who were trying to help him and reprint his suicide note. The ministers ask him if he thinks that he is like Spira. Child replies: 'Spira's condition was nothing to mine; for wrath is come and [is] coming on me to the utmost, because I have forsaken that which I believe to be true, to embrace that which I knew to be false, thro' slavish fear to keep myself from sufferings.'[87] They conclude with a statement, allegedly written by Child, in which he admits that he had renounced the Baptist faith and issued his call for church unity at the instigation of the devil.[88] Tagged on to a seventeenth-century narration of Spira's story, which was immensely popular among Baptists and Methodists, this tract was reissued in 1715, 1718, 1734, and 1770.[89] The Spira *topos* thus allowed Plant and Dennis to transform the disaster of Child's suicide into a warning that would stiffen the resolve of the faithful in the face of persecution. The stories of Spira and Child conveyed two related messages to distressed sectarians: true peace of mind would be found only through adherence to their faith, no matter how bad the persecution might seem, and conforming to a religion that they had rejected as false would bring even greater guilt and misery. This had been the point of Spira's tale originally, and it is probably no accident that stories of new Spiras multiplied in the 1680s and 1690s: persecution of the dissenters peaked in the 1680s, and even after the Toleration Act of 1689, they were rightly concerned that it might resume.[90] In addition to comparisons of Spira and Child, two books called *The Second Spira* appeared in 1692 and 1693, followed within the next five years by at least five more 'Spira' stories.[91] Wesley republished both Bacon's original version of the Spira story and one of the second Spiras in the *Arminian Magazine* at the end of the eighteenth century.[92] Even when they were not being persecuted by the authorities, dissenters

[87] T. Plant and B. Dennis, *Mischief of Persecutions Exemplified* (London, 1688), 27.

[88] Ibid. 39–42.

[89] B.H., *A Relation of the Fearful Estate of Francis Spira . . . As Also the Miserable Lives and Woful Deaths of Mr. John Child . . . and Mr. Geo. Edwards* (London, 1770).

[90] M. Watts, *The Dissenters* (Oxford, 1985), 263.

[91] These are conveniently listed in Trosse, *Life*, 18.

[92] *Arminian Magazine*, vi (1783), 24–8, 79–83, 132–3; x (1787), 354–6, 412–15, 465–8, 526–9, 582–5, 634–7.

and Methodists were reviled by their orthodox neighbours, and they often confided to their diaries fears that they would lose heart and yield to the pressures to conform. Spira thus became a sectarian saint, and his example could be used to neutralize the shock that the suicide of one of the faithful caused and turn it into a lesson that renewed the psychological fortitude of the sect.

At the height of the vogue for 'second Spiras', at the end of the seventeenth and beginning of the eighteenth centuries, the story was also integrated into attacks on 'atheists'.[93] True atheists were rare, but in the volatile religious climate of the time, people who repudiated particular doctrines or embraced some of the ideas of the deists were labelled as atheists. Easily the most interesting of the polemics blaming suicides on atheism was John Smith's account of the beliefs and death of George Edwards. Edwards was a prosperous Essex man, raised in a strict religious household, who began to develop his own heterodox theology when he was in his forties. He read books by prominent authors who advocated rational religion, and he began to question the truth of Christian beliefs and even of the scriptures themselves. He denied, for instance, that the existence of God could be proved from the universality of beliefs in divinity, since those beliefs were so various and contradictory. He wondered if all men are descended from Adam how some of them could be black. Views like this aroused the ire of Smith, his minister, and seem also to have set him at odds with his family and neighbours. His wife refused to sleep with him, accusing him of promiscuity and of having a venereal disease. Finally, on 4 January 1704 Edwards rigged up three guns to fire simultaneously, pointed them at himself, and set them off when his wife entered the house. Smith had no doubt as to the fundamental cause of Edwards's death. He railed at atheists, the men who uphold the principles of Hobbes, Spinoza, and the neo-Epicurean, Walter Charleton. He compared Edwards with the deist Charles Blount, who had killed himself two decades earlier, and argued that atheism deprived men of reason and God's grace. They were left vulnerable to Satan's wiles and to their own desperate passions.[94]

Religious polemics easily elided with political polemics, for sectarian rivalries continued to influence politics throughout the seventeenth century. The suicides of politically important people did not, therefore, escape the attention of writers gripped by 'the rage of party'. The death

[93] For an example, see T. James, *Spira's Despair Revived* (London, 1694).
[94] J. Smith, *The Judgment of God upon Atheism and Infidelity*, 2nd edn. (London, 1704).

of Robert Long, a participant in Monmouth's Rebellion, was mentioned briefly in the last chapter. Long, also known as Baker, had been a captain in the Western Rebellion, Monmouth's desperate attempt in 1685 to supplant James and impose a radical Whig programme. Monmouth's aims seemed to Tories to be the very antithesis of legitimate government: instead of divine right, Monmouth stood for parliamentarianism, even republicanism; instead of the established church, he stood for the dissenters. The author of a manifestly Tory account of his death strove to equate Long's rebellion against the king with his repudiation of God. Self-murderers, he began, defy their creator. Heedless of their future state, they are prey to 'the Enemy of Mankind' who heightens 'the Sence of their Guilt into that of a desparate Despair'. Long, he explains, had been an inn-keeper at Shaftsebury, but he was dissatisfied and so he joined the rebels. After their defeat he fled to London, where he was recognized and captured. Cast into Newgate and charged with treason, Long grew very melancholy. There was 'a kind of Wildness' in his countenance. On 20 October 1685, he barricaded his room shut and hanged himself. The author notes that the coroner's jury found him *felo de se*, 'or, that Through his Despair, occasioned by the Horrour of his Guilt, he laid Violent Hands upon himself'.[95]

The most spectacular of all the political suicides of the late seventeenth century was that of the Whig grandee, Arthur Capel, earl of Essex. Essex was a leading Whig politician, and together with three other party grandees, the duke of Monmouth, Lord Russell, and Algernon Sidney, he was arrested in 1683 and charged with plotting to assassinate the king and the duke of York. The Rye House Plot, like the Popish Plot before it, fed on partisanship and religious bigotry and grew into a monstrous and dangerous confusion of fact and fiction. The confusion continues to this day. Many historians have denied that there was a Rye House Plot; its latest student, Richard Ashcraft, has no doubt that there was. He is almost certainly right. He succeeds in showing that Essex's circle was hatching some sort of conspiracy to resist government tyranny, and that as their conspiracy grew, it became an assassination plot. Essex was confused and deeply dismayed by his arrest and the hysteria that followed the plot's discovery. Confined in the Tower

[95] *A Sad and Dreadful Account of the Self-Murther of Robert Long, alias Baker* (London, 1685).

awaiting trial on charges of high treason, he cut his throat on 13 July 1683.[96]

For the Whigs, Essex's suicide heaped calamity on calamity until they built up to catastrophe. The news of his death caused a sensation at Lord Russell's trial and wrecked his defence. William, Lord Howard of Escrick, a main prosecution witness, began his testimony in a low and almost inaudible voice. When the Lord Chief Justice and a member of the jury admonished him to speak more loudly, he answered: 'There is an unhappy accident happened that hath sunk my voice: I was but just now acquainted with the fate of my lord of Essex.' Serjeant Jeffreys recalled this poignant moment in his summation to the jury, declaring that Essex would not have killed himself except 'to avoid the methods of public justice'. The jurors allegedly reported later that Essex's suicide weighed more heavily with them than the evidence presented against Russell by the prosecution.[97] Skilfully publicized by the government in newsheets and a pamphlet that was a transcript of the coroner's inquest, it fortified the public conviction that the Whig radicals were guilty of treason.[98] One 'Anti-Jack Presbyter' took up the official version of events and turned it into execrable verse. He had no doubt about Essex's guilt, or his subsequent fate:

> Some do affairs, that 'twixt such *Acts* and *Death*,
> Some may *repent*, even at his last *breadth* [*sic*].
> I fear, there is, (after so foul a *Sin*,)
> Too narrow a *gap* to let *Repentence* in.[99]

Perhaps the most damaging aspect of the Tory case was the repeated assertion that Essex had defended suicide as a justifiable act in certain

[96] R. Ashcraft, *Revolutionary Politics and Locke's Two Treatises of Government* (Princeton, 1986), ch. 8. See also, D. J. Milne, 'The Results of the Rye House Plot and their Influence upon the Revolution of 1688', *Transactions of the Royal Historical Society*, 5th ser., i (1951), 91–108; K. H. D. Haley, *The First Earl of Shaftesbury* (Oxford, 1968), 707–24; L. G. Schwoerer, 'William, Lord Russell: The Making of a Martyr, 1683–1983', *Journal of British Studies*, xxiv (1985), 49–50; J. Carswell, *The Porcupine: The Life of Algernon Sidney* (London, 1989), ch. 15. Many of the pertinent sources, together with accounts of the trials of the plotters, are conveniently gathered together in W. Cobbett, T. Howell, *et al.* (eds.), *Cobbett's Collection of State Trials* (London, 1811), ix, cols. 358–1372.

[97] *State Trials*, ix, cols. 602, 633, 800.

[98] *An Account of How the Earl of Essex Killed Himself in the Tower of London* (London, 1683).

[99] *A New Poem on the Dreadful Death of the Earl of Essex Who Cut His Own Throat in the Tower* (n.pl., n.d.).

circumstances. The coroner's jury itself may have been informed that the earl held this view, still identified with free-thinkers, deists, and libertines. A few years later, a juror recalled that a Major Hawley had told him at the time of the inquest that although Essex's suicide might surprise some who did not know him, those who did were well aware 'That it was a Fixt principle with my Lord, that any man might cut his throat, or otherwise dispose of his life as he thought fitt to auoid a Dishonorable & Infamous Death'.[100]

Whig sympathizers were understandably reluctant to believe that Essex had actually committed suicide, and so were some others, like John Evelyn, who knew the earl to have been a deeply religious man.[101] The rumour that Essex had been murdered rapidly spread, and the government grew exceedingly alarmed. 'The faction have some great villainy in prospect', Robert L'Estrange wrote anxiously to Secretary Jenkins, 'The murder of the Earl of Essex is the main point they trust to and the next step will make a sham plot of this conspiracy. . . . They look for a parliament and hope for such a one as will be prevailed on to believe this to be a Popish plot.'[102] A rash party zealot named Lawrence Braddon set out to prove that Essex had been killed on the orders of the duke of York and, perhaps, the king himself. Braddon's speculations were circulated by his confederate, Hugh Speke, and after repeated examinations, they were arrested and convicted for suborning witnesses.[103] Braddon was kept in prison until the flight of James II. The cry of murder was taken up by others, the most notable of whom was Robert Ferguson, a leading figure in the conspiracy itself. Safe in exile in Holland, Ferguson wrote a pamphlet in 1684, protesting that Essex had never condoned suicide, challenging some of the forensic evidence in the printed inquisition, and calling attention to irregularities in the inquest.

[100] BL, Harleian MS 1221, fo. 317. See also *CSPD, 1 July–30 Sept. 1683*, 202; G. Burnet, *Burnet's History of My Own Times*, new edn., ed. O. Airy, Part I (Oxford, 1900), ii. 398–9; H. C. Foxcroft (ed.), *A Supplement to Burnet's History of His Own Time* (Oxford, 1902), 119; *State Trials*, ix, col. 1234.

[101] J. Evelyn, *The Diary of John Evelyn*, ed. E. S. de Beer (Oxford, 1955), iv. 326–7.

[102] *CSPD, 1 July–30 Sept. 1683*, 335–6. See also ibid. 197, 204, 234–4, 313, 332, 353, 380, 416; *CSPD, 1 Oct. 1683–30 Apr. 1684*, 227, 283, 296, 303.

[103] *CSPD, 1 July–30 Sept. 1683*, 174, 215, 228, 313, 323, 331, 336–7, 341–2, 366–7, 371–2, 430; *CSPD, 1 Oct. 1683–30 Apr. 1684*, 10, 24, 58, 75, 146, 218, 234; *State Trials*, ix, cols. 1127–224; Foxcroft, *Supplement to Burnet's History*, 123; N. Luttrell, *A Brief Relation of State Affairs* (Oxford, 1857), i. 286–7, 299–300, 306.

Ferguson's piece was immediately translated into French, Dutch, and Flemish.[104]

The discovery of the Rye House Plot demolished the Whig party; Russell and Sidney were executed, Monmouth was exiled, and the Tories secured an unshakeable grip on the government until the Glorious Revolution. The belief that Essex had been murdered nevertheless survived and resurfaced periodically.[105] John Locke wrote a manuscript insisting that Essex had not killed himself.[106] The Revolution rehabilitated the Whigs and rekindled the controversy over Essex's suicide. The Convention Parliament quickly established a committee to investigate the Rye House Plot, with the aim of exonerating the Whig martyrs of 1683. Braddon was in the forefront of an effort to prove once and for all that Essex had been murdered. He recorded the testimony of witnesses who swore that the razor that had killed the earl had been found outside his cell, not inside it behind locked doors as the official version had it. One woman claimed to have overheard a group of papists conspiring to murder Essex before the deed. The duke of York, she asserted, had first suggested poisoning, and when that had proved impossible, 'his Highness ordered his throat to be cut'.[107] Despite the Whigs' eagerness to restore Essex's honour and to blacken James's, the official investigation of the earl's death ran aground on the implacable opposition of his widow. The earl of Clarendon learned from the duchess of Beaufort that in 1689, as the proceedings were getting under way, Lady Essex had sent for her, her husband, other relatives, and a group of politicians and had demanded that the inquiry be dropped: 'She had declared that she believed he killed himself; and therefore desired that the business might fall.'[108] Frustrated in his aim to achieve an official endorsement for his

[104] R. Ferguson, *An Enquiry Into, and Detection of, the Barbarous Murder of the Earl of Essex* (London, 1684); Ashcraft, *Revolutionary Politics*, 380–2. Cf. *An Account of the Murder of the Earl of Essex* (London, 1688), which is substantially the same. Another, more explosive broadsheet, naming the duke of York as Essex's assassin, may have been written at the same time; a summary is in PRO, KB 15/40, 414–19.

[105] *State Trials*, ix. cols. 1232–3, 1335, 1339; BL, Sloane MS 78, fos. $1^r$–$22^v$; Ashcraft, *Revolutionary Politics*, 380–2, gives other references.

[106] Ashcraft, *Revolutionary Politics*, 380.

[107] BL, Harleian MS 1221, fos. 295–7; *State Trials*, ix. cols. 1223–30, 1327–31.

[108] *The Correspondence of Henry Hyde, Earl of Clarendon, and of his Brother, Lawrence Hyde, Earl of Rochester; With the Diary of Lord Clarendon from 1687 to 1690 . . . and the Diary of Lord Rochester During his Embassy to Poland in 1676*, ed. S. W. Singer (London), ii. 277. Braddon later confirmed this story, *State Trials*, ix, col. 1329. It is this piece of evidence, more than anything else, that makes us doubt Ashcraft's argument that Essex may actually have been murdered, perhaps by John Holland, the chief suspect in the 1689 investigation: Ashcraft, *Revolutionary Politics*, 380–1 n. 190; *An Account of the Taking of Captain Holland* (London, 1689).

version of Essex's death, Braddon returned to propaganda. He published two detailed expositions of his theory and the evidence supporting it in 1689.[109] Like many conspiracy theorists, he had little difficulty in locating anomalies in the official statements, suspicious departures from routine procedures, and ambiguities in the forensic evidence. His efforts kept the issue alive for another sixty years or so. When Bishop Burnet's account of his life and times appeared posthumously in 1724, the Whig case was damaged by the defection of the dignitary closest to the participants. Burnet admitted that 'Lord Essex had got into an odd set of some strange principles, ... and seemed to approve of what ... the earl of Northumberland did, who shot himself in the Tower after he was arraigned'. He also recalled that Essex had been subject to 'very black fits of the spleen'. Braddon's sincerity Burnet did not question, but he disavowed his theories and called him 'an honest but enthusiastical man'.[110] This assault on his character provoked the aged zealot to issue one last pamphlet defending his views.[111] No matter how much testimony was amassed on either side, though, it was party passion that sustained the theory that Essex had been murdered. Whig historians alluded to the murder theory; Tory polemicists denounced them for their duplicity.[112]

The use of suicide for religious and political reasons depended on a common set of assumptions about its significance. As long as most people continued to believe that self-killing was a heinous, even diabolical act, the suicide of a prominent religious or political figure was a disaster for his confession, sect, or party. The charge that Essex had got hold of some 'strange principles' points to one of the sets of ideas that was eventually to replace the diabolical interpretation of suicide. The Whigs were associated with republicanism in political theory, and the

[109] [L. Braddon], *Murder Will Out; or, a Clear and Full Discovery that the Earl of Essex did not Murder himself, but was Murdered by Others* (London, 1689), reprinted in *A Collection of Scarce and Valuable Tracts ... of the Late Lord Somers*, ed. W. Scott, 2nd edn. (London, 1813), iv. 65–71; [Braddon], *Innocency and Truth Vindicated* (London, 1689), reprinted in John Somers, *A Collection of Scarce and Valuable Tracts*, ed. W. Scott, 2nd edn. (London, 1813), iv. 72–174.

[110] Burnet, *Burnet's History*, ii. 398–9; Foxcroft, *Supplement to Burnet's History*, 119–23.

[111] L. Braddon, *Bishop Burnet's Late History Charged with Great Partiality and Misrepresentation, to Make the Present and Future Ages Believe, That Arthur Earl of Essex Murdered Himself* (London, 1725), reprinted with additional comments in *State Trials*, ix, cols 1229–332.

[112] *State Trials*, ix, cols. 1230–1, cites some of the chief disputants. See also W. Kennett, *A Complete History of England* (London, 1706), iii. 409; R. North, *Examen; or an Enquiry into the Credit and Veracity of a Pretended Complete History* (London, 1740), 400–5.

allusion to Essex's opinions undoubtedly refers to the Roman notion that political suicide, like that of Cato, could be the most glorious sort of death. The association of Essex and Cato was an almost unavoidable one, since Cato had killed himself as a protest against a tyrannical regime. Interestingly, no one in the Whig party capitalized on the association, even after 1688, preferring instead the tactic of claiming that Essex's death was a murder. The reasons for this reticence about making a suicide into a political martyr will be clearer after we have examined the undertow and eddies of opinion, classical and medical, that flowed against the main tide of sentiment condemning self-murder.

## CONCLUSION

Our argument in these first two chapters has been that for a little more than a century and a half, from about 1500 until after 1660, suicide was punished more severely than ever before or afterwards. Although research on the subject is still too inchoate to permit confident generalizations, it appears that suicide was penalized more severely in England than in any other nation. About enforcement of the law of suicide in Germany, Spain, and Italy, very little seems to be known; some information about France and parts of Switzerland is available. French law, really a collection of regional customs and codes, stipulated different punishments in different regions of the country. In some places, the penalties were horrific by English standards; in others they were mild or non-existent. Throughout France, scholars generally agree, the laws against self-murder were very seldom applied. And after they were standardized in 1670, in an ordinance decreeing that every convicted suicide should forfeit his goods and be drawn on the hurdle to a profane grave, they were enforced even less often. Counter-Reformation theologians were no more tolerant of suicide than Protestant ones, but in France at least they failed to achieve the full backing of the crown until Enlightenment notions had already begun to erode the élite's willingness to enforce laws punishing suicide.[113] Apparently, the only countries apart from England that attempted to enforce regulations against self-murder systematically were the Swiss city-states, Geneva and Zurich. In both of those cantons Calvinist regimes attempted to impose rigorous religious

[113] A. Bayet, *Le Suicide et la morale* (Paris, 1922), 602–9, 668–73; J. McManners, *Death and the Enlightenment* (Oxford, 1981), 409–11.

ideals on their citizenry, and the stigmatization of self-killing was a by-product of their efforts. The campaign against suicide began in both places in the seventeenth century, later than it did in England, and involved milder sanctions than those imposed in England. Suicides were often convicted but seldom punished severely. In Switzerland as in France, religious efforts to reform the punishment of suicide achieved the support of the authorities too late to flourish before opposing trends began to challenge them.[114]

What seems to have made England distinctive, at least in this lugubrious way, was the early coincidence of governmental and religious reform. The 'Tudor revolution in government' and the Protestant Reformation extended the powers of the state and the ideas of the church into local villages far more pervasively than they had ever intruded before. They transformed the enforcement of the law and completed the Christianization of popular religious beliefs about suicide. Many social historians have argued that the rise of the nation state and the religious changes of the sixteenth century began the erosion of popular culture, a process that was completed in the eighteenth century, as the élite finally withdrew from demotic recreations and rituals and repudiated rustic beliefs about the world.[115] The history of suicide in early modern England tells a somewhat different story. The initial effect of the changes that occurred in the sixteenth century was to reinforce abhorrence of suicide. A common stereotype of self-murder, shared by men and women of every rank, determined the response to the deed. It was a stereotype that fused elements of élite belief and demotic folklore. The clerical élite contributed an increased emphasis on the menace that Satan posed to Christian souls; the laity contributed the beliefs about ghosts and rituals of desecration that dramatized the supernatural ramifications of self-murder. The correspondence between learned ideas about suicide and those of the common people was not perfect, of course, and we shall see that the prevailing stereotype was challenged by other attitudes. But thanks to the government's anxiety to extend and improve the effectiveness of its judicial institutions and the church's drive to heighten religious devotion, there was a large area of overlap, an area coloured with the darkest hues of fear and hatred.

114 L. Haeberli, 'Le Suicide à Genève au XVIII^e siècle', in *Pour une histoire qualitative* (Geneva, 1975), 115–29; M. Schär, *Seelennöte der Untertanen: Selbstmord, Melancholie und Religion im Alten Zürich, 1500–1800* (Zurich, 1985).

115 The most vigorous version of this theme is R. Muchembled, *Culture populaire et culture des élites* (Paris, 1978). See also, P. Burke, *Popular Culture in Early Modern Europe* (New York, 1978).

# 3

# *Opposition and Ambivalence*

THE prevailing attitude to self-destruction in sixteenth- and seventeenth-century England, it must be emphasized, was profoundly hostile. Punishment of suicide was unprecedented and unparalleled in severity. And yet like an astrological conjunction this unity of attitude and action was temporary, a coincidence of views that were moving in different and sometimes opposed directions. Both at the local level, among village communities, and at the national level, among the educated élite, it is possible to detect signs of ambivalence about the punishment of suicide that appeared even as attitudes and responses were hardening. Literary critics and cultural historians influenced by post-structuralist thought have taught us to be sensitive to the ways in which texts tend to subvert themselves. They imply their own negations, and in the awareness of opposition one finds the key to deconstructing them. Very few social historians have found the post-structuralist programme an attractive one, and we do not propose to advance it here. But it is helpful to think of cultural change in terms of oppositions and subversions, for beliefs and the behaviour that expresses them are dynamic and unstable entities. The prevailing hostility to suicide in early modern England was the result of political and religious changes that were themselves the product of a highly complex set of events and forces. The centralization of the state and the Protestant Reformation had consequences no one could have intended or predicted. They also generated tensions that moderated their course and content, limiting the reach of the crown's power and frustrating the attempt to impose religious unity.

## OPPOSITION TO FORFEITURE

Despite popular abhorrence of suicide in the sixteenth and seventeenth centuries, the savagery of official reactions to the crime fostered opposition to them. The rise in the *felo de se* verdict, even more than the contemporary rise in witchcraft prosecutions, created resentments and doubts that led eventually to its repudiation. There was a striking disjunction between popular attitudes to the secular and the religious penalties for self-murder. Ritual burials seem normally to have been carried out. Although their savagery was occasionally tempered for reasons we cannot now know, they were genuine popular customs in which crowds of people sometimes participated.[1] Forfeiture, on the other hand, was very often evaded or resisted. Juries willingly returned verdicts of *felo de se*, but they disliked depriving the suicide's heirs and occasionally colluded in attempts to evade forfeiture. Reverence for the rights of inheritance is the central value of any agrarian society. The law of self-murder pitted that powerful sentiment squarely against demotic horror of the crime.

The crown's claim to the property of self-murderers was fiercely resented by local communities, perhaps even more than it had been in the Middle Ages, when it was rarely exercised. There are hundreds of suits in the surviving records of Star Chamber in which families, neighbours, and coroners and their juries were charged with concealing the goods of suicides. Imaginative gambits were sometimes devised to deceive royal officials; stupidly transparent ploys were evidently just as common. Defendants in Star Chamber swore on their oaths that gangs of strangers descended on the homes of self-murderers and carried off their goods immediately after their deaths.[2] Samuel Pepys joined in one such demonstration of hostility to forfeiture in 1668. As Anthony Joyce lay dying of an illness contracted in an attempt to drown himself, Joyce's wife distributed the household goods to his friends and neighbours. Pepys, who was her cousin, got a set of flagons. She was afraid that her husband would be found *felo de se*, since his death was the result of his suicide attempt; Pepys was afraid he would be caught with goods that

[1] For crowds at burials, see J. C. Cox, *The Parish Registers of England* (London, 1910), 114; PRO, STAC 4/7/14; KB 9/588/2, m. 237; KB 29/189/2d; T. R. Murphy, '"Woful Childe of Parents Rage": Suicide of Children and Adolescents in Early Modern England, 1507–1710', *Sixteenth Century Journal*, xvii (1986) n. 34.

[2] See, e.g., PRO, STAC 8/1/29; STAC 2/1/107, 108, 110; STAC 4/3/35; STAC 5/A3/8; STAC 8/1/29; STAC 8/1/32, 38.

should have been forfeited. He scurried home 'in great fear all the way of being seized; though there was no reason for it, he not being dead; but yet so fearful I was'.[3] Some reports of crowds taking away the goods of strangers were legal fictions that masked disputes over the rights to them. But others, like Pepys's account, plainly record real popular actions—a kind of informal probate of the suicide's goods in which people who would have been heirs to part of the property participated to help the family and themselves. Another common ploy was to claim that the deceased's debts, which were normally settled before the crown was paid, exceeded the value of his chattels. A particularly dim-witted Cumberland jury reported in 1655 that John Fisher's forfeitable property was worth £56. 7*s*. 1*d*. and that his debts, which were to be paid out of that property, also amounted to £56. 7*s*. 1*d*.[4] Families frequently resorted to the bold-faced lie, swearing that they were ignorant of property that informants alleged the deceased had owned or that he had deeded all his goods away before his death.[5] Coroners and juries were occasionally charged with undervaluing the goods of suicides, a practice that was undoubtedly rather common.[6]

Some juries allowed themselves to be talked into returning bogus verdicts, claiming, for instance, that a highly suspicious drowning had been an accidental death. Alexander Gooddyn's relatives, together with seven sympathetic jurors, tried to coerce the rest of the jury to find that Gooddyn had been killed by 'John above the Winde', that is, by some unknown person. At first the jurors rebelled, declaring 'that yf John above the winde was the devell then woulde they find him the occasion of his death, otherwise they wuld not agree'. Eventually, however, they agreed reluctantly to return a verdict of misadventure.[7] Perhaps to forestall a challenge, a Norwich coroner returned a set of depositions

[3] S. Pepys, *The Diary of Samuel Pepys*, ed. R. Latham and W. Matthews (London, 1970–83), ix. 32–4, 49, 78.

[4] Cumbria RO, D/Lec/CR, 1/3. See also PRO, STAC 5/A5/39; STAC 5/A24/6; STAC 8/1/39–41; STAC 8/3/18.

[5] This was so frequent that it would be impractical to try to list examples. It should be emphasized that the great majority of the Star Chamber disputes over suicides involve allegations of property concealed by juries, local officials, or neighbours.

[6] For examples, see PRO, STAC 5/A2/7, 14; STAC 5/A4/34; STAC 5/A59/10a. No final determinations in such cases seem to be extant, and so it is impossible to guess just how commonly or flagrantly juries undervalued goods. Inquisitions in which the forfeiture hovered at or just above the coroner's fee (13*s*. 4*d*.) seem suspiciously numerous. On the other hand, King's Bench monitored the amounts reported closely, and so gross abuse was probably not the norm.

[7] PRO, STAC 5/A12/19.

together with his inquest on the death in 1598 of John Wilkins, a grocer. Wilkins had died a week or so after cutting his throat, but the jury had returned a verdict of natural death (*ex visitatione divina*). Although medical men were very seldom summoned after suicide attempts and almost never appeared as witnesses at inquests in this period, a doctor and three surgeons were produced at this one to testify that the wound Wilkins had given himself was not mortal. The jury carefully noted that Wilkins's illness began *before* he cut his throat—the law otherwise would have counted him as a *felo de se*, whether or not the wound had been fatal. The whole story is too good to be probable, though of course it may nevertheless have been true.[8]

Juries also occasionally used the *non compos mentis* verdict or returned a mixed or ambiguous verdict in an attempt to acquit suicides of self-murder and save their property from forfeiture.[9] This practice was an extension of medieval juries' habit of sparing their neighbours by returning lenient verdicts. It was not uncommon during the reign of Henry VIII, when the crown began to reform enforcement of the law. *Non compos mentis*, mixed, and ambiguous verdicts were returned more often in the 1530s than they were at any time until the 1660s. They amounted to just over 10 per cent of the suicides reported to King's Bench; for the whole period 1485 to 1660 they accounted for 1.3 per cent of reported suicides. Some of the mixed and ambiguous verdicts were merely clerical errors: *non compos mentis* returns that were marked *felo de se* mistakenly by King's Bench clerks or garbled verdicts set down by coroners as yet unfamiliar with the new procedures. But the pattern of *non compos mentis*, mixed, and ambiguous verdicts over time confirms the impression that the majority of them represent attempts to find a way to acquit suicides and save their property from forfeiture. They were comparatively frequent when the crown began to enforce the law more vigorously, in the early sixteenth century, fell rapidly after the court of Star Chamber began to prosecute evaders, and rose sharply during the 1640s, when the Civil War temporarily wrecked the whole system of

[8] KB 9/703/mm. 110a–111. For other examples of suspicious or bogus verdicts, see STAC 5/A1/21; STAC 5/A6/6; STAC 5/A17/40; STAC 8/2/42; STAC 8/3/14; PRO, KB 9/514, m. 97; KB 9/588, pt 2, m. 202; KB 9/560, m. 109; KB 9/576, mm. 124–8; KB 9/1094, unnumbered (a homicide by 'John ultra Luna'); and our personal favourite, a man who allegedly fell on his knife while playing football, KB 9/448, m. 44.

[9] Mixed and ambiguous verdicts deserve a little explanation. Mixed verdicts usually resulted from the decision of an official of the court to change the inquisition to read *felo de se* instead of *non compos mentis*; ambiguous verdicts included language that both condemned and spared the deceased.

enforcement. In the 1650s, the governments of the Commonwealth and Protectorate cracked down again. This explains why there was a shift from *non compos mentis* to mixed verdicts as the largest proportion of attempted acquittals. The clerks of King's Bench were challenging more *non compos mentis* returns, reclassifying them as potential *felones de se*. (See Fig. 3.1.)

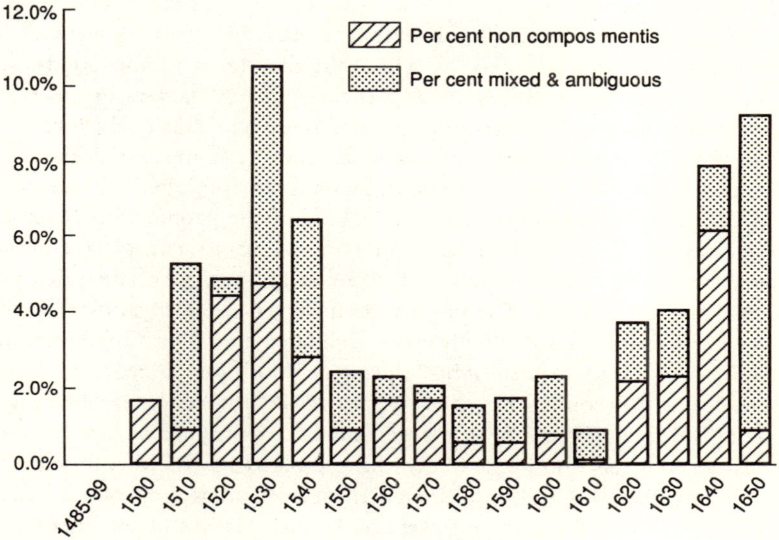


FIG. 3.1. Suicides acquitted by juries, 1485–1659
*Source*: PRO, KB 9, 10, 11, 140; PL 26; HCA 1.

Resentment of the crown's right to the goods of suicides may have been exaggerated by unrealistic fears. Almoners, after all, were supposed to be merciful to poor families. But there are plenty of tales of official greed in the records, and some of them were surely true. This one cannot be doubted, because the key information, on which the almoner sued, only came to light after the composition had been agreed upon. Following the suicide of a Bedford apothecary named Robert Taylour, the burghers of the town prevailed upon Robert Ridge to act as the guardian of Taylour's children, who seem to have been orphaned by his death. Ridge posted off to London, where he met with the king's almoner, who was none other than the saintly Lancelot Andrewes. (His rigorous condemnation of self-murder was quoted earlier in this book.) Ridge explained the situation and estimated the value of Taylour's goods at

£16. 12*s*.; the coroner's jury had appraised them at a still lower figure, just £10. Andrewes and his deputy compounded for a sum of £4 in lieu of the full amount of the estate. The almoner, in other words, took one-fourth of the property to be used to support Taylour's children. It matters not that he subsequently learned from two of the town's bailiffs that they believed Taylour's goods to have been worth far more, about £50. As an act of charity, this deed was passing strange.[10]

Still more offensive to local sentiment than the almoners were corporations and private persons who held the rights to the goods of suicides and to deodands in a particular manor, town, or liberty. Monarchs had over the centuries granted these windfalls to the lords of the manors, corporations, and royal servants. In some instances, it is impossible to tell how many, the right was sold and inherited with the property to which it was attached.[11] Many of the people who claimed suicides' goods were absentees, and some of them seem to have been previously unknown to the survivors or neighbours who later tried to challenge their rights. The improved efficiency of the royal machinery for confiscation must initially have facilitated the ability of franchise holders to exercise their rights. Coroners were more effective and inquisitions that could serve as proof of a *felo de se* were regularly filed in King's Bench. These lesser lords were neither constrained by custom nor restrained by law: nothing obliged them to behave mercifully. In seizing property that was rightfully theirs, they were often remorseless. The disposition in 1595 of the property of Thomas Graves of the liberty of Writtle in Essex gives some sense of the catastrophe that could befall the survivors of suicides who died in one of these legal enclaves. The goods in Graves's house, worth 9*s*., were granted to his widow. His firewood and crops were sold for £4. 3*s*. 8*d*. The widow's half-yearly rent of £1 was paid out of that sum and of the rest she received at best 10*s*. The steward and the coroner got £1. 6*s*. 3*d*. between them.[12] The lord of the manor of Writtle was comparatively merciful: some other lords swal-

[10] PRO, STAC 8/3/38; KB 9/730, m. 561. If the normal fees were charged by the coroner and the court of King's Bench, an additional 19*s*. 12*d*. would have been paid to them.

[11] For examples, see *Calendar of the Patent Rolls, Edward VI*, v. 98; PRO, STAC 5/A4/14; STAC 5/A59/8.

[12] Essex County RO, D/DP/M 607/12; PRO, STAC 5/A40/15, PRO, KB 9/777, m. 33; Cumbria RO, D/Lec/CR I, 1/2; F. G. Emmison, *Elizabethan Life: Home, Work and Land* (Chelmsford, 1976), 213; O. Heywood, *His Autobiography, Diaries, Anecdote and Event Books*, ed. J. Horsfall Turner (Brighouse and Bingley, 1882–5), ii. 173. For a somewhat later contemporary's confirmation of this conclusion, see Umfreville, *Lex coronatoria*, 106–7.

lowed up everything they could grab. Nor were franchise holders hesitant to pursue defaulters for trivial sums that heirs had been allowed to keep for reasons of charity. Manorial officials fined the village of Witham, also in Essex, £15 in 1666 because its inhabitants left 15*s*. 6*d*. in the hands of William Baker's widow and failed to return it to the authorities.[13] Some of the almoners' suits in Star Chamber seem to have been initiated by families who expected to get more favourable treatment from the crown than from a lesser lord who claimed their property.[14]

The royal right to the goods of suicides was thus complicated by the crown's habit of using it as a form of patronage. On the one hand these grants created an identity of interest between the monarch and the landed classes: both groups profited from the strict enforcement of the law. On the other, they led to conflicts between royal officials and manorial lords who claimed the goods of suicides by an old patent. In all of these disputes, whatever their form, the rights of one lord, the crown, were pitted against those of another with absolute clarity. A gang of men, mostly weavers and husbandmen, who carried off the property of George Hawkins, a Devon farmer, on behalf of a rival claimant abused the deputy almoner, saying that he was no honest man to be prying into other gentlemen's titles.[15] The importance of quarrels between the crown and the lords of franchises in eroding support for the law after 1660 will be discussed in a later chapter. In this context, it is sufficient to stress that the fragmentation of the crown's rights often led to situations in which a person intent on stripping the survivor of his or her goods suddenly appeared in the community immediately after a shocking death. In the worst cases of all, both the crown and a lesser lord descended on the heirs, demanding all or part of the suicide's chattels.[16] Even if the almoners had been more benign figures than contemporaries seem to have taken them to have been, the right of forfeiture was bound to cause conflict. In 1593 one coroner boldly (and falsely) declared to a sympathetic jury: 'In the time of popery the goods of felons of themselves were distributed by the Almoner to poor people in hospitals and such like, but in these days . . . the Almoner had nothing to do with

[13] Essex County RO, D/P 30/28/9.

[14] PRO, STAC 5/A28/8 is a good example. See also, STAC 5/A19/10; STAC 5/A37/10; STAC 5/A40/16; STAC 5/A58/4.

[15] They were apparently acting on behalf of Lewis Pollard, who had bought or inherited the rights to the goods: PRO, STAC 5/A59/31; STAC 5/A41/7. See also, STAC 5/A1/16; STAC 5/A2/28; STAC 5/A3/11, 33, 36; STAC 5/A5/18; STAC 5/A19/19, 30; STAC 5/A26/15, 34; STAC 5/A40/16.

[16] See e.g., PRO, STAC 5/A3/33; STAC 5/A20/37.

the said goods, chattels and debts . . . but the same was to pass by administration to the next of kindred.'[17] His assertion was bad history and worse law, but it expressed a real and legitimate resentment.

Like many other popular resentments, antagonism to the fiscal penalties for self-murder was voiced openly in the Interregnum. Radical reformers disliked the whole idea of forfeiture for felony. In the third *Agreement of the People*, the Levellers complained that the confiscation of criminals' estates, contributed to the 'wickedness, misery and beggary' of 'all sorts of people', and demanded that the practice be abandoned, except in cases of high treason.[18] Expressing a sentiment that would often be voiced against forfeiture in the future, John March declared in 1651: 'I think there cannot be a more rigid and tyrannical Law in the world, that the children should thus extremely suffere for the crime and wickedness of the Father; the innocent for the nocent.'[19] When the parliamentary commission headed by the great jurist Matthew Hale undertook its attempt at law reform in 1652, it included in its proposals the suggestion 'That such as kill themselves shall not forfeit any thing by Reason thereof, unless at the Time of the Fact committed they be under Restraint or Prosecution for some capital Offence'.[20] Both the Rump and Barebone's Parliament failed to act on most of the reforms proposed by the Hale Commission, but radicals continued to mention abolition of forfeiture for *felo de se* in their programme. William Sheppard had the law of suicide in mind, along with many other laws, when he called in 1656 for the abolitiion of 'Laws that are or seem to be hard, cruel, burdensome and oppressive to the people'.[21] Three years later, the Quaker Edward Billing reiterated the argument that the goods of felons should pass freely to their heirs.[22]

As the language of the reformers sometimes implied, antagonism to

[17] PRO, STAC 5/A1/21.

[18] D. M. Wolfe (ed.), *Leveller Manifestoes of the Puritan Revolution* (New York, 1944), 407. See also, A. S. P. Woodhouse (comp.), *Puritanism and Liberty* (Chicago, 1951), 365; D. Veall, *The Popular Movement for Law Reform, 1640–1660* (Oxford, 1970), 131.

[19] J. March, *Amicus Reipublicae* [sic]: *The Common-Wealths Friend* (London, 1651), 109. See also, W. Thomlinson [or Tomlinson], *Seven Particulars* (London, 1658), 18.

[20] John Somers, *A Collection of Scarce and Valuable Tracts*, ed. W. Scott, 2nd edn. (London, 1813), vi. 177.

[21] W. Sheppard, *England's Balme; or, Proposals By Way of Grievance and Remedy; Humbly Presented to His Highness and the Parliament; Towards the Regulation of the Law, and Better Administration of Justice* (London, 1656), 15, 196, 206, 214. Notice that the application of these passages specifically to suicide is indicated by index references and marginalia.

[22] R. M. Rogers, 'Quakerism and the Law in the English Revolution', *Canadian Journal of History*, xxii (1987), 171.

forfeiture had a basis in conflicting class interests. William Cole, for example, condemned all kinds of forfeiture in radical terms:

> Hence it came to pass [after the Conquest] that all penal Laws were made for the benefit of the King, the Lords of Manors, and other great Officers who were the King's Creatures; This was and still is the ground and reason why . . . the estates of Offenders were forfeited by Law to the King, or lord of the Manor.[23]

Lords, including the crown, profited from punishing suicide; tenants, indeed everyone who paid the poor rates, did not. Families whose goods were taken from them by the almoners or by franchise holders were apt to fall into poverty and become a financial burden to the parish. Government reform and religious reformation might discipline juries and strengthen public antagonism to the crime of self-murder, but they could not entirely overcome this inherent conflict of interests between lords and tenants, government and local communities. And yet while it is essential to point out that the extension of royal authority and ruling-class privilege created a conflict of economic interest between classes, it is also important to note that the lines were not as sharply drawn as old-style economic materialists might have predicted. For the tension was as much between the state and local communities as it was between classes. As the government increasingly interfered in local affairs, it unwittingly sharpened the resentment of the parish gentry, the middling sort, and, in all likelihood, the common people. Localism, as countless historians have reminded us, was a powerful sentiment, one that was far more self-conscious than class solidarity. Indeed, most of the time juries that tried to deceive the crown were probably moved chiefly by sympathy for the suicide's survivors. A jury caught undervaluing the goods of Thomas Chennell by about £40 in 1588, for instance, explained that they had done so in order to compensate John Ticknor for acting as the guardian of Chennell's child.[24] Arthur Barnes allegedly bribed the jury to bring in a verdict of natural death after his brother's suicide in 1617. Arthur explained that the sudden deaths of two of William's sisters and one of their husbands had left a total of fourteen children, three poor widows, and an elderly matriarch who were 'to have some relief and maintenance out of the estate and goods of the said William Barnes'.[25]

[23] W. Cole, *A Rod for the Lawyers* (London, 1659), 6. Cole does not mention suicide specifically, but his arguments and his (false) assertion that forfeiture was not practised in Kent comprehend forfeiture for *felo de se*. He also protests against deodands.

[24] PRO, STAC 5/A2/14.

[25] PRO, STAC 8/2/46. Such claims were commonplace.

In cases like this charity, class interest, local solidarity, and traditional values concerning inheritance set up eddies of defiance, strong local forces of resistance that complicated the current of change.

## THE CLASSICAL TRADITION

The tide of hostility toward suicide among the educated élite was also accompanied by an undertow of opposition. Even as administrative and religious reform intensified the conviction that suicide was a diabolical crime, the revival of classical philosophy and science fostered renewed awareness of more tolerant attitudes. These attitudes were the product of Renaissance humanism, which was also one of the foundations of the Protestant Reformation. It is not surprising, therefore, that philosophical and theological discussions of suicide in the sixteenth and seventeenth centuries drew on an identical set of arguments and examples. More importantly, although conservative opinion was certainly more influential than liberal arguments, the discussion of suicide by both its detractors and its defenders tended to be self-subverting. The arguments of both sides, in other words, implied their opposites. Because of the Renaissance fondness for the rhetorical device of opposition, this habit of publicizing contradictory ideas about self-destruction was often a conscious strategy.

Renaissance humanism was, as everyone knows, grounded on a profound reverence for classical literature, philosophy, and history. Humanist intellectuals were inescapably aware of Roman customs and Stoic arguments in defence of suicide, and these views were given greater currency in the literature of the age.[26] The French sceptics, Montaigne and Pierre Charron, discussed Stoic arguments in favour of suicide, concluding that self-destruction was a legitimate way to end a life of unremitting pain. Both Montaigne's *Essayes* and Charron's *Of Wisdome* appeared in English translations during the first decade of the

[26] Wymer, *Suicide and Despair*, chs. 4–7, *passim*; T. Spencer, *Death and Elizabethan Tragedy* (New York, 1960), 141, 158–79, 218, 233, 251, 252; C. Leech, 'Le Dénouement par le suicide dans la tragédie élisabethaine et jacobéenne', in J. Jaquot (ed.), *Le Théâtre tragique* (Paris, 1962), 179–97; P. D. Green, 'Doors to the House of Death: The Treatment of Suicide in Sidney's *Arcadia*', *Sixteenth Century Journal*, x (1979), 17–27.

seventeenth century; both were often reprinted afterwards.[27] Readers of Lucretius and of Plutarch knew of Epicurean as well as Stoic apologies for suicide. Examples of suicides by classical heroes were familiar to everyone. What educated Elizabethan could have been ignorant of the deaths of Lucretia, Cato, or Brutus? Their encomiums could be read by every schoolboy with little Latin and less Greek; their virtues were praised in English poetry and plays. George Chapman made Cato the unquestioned hero of *Caesar and Pompey*. The play ends with Cato's suicide, a terrible death that the Chapman presents as a wholly noble deed. Just about to fall on his sword, the great Roman addresses the gods and leaves no doubt that he expects to meet them in heaven:

> Now wing thee, dear soul, and receive her, heaven.
> The earth, the air, and seas I know, and all
> The joys and horrors of their peace and wars,
> And now will see the gods' state, and the stars.[28]

And Ben Jonson made Arruntius ask in his *Sejanus*:

> 'Tis we are base,
> Poor, and degenerate from th'exalted strain
> Of our great fathers. Where is now the soul
> Of godlike Cato?—he that durst be good
> When Caesar durst be evil.[29]

So far as we know, no Englishman followed the French sceptics' example and ventured to publish a fully developed Stoic or Epicurean defence of suicide, but these radical ideas had greater currency than one might suppose. Thomas More permitted suicide in his Utopia, although he condemned it elsewhere. For Utopia was an ideal society constructed out of the building-blocks of pagan philosophy. When they are ill with an incurable disease, the Utopians might kill themselves with the permis-

[27] M. E. de Montaigne, *Montaigne's Essays*, trans. J. Florio (1603; repr. London, 1965), ii. 26–41; P. Charron, *Of Wisdome, Three Bookes*, trans. S. Lennard (London, [1608]). For a more accurate translation of Montaigne, see *The Complete Essays of Montaigne*, trans. D. M. Frame (Stanford, 1965), 251–62. Note also his essay in praise of Cato the Younger, which is interestingly expounded by J. Starobinski, *Montaigne in Motion*, trans. A. Goldhammer (Chicago, 1985), 70–5. Another useful commentary is M. A. Screech, *Montaigne and Melancholy* (London, 1984), 43–6.

[28] G. Chapman, *The Plays of George Chapman*, ed. T. M. Parrott (New York, 1961), ii. 398, *The Tragedy of Caesar and Pompey*, v. ii. 157–61.

[29] B. Jonson, *Sejanus*, ed. J. A. Barish (New Haven, 1965), i. 87–90.

sion of their priests. One who does so 'will act wisely, since by death he will put an end not to enjoyment but to torture. . . . It will be a pious and holy action.'[30] In 1578, when he was still an undergraduate at Cambridge, John Harington wrote a dialogue on the legitimacy of self-killing that displays familiarity with the arguments of the ancients. The piece is an inept performance, an anachronistic debate between Samuel, Saul, and Solomon, who keep referring to post-Christian and even contemporary events. Its most daring assertion—that whenever a man has a 'necessary cause' to die, his suicide is vindicated, for 'yt is no matter what death a man dyeth'—smacks of Epicureanism.[31] Sir Thomas Browne worried that some preachers had grown so fond of Stoicism that they 'allow a man to be his owne *Assassine*, and highly extoll the end and suicide of *Cato*'.[32] This was an exaggeration, if the printed sermons are any gauge, but John Sym also worried that people killed themselves because of the 'frequent *examples* both of *heathens* and *Christians*, who have done the same, and are celebrated, and famous in *histories*'.[33]

Epicurean arguments defending suicide were far more antagonistic to religious orthodoxy than Stoic ones, because they were grounded ultimately on Epicurus' materialism. Educated Englishmen were familiar with the philosopher's views from ancient texts and translations, but it was not until the Interregnum, when the virtual collapse of censorship afforded an opportunity to publish radical ideas without much risk of reprisal, that his defence of suicide was fully expounded by a modern author. In 1656 Walter Charleton published an edition of Epicurus' *Morals* with a long opening commentary. Physician to Charles I and friend of Hobbes, Charleton was a decidedly unusual thinker and a prolific writer. 'In religion he was a High Churchman, in philosophy an Epicurean, and in politics one of the last old royalists.'[34] A strange combination, indeed, and one that he had some difficulty reconciling. Charleton firmly rejected Epicurus' argument that the soul is mortal, but he was of two minds about his master's views on suicide. Writing as a 'as a *Christian*', Charleton declares, 'I hold [Epicurus' defence of suicide] to be a bloody and detestable opinion, because expressly repugnant to the *Law* of *God*'. But as a 'meere *Philosopher*', Charleton ably recites the Epicurean argument that men are free to commit 'Selfe-Homicide in case

30 T. More, *Utopia*, ed. E. Surtz (New Haven, 1964), 108–9.
31 BL, Add. MS 27, 632, fo. 125$^r$.
32 Browne, *Selected Writings*, 50.
33 Sym, *Lifes Preservative*, 252.
34 *DNB*, s.v. 'Charleton, Walter'.

of intolerable and otherwise inevitable Calamity'. So although he condemns suicide as a sin, he also can agree with Epicurus that the law of nature obliges men to seek good and fly evil. When life itself 'degenerates into an *Evill*' suicide becomes 'an absolute accomplishment of the Law of Self-praeservation'.[35]

Unquestionably the most astonishing rejection of prevailing attitudes to suicide was John Donne's *Biathanatos*, which expounded the 'Paradox or Thesis, that Self-Homicide is not so naturally Sin that it may never be otherwise'.[36] Donne eschewed classical arguments and examples and relied instead on theological analysis and authorities to prove that suicide was not always contrary to divine, natural, and civil law. He stressed in particular that self-killing is nowhere explicitly forbidden in scripture, and that many suicides in the history of the church had been excused and even venerated as martyrs of the faith. His arguments are complex, deliberately conforming to the methods of 'scholastic and artificial men', and they are exceedingly radical. Donne observes that the only place in the scriptures that is generally agreed to prohibit self-murder is the Sixth Commandment, on which Augustine founded his case against suicide.[37] But, Donne stresses, Augustine was compelled to admit that the commandment ignores occasions on which killing is legitimate, for example, in war or to punish criminals. He also shows that Augustine's lame argument that biblical and early Christian suicides were permissible because they were carried out by the secret command of God is mere supposition.[38] At one vertiginous moment, he actually asserts that Christ's passion is the model suicide.[39] Donne's book was unique. It was unprecedented, and it was unimitated.[40] All other defences of suicide relied mainly on classical arguments and precedents.

Both the rhetoric of contemporary apologies for suicide and the cultural context within which they appeared expressed ambivalence about the philosophical and religious significance of self-killing. What More permitted the humanist saints in Utopia to do, he would in no wise permit Christians. Of all the fears one can experience, he wrote in *A*

35 W. Charleton (ed.), *Epicurus's Morals* (London, 1656), sigs. d1$^{v}$–d2$^{v}$.

36 J. Donne, *Biathanatos*, ed. M. Rudick and M. P. Battin (New York, 1982), 1.

37 Ibid. 147.

38 Ibid. 181.

39 Ibid. 169–70.

40 It had, of course, partial precedents in the works of continental casuists, such as Franciscus de Victoria and Gregory Sayre, and some of his assertions—mostly those made by others independently—were repeated by later writers: Donne, *Biathanatos*, pp. xxvi–xxviii.

*Dialogue of Comfort Against Tribulation*, the most horrible is 'where the devill temptith a man to kyll and destroy hym selfe'.[41] Charleton made the split between his philosophical persona and his Christian identity explicit, as we have seen. More obviously than Donne, whose subtitle he surely had in mind, Charleton finds a refuge from a deeply disturbing contradiction in paradox. In his philosophical persona, he can feel free, 'without being unreasonably Paradoxicall, [to] adventure to dispute, whether it be so highly repugnant to the *Law* of *Nature*, as men have generally conceived'.[42]

The most famous discussions of suicide—Montaigne's *Essayes* and Sidney's *Arcadia*—are inherently contradictory. Montaigne's sceptical self-doubt was the basis for all of his thought, and it suffuses his remarks on suicide. 'If, as some say, to philosophate be to doubt; with much more reason, to rave and fantastiquize, as I doe, must necessarily be to doubt', his essay on 'A Custome of the Ile of Cea' begins. And throughout this meditation on voluntary death, he constantly shifts between affirmations of the Stoic defence of suicide and traditional condemnations of it. Death is, as the Stoics maintained, the key to unlocking the chains of suffering. '*Death is a remedy against all evils*', he writes echoing Seneca, 'The voluntariest death, is the fairest.' No law can rightly forbid suicide: 'As I offend not the lawes made against theeves, when I cut my own purse . . . : so am I nothing tied unto lawes made against murtherers, if I deprive my selfe of mine owne life.' Yet, Montaigne notes almost immediately, 'But this goeth not without some contradiction'. There is the ancient argument that suicide is a form of desertion, and so God and the state have the power to forbid it. Montaigne wrote a whole separate essay in praise of Cato, but in it he declares: 'There is more constancie in using the chaine that holds us, than in breaking the same; and more triall of stedfastnesse in *Regulus* than in *Cato*.' To flee life to avoid pain, he concedes, is pointless; yet when Montaigne at last concludes his essay, he is of the opinion that 'Grieving-smart [unbearable pain], and a worse deathe seem to me the most excusable incitations'. Montaigne thus both advanced the Stoic defence of suicide and condemned it.[43]

The same tension between irreconcilable sentiments is evident in the old *Arcadia*. Here the structure of the discussion arises not from Sidney's reflexive doubt but from his use of the rhetorical device of opposition

[41] T. More, *The Complete Works*, xii: *A Dialogue of Comfort Against Tribulation*, ed. L. L. Martz and F. Manley (New Haven, 1976), 122.
[42] Charleton, *Epicurus's Morals*, sigs. d1$^v$–d2$^v$.
[43] Montaigne, *Montaigne's Essays*, ii. 26–8, 41.

—a device fundamental in Renaissance philosophy and literature. Realizing that he and Philoclea face disgrace and execution after they have been discovered in bed together, Pyrocles concludes that his suicide will save her. In his prayer to Jove and his subsequent attempt to persuade Philoclea that his action would be right, Pyrocles relies mainly on the Stoic argument that no one is obliged to live when his death may promote some greater good, and in fact suicide in such circumstances is consonant with natural law: 'It is the right I owe to the general nature that (though against private nature) makes me seek the preservation of all that she hath done in this age.'[44] Philoclea offers several objections to this, also drawing mainly on arguments advanced by classical philosophers. Quoting Pythagoras' famous metaphor, she tells him that wise men have maintained that God has 'appointed us captains of these our bodily forts, which without treason to that majesty were never to be delivered over till they were redeemed'.[45] Ultimately, Philoclea persuades Pyrocles not to kill himself, but it is his love for her and not her arguments that causes him to change his mind. The philosophical debate is therefore left unresolved.[46]

Modern literary critics have discerned the same tendency to self-contradiction (or at least to opposition) in Donne's *Biathanatos*. An influential group of commentators maintain that the book is inherently a paradox—as indeed it declares itself to be in the subtitle. They argue ingeniously that we are not supposed to take Donne's argument literally. Rather we should read it as a deliberately obfuscatory and contradictory satire on scholasticism and casuistry. There is certainly merit in pointing out the way in which Donne's language at once advances and sabotages his argument. Consider again the book's subtitle: 'That Self-Homicide is not so naturally Sin that it may never be otherwise'.[47] Two negatives almost a positive make. On the other hand, the most persuasive critics of *Biathanatos*, Michael Rudick and M. Pabst Battin, have disputed this view and demonstrate that Donne does advance a logically coherent argument exculpating suicide. But what an argument it is! Having come

[44] P. Sidney, *The Countess of Pembroke's Arcadia*, ed. J. Robertson (Oxford, 1973), 293.

[45] Ibid. 294.

[46] Ibid. 292–8. For a discussion of this debate and the other suicides in *Arcadia*, see Green, 'Doors to the House of Death', 17–27. Despite the merits of Green's article, a closer analysis of the classical and Christian sources on which Sidney drew would repay the effort.

[47] A. E. Malloch, 'The Techniques and Function of the Renaissance Paradox', *Studies in Philology*, liii (1956), 203; R. Colie, *Paradoxia Epidemica: The Renaissance Tradition of Paradox* (Princeton, 1966), 500–1; J. Webber, *Contrary Music: The Prose Style of John Donne* (Madison, Wis., 1963), 5, 10; Donne, *Biathanatos*, 1.

to the end of his labyrinthine demonstration that suicide is not absolutely forbidden by divine, natural, or civil law, Donne abjures any attempt to specify the circumstances in which suicide might be permitted: 'I abstained purposely from extending this discourse to particular rules or instances, both because I dare not profess myself a master in so curious a science, and because the limits are obscure and steepy [*sic*] and slippery and narrow, and every error deadly.'[48] The final paradox of *Biathanatos*, Rudick and Battin maintain, is that it makes a powerful case against the prohibitions to self-killing without advancing a set of arguments that would justify modern suicides. Since the sacrifice of Christ is the model suicide, no death that does not match its purity of motive can be free from deadly sin. No wonder, as they remark, *Biathanatos* has been so often misunderstood. The negatives are never fully transformed into a positive, except in one inimitable instance.[49]

Donne was the only English clergyman of his era to suggest in print that suicide might be defensible. Clerics resoundingly rejected classical palliations of suicide, Sir Thomas Browne's worries about their soundness on that score notwithstanding. After reviewing classical arguments in favour of suicide, even the eirenical Burton was roused to conclude with a torrent of denunciation. 'But these are false and pagan propositions, profane Stoical paradoxes, wicked examples; it boots not what heathen philosophers determine in this kind, they are impious, abominable, and upon a wrong ground.'[50] Pious laymen, whether they were papists or Protestants, were equally adamant. Sir Thomas More set the tone. 'Take for the sample *Cato uticensis* which in Afryque killed hym selfe', he proposed. 'S Austyn well declarith ... that there was no strength nor magnanimyte therein but playne pusillanimite and Impotency of stomacke.'[51] John Donne was so apprehensive about the reception of *Biathanatos* that he refused to permit its publication in his lifetime and presented the manuscript to Sir Robert Ker with the comment that it was 'a book written by Jack Donne and not by Dr. Donne'. It was not finally printed until 1647.[52] Despite the public's familarity with Roman

48 Donne, *Biathanatos*, pp. lxxxii–lxxxiv, 193.

49 Ibid., pp. lxxxiii–lxxxiv.

50 R. Burton, *The Anatomy of Melancholy*, ed. H. Jackson (London, 1972), i. 438. For rejections of classical arguments and examples, see J. King, *Lectures Upon Jonas, Delivered at Yorke in ... 1594*, 6th edn. (London, 1618), 184–90; W. Vaughan, *The Golden Grove*, 2nd edn. (London, 1608), chs. 23–4; G. Abbot, *Exposition upon the Prophet Jonah* (London, 1600), 128–30.

51 More, *Dialogue of Comfort*, 130. The documents relevant to Sindercombe's case are conveniently reprinted in *Cobbett's Complete Collection of State Trials*, v (London, 1810), esp. col. 836, where Edward Sexby compares him with Brutus and Cato.

52 Donne, *Biathanatos*, pp. ix–x, xv, 4.

examples, no actual suicide was praised as an honourable death before 1650.

And yet the arguments of writers hostile to classical defences of self-killing also display a tendency to imply their contradictions. Burton's review of the opinions of his opponents is thorough to the point of advocacy. He provides effective synopses of the arguments of the most prominent classical authorities, together with apposite quotations. 'How many myriads besides in all ages might I remember', he asks in the midst of his discourse, '*qui sibi letum Insontes peperere manu* [who though innocent committed suicide]?'[53] The opponents of suicide were forced repeatedly to acknowledge the uncomfortable examples Burton recalled. 'Truely I say', exclaimed Anthony Anderson in a sermon, 'that neyther *Cato*, *Razias*, Lucretia, Curtius, or his lyke, are sure warrants to thee.' Noting early Christian parallels, he goes on to declare that they were contrary to the Sixth Commandment, but then concedes that Augustine allowed that there was something lawful in their deaths.[54] The case of Samson proved a constant source of anxiety. For whatever else Samson had done, he had certainly taken his own life. Most theologians preferred Augustine's gloss—he must have done so at the secret command of God. But a few, implicitly granting that there is no mention of such a command in the Bible, argued that his death was an exception to the rule. The Puritan casuist William Ames was surprisingly bold on this score, citing Samson to prove that although suicide was forbidden, 'it is lawfull . . . sometimes to expose oneself to such a danger, by which death must necessarily though indirectly follow'.[55] In fact the constant reiteration of classical and early Christian examples merely called attention to the weakness of the scriptural foundations of the prohibition. Writing in the aftermath of the publication of *Biathanatos*, George Mackenzie achieved a level of self-contradictory argument that easily surpassed the mark set by his predecessors. He declared that no biblical text forbade it because God knew man's natural aversion to self-destruction was stronger than any law. On the other hand, the Lord did not want to mention it, lest he implant the idea that such a sin was possible. It is strange, Mackenzie finally concludes this disastrous argument, that no biblical suicides are explicitly condemned.[56]

53 Burton, *Anatomy of Melancholy*, i. 436.

54 Anderson, *Shield of Our Saftie* (London, 1581), sigs. Kiiii [*sic*], L2$^{r}$.

55 W. Ames, *Conscience, with the Power and Cases Thereof* (London, 1639), 185 (mispaginated, 185–6 are between 180–2).

56 G. Mackenzie, *Religio Stoici* (Edinburgh, 1665), 84–5.

Contemporary playwrights exploited both the religious condemnations and classical exculpations of suicide. Imogen in *Cymbeline* is stayed from stabbing herself by the thought that suicide is forbidden by God:

> Against self-slaughter
> There is a prohibition so divine
> That cravens my weak hand.[57]

And yet in other tragedies, Shakespeare's characters commit pitiable or heroic suicides, as everyone knows. Rowland Wymer has recently argued that the dramatic possibilities and moral complexities of suicide were most effectively presented when authors endorsed fully neither the Christian nor the classical perspective. Shakespeare, whose prismatic imagination displayed the colours in the spectrum of attitudes more fully than anyone else's, is once more the best example. In *Hamlet* he presents the entire range of opinion about the legitimacy and morality of suicide. Moreover, he assigns varying opinions to characters who represent the groups that held them most strongly. Hamlet and the members of Claudius's court are inclined to Stoicism, and they tend to regard suicide as a moral and ethical problem. Hamlet himself debates whether suicide is an act of nobility and courage—the problem at the heart of Stoic discussions of self-killing, as Montaigne also recognized. The fear of divine punishment overwhelms the famous question that begins his soliloquy on suicide, but Hamlet does not conclude it is contrary to divine law, merely that it is impossible to know whether it will be punished:

> Who would fardels bear,
> To grunt and sweat under a weary life,
> But that the dread of something after death,
> The undiscovered country from whose bourn
> No traveller returns, puzzles the will,
> And makes us rather bear those ills we have
> Than fly to others that we know not of?[58]

Assuming that Ophelia committed suicide while she was mad, Gertrude and Laertes pity and excuse her. The 'churlish priest' and the plebeian

[57] W. Shakespeare, *Cymbeline*, in his *Complete Works*, ed. G. B. Harrison (New York, 1952), III. iv. 76–8; Wymer, *Suicide and Despair*, 32.

[58] Shakespeare, *Hamlet*, III. i. 76–82. In the pages that follow, we rely heavily upon Wymer's thoroughly researched and lucidly expounded treatment of suicide in Jacobean drama.

grave-diggers, on the other hand, complain that she ought to have been buried profanely and suggest that rank has overswayed justice in securing even the truncated rites performed for her. The priest snaps at Laertes:

> Her death was doubtful,
> And but that great command o'ersways the order,
> She should in ground unsanctified have lodged
> Till the last trumpet; for charitable prayers,
> Shards, flints, and pebbles should be thrown on her.

The grieving brother answers back in anger:

> I tell thee, churlish priest,
> A ministering angel shall my sister be
> When thou liest howling.[59]

How often the families of suicides must have protested in much the same way the desecration of their loved ones' bodies![60]

## HONOUR, LOVE, AND MELANCHOLY

Two medieval traditions more favourable to suicide than religion and folklore were revived in the sixteenth and seventeenth centuries: chivalry and courtly love. Elaborate codes of behaviour for the military aristocracy and their ladies, these intersecting sets of values may be described as the basis for a comprehensive subculture—an ideology, a set of literary and symbolic conventions, and an ethical system that was at odds with the moral teachings of the church on many points. Many features of 'classical' chivalry and courtly love were obsolete by 1500, but both still strongly influenced the ruling classes' conception of suicide, perhaps more strongly than ever. The Tudors revived chivalry and absorbed courtly love into the cult of romance that flourished at court and among the literati, especially during Elizabeth's reign.[61] Their importance would perhaps be more obvious to us today had Henry VIII's elder brother Arthur lived to assume the throne. The Tudor

[59] Shakespeare, *Hamlet*, v. i. 250–4, 262–4.

[60] For fuller discussions, see Wymer, *Suicide and Despair*, 29–36; M. MacDonald, 'Ophelia's Maimèd Rites', *Shakespeare Quarterly*, xxxvii (1986), 309–17; J. V. Holleran, 'Maimed Funeral Rites in *Hamlet*', *English Literary Renaissance*, xix (1989), 65–93.

[61] H. Haydn, *The Counter-Renaissance* (New York, 1950), ch. 9; A. B. Ferguson, *The Indian Summer of English Chivalry* (Durham, NC, 1960).

aristocracy was very fond of tournaments, old treatises, and chivalric romances. In the conditions of the sixteenth century, both chivalry and courtly love were necessarily modified by rival traditions and new social realities. Chivalry was perhaps more drastically affected than courtly love, which had always been a more purely literary tradition. Humanist intellectuals propounded a new ideal of nobility that stressed learning and public service, rather than martial prowess. The age of the great territorial magnates, whose fortified castles and armies of retainers manifested their military power, was fading, and the military aristocracy was slowly being transformed into a political élite. The new chivalry was therefore increasingly artificial—an anachronistic set of ideals that were overlaid with newer attitudes and practices.

The principal legacy of chivalry, as Maurice Keen has stressed, was its conception of personal honour, a sense of selfhood that depended not only on lineage but also on the aristocrat's social accomplishments: his skills in war and play, his service to the crown, his behaviour toward his peers, toward his inferiors, and toward women of his own rank.[62] An aristocrat whose conduct belied his estate forfeited his social identity. If anything, the changing role of the nobility in society intensified the élite's obsession with personal honour. As Lawrence Stone taught us long ago, the duel replaced bastard-feudal melées as the favoured form of aristocratic violence in the sixteenth century. The elaborate Italian code of fighting, with its degrees of injury and strict etiquette of combat, was rapidly domesticated. Violence and honour proved inseparable. Handbooks and courtly literature emphasized that death was preferable to dishonour. A gentleman had to fight to avenge an insult, if it were sufficiently grave, and it was cowardly to refuse a challenge. 'Everie injurious action not repulsed', asserted Sir William Segar, 'is by common consent of all Martiall minds holden a thing dishonourable, infamous, and reproachfull; it cannot be, but at some times and occasions such questions and quarrells shall arise, as necessarilie must receive triall by the Sword. And *Cicero* saith, that hee who repulseth not an injury, being able, offendeth no lesse, than if he had abandoned his friends, parents and countrie.'[63]

[62] M. Keen, *Chivalry* (New Haven, 1984), 249.

[63] W. Segar, *The Book of Honour and Arms (1590)*, ed. D. Bornstein (New York, 1975), sig. A2$^r$. For general treatments of the code of honour, see L. Stone, *The Crisis of the Aristocracy* (Oxford, 1965), 242–50; A. J. Fletcher, 'Honour, Reputation and Local Officeholding in Elizabethan and Stuart England', in A. J. Fletcher and J. Stevenson (eds.), *Order and Disorder in Early Modern England* (Cambridge, 1985), ch. 3; M. James, *English Politics and the Concept of Honour, 1485–1642*, Past and Present Supplement, 3 ([Oxford], 1978), which is indispensable.

That death was preferable to dishonour was one of the shibboleths of the age. And however much moralists and royal ministers tried to curb the murderous fad for duelling, no one really doubted that there were situations in which the maxim was a moral imperative. It was more difficult to decide what sorts of occasions were worth dying for and what sorts of deaths were permissible. Clerical opponents of suicide condemned Cato and Lucretia, but they admired the Marian martyrs for submitting to death rather than apostasizing. 'There be two sorts of voluntarie deaths', wrote one of them, 'the one lawful and honest, such as the death of Martyrs, the other dishonest and unlawful', such as the death of Peregrinus Proteus, the cynic who immolated himself, according to Lucian's fictionalized biography.[64] Laymen acknowledged a wider range of circumstances in which death was ennobling. Thus soldiers who fought on against impossible odds in the service of their countries were undoubtedly heroic. Sir Walter Ralegh immortalized Sir Richard Grenville, who attempted to persuade the crew of the *Revenge* not to surrender to the Armada when their ship was hopelessly overpowered, saying 'they should not now shorten the honour of their nation by prolonging their own lives for a few hours, or a few days'.[65] And in practice the crown was consistently lenient toward aristocrats who duelled to avenge their honour.

The forms of honourable death elided into outright suicide. Noble acts of sacrifice were not always easy to distinguish from baser kinds of self-destruction, as the long-standing debate over the death of Samson plainly showed. In his *Honourable Reputation of a Soldier*, George Whetstone retold a true story that neatly illustrated the ambiguities that could arise. Confronted by French forces that far outnumbered his own, the earl of Shrewsbury declared it was his duty to stand and die but advised his son Viscount Lisle to flee the field of battle. The old man was already covered with the honour of his many victories; the youth had a long life still before him, and his services would outweigh any dishonour his 'timourous flight' might bring him. Lisle, of course, chose to stand fast and die beside his parent. 'This precise preservation of honour', Whetstone remarks uneasily, 'neither the divines, nor many politick Martial-

[64] M. D. Faber, 'Shakespeare's Suicides: Some Historic, Dramatic and Psychological Reflections', in E. S. Shneidman (ed.), *Essays in Self-Destruction* (New York, 1967), 31–2.

[65] W. Ralegh, *Selected Writings*, ed. G. Hammond (Harmondsworth, 1986), 70. Ralegh himself seems to have doubted the wisdom, and perhaps the ethics, of Grenville's behaviour; that was not, however, how his narrative was or has been usually read. For a discussion, see C. B. Watson, *Shakespeare and the Renaissance Concept of Honor* (Princeton, 1960), 116.

ists, do allowe: the one absolutely reproving desperate ende; the other forbidding a man willfully to die, when by his death, hee neither benefiteth his frend, nor hurteth his enemie. And yet, the greatness of these mens courages, are to be honoured, although not necessary to be followed. But necessity many times approveth resolute bouldness, to be honorable, profitable, and necessarie.'[66] There was, as this example shows, an inescapable contradiction between religious prohibitions against suicide and aristocratic notions of honour. The code of honour was individualistic and social; religious imperatives were general and transcendant. The man of honour asked how his death would affect his reputation; the Christian asked how it would affect his soul.

Humanism tempered the chivalric code's emphasis on military honour in many ways, but it merely heightened the discrepancy between the code of honour and Christianity with regard to suicide. At least one popular handbook for gentlemen, *The Courtier's Academie*, simply advocated the Stoic solution in cases where honour was at stake. 'A man of honour shuld alwaies preferre death, before infamous saftie', asserts its author, Count Romei, citing Aristotle to prove the platitude. 'And upon this foundation the Stoickes in some cases permitted the violent killing of one's selfe to avoide a dishonorable life.'[67] For the most part, however, moralists did nothing to reconcile the man of honour's obligation to die rather than be dishonoured with his duty to God. In his influential dialogue on civic duties, for example, the comically named Lodowick Bryskett calls attention to 'the ancient Romanes, who held it the part of a stout heart, for a man to kill himselfe rather then to suffer shame or servitude, as we reade that *Cato* did, and *Cassius* and *Brutus*'. Bryskett plainly disapproves of self-murder, and he immediately resumes his review of the authorities (including Aristotle) condemning it. But he does not refute the Stoic ideals and examples he introduces, a fact to which he calls attention by opening the passage mentioning them with the phrase: 'But to omit the judgement of the ancient Romanes . . .'.[68] Similar juxtapositions of Christian cautions and Stoic mandates also appear in widely read handbooks by La Primaudaye, Whetstone, and others.[69]

66 Quoted in Watson, *Shakespeare and Honor*, 121–2. See also, *DNB*, s.v. 'Talbot, John'.

67 Quoted in Watson, *Shakespeare and Honor*, 120–1.

68 L. Bryskett, *Literary Works*, ed. J. H. P. Pafford ([?London], 1972), 182–3; R. Wymer, 'Lodowick Bryskett and Renaissance Attitudes to Suicide', *Notes and Queries*, NS 32 (Dec. 1985), 480–2.

69 Watson, *Shakespeare and Honor*, 121.

The dramatists did little to harmonize the contradictions between the code of honour and Christianity. In Massinger's *A Very Woman*, Cardenes falls into despair after provoking a duel in which he is badly wounded. He resolves to kill himself to atone for his dishonourable behaviour:

> Then in honour
> Wronging him so, I'll right him on my self;
> There's honour, justice, and full satisfaction
> Equally tender'd; 'tis resolv'd, I'll do't.

The doctor, Paulo, however, urges him that it is 'Honour to dare to live, and satisfie'. True honour, in other words, demands fortitude and reconciliation; false honour leads to suicide.[70] As Wymer points out, such a neat formulation of the problem is unusual. The supreme expression of the conflicting moralities occurs, as he shows, in *Othello*. To see Othello's suicide merely as an attempt to restore his honour traduces the subtlety of the play's handling of the concept of honour. But the curmudgeonly critic Thomas Rymer had no time for subtlety. He thought that Othello's single honourable action was his suicide: 'We see nothing done by him, nor related concerning him, that comports with the condition of a General, or, indeed of a Man, unless the killing himself, to avoid a death the Law was about to inflict upon him.'[71] Great writers like Shakespeare seized on the irreconcilable demands of honour and faith to enrich the thematic and psychological complexity of their depictions of suicide. Their readers were more likely to interpret such deaths, as Whetstone realized, in terms of their own roles—as moralists or martial minds. For those among the governing élite who played two roles, as Christians and as gentlemen, the legitimacy of a suicide depended on the scene it ended.

Chivalry and courtly love were so closely linked in aristocratic culture that they often seem merely to have been two aspects of the same code of conduct. Chivalry was how men of honour were to behave toward other gentlemen; courtly love was how gentlemen were to behave toward ladies. Suicide was as much a part of the courtly-love tradition as it was of chivalry. The tradition of tragic love-suicides was as old as western thought. Classical prototypes—the stories of Dido and Aeneas, Antony and Cleopatra, Pyramus and Thisbe—were preserved in the

[70] Wymer, *Suicide and Despair*, 87–8.

[71] Ibid. 93. It is possible, of course, that Rymer was being cynically ironic. If so, his cynicism and irony turn on the fact that some people thought suicide could be honourable in such circumstances.

Middle Ages. Chaucer celebrated all of these famous lovers in his *Legend of Good Women*, describing the suicides of Dido, Cleopatra, and Thisbe without a hint of condemnation. In his version of the story of Pyramus and Thisbe, suicide is the means by which the lovers achieve a perfect and eternal union, denied to them on earth. Taking up her dead lover's sword, Thisbe exclaims:

> And thogh that nothing, save the deth only,
> Mighte thee fro me departe trewely,
> Thou shalt no more departe now fro me
> Than fro the deth, for I wol go with thee.[72]

Although Chaucer's source was Ovid, this sentiment was entirely consistent with the view of love-suicide in courtly literature, where, Bayet remarks, 'One can say without exaggeration that, for the lover and his lady, suicide is correct [*élégant*], obligatory in several instances'.[73] Courtly love, like chivalry, was an ethical system with its own doctrines—doctrines that were notoriously at odds with Christian moral teachings. In the hermetic world of courtly values, suicide could become an act of transcendent self-sacrifice, and the pangs experienced by lovers betrayed or abandoned excused even deaths that were motivated by despair.

Many of the conventions of courtly love survived long after the disappearance of the cultural milieu in which they arose and flourished. The notion that love-suicide was an ennobling act was one of them. Love and death were inextricably linked in Renaissance tragedy. 'Love's martyrs must be ever, ever, dying', sings Penthea in Ford's *The Broken Heart*, echoing a thought that may well have occurred to the play's audience.[74] And when lovers died, as die they must, they chose frequently to take their own lives. The prototypical love tragedy, *Gismond of Salern* (1567–8), restates the courtly doctrine that lovers who kill themselves are united in death as Cupid's votaries. A violent story of jealousy and murder, the play tells of a young woman, recently widowed, whose possessive father Tancred refuses to allow her to remarry. She takes a lover, and when Tancred discovers them in bed, he murders the young man sadistically. Grief-stricken, Gismond poisons herself, dying confident that she will soon join her beloved in paradise:

[72] G. Chaucer, *The Legend of the Good Women*, in his *Works*, ed. F. N. Robinson, 2nd edn. (Boston, 1957), ll. 896–9.

[73] A. Bayet, *Le Suicide et la morale* (Paris, 1922), 485.

[74] J. Ford, *The Broken Heart*, in *John Ford: Three Plays*, ed. K. Sturgess (Harmondsworth, 1970), IV. iii. 153.

Now passe I to the pleasant land of love,
Where heavenly love immortall flourisheth.[75]

It is the assurance that suicide may be a means to consummate love forever that places the deaths of Antony and Cleopatra in Shakespeare's play beyond the moralizing condemnation of didactic writers like Thomas Beard and William Vaughan. Shakespeare also invokes the Roman ideal of honourable suicide in his treatment of Antony's death, which at once preserves his honour and his passion.[76] Believing that Cleopatra has already killed herself, Antony exclaims that he is dishonoured by her courage; she has by her own hand conquered herself and so conquered Caesar, who would have conquered her. He fails to persuade his servant, named Eros, to kill him—Eros slays himself instead. And at last he summons the courage to follow their example:

My Queen and Eros
Have by their brave instruction got upon me
A nobleness of record. But I will be
A bridegroom in my death, and run into 't
As to a lover's bed.[77]

The convention that love-suicide might be free from the taint of sinful despair directly contradicted Christian attitudes to self-murder, and Renaissance writers were aware of the danger of promoting sinful actions. Some of them, drawing on an ancient medical tradition, depicted love as a dangerous disease. Literary examples of lovers driven to such extremes of melancholy that they attempt or succeed in killing themselves abound. A melancholy lover in John Davies's *The Scourge of Folly*, for instance, 'seeks a rope, and then ... a knife'.[78] The affinity of melancholy and despair and the contemporary distrust of the passions render such suicides morally ambiguous. As Wymer shows, the Jailer's daughter in Fletcher and Shakespeare's *Two Noble Kinsmen* wavers in her suicidal moods between the certainty of damnation for self-murder and the conviction that if she merely died from the natural effects of love, she would in death 'do nothing all day long | But pick Flowers with

[75] Wymer, *Suicide and Despair*, 113–4. For another analysis of *Gismond*, see R. Stilling, *Love and Death in Renaissance Tragedy* (Baton Rouge, La., 1976), ch. 1.

[76] Wymer, *Suicide and Despair*, 128–3.

[77] Shakespeare, *Antony and Cleopatra*, IV. xv. 97–101.

[78] Quoted in L. Babb, *The Elizabethan Malady* (East Lansing, Mich., 1951), 168. See also Wymer, *Suicide and Despair*, 118–9.

*Proserpine*'. What sets her apart from many of the heroes and heroines in love tragedy is her recognition that killing herself will lead to perdition and not to the lover's paradise: 'if one be mad, or hang, or | Drown themselves, thither they goe [to hell]'.[79] But perhaps the most effective juxtaposition of the contrary moralities of courtly love and Christianity is a sonnet in which Michael Drayton compares his mistress to an evil spirit, tempting him to murder himself:

> An evill spirit your beauty haunts me still,
> Where-with (alas) I have been long possest,
> Which ceaseth not to tempt me unto ill.
> . . . . . . . . .
> Before my face, it layes all my dispaires,
> And hastes me on unto a suddaine death;
> Now tempting me, to drowne my selfe in teares,
> And then in sighing to give up my breath;
> Thus am I still provok'd, to every evill,
> By this good wicked spirit, sweet Angel devill.[80]

Drayton's poem fuses desire and damnation, erotic and suicidal temptation, into an emotional and spiritual oxymoron.

Medical writers, reviving classical psychology, popularized the concept of love-melancholy and warned of its pernicious effects. Robert Burton, whose treatment of the theme was exhaustive, was pessimistic about the prognosis for lovers afflicted with the malady: 'Death is the common catastrophe of such persons.'[81] But Burton and other medical writers also advanced another set of views that further complicated the prevailing notion that suicides were wilful rebels against the laws of God and nature. Peter Barrough, whose medical textbook was reissued for three generations after its first publication in 1583, observed that people suffering from melancholy 'desire death, and do verie often behight and determine to kill them selves'.[82] His words were echoed in La Primaudaye's popular *The French Academie*, which warned that the black humour caused 'some to grow so far as to hate themselues, and so fall despaire, yea many kil and destroy themselues'.[83] And Burton, in his famous *Anatomy of Melancholy*, declared that religious and legal condem-

[79] Wymer, *Suicide and Despair*, 121.
[80] *Minor Poems of Michael Drayton*, ed. C. Brett (Oxford, 1907), 34; Wymer, *Suicide and Despair*, 112 3.
[81] Burton, *Anatomy of Melancholy*, iii. 187.
[82] P. Barrough, *The Method of Physick* (London, 1596), 46.
[83] Quoted in Babb, *Elizabethan Malady*, 105.

nation for suicide ought to be suspended for people who had been sorely afflicted with the disease for a long time: 'In some cases those hard censures of such as offer violence to their own persons ... are to be mitigated, as in such as are mad, beside themselves for the time, or found to have been long melancholy, and that in extremity.'[84] Melancholy was the most fashionable malady of the age, and gloomy lovers, sad philosophers, and unhappy religious fanatics throng through its literature. A character in one of Chapman's plays who has lost his wife falls into a long, suicidal torpor, which he explains in humoral terms:

> A kind of false, sluggish, and rotting sweetness
> Mix'd with a humour where all things in life
> Lie drown'd in sour, wretched, and horrid thoughts.[85]

'I am mop't', exclaims the lovesick maid in *The Two Noble Kinsmen*, using a synonym for one sort of melancholy, 'Let not my sence unsettle | Least I should drown, or stab or hang myself'.[86] And of course the most famous meditation on suicide in English literature is voiced by Hamlet, who declares himself melancholy before he speaks it and is diagnosed as a melancholic after he has finished his soliloquy and abused Ophelia: 'There's something in his soul | O'er which his melancholy sits on brood'.[87] That melancholy was frequently the prelude to suicidal thoughts was a commonplace.

## CONCLUSION

Literary scholars and historians have often asserted that there was a progressive liberalization of attitudes to suicide in the sixteenth and seventeenth centuries. Accepting the arguments of Fritz Eisinger and W. E. H. Lecky, for instance, Curtis Watson declares: 'The Christian taboo was strong against it, but as the 16th century progresses Christianity has less and less of a hold, and increasing approval is demonstrated.'[88] This judgement contains a germ of truth, but it also illustrates how easy it is to oversimplify the course of change. At the very same time that

[84] Burton, *The Anatomy of Melancholy*, iii. 439.
[85] Quoted in Babb, *Elizabethan Malady*, 106.
[86] J. Fletcher and W. Shakespeare, *Two Noble Kinsmen*, ed. G. R. Proudfoot (London, 1970), III. ii. 25, 29–30; Babb, *Elizabethan Malady*, 166.
[87] Shakespeare, *Hamlet*, III. ii. 171–3.
[88] Watson, *Shakespeare and Honor*, 118.

humanism was fostering awareness of more tolerant attitudes to suicide, government reform and clerical evangelism were deepening popular hostility to it. There can be no doubt which current of opinion was stronger in the sixteenth and early seventeenth centuries. There were suicides for honour occasionally, and many men and women slew themselves for love, as we shall see in a subsequent chapter. But no one praised the men of honour for the way they died; no one excused actual suicides on the grounds that they had committed a crime of passion. When the earl of Northumberland killed himself in the Tower of London, his Catholic co-religionists claimed his death was murder, rather than praising him as a modern Cato.[89] Miles Sindercome, the man who tried to assassinate Oliver Cromwell, was hailed as a Cato and a Brutus by his republican fellow-conspirator, Edward Sexby, in 1657.[90] He was, however, the solitary suicide esteemed as a political martyr during the century, and the government's savage reaction to his death certainly outweighed the words of its radical opponent. There are no examples at all of love-suicides who received lenient treatment or were eulogized as real Romeos, actual Juliets.

Juries, as we know, ignored not only these extenuating circumstances, but also refused to adopt the more tolerant perspective advocated by some medical men. The palliating ideas of medical writers were simply absorbed into the religious interpretation of the crime. John Sym declared that Satan preyed particularly on people plagued by melancholy, 'speaking to and persuading a man to kill himself'.[91] This point was reiterated by Robert Burton and William Perkins, who stressed that melancholy was the *balneum diaboli*, the devil's bath, that enables him to torment the down-hearted and bring them to despair.[92] Melancholy and diabolical temptation were not, therefore, incompatible explanations for suicide. It was widely believed that Satan could influence people's minds by natural or supernatural means, and treatise after treatise warned the godly to be especially careful when they were melancholy. Literary works implied the same belief. Just before his soliloquy, Hamlet worries that his father's ghost may be a demon:

[89] *DNB*, s.v. 'Percy, Henry'; *Complete Peerage*, ix. 730–2; J. Lingard, *The History of England* (Dublin, 1874), vi. 102–3.

[90] W. Allen [E. Sexby], *Killing No Murder*, in *The Harleian Miscellany*, ix (London, 1810), 306; *State Trials*, v, col. 836.

[91] Sym, *Lifes Preservative*, 246–7.

[92] Burton, *Anatomy of Melancholy*, i. 429, iii. 395; W. Perkins, *The Workes of that Famous and Worthy Minister of Christ in the University of Cambridge, Mr William Perkins* (London, 1626–31), ii. 46–7, iii. 381.

The spirit that I have seen
May be the Devil, and the Devil hath power
To assume a pleasing shape. Yea, and perhaps
Out of my weakness and my melancholy,
As he is very potent with such spirits,
Abuses me to damn me.[93]

Prior to the middle of the seventeenth century, the widespread acceptance of the notion that melancholy folk were especially vulnerable to Satan's wiles did not excuse those who succumbed and killed themselves. Indeed, one of the most uncompromising advocates of the notion that suicide was not the consequence of natural disease but the product of divine vengeance and diabolical temptation was the author of the earliest English treatise on melancholy, Timothy Bright.[94] Evidence of melancholy moods was frequently advanced in Star Chamber cases and at inquests to prove that dead people had been self-murderers.

Local resentment to forfeiture and élite fascination with classical ideas about suicide were nevertheless significant. Although they did not arrest the growing severity of practice and opinion in the sixteenth and early seventeenth centuries, they were the preconditions for the spread of a more tolerant and secularized approach to suicide in the eighteenth century. Opposition to forfeiture complicated responses to actual suicides in the Tudor and Stuart period, pitting the interests of lords against those of tenants, sharpening the tensions between the crown and local communities, and creating ambivalence between abhorrence and sympathy. The popularization of classical philosophies and historical events and the survival of chivalry and courtly love fostered an awareness that people might kill themselves for reasons other than diabolical despair. These traditions, as conventional as they were, provided playwrights and poets with the opportunity to fashion morally complex and psychologically powerful depictions of self-destruction that must certainly have influenced their readers. It was not simply a question of contrasting contradictory moralities: the interplay of philosophical and moral contraries, implicit and explicit, complicated the problem of judging suicide, even as the actual process of judgement became increasingly severe. The apparent consistency of belief and behaviour in the sixteenth and early seventeenth centuries thus concealed a deepening ambivalence toward suicide, expressed in the behaviour of local com-

93 Shakespeare, *Hamlet*, III, i. 627–32.
94 T. Bright, *A Treatise of Melancholie* (London, 1586), 193, 208–9, 225–30, esp. 228.

munities and in the lay literature of the educated élite, that was generated by social, political, and intellectual changes. These tensions and contradictions explain both the nature and the speed of the decline of severity after about 1660.

# II

# THE SECULARIZATION OF SUICIDE

What Cato did, and Addison approved
Cannot be wrong.

Eustace Budgell, untitled
suicide note (1737)

I thought of Chatterton, the marvellous Boy,
The sleepless Soul that perished in its pride.

William Wordsworth, 'Resolution
and Independence' (1802)

# 4

# *The Revival of Leniency*

ATTITUDES to suicide changed profoundly in the century and a half following the English Revolution. Judicial and ecclesiastical severity gave way to official leniency and public sympathy for most people who killed themselves. This transformation was a complex phenomenon. The views of particular classes and groups altered at different times and for different reasons; the actions of officials and institutions did not simply reflect public opinion. The signs of change were apparent even before the Restoration. Freed temporarily from crown supervision during the civil war, juries began to return higher numbers of *non compos mentis* and ambiguous verdicts, and although the governments of the 1650s re-established the effectiveness of King's Bench, its challenges did not halt the upward trend in acquittals. John Donne's *Biathanatos* was belatedly published in 1647, after censorship had collapsed. The trend toward more lenient responses and more liberal attitudes to suicide accelerated after 1660. By the last three decades of the eighteenth century, *felo de se* verdicts had become as rare as *non compos mentis* ones had been two centuries earlier. And although there were persistent calls to retain the old punishments and protests against tolerance, the weight of lay opinion swung back against severity. Classical philosophy and medical science, which had been the basis for dissenting opinions in the sixteenth and seventeenth centuries, dominated Georgian thinking about suicide. Radical defences of self-killing were published and widely read; admiration for classical suicides became more general and more unapologetic than ever before; upper-class laymen came to regard suicide as a rational choice or a medical calamity.

And yet the law against suicide was not altered until the nineteenth century. The savagery of the traditional reaction to suicide was mitigated by the increasing suspension of the law case by case, rather than by reforms promulgated by Parliament or by the officials at Westminster. The locus of change was therefore the coroner's jury, which became increasingly reluctant in the later seventeenth and eighteenth centuries to enforce the penalties for self-murder. The decisions made by coroners' juries are especially significant and revealing. They were influenced by the changing attitudes of the governing élite as well as by the moral conservatism of local communities. At the same time, the verdicts that juries returned determined what the community's response to suicidal deaths would be. Neither the official penalty of confiscation nor the popular sanction of ritual desecration could be performed unless a jury brought in a verdict of *felo de se*. The mysterious alchemy of the coroner's inquest transmuted the insubstantial stuff of attitudes and beliefs into the tangible matter of collective action.

## THE CORONER'S JURY

A close look at coroners and their juries is necessary if we are to understand the changes that occurred in the societal reaction to suicide. Coroners were elected to their posts by the freeholders of their counties or selected according to the custom of the liberty or borough that they served. Their numbers varied from county to county; between two and six seems to have been the usual complement for a shire, but it should be remembered that every county also contained special jurisdictions with their own coroners.[1] At least until the mid-eighteenth century, it

[1] The leading authority on the office of the coroner from the Middle Ages until modern times is R. F. Hunnisett. The most important of his works in the present context are *Wiltshire Coroners' Bills: 1752–1796*, Wiltshire Record Society, xxxvi (Devizes, 1981); 'The Importance of Eighteenth-Century Coroners' Bills', in E. W. Ives and A. H. Manchester (eds.), *Law, Litigants, and the Legal Profession* (London, 1983), 126–39; *Calendar of Nottinghamshire Coroners' Inquests*, Thoroton Society Record Series, xxv (Nottingham, 1969). Other useful sources include T. R. Forbes, *Crowner's Quest*, Transactions of the American Philosophical Society, lxviii (Philadelphia, 1978); J. D. J. Havard, *The Detection of Secret Homicide* (London, 1960), 18–20; *Report of the Committee on Death Certification and Coroners*, Cmnd. 4810 (Nov. 1971); J. A. Sharpe, *Crime in Seventeenth-Century England: A County Study* (Cambridge, 1983), 33–4; J. C. Cox, *Three Centuries of Derbyshire Annals* (London, 1890), i. 66–95, ii. 283. The last is particularly informative. We have assembled additional evidence, too fragmentary and cumbersome to cite, from inquests and scattered references in other documents on the backgrounds of coroners in Cumberland, Norwich, Westminster, Middlesex, and the City of London.

was unusual for coroners to be medical men. The office was essentially a local one, held by a man of some standing in his county or community. Coroners were required to own enough property to bear the cost of any fines and amercements that they might be charged, and the statutory fine for failure to hold an inquest was 100*s*. They were customarily drawn from the ranks of the gentry. Remarking that the coroners in Tudor Nottinghamshire were all members of families of long-established landowners, R. F. Hunnisett asserts that they 'were elected from among those county families which from time to time provided sheriffs, escheators, justices of the peace and other of the more eminent local officials'.[2] The men themselves may have been a little less exalted than the breeding of the Nottinghamshire coroners suggests. Sir Thomas Smith commented that they were chosen from among 'the meaner sort of gentlemen', and he was almost certainly right.[3]

Because the inquest was an occasional institution and jurors were hurriedly summoned from the immediate area, even less is known about them than the coroners. They were usually selected from the men of the deceased's village or nearby communities: some of them, often perhaps all of them, were his neighbours and knew him well.[4] In the Middle Ages, the distinction between witnesses and jurors was blurred; in the early modern period some jurors may still have been chosen from the list of candidates because of their acquaintance with the dead person and his affairs. It is impossible to be certain precisely what the minimal qualifications for serving on coroners' juries were. Although the evidence is very scanty, it seems plain enough that jurors were usually of middling rank, mostly husbandmen and craftsmen, but that more exalted persons served on juries deliberating the deaths of gentlemen and ladies in some rare instances. A more or less typical jury charged with concealing the true cause of Edward Langford's death included three husbandmen, a baker, and a schoolmaster, for instance.[5] J. A. Sharpe believes, no doubt correctly, that coroners' jurors were mostly men of the type who served

[2] Hunnisett, *Calendar of Nottinghamshire Coroners' Inquests*, pp. xi–xii.
[3] T. Smith, *De Republica Anglorum*, ed. M. Dewar (Cambridge, 1982), 108.
[4] Cox, *Three Centuries of Derbyshire Annals*, i. 80–2, prints documents showing the process of selection at work.
[5] J. Miller and K. H. Rogers, 'The Strange Death of Edward Langford', *Wiltshire Archaeological and Natural History Magazine*, lxii (1967), 105–8.

on other juries and as constables and churchwardens.[6] The coroner's jury was therefore representative of the middling ranks of the local community and often very familiar with the deceased and his family.

The attitudes of the coroner and jurors inevitably influenced their decisions, and their views were shaped by many factors other than the ostensible facts of the case. Furthermore, the coroner and jurors were subject to pressures that sometimes placed them at odds with higher authorities or with each other because of their very different official and social positions. As royal officials, the majority of coroners were supervised by the justices of the assizes and by the deputies of the king's almoner. When verdicts were contested or forfeited property was allegedly concealed, the whole jury might be sued in Star Chamber, but it was the coroner who bore the largest responsibility for the jury's actions and it was he who dealt directly with the officials of the crown. In many liberties and towns, coroners were selected by the lord or corporation who possessed the right to the goods of felons. Coroners were therefore more apt than their jurors to interpret the law narrowly and to preserve the right of the king or franchise holder. Jurors, on the other hand, were necessarily sensitive to local opinion and aware of the consequences for the survivors of a *felo de se* verdict. A pauperized family was a burden to the community that the jurors represented. Attitudes to suicide itself could also differ between the coroner and his jurors. Coroners were literate and aware of the legal rules and procedures regarding suicide. They had access to books that propounded new ideas about suicide; they were members of the ruling élite and shared its

[6] J. A. Sharpe, *Crime in Early Modern England* (London, 1984), 76. See also, J. S. Cockburn and T. A. Green (eds.), *Twelve Good Men and True: The Criminal Trial Jury in England, 1200–1800* (Princeton, 1988), 162–3, 182–213, 250, 305–57. The ranks of jurors are impossible to determine precisely except through a thorough examination of the surviving records for a locality, a task beyond the scope of this national study of suicide. Occasionally, however, jury lists and depositions that give occupations or hint at them survive. The generalization in the text is based on shards of such information from Cumberland, Norwich, Westminster, London, and Essex in the later 17th and 18th centuries. The jurors who were summoned to the Tower to judge the death of Miles Sindercombe may have been atypical, for the deceased was an important political prisoner. But their ranks are generally consistent with those on other juries: 'Merchants, and other substantial House-keepers of the Tower Liberty': *The Whole Business of Sindercome* (London, 1657), 13. The jury in the case of the earl of Northumberland in 1585 was also called 'substantiall': R. Holinshed, *Holinshed's Chronicles*, 6 vols. (London, 1807–8), iv. 602. Judge Jeffreys maintained that the jurors in the death of the earl of Essex in 1683 were 'several persons of quality. . . . Several of them were esquires and persons of note': W. Cobbett, T. Howell, *et al.* (eds.), *Cobbett's Collection of State Trials*, ix (London, 1811), col. 1207. For a jury made up mostly of local gentlemen, see *The Annual Register*, xxxix (1797), 12.

culture. Jurors, in contrast, were very frequently illiterate in the sixteenth and seventeenth centuries; men who could only make their marks on the inquest or depositions still sometimes served on coroner's juries in the eighteenth century. The legal lore about suicide that such men learned was taught by the coroners themselves during inquests, by the clergy in sermons, and by popular literature and folk tradition.

The authority enjoyed by coroners was very great, and they could determine the outcome of inquests. Complaining in 1700 about the growing tendency to suspend the laws against suicide, John Adams placed the blame on the coroner:

> Though I have hitherto applied my self to the Jury, 'tis certain that their Verdict depends much upon the Coroner. . . . 'Tis he that *summons* whom he *pleases* to be of the Jury, and to these he gives *what Charge he pleases*; the Examination of the Witnesses, the Summing up the Evidence is done *by him*: so that unless there happen to be upon the Jury Men of Conscience, Courage, and Understanding (which may easily be avoided if the Coroner thinks fitting) they will be apt to be led by him implicitly.[7]

The coroner's views did not, however, invariably prevail. Throughout the period some juries occasionally displayed independence and even defiance. Very detailed records survive for two late seventeenth-century cases. Anthony Joyce, the husband of Samuel Pepys's cousin, cast himself into an Islington pond in 1668. Pulled from the water, he fell ill with a fever that soon killed him. Legally, Joyce was a *felo de se*; his discourse was very sensible, and he confessed that he had attempted suicide. But in spite of pressure by the coroner (or foreman) and by persons with designs on the dead man's goods, the jury eventually declared that Joyce had died a natural death.[8] A similar incident occurred in remote Cumberland almost thirty years later. After declaring to several of his neighbours that he was utterly miserable and 'that God had forsaken him and the devill had gotten holden of him', John Atkinson slashed his throat. He lingered for three days, then died of a 'melancholy fever'. The verdict of a somewhat irregular and hasty inquest, natural death, enraged the duke of Somerset, who possessed the right to the

[7] J. Adams, *An Essay Concerning Self-Murther* (London, 1700), 128.

[8] S. Pepys, *The Diary of Samuel Pepys*, ed. R. Latham and W. Matthews (London, 1970–83), ix. 32–4, 49, 78. Pepys first wrote that opposition to the verdict came from the coroner, then crossed out the word and substituted 'foreman'. In either event, the whole tale demonstrates that the jury held fast against considerable pressure from people who stood to gain from a *felo de se* verdict and who were able to control the procedures of the inquest.

property of felons, and he ordered a second inquest. The body was disinterred and the coroner of the liberty delivered a stern charge to the new jury that detailed the duke's rights, the meaning of the *felo de se* verdict, and the penalties of forfeiture. He carefully avoided any mention of the *non compos mentis* alternative, and yet that was the verdict the second jury brought in.[9]

## THE DYNAMICS OF CHANGE

Coroners' juries palliated the law of suicide in two ways, by colluding with families to frustrate the rights of the crown and lesser lords and by excusing increasing numbers of suicides as persons *non compos mentis*. These two methods of evading the penalities for suicide had different motivations and implications. Resistance to forfeiture was an expression of local communities' long-standing resentment of the crown and its privileges. It expressed tensions that were generated by the contradictory interests of local communities and the monarchy and of humble ratepayers and privileged landlords. The rise of the *non compos mentis* verdict began as just another strategy for avoiding forfeiture, but it eventually came to embody a profound change in beliefs about suicide itself. Used more and more frequently, it was the tangible expression of the secularization of suicide, of the opinion that self-destruction was in itself an act of insanity, an end more to be pitied than to be scorned. The causes of this change are more difficult to identify with confidence than the causes of the decline of forfeiture. They owed something to Enlightenment thought and to the increasing prestige of science, including medical science. But they can also be traced to the orthodox élite's reaction against religious enthusiasm and Catholic miracle-mongering. Élite opinion changed much more rapidly than popular belief. At some point during the mid-eighteenth century the men of middling rank who served as coroners' jurors adopted the medical interpretation of suicide.

Resistance to forfeiture proceeded more rapidly than the secularization of suicide verdicts. There was a precipitate fall in the number of inquisitions reporting forfeited goods in the 1640s. This was undoubtedly the consequence of the turmoil caused by the civil wars, which temporarily destroyed the whole system for returning coroners' inquisitions. The Interregnum governments strove to restore the government's

[9] Cumbria RO, D/Lec/CR I, 5/3. See also Sharpe, *Crime in Seventeenth-Century England*, 34, 231 n. 109.

profits, and they succeeded in driving up the average value of the forfeitures they collected to almost £50, almost twice the level achieved during any other period.[10] But they failed to improve the percentage of inquisitions reporting goods. Because many suicides were women or paupers, that figure had never exceeded 40 per cent by much. Wives could not legally own property; financial ruin was a common motive for self-killing. After 1660, however, the proportion of inquisitions mentioning confiscated property worth anything at all fell steadily in every decade, from about 35 per cent in the 1660s, to about 25 per cent in the 1680s, to about 13 per cent in the first ten years of the eighteenth century. (See Table 4.1.) And when juries reported goods to seize, they set their worth at figures that were lower and lower. In the 1660s about one-third of the forfeitures reported in inquests to King's Bench were valued at sums higher than one pound, and some of them brought the crown hundreds of pounds; by the period 1710–14 only 6.7 per cent of forfeitures were worth more than a pound, and there were no windfalls of

Table 4.1. *Goods Reported to King's Bench, 1660–1714*

| Years | Suicides | Goods | % reporting goods | % £1 or more |
|---|---|---|---|---|
| 1660–4 | 334 | 122 | 36.5 | 30.5 |
| 1665–9 | 293 | 97 | 33.1 | 27.1 |
| 1670–4 | 241 | 72 | 29.9 | 30.3 |
| 1675–9 | 219 | 55 | 25.1 | 22.0 |
| 1680–4 | 256 | 68 | 26.6 | 22.8 |
| 1685–9 | 177 | 44 | 24.9 | 19.6 |
| 1690–4 | 256 | 59 | 23.0 | 21.0 |
| 1695–9 | 216 | 43 | 19.9 | 19.3 |
| 1700–4 | 181 | 30 | 16.6 | 17.0 |
| 1705–9 | 170 | 17 | 10.0 | 11.2 |
| 1710–14 | 156 | 12 | 7.7 | 6.7 |
| TOTALS | 2,499 | 619 | 24.8 | 23.1 |

*Note*: The figures given for 'goods' include only those inquisitions in which chattels were valued, i.e., were assessed at a sum larger than nothing, but the percentage of forfeitures rated at one pound or more is the proportion of all inquisitions in which goods were reported, even if they were valued at nothing.

*Source*: PRO, KB 9, 10, 11, 140; PL 26; HCA 1.

[10] This figure was elevated considerably by a single, huge forfeiture of £8,875, the chattels of William Toomes, esq., who killed himself in 1655: KB 9/866/2, mm. 141–3. The next largest windfall for the whole period was less than half that amount.

fifty pounds or more at all. Juries were declaring openly that yeomen and even gentlemen whom they judged to have been self-murderers either possessed no chattels or owned goods that were worth only trivial sums.[11]

In other words, the proportion of cases in which suicides were supposed to have had no goods at all or in which juries simply ignored the matter grew as the value of the forfeitures that did take place shrank. Even allowing for the distortions that are caused by missing inventories and by procedures that were inconsistent and shifting, the king's right to the goods of suicides was obviously severely eroded by noncompliance between the Restoration and the accession of George I. All of the old gambits were employed to conceal property from the authorities. By the reign of Queen Anne juries were plainly on the side of the survivors, openly declaring that there were no goods to forfeit, flagrantly undervaluing those they did report, and brazenly ignoring their duty to inventory and confiscate property.

The decline of forfeiture could not have occurred without the weakening of the government's ability and resolve to enforce the law of suicide. As long as the Tudor system of enforcement remained in place, the activities of coroners and their juries were too closely supervised to permit massive evasion. During the English Revolution the legal and institutional basis for forfeiture was challenged, and after the Restoration the governing élite's support for the law of suicide eroded rapidly. In a series of events rich in irony the instruments with which the crown had enforced the law were destroyed or weakened. Star Chamber was abolished in 1641, and the supervision of coroners henceforth reverted solely to King's Bench, a much more cumbersome and less effective tribunal. The Long Parliament was certainly not thinking about the law of suicide when it struck down Star Chamber. Its members were concerned to dismantle the institutions that had made the royal prerogative a danger to religion and property. An immediate effect of the disappearance of Star Chamber was that juries started to return many more *non*

[11] Examples of yeomen whose goods seem patently to have been undervalued are too numerous to cite. For gentlemen see PRO, KB 11/20/2, m. 3 (Rowland Morgan, gent., no goods, 1702); KB 11/21/8, m. 12 (John Cheveley, gent., 26*s*., 1707); KB 11/18/2, m. 14 (John Gooch, gent., no goods, 1698); KB 11/17/2/4, m. 1 (James Thomas, gent., no goods, 1693); KB 11/12/3, m. 31 (James Prade, armiger., no goods, 1685); KB 10/3, m. 2 (Arthur Capel, earl of Essex, no goods, 1683). Essex was a very special case, and the disposition of his goods was a political issue: H. C. Foxcroft, *A Supplement to Burnet's History of My Own Time* (Oxford, 1902), 100, gives an account of what happened to Essex's property. Many more gentlemen and aristocrats who killed themselves were simply declared to have been *non compos mentis*.

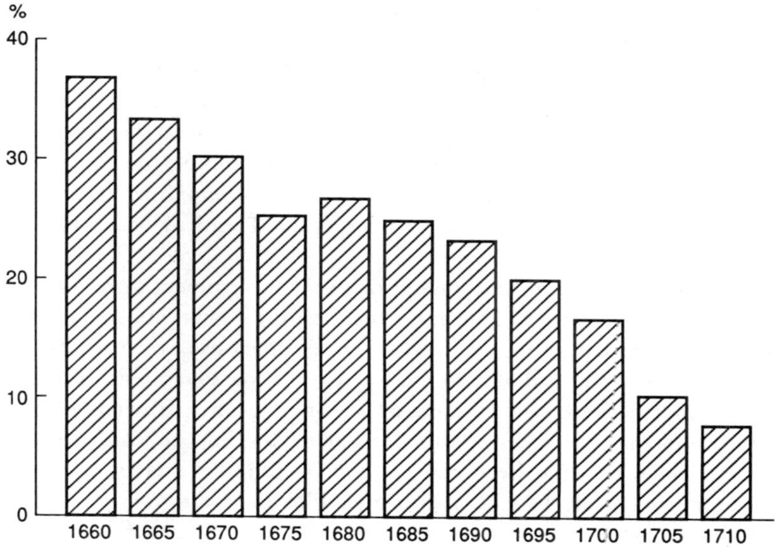


FIG. 4.1. Goods reported to King's Bench, 1660–1714
*Source*: PRO, KB 9, 10, 11, 140; PL 26; HCA 1.

*compos mentis* verdicts, attempting, no doubt, to avoid paying forfeitures. Eventually, on 6 May 1650, Francis Walsall presented papers to the Council of State 'concerning the goods of felo's de se'. The matter was referred to John Milton, who was charged with moving the Lords Commissioner of the Great Seal to 'take what course therein for the advantage of the Commonwealth as they shall thinke fit'.[12] It is difficult to tell precisely what they did. But they certainly jolted the Upper Bench into challengng lenient verdicts, and they may also have been responsible for the reappearance of the almoner as a government official.[13] Thus at

[12] *CSPD, 1650*, 142; J. M. French, *The Life Records of John Milton*, Volume ii, *1639–1651* (New Brunswick, NJ, 1950), 307. For Walsall, see J. and J. Venn, *Alumni Cantabrigienses*, s.v. 'Walsall, Francis'. The Commonwealth and Protectorate governments were more rigorous and successful in enforcing the law than either the regimes of the 1640s or of Charles I had been. The reasons for their severity and their success, aside from penury and a penchant for fiscal expedients, are not clear.

[13] Most of the 60 mixed verdicts in the records of the Upper Bench (King's Bench) for the 1650s were originally *non compos mentis* verdicts that were altered by the clerks of the court, almost certainly as a prelude to challenging them. Together with the six straight *non compos mentis* verdicts, they amounted to some 9.2% of the suicides reported. The almoner throughout much of the 1650s was Nicholas Bernard, DD, one of Oliver Cromwell's chaplains: for references to him and his work, see PRO, KB 9/879/3, mm. 282–3; KB 29/307–8; *DNB*, s.v. 'Bernard, Nicholas'.

almost the precise moment that the Hale Commission was proposing the abolition of forfeiture for suicide, the Council of State was taking steps to reinforce it. This contradiction of practice and principle will sound familiar to students of the English Revolution. Although the parliamentarians rebelled against the centralization of authority and the use of the royal prerogative in ways that seemed to them to impinge on traditional rights, their governments were of necessity as committed to central control and as jealous of their revenues as any Tudor or Stuart regime had been.

The failure of reform and reassertion of the government's prerogative caused the resumption of disputes between the crown and owners of patents granting them the rights to the goods of felons of themselves and to deodands. And royal officials were no longer able to use Star Chamber to intimidate those who challenged its privilege in particular places. Some suits may have been brought in Exchequer, but the main arena of battle seems to have been King's Bench. Judging merely by cases recorded in extant Law Reports, squabbles over the law of suicide produced some important precedents that seem in general to have favoured the rights of survivors as against those of the crown and lords of liberties.[14] The heaviest blow of all against forfeiture for self-murder was, ironically, struck on behalf of the very persons who profited most from it. In 1693 parliament passed a statute that severely weakened the ability of King's Bench to enforce the law of suicide. The statute of 4 & 5 William and Mary, c. 22, tipped the balance in disputes between the crown and the holders of royal patents over who had the right to the goods of suicides decisively in favour of the latter. It made it unnecessary for an inquisition to be filed in King's Bench before a suicide's property could be claimed, established a cheap and simple way to record one's patent with the court, and made the officials of the court liable to a fine of £5 if they infringed the rights of rival claimants.[15] The clerks of the Crown Office complained as the statute was passing through parliament that it would 'render the Business of the said Office wholly impracticable', and their political hyperbole eventually proved prophetic. Looking back at the end of the eighteenth century, Henry Deathy, an official of King's Bench, observed that 'some time after the passing of the Act . . . the coroners discontinued returning their Inquisitions into the Court of Kings Bench & of course all Proceedings upon such Inquisitions were discontinued likewise'.[16] The statute of 1693 was

[14] See e.g., Barclay's Case (1658); *Rex* v. *Ripley* (34 Chas. II); *Rex* v. *Clark* (1 Anne); *Rex* v. *Atkinson* (1701); *Rex* v. *Stuckley* (1701).

[15] The act was made perpetual by 7 & 8 William III, c. 36.

[16] *Journal of the House of Commons*, x (1688–93), 742; PRO, KB 33/25/2.

designed to protect the rights of property-owners at the expense of the crown's ability to exercise its own prerogative. The point was not lost on the House of Commons. Summarizing the objections made to the bill in debate, Narcissus Luttrell commented that 'it entrenched upon the rights of the Crown'.[17]

The 1693 statute was an expression of the cult of private property that the English Revolution and the Revolution of 1688 had fostered. 'There is a thing called Property', wrote Bolingbroke, 'that the People of England are fondest of.'[18] Whatever their political allegiances, a majority of the gentlemen of late seventeenth- and eighteenth-century England shared Locke's view that no government might 'take to themselves the whole or any part of the Subjects *Property* without their own consent'.[19] The statute of 1693 epitomized the post-revolutionary mood. It was also an ill-calculated action that eventually destroyed the very rights that it was meant to protect. For the rights to the goods of suicides and to deodands were a *shared* prerogative. Their exercise by holders of royal patents depended ultimately on respect for the law from which they were derived and on the principle it implied.[20] Handcuffed in its attempts to proceed against manorial lords who claimed the goods of self-murderers, King's Bench lost interest not only in supervising coroners but also in affording protection to patent-holders who were sued by heirs. The distinguished jurist Michael Foster summed up the court's recent practices: 'It hath frequently interposed it's [*sic*] Authority . . . in the Case of Suicide, *in Favour of the Subject and to Save the Forfeiture*, but will not do it in either case *to his Prejudice*.'[21] Following Foster, Blackstone made the same point in his far more widely read *Commentaries on the Laws of England*. After observing that juries routinely undervalued deodands, a right that was always linked with the right to the goods of self-

[17] N. Luttrell, *The Parliamentary Diary of Narcissus Luttrell, 1691–1693*, ed. H. Horwitz (Oxford, 1972), 348. We are grateful to Professor Henry Horwitz for discussing this act with us.

[18] Quoted in H. Nenner, *By Colour of Law: Legal Culture and Constitutional Politics in England, 1660–1689* (Chicago, 1977), 39. For the importance of property rights in the constitutional history of the early 17th century, see J. P. Somerville, *Politics and Ideology in England, 1603–1640* (London, 1986), 145–63.

[19] Quoted in J. Tully, *A Discourse on Property: John Locke and His Adversaries* (Cambridge, 1980), 171.

[20] V. Morgan, 'Whose Prerogative in Late Sixteenth and Early Seventeenth Century England?', *Journal of Legal History*, v (1984), 39–64, provides an interesting discussion of the extent to which the king's prerogative rights were shared with others or exploited by them.

[21] M. Foster, *A Report of Some Proceedings on the Commission of Oyer and Terminer and Gaol Delivery for the Trial of the Rebels in the Year 1746* (Oxford, 1762), 266.

murderers, he remarked: 'The court of king's bench hath generally refused to interfere on behalf of the lord of the franchise, to assist so odious a claim.'[22]

The constitutional disputes that culminated in the Civil War and Revolution of 1688 encouraged the governing élite to become disenchanted with forfeiture as a punishment for self-murder. Although they had little in common with the humble folk who resisted the law's enforcement or the radicals who called for its abolition in the Interregnum, Georgian gentlemen were equally bothered by a law that seized property that ought to have been inherited by the innocent to punish people already dead. Few were eager to defend common criminals and traitors, the chief targets of the penalty of forfeiture, but parliament nevertheless nearly abolished forfeiture for high treason in 1709. Carried away with himself in debate on this matter, Bishop Burnet declared in the House of Lords that 'it was neither just nor reasonable to set the children to begging for their father's faults'. Forfeiture, he claimed, 'was never the practice of free governments'.[23] The issues raised by any attempt to limit or abolish forfeiture were exceedingly complex and controversial. There were many reasons, political and philosophical, for opposing its abolition. But in general there is little doubt that the forfeiture of property as a penalty for crime, and for suicide more particularly, was inconsistent with the ruling élite's profound reverence for private property.

As the eighteenth century progressed, more and more writers protested that the law was unjust. Echoing the words of radical law reformers, Defoe remarked as early as 1704 that society was inclined to pity the family: 'the children should [not] be starv'd because the Father has destroy'd himself'.[24] Even the opponents of palliating the law of suicide

22 W. Blackstone, *Commentaries on the Laws of England*, 2nd edn. (Oxford, 1766), i. 302. In later editions the word 'inequitable' was substituted for 'odious'. The last case in King's Bench regarding deodands that Henry Deathy could find in about 1799 was *Rex* v. *Williams*, 5 Geo. III, 1765: KB 33/25/2.

23 7 Anne, c. 21; Blackstone, *Commentaries on the Laws of England*, iv. 377–8; W. Cobbett, T. Howell, *et al.* (eds.), *Cobbett's Parliamentary History of England*, vi. (London, 1810), cols. 796–7. Blackstone comments interestingly that juries had become unwilling to find defendants liable to forfeiture when they fled to avoid prosecution: 'forfeiture being looked upon, since the vast increase of personal property of late years, as rather too large a penalty for an offence, to which a man is prompted by the natural love of liberty', Blackstone, *Commentaries*, iv. 380.

24 *Defoe's Review*, ed. A. W. Secord (New York, 1938), [*Review* no. 60 (30 Sept., 1704)], 255. See also Adams, *Essay Concerning Self-Murther*, 29; W. Fleetwood, *The Relative Duties of Parents and Children, Husbands and Wives, Masters and Servants, Consider'd in Sixteen Sermons: With Three More Upon the Case of Self-Murther* (London, 1705), 476.

acknowledged that forfeiture offended the public's sense of justice. Suicide, wrote one of them in 1754, pillages 'the widow and the orphans of the felon, thus heaping one calamity upon another. . . . The extreme and evident cruelty of this law has produced an almost constant evasion of it.'[25] Other commentators agreed. A thoughtful critique of the law written by an anonymous author in 1776 deplored the frequency with which false verdicts were returned. He confirmed the view of less expert writers that 'the people are prepossessed with an opinion, that the Law, in the particular before us, is grievous and unreasonable'. Coroners and their juries, he maintained, shared this prepossession, and they did not abandon it when they took their oaths.[26] Although he defended forfeiture as reasonable and just, Charles Moore nevertheless concluded that parliament should repeal it. Public sentiment held that the law 'militates against all private feelings and is deemed severe on the innocent', and so he concluded that the best course would be to abolish forfeiture altogether and enforce more strictly the punishments disgracing the suicide's corpse and reputation.[27]

The second way that juries suspended the penalties for suicide was to bring in increasing and finally overwhelming numbers of *non compos mentis* verdicts. Less than 7 per cent of the suicides reported to King's Bench were declared to have been insane in the early 1660s, but the proportion more than doubled in the next two decades. In the 1690s around 30 per cent of suicides were brought in *non compos mentis*, and lunacy verdicts exceeded 40 per cent in the early eighteenth century (see Table 4.2 and Fig. 4.2).

The decay of the practice of returning coroners' inquisitions to King's Bench in the eighteenth century means that fewer and fewer documents enabling us to trace the rise of the *non compos mentis* verdict survive in the archives of the central courts. But there is one series of records in King's Bench and others from local jurisdictions that illustrate the trend in the otherwise poorly documented years between 1714 and about 1740. The long run of inquisitions for the city of Norwich is perhaps the best set of such records for the period.[28] *Non compos mentis* verdicts exceeded *felo*

[25] *Gentleman's Magazine*, xxiv (1754), 507.

[26] *Considerations on Some of the Laws Relating to the Office of a Coroner* (Newcastle, 1776), 53–4.

[27] Moore, *Full Inquiry into Suicide*, i. 336–7, 339. See also, *Gentleman's Magazine*, xix (1749), 341–2; C. Fleming, *A Dissertation upon the Unnatural Crime of Self-Murder* (London, 1773), 17; R. Hey, *A Dissertation on Suicide* (Cambridge, 1785), 24–5, 82, 85; A. Smith, *The Theory of Moral Sentiments*, ed. D. D. Raphael and A. L. Macfie (Oxford, 1979), 287.

[28] A few West Country counties continued to return inquisitions to King's Bench for the early 18th century and they have been preserved in PRO, KB 13. The ratios of *felo de se* to *non compos mentis* verdicts in them are given in the Appendix. Norwich Inquisitions.

Table 4.2. *Suicide Verdicts Returned to King's Bench, 1660–1714*

| Years | *Felo de se* | *Non compos mentis* | Per cent *non compos mentis* |
|---|---|---|---|
| 1660–4 | 311 | 23 | 6.9 |
| 1665–9 | 262 | 31 | 10.6 |
| 1670–4 | 213 | 28 | 11.6 |
| 1675–9 | 196 | 23 | 10.5 |
| 1680–4 | 220 | 36 | 14.1 |
| 1685–9 | 143 | 34 | 19.2 |
| 1690–4 | 186 | 70 | 27.3 |
| 1695–9 | 151 | 65 | 30.1 |
| 1700–4 | 107 | 74 | 40.9 |
| 1705–9 | 95 | 75 | 44.1 |
| 1710–14 | 93 | 63 | 40.4 |
| TOTALS | 1,977 | 522 | 20.9 |

*Note*: All mixed and ambiguous verdicts have been disregarded.
*Source*: PRO, KB 9, 10, 11, 140; PL 26; HCA 1.

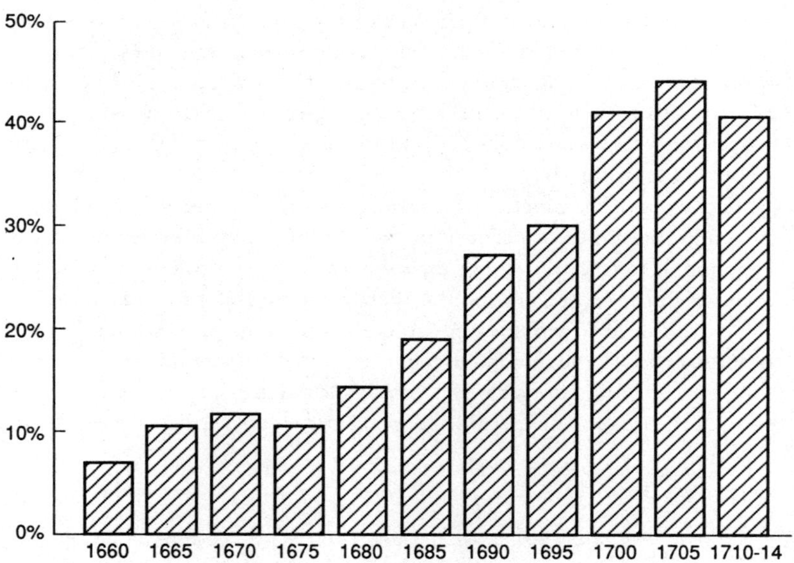


FIG. 4.2. *Non compos mentis* verdicts, 1660–1714
*Source*: PRO, KB 9, 10, 11, 140; PL 26; HCA 1.

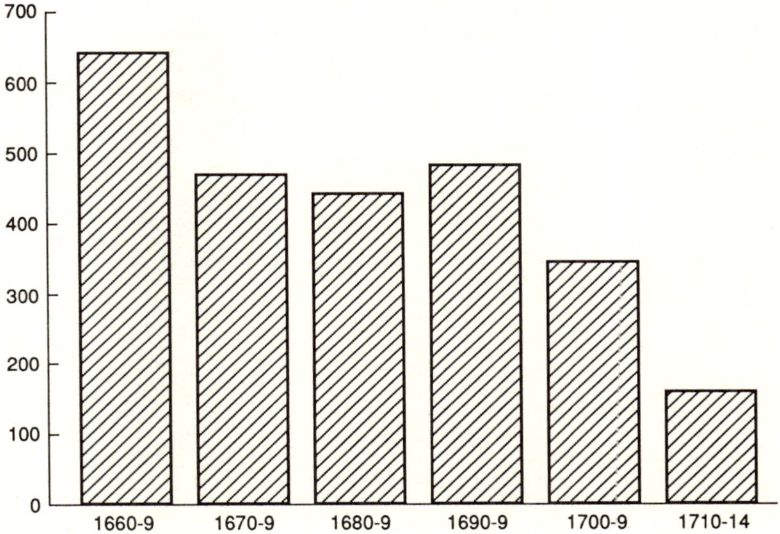


FIG. 4.3. Suicides reported to King's Bench, 1660–1714
*Source*: PRO, KB 9, 10, 11, 140; PL 26; HCA 1.

*de se* there early in the eighteenth century. By the 1710s and 1720s over 90 per cent of all suicides were judged insane, and after a period of more rigorous enforcement of the law, *non compos mentis* became in the last three decades of the century the only suicide verdict that Norwich coroners returned (see Table 4.3).[29] Several runs of coroners' inquisitions and bills from the second half of the eighteenth century tell a similar tale. Regardless of the character of the locality, from remote Cumberland to London itself, *non compos mentis* had become the usual verdict in cases of suicide by the last third of the century (see Appendix 2).

The rise of the *non compos mentis* verdict was prompted initially by its attractiveness as a way of escaping the fiscal penalties for self-murder, and for a long time this no doubt remained a major aspect of its appeal to coroners' juries. Bishop William Lloyd, the king's almoner, was dismayed to learn late in 1689 that Francis Bonney's 'widow had got the Coroner's jury to bring him in *non compos mentis*'. Bonney was a London

[29] A matching pattern may be observed in smaller scale in Cumbria RO, Coroners' Inquest Records for the Liberties of Cockermouth and Egremont, 1693–1800, D/Lec/CR I.

Table 4.3. *Suicides in Norwich, 1670–1799*

| Years | *Felo de se* | *Non compos mentis* | Per cent *non compos mentis* |
|---|---|---|---|
| 1670–99 | 12 | 5 | 29.4 |
| 1700–9 | 0 | 0 | 0 |
| 1710–9 | 1 | 17 | 94.4 |
| 1720–9 | 1 | 10 | 90.9 |
| 1730–9 | 8 | 26 | 76.5 |
| 1740–9 | 13 | 25 | 65.8 |
| 1750–9 | 16 | 40 | 71.4 |
| 1760–9 | 2 | 32 | 94.1 |
| 1770–9 | 0 | 27 | 100 |
| 1780–9 | 0 | 11 | 100 |
| 1790–9 | 0 | 5 | 100 |
| Totals | 53 | 198 | 78.9 |

*Source*: Norwich Inquisitions.

goldsmith who had posted a recognizance of £1,000 for John Grant, who had absconded. In the end the bishop apparently had to content himself with collecting the recognizance, which he assigned 'to several charities'.[30] The widow of Hugh Richardson sought the advice of the attorney, Joseph Chesshyre, after her husband drowned himself in 1705. Richardson's goods had been claimed by the lord of the manor of Cockermouth and Egremont in Cumberland. 'I doe advise', Chesshyre responded, 'if the fact will bear it and it can be made out that H. Rich. was non compos mentis at the time he drowned himself . . . that you prove the will . . . and say he was non compos mentis.'[31] The increasing frequency of *non compos mentis* verdicts in the 1680s and 1690s, however, signalled the beginning of a fundamental change in the cultural meaning of suicide. For unlike the other methods of avoiding forfeiture, declaring that suicides were mad unavoidably challenged durable popular beliefs about the crime. A *non compos mentis* verdict was an implicit rejection of religious and folkloric interpretations of suicide that condemned it utterly in favour of medical explanations that excused it. During the long period in which the attitudes of juries to suicide were gradually

[30] *Calendar of Treasury Books, 1689–92*, ed. W. A. Shaw (London, 1931), 319, 456, 497, 746,2010 (continuous pagination). We are grateful to Robert Buchholz for this citation and for his help with the office of the king's almoner in the later 17th century.

[31] Cumbria RO, D/Lec/CR I, 14/2.

changing, roughly for a century after 1680, the law against self-murder was enforced selectively. This transitional phase in the secularization of suicide deserves special attention despite dismaying gaps in the records for the period because the pattern of juries' decisions reveals a partial picture of the social values that guided the behaviour of ordinary people in Georgian England.

## SELECTIVE ENFORCEMENT

With each passing decade of the eighteenth century, juries that were disposed to treat suicides mercifully accepted testimony describing less and less severe mental disorders as evidence of insanity. They were not, however, invariably disposed to be merciful, and for a long time a substantial number of suicides continued to be judged *felones de se*. Self-murder remained the majority verdict through 1714 among the inquisitions returned to King's Bench. About one in four Norwich suicides was a *felo de se* in the first half of the eighteenth century. In the liberties of Cockermouth and Egremont in Cumberland, where the local lords were jealous of their rights to the goods of suicides, almost half of the thirty-nine suicides from 1700 to 1775 were *felones de se*. Even after 1760 *felo de se* verdicts were not rare in some places: they accounted for about one in six of the Wiltshire suicides from 1752 to 1796.[32] Thus although the increasing use of the *non compos mentis* verdict greatly mitigated the societal reaction to suicide, juries extended mercy in a discriminating manner throughout much of the eighteenth century.

The criteria for distinguishing those to be pardoned from those to be condemned were seldom simply psychological. Evidence about the mental state of the deceased was considered in the light of many other factors that heightened or lessened its significance, and it was interpreted very flexibly. In particular, testimony that the deceased had been melancholy and low-spirited might be construed either as proof of self-murder or as evidence of insanity. Thomas Law, a Cheshire clergyman who had come to London after losing his post as a chaplain, was observed to have been 'melancholy and discontented' before he killed himself in 1684, but he was nevertheless declared a *felo de se*.[33] The London family with whom Dorcas Pinkney, a children's coat-maker,

[32] Norwich Inquisitions; Cumbria RO, D/Lec/CR I; Hunnisett, *Wiltshire Coroners' Bills*.
[33] *The Sad and Dreadful Relation of a Bloody and Cruel Murther Committed by Mr. Thomas Law, a Minister, in Heart-Street, Covent-Garden Upon his own Person* (London, 1684).

lodged and worked noticed that she was 'much dejected with Melancholy' before her suicide in 1686. But her conviction as a *felo de se*, unlike Thomas Law's, was set aside because she was found to have been 'Distracted'.[34] Witnesses who appeared before juries in early eighteenth-century Cumberland described the profound melancholy of Ann Garnett, Thomas Rothery, Robert Ravell, Joshua Rumball, and Abraham Bank in very similar terms, but only Garnett, Rumball, and Bank were declared *non compos mentis*.[35] A critic who was familiar with the practices of coroners' juries remarked in 1776 that they brought in one verdict or the other 'without having even a shadow or presumption of Proof to support them. . . . Their Judgments in general are the effect of Caprice and Partiality.'[36]

The scarcity of extant depositions and other descriptions of ordinary people's suicides makes it impossible to be certain why one verdict or the other was returned in the overwhelming majority of cases. Some clues to the social factors that influenced juries' decisions do survive, though. Rank mattered. The *Connoisseur* in 1755 railed that the difference between a self-murderer and a pitiful suicide was the size of his fortune: 'A pennyless poor dog . . . may perhaps be excluded from the church yard; but the self-murder by a pistol genteelly mounted or the Paris-hilted sword qualifies the polite owner for . . . a pompous burial and a monument setting forth his virtues in Westminster Abbey.'[37] This was a cynical exaggeration, but it was not entirely wrong. Throughout the period, aristocrats and gentlefolk were treated more leniently than their social inferiors, and everyone knew it. Shakespeare had made the grave-diggers in *Hamlet* complain of Ophelia: 'If this had not been a gentle-woman, she should have been buried out o' Christian burial.'[38] We know of no great ladies of the court who killed themselves, but other cases show that the grave-diggers' complaint was fully justified. When the despicable earl of Berkshire shot himself with his crossbow in 1622, for example, the court directed letters to the coroner, ordering that 'the evidence touching the earle of Berkshires manner of death must not be urged, but the matter made as fair as possible'. The pressure worked: the

[34] *Sad and Dreadful news from Dukes-place near Aldgate; or, a true Account of a Barbarous and Unnatural self-murther committed by Dorcas Pinkney* (London, 1686).

[35] Cumbria RO, D/Lec/CR I, 20/2, 22/1, 26/1, 36/6, 43/4.

[36] *Considerations on the Office of a Coroner*, 45–6.

[37] [G. Colman and B. Thornton], *Connoisseur* (London, 1755), no. 50, 298.

[38] W. Shakespeare, *Hamlet*, in his *Complete Works*, ed. G. B. Harrison (New York, 1952), v. i. 26–8.

jury duly ruled the earl *non compos mentis*.[39] A far more obscure member of the nobility, the twenty-two-year-old daughter of Henry, Lord Mordaunt, leaped out of a high window on 5 April 1610. She survived the fall, and afterwards tried to drown herself. Five days after her first suicide attempt, she died, perhaps from her injuries, perhaps from an illness contracted because of her suicide attempts. Although by law her death ought to have been ruled a *felo de se*, the jury evidently took advantage of the fact that she had not perished immediately and returned a judgment of accidental or natural death.[40] The tendency to acquit men and women of quality only intensified after the Restoration. With the exception of the earl of Essex, none of the noblemen who is known to have killed himself after that time was judged a self-murderer.[41]

There can be no doubt that men and women of quality were less likely to be judged self-murderers. In the Tudor and Stuart centuries, 67 per cent of peers and gentlemen whose deaths were reported to the government were convicted; 93 per cent of their social inferiors met the same fate. The ratio of *felo de se* to *non compos mentis* verdicts, in fact, precisely mirrored the social hierarchy. The vast advantage of gentle status is plainly evident in the inquisition data, and so is the lesser advantage that yeomen enjoyed over husbandmen, husbandmen over labourers, and labourers over servants and apprentices. (See Table 4.4.) Gentility was least important in the second half of the sixteenth century, when enforcement of the law was most rigorous and 90.9 per cent of gentlemen and ladies were convicted; it became increasingly significant after 1650, when enforcement relaxed and only 51.1 per cent were. The much more fragmentary and less revealing statistics for the Georgian period tell the same story, in a somewhat different register. Very few gentlemen were returned *felo de se*, but men and women of humble rank were spared much more often, and in increasing numbers. The three gentlemen who

39 The crown's intervention was unusual; it was prompted by the duke of Buckingham, whose brother had designs on the fortune of the earl's daughter: *The Letters of John Chamberlain*, ed. N. E. McClure, American Philosophical Society, Memoirs xii, Parts i–ii (Philadelphia, 1939), ii. 423; S. D'Ewes, *The Diary of Sir Simonds D'Ewes (1622–1642)*, ed. E. Bourcier (Paris, n.d.), 64, 159–60; *DNB*, s.v. 'Norris, Francis'; PRO, KB 9/766/2, m. 246.

40 Bodl., Ashmole MS 334, fos. 120$^{v}$–121$^{r}$. No inquisition reporting her suicide was returned to King's Bench. Sir John Fites (or Fitz) was found *non compos mentis* despite the murderous rampage that preceded his suicide: PRO, KB 9/1077, mm. 12–3; Chapter 1 above. Thomas Hoyle, the York alderman and MP, was returned *non compos mentis* in 1650, almost certainly in part because of his social stature and his influential friends: M. F. Keeler, *The Long Parliament, 1640–1641* (Philadelphia, 1954), 224–5.

41 For a comment on this trend, see F. Ayscough, *A Discourse against Self-Murder* (London, 1755), 13–14.

Table 4.4. *Social Status of Suicides, 1485–1714*

| Status | *Felo de se* | | *Non compos mentis* | | Mixed | |
|---|---|---|---|---|---|---|
| | N | % | N | % | N | % |
| Peers/Gentlemen | 131 | 67.2 | 53 | 27.2 | 11 | 5.6 |
| Yeomen | 394 | 86.6 | 45 | 9.9 | 16 | 3.5 |
| Husbandmen | 804 | 92.3 | 53 | 6.1 | 14 | 1.6 |
| Labourers | 1,436 | 94.1 | 68 | 4.5 | 21 | 1.4 |
| Servants/Apprentices | 311 | 99.0 | 3 | 1.0 | 0 | 0 |
| Craftsmen | 1,014 | 93.5 | 55 | 5.0 | 16 | 1.5 |
| Others | 2,611 | 93.8 | 120 | 4.3 | 54 | 1.9 |
| TOTALS | 6,701 | | 397 | | 132 | |

*Notes*: Includes only persons whose status was indicated in the inquisition reporting their suicide. Status groups include adult males and their wives and children. The category 'craftsmen' is extremely heterogeneous, socially and economically.

*Source*: PRO, KB 9, 10, 11, 140; PL 26; HCA 1.

killed themselves in Wiltshire after 1751, for example, were all judged lunatics, but so were 271 persons of lesser rank.[42] Mercy was no longer the virtually exclusive privilege of the nobility, as it had been before the English Revolution.

The immunity of the rich to *felo de se* verdicts was assured partly by the opportunities that their wealth provided for their families. Their survivors took care to produce medical witnesses to testify that the suicide had been unbalanced. When the duke of Bolton shot himself in 1765, for example, an eminent physician, Sir Clifton Winteringham, and an apothecary appeared at the inquest to swear that he was suffering from a fever that 'was capable of depriving his Grace of his Senses'.[43] Medical men rarely appeared at inquests on men and women of lesser rank, except when they had been summoned to try to save their lives. And of course the rich could easily afford simply to bribe the coroner and his jurors. Bribery has left few records, for obvious reasons. On the back of the inquisition returning as *non compos mentis* Edward Walsingham,

[42] Hunnisett, *Wiltshire Bills*.

[43] Westminster Inquisitions, duke of Bolton (5 July 1765). For an excellent example of how carefully testimony was mustered to prove the insanity of notables who killed themselves, see the case of John Powell, a treasury official in political trouble, who died in 1783. The inquest was orchestrated to present four witnesses to describe the discovery of his body, eight witnesses 'to prove the State of Mr. Powell's mind for some time before his Death' and two witnesses to testify to the state of his mind the day before he killed himself: Westminster Inquisitions, John Powell (26 May 1783).

doubtless a member of the famous Norwich family of that name, someone wrote 'fee paid by the relations', but this was exceptional.[44] Some critics complained that bribery was widespread.[45] Defoe, however, thought that it was less important than sympathy in securing favourable verdicts, and given the long history of hatred of forfeiture we are inclined to agree with him.[46]

When jurors judged the deaths of aristocrats and gentlemen, their sympathy was born of deference; but most suicides were, of course, neither noble nor rich. Those for whom juries were most likely to feel compassion were prosperous and responsible persons of good reputation whose survivors would be greatly injured if their property were seized. The most likely candidate for a *non compos mentis* verdict was thus a man of some property and good reputation who was the head of a household. Testimony about the mental state of the deceased was likewise most persuasive when it was given by witnesses whose status or character commanded the jury's respect. In 1734, a time when juries in the liberty of Cockermouth and Egremont still commonly returned *felo de se* verdicts, the support of Jennet Millsell, 'a Neighbour and a devout woman well stricken in Years', helped win Abraham Bank's acquittal. She testified that he had been long melancholy, like several of his ancestors, and that she had visited him frequently, 'to read to him out of the Holy Scriptures and other good books and to sing Psalms and pray to him', attempting to drive off his gloomy thoughts.[47] Displays of neighbourly pity could move juries to mercy even when the deceased had not been a person of importance. No fewer than five women described how Hannah Baldwin had been left penniless and pregnant when her husband died and said she had been melancholy ever since. Her plight had obviously distressed those who had known her, and the jury brought in a verdict of lunacy.[48]

Conversely, it is safe to say that eighteenth-century *felones de se* were often marginal members of the community in which they died: criminals, people in disgrace, servants, apprentices, abject paupers, or strangers. Men and women who tried to escape punishment for crimes by killing themselves were invariably convicted as self-murderers throughout the century. A London mob was so incensed by the suicide of a murderer

44 Norwich Inquisitions, Edward Walsingham (20 Mar. 1759).
45 Adams, *Essay Concerning Self-Murther*, 29; [Colman and Thornton], *Connoisseur*, 298.
46 Defoe, *Defoe's Review*, 255.
47 Cumbria RO, D/Lec/CR I, 43/4.
48 Essex County RO, D/DHt, T 140/100.

named James Newth that they exhumed his body from the crossroads and mutilated it. The rituals of desecration were not punishment enough for him.[49] Posthumous prosecution of criminal suicides is easy to understand. Juries were also disinclined to spare many whose offences were much less serious. A Cheshire girl who was judged a self-murderer in 1740 was 'suspected of being with Child of a bastard'.[50] Mary Grave, a Cumberland *felo de se*, was a 'poor man's daughter' who possessed nothing to forfeit.[51] Strangers who could not be identified, like the man whose decayed body was found in Dorset in 1724, were prime candidates for *felo de se* verdicts.[52] And so, perhaps, were soldiers.[53] The people condemned as *felones de se* in eighteenth-century Norwich included poor weavers and labourers, two women rumoured to have been in trouble because of illicit pregnancy and embezzlement, and unmarried youths who had no dependants.[54] These were men and women with whom the jurors, as representatives of the local community, had at best weak ties of sentiment and obligation.

Juries sometimes found solid citizens guilty of self-murder. The *Norwich Mercury* wondered at the suicide and conviction of Henry Hudson, a journeyman weaver who 'was always esteem'd a careful industrious Man, lifed regularly, and maintain'd his Family in a handsome manner'.[55] Such men were not normally returned *felo de se*. Very occasionally it is possible to guess why an otherwise respectable citizen was found guilty of his own death. Robert Ravell's daughter and one of his neighbours testified that he had been melancholy and disturbed in mind a long time before his suicide in 1717. He was condemned anyway. Ravell was an old man, who had been maintained for many years by his children to whom he had given over his property: his

49 *Gentleman's Magazine*, v (1735), 557–8.

50 PRO, CHES. 18/3, Sarah Browne (1740).

51 Cumbria RO, D/Lec/CR I, 39/3. For other paupers or propertyless dependants, see ibid. 53/2; Dorset RO, D131/X8.

52 Dorset RO, D131/X8.

53. See e.g., Somerset RO, D/B/bw 1917/50, Thomas Ubank (1743).

54 See e.g., Norwich Inquisitions, James Quailes (16 June 1692), a woolcomber who dwelt in the pesthouse; John Fletcher (4 May 1692), a 14-year-old apprentice weaver; Ann Letree (4 May 1730), very poor and with child (see also *Norwich Mercury*, 2–9 May 1730); Daniel Alborough (7 Jan. 1735), a poor man (and *Norwich Mercury*, 3–10 Jan. 1735/6); Samuel Lane (23 Sept. 1737), a mason's labourer (and *Norwich Mercury*, 17–24 Sept. 1737); Susan Ward (17 Aug. 1737), allegedly stole some yarn (and *Norwich Mercury*, 13–20 Aug. 1737). Because of concealment, it is obviously impossible to know how many of the 18th-century *felones de se* who were said to have had no goods, the overwhelming majority of them, were actually paupers.

55 *Norwich Mercury* (19–26 May 1739); Norwich Inquisitions, 25 May 1739.

conviction as a self-murderer neither deprived his heirs nor added to the burdens of the parish.[56] Another Cumberland man, Robert Lowthian, was a farmer of some substance. He killed himself in 1718 and was found a *felo de se*; his family forfeited over forty pounds. The testimony about Lowthian's state of mind was conflicting. His wife said he was perfectly sane; his son and a friend spoke of previous suicide threats, melancholy, and distress. But perhaps the crucial fact brought out at the inquest was that Lowthian's troubles could be traced to a dispute between him and his neighbours that had ended up before the bench of quarter sessions. His principal adversary, John Moreland, swore at the inquest that he had known Lowthian for over forty years and had 'never heard he was in any way melancholy but since this accident happened'. Robert Lowthian was a man whose own wife would not defend him and who had alienated his neighbours as well.[57]

One class of person whom juries treated with unexpected leniency was debtors. None of the men and women who killed themselves while imprisoned in King's Bench for debt in the reign of George III was judged a *felo de se*.[58] A similar tendency to treat those who had fallen on to hard times mercifully may be detected in newspaper stories and inquisitions from other jurisdictions as well. It is tempting to see this pattern as evidence of popular hostility to the law of debt, which was heatedly criticized throughout the century. It shows in any case that juries discriminated among the dead not merely according to their rank and fortune, but also according to the circumstances that had brought about their desperate act. Men and women of good character whose downfall was the result of economic misfortune and their creditors' greed were the objects of pity.[59] Those who had always been paupers were less likely to command sympathy. So were usurers. *Fog's Weekly Journal* reported in 1731 that a Shropshire shoemaker had been found *felo de se* and 'a considerable Sum of Money he had out at Usury' had been forfeited. His neighbours said that prior to his death they had argued with him over whether he would be assessed to 'pay to Church and Poor'. He had declared that he would kill himself rather than pay his share, and when they charged him, he did just that.[60]

56 Cumbria RO, D/Lec/CR I, 26/1.

57 Cumbria RO, D/Lec/CR I, 27/4; Q/1/2, 429. This Minute Book has faded too much to tell any longer what the charges were.

58 PRO, KB 14/2–3, 8, 9.

59 The best discussion of popular sympathy for arrested debtors is P. H. Haagen, 'Imprisonment for Debt in England and Wales', Ph.D. thesis (Princeton, 1986), 42–3, 107–12.

60 *Fog's Weekly Journal*, no. 130 (20 Mar. 1731).

The factors that juries weighed cannot be fully recovered—the records are too fragmentary and the facts that influenced them were too varied to support detailed arguments. But there is enough evidence to conclude with confidence that the suicide's social standing, his personality, his relationships with his neighbours, and his survivors' claims on the community's sympathy all played a part in determining verdicts. Historians have long been aware that the flexible application of a savage criminal code was characteristic of the period, but they have often disagreed about the social significance of discriminatory enforcement. The practices of coroners' juries lend support to Peter King's radical recension of Douglas Hay's thesis that the selective exercise of mercy was a 'ruling-class conspiracy'.[61] The law of suicide was applied in ways that expressed the social values of the period, and those values included reverence for rank. But even if exalted and rich people benefited from the discretionary powers of coroners and their juries more often than the destitute, the pattern of enforcement did not *simply* serve the interests of the ruling classes. Resistance to forfeiture and the use of the *non compos mentis* verdict eroded the privileges first of the crown and then of the lords of liberties. The defiant behaviour of the juries in the case of John Atkinson, discussed above, illustrates the inability of grandees to protect their rights against panels determined to exculpate a suicide. Mercy was also often extended to men and women of very humble social standing. King shows that the men of middling status who served on juries in criminal trials in the later eighteenth century enjoyed considerable independence and that they took into account a wider range of factors than social class in exercising their discretionary powers. Coroners' juries a half-century earlier behaved similarly. They were in effect mediators between the values and interests of the governing élite and the sentiments of the local community.

## SECULARIZATION AND SOCIAL CONTROL

Throughout the age of Walpole, the *non compos mentis* verdict was thus

[61] P. King, 'Decision-Makers and Decision-Making in the English Criminal Law, 1750–1800', *Historical Journal*, xxvii (1984), 25–58; D. Hay, 'Property, Authority and the Criminal Law', in D. Hay, P. Linebaugh, J. G. Rule, E. P. Thompson, and C. Winslow (eds.), *Albion's Fatal Tree* (New York, 1975). See also J. Langbein, 'Albion's Fatal Flaws', *Past and Present*, no. 98 (Feb. 1983), 96–120; C. B. Herrup, 'Law and Morality in Seventeenth-Century England', *Past and Present*, no. 106 (Feb. 1985), 102–23; id., *The Common Peace: Participation and the Criminal Law in Seventeenth-Century England* (Cambridge, 1987).

an instrument of discretionary justice, wielded by men of the middling classes. Acting as members of the ruling groups of their villages and neighbourhoods, coroners' juries dispensed savagery and sympathy in ways that reinforced the values that contemporaries meant when they used the word 'respectable', one of the weightiest terms in the lexicon of social life.[62] It implied probity, thrift, orderliness, and cordiality—all the qualities that made a man or woman a good neighbour, a valued member of his or her community. During the reign of George III, however, juries virtually stopped punishing suicide itself: over 97 per cent of the suicides recorded in the last three decades of the eighteenth century were declared to have been lunatics. Men and women of every class and kind were spared the penalties for self-murder—paupers, apprentices, and servants, even total strangers, were treated mercifully. In the vast majority of cases, therefore, suicide was regarded as a secular calamity—the consequence of mental disease—rather than a diabolical crime. But the law of self-murder was not abolished, and juries continued to enforce it from time to time, using the *felo de se* verdict principally as a means of penalizing men and women who would otherwise have escaped punishment for crimes and other anti-social actions. Most suicides were routinely excused, but occasionally the law and rituals condemning self-murder were invoked to stigmatize the dead for some antecedent offence.

Whatever their private views about the causes of self-destruction or its religious implications, juries in the last decades of the eighteenth century acted on the belief that suicide was an insane action. The rituals of judgement and desecration that had dramatized the supernatural evil of self-murder declined as more and more juries returned verdicts that labelled suicides as innocent mad people. The rites of profane burial could not be performed unless a verdict of *felo de se* was returned. Alarmed traditionalists recognized the importance of the rise of the *non compos mentis* verdict long before it actually became routine, and they rightly insisted that the shifting pattern of verdicts expressed a new interpretation of suicide. As early as 1700 John Adams had complained: 'There is a General Supposition that *every one* who kills himself is *non Compos*, and that nobody wou'd do such an Action unless he were Distracted.'[63] Laymen and divines repeated this charge so often that it

62 'Respectable' in this sense seems to have become common usage in the 18th century; 'reputation' and its derivatives was the commonest Tudor and Stuart synonym.

63 Adams, *Essay Concerning Self-Murther*, 120–1.

became an axiom of eighteenth-century discussions of the law of suicide and its enforcement.[64]

The critics exaggerated the speed with which coroners' juries embraced the secular, medical interpretation of suicide. There is no doubt, however, that during the reign of George III juries all over the country liberalized their notions of what constituted exculpating insanity. Evidence of distress and gloom that would have supported a *felo de se* verdict before the Civil War was interpreted as the symptoms of lunacy. Almost any sign of melancholia was sufficient to prove insanity, and many people were excused who had suffered some quotidian disappointment. Since few people kill themselves without displaying any emotional distress, this meant that almost everyone was excused more or less automatically. Unfortunately, it is impossible to quantify meaningfully the enormous range of symptoms of mental disorder that were regarded as proofs of lunacy by eighteenth-century juries.

The rich or influential produced medical experts, physicians, and surgeons, who often swore that they had suffered from highly specific mental or physical illnesses.[65] The poor were usually defended by the testimony of their families and neighbours, rather than by medical men. They naturally used psychiatric jargon less often, but they, too, regarded 'low spirits' as a sufficient psychological explanation for suicide. There are few detectable differences of substance between testimony presented by or on behalf of members of the élite and the common people. The rich were perhaps somewhat more likely to be excused because of physical illnesses, which were not as shameful as mental afflictions, the poor perhaps more likely to have been mad from drink. There seems to have been some ambivalence on the part of many witnesses and jurors about whether or not people who were drunk when they killed themselves were *non compos mentis*. At the inquest into the suicide of Elizabeth Sadler, who had poisoned herself in 1767, her husband testified that she had

64 *Defoe's Review*, 255; Fleetwood, *Relative Duties of Parents and Children*, 482; I. Watts, *A Defense against the Temptation to Self-Murther* (London, 1726), 48–9; *Self-Murther and Duelling the Effects of Cowardice and Atheisim* (London, 1728), 4; *Gentleman's Magazine*, xix (1749), 341; *A Discourse upon Self-Murder*, 2nd edn. (London, 1754), 14; Ayscough, *Discourse against Self-Murder*, 13; *Duelling and Suicide Repugnant to Revelation, Reason, and Common Sense* (London, 1774), 11. Two authors who approved of the practice were J. Jortin, *Sermons on Different Subjects*, 3rd edn. (London, 1787), v. 147–8; W. Rowley, *A Treatise on Female, Nervous, Hysterical, Hypochondriacal, Bilious, Convulsive Diseases . . . With Thoughts on Madness, Suicide, &c* (London, 1788), 342–3.

65 See, e.g., Westminster Inquisitions, duke of Bolton (6 July 1765); John Brown, DD (23 Apr. 1766); Dame Elizabeth Anderson (6 March 1769); William Scrine, MP (8 Mar. 1783); Lady Jane Crawford (6 May 1794); Thomas Smith, Esq. (28 Dec. 1799).

sometimes been disordered and unable to answer questions reasonably. Three of her friends, however, admitted that her distress was due in large part to intoxication, and one remarked candidly that she was not always in her perfect senses, 'but whether it was owing to her Drinking or otherwise, this deponent cannot say'.[66] Sadler was judged a lunatic, but a few habitual drunkards were found *felo de se*.

When the victim was not a criminal or person of ill repute, however, late eighteenth-century juries frequently assumed that suicidal behaviour was itself enough to justify a lunacy verdict. In March 1774, for example, juries at Westminster found both Elizabeth Mobbs and Daniel Miller to have been insane because they had made earlier attempts on their lives. Mobbs's husband testified that just before her death she had pawned her dress and told him she would not need it again. She was sometimes intoxicated, but there was no other indication that she was mentally disturbed apart from the fact that she had tried to drown herself in the Serpentine the summer before. Miller had made repeated suicide attempts in the three weeks before he finally succeeded, and his wife had been afraid to leave him alone.[67] A century or so earlier, previous suicide attempts would have been evidence to support a verdict of *felo de se*. But the most convincing evidence that juries had accepted the notion that suicide itself was a sign of madness is that unidentified people who were found drowned were returned *non compos mentis*. The jury deliberating on the death of a man dragged out of the Serpentine in 1760, for example, concluded that 'being Lunatick and not of Sound Mind, Memory and Understanding . . . [he] Voluntarily threw himself into the said Water'.[68] A dozen years later a witness at the inquest on an anonymous woman testified that he had seen her walking in the rain by the Thames. At first he said he did not know how she drowned, but later in the inquest he added that he 'thinks she drowned herself and was not in her senses'.[69] In some cases coroners may have pressured juries to interpret psychological evidence leniently, but the content of depositions indicates that late

[66] Westminster Inquisitions, Elizabeth Sadler (6 July 1767).

[67] Westminster Inquisitions, Elizabeth Mobbs (1 Mar. 1774), Daniel Miller (9 Mar. 1774). See also, Westminster Inquisitions, John Ryley (3 June 1762), Thomas Bull (6 June 1767), William Corry (3 Aug. 1763), Thomas Clayton (4 May 1764), Elizabeth Horrell (27 Nov. 1765), George Fisher (24 June 1771), Richard Boughen (30 July 1771), Gavin Shiells (11 Dec. 1773), Francis Life (14 Dec. 1778), Lawrence Kennedy (19 June 1786).

[68] Westminster Inquisitions, Unidentified Man (1 May 1760). See also ibid., Unidentified Man (22 Feb. 1766), Unidentified Man (3 June 1767), Unidentified Woman (8 June 1773), Unidentified Woman (5 Apr. 1779), Unidentified Woman (29 July 1782), Unidentified Woman (31 May 1799). Norwich Inquisitions, Unidentified Man (21 May 1762).

[69] Westminster Inquisitions, Unknown Woman (3 Sept. 1772).

eighteenth-century juries needed little prompting to regard suicide as the consequence of insanity.

Selective enforcement survived in spite of the secularization of juries' attitudes to suicide, but the *felo de se* verdict was used much more sparingly than before. Its targets were for the most part people who killed themselves to avoid punishment for crimes or who had committed other misdeeds. Juries seem to have felt that such suicides were not irrational in the usual sense, or if they were, that it was still necessary to punish them. Ten of the fifteen persons found *felo de se* in London between 1760 and 1799, for example, had been accused of breaking the law.[70] Another was a drunkard who had paid his rent only once in the nine months he had been lodging with his landlord.[71] Yet another was a soldier who had grumbled about an order to mount the guard and left a suicide note in which he blamed his insubordination on his sergeant: 'The Instigation of this Unhap Afair', he declared, 'was by the Ill Usage by William Stevans Sarjeant of the Same Company.'[72] None of the remaining three had led blameless lives.[73] Commenting on the lunacy verdict returned on John Powell, a paymaster who killed himself in 1783 after being accused of peculation, the *Gentleman's Magazine* observed correctly that 'had a criminal in Newgate, under the apprehension of an approaching trial for his life, made use of the same means to his destruction, very few juries would have hesitated to have given a contrary verdict'.[74]

One of the London self-murderers accused of a crime was David Mendes. He had been suspected of murdering his uncle, a Mr Silva, and

[70] Westminster Inquisitions, Richard Liff (20 Oct. 1761), felony; Elizabeth Beck (13 Apr. 1762), theft; Jacob Miers (2 Oct. 1772), attempted murder; Charles Price (25 Jan. 1786), forgery; George Pricard (16 June 1791), theft; William Millar (12 Nov. 1795), forgery; London Inquisitions, Lawrence Jones (9 Dec. 1793), awaiting execution; David Mendes (26 Jan. 1793), suspected of murder; Anonymous Man (6 July 1799), arrested for theft; Hannah Horton (9 July 1794), accused of theft.

[71] Westminster Inquisitions, Richard Dawes (9 Jan. 1787).

[72] Westminster Inquisitions, James Holt (14 Oct. 1782).

[73] Westminster Inquisitions, William Bold (4 Apr. 1765), left a note admitting an addiction to lewd women and drink; Charles Holloway (2 May 1765), a prisoner who received five votes to spare him; Sarah Hopkins (21 June 1792), drunkenness but no other details. For other examples see PRO, PL 26/293, James Burns (1 October 1791); L. Radzinowicz, *A History of English Criminal Law and its Administration from 1750* (New York, 1948), i. 195–9.

[74] *Gentleman's Magazine*, lii (1783), pt. 1, 539. The author goes on to complain that 'suicide is too much the fashion of the present day to be considered only as an act of a lunatic', but he does not dispute the verdict in Powell's case, exaggerating, in fact, the evidence for his insanity that was presented at the inquest: cf. ibid., pt. 2, 613–14; Westminster Inquisitions, John Powell (26 May 1783).

his uncle's wife in 1793, but the charges against him were dropped for lack of evidence. Soon, however, new facts came to light and it was rumoured that he was about to be rearrested; to add to his troubles, one of his children died the same week. He committed suicide on 26 January. The inquest became, in effect, Mendes's posthumous trial for the Silva murders. Solomon Israel testified that at Silva's funeral Mendes had complained of how miserable he was because of the accusations against him; but if this implied that Mendes was innocent, the fact that he 'did not go to mourn on the side of the hall with the other relatives of Silva' must have weighed against him in the eyes of the Portuguese Jewish community and, ultimately, the jurors. The jury found him guilty of self-murder, and he was buried in the public highway. It was not the taking of his own life that made his suicide worthy of punishments that were by then very seldom exacted: it was the probability that he had committed the murders of which he was accused.[75]

Mendes's suicide and its circumstances were widely publicized by the newspapers. The press reinforced the assumption that *felo de se* verdicts were a means of punishing anti-social actions posthumously, rather than a penalty for suicide itself. The newspapers and reviews published lurid accounts of the crimes committed by suicides and reports of the ritual burials of malefactors. In 1790, for example, *The Times* paraphrased a letter from Lincolnshire describing a 'horrid affair'. A woman who 'farmed the poor' at the Epworth workhouse poisoned sixteen of her charges, killing four of them, and afterwards fatally dosed herself with arsenic as well. Shocked by the magnitude of her crime, the coroner's jury not only brought her in *felo de se* but also ordered her body buried in the public highway with *two* stakes driven through it.[76] Elaborations on the ancient rites of desecration seem to have been invented to disgrace notorious criminals in other cases as well. A thief named Jones who had robbed a banker's clerk in 1793 hanged himself in his cell, 'to evade the operations of public justice'. He was 'brought out of Newgate, extended

75 London Inquisitions, David Mendes (26 Jan. 1793); *The Times*, no. 2518 (Jan. 28, 1793), 4; *Annual Register*, xxxv (1793), 5 6.

76 *The Times*, no. 1715 (23 June 1790), 3. See also no. 283 (21 Nov. 1785), 3; no. 494 (22 July 1786), 3; no. 761 (31 May 1787), 3; no. 4224 [misnumbered] (7 July 1798), 3; no. 4298 (3 Oct. 1798), 3; *Annual Register*, iii (1760), 130; viii (1765); xxii (1779), 207; xxxv (1793), 58; xxxvi (1794), 13; xl (1798), 57; *Gentleman's Magazine*, xxx (1760), 440; liv (1784), 868. It ought to go without saying that not every newspaper story about a *felo de se* depicted the suicide as a malefactor. Many gave no details at all; others strayed from the usual pattern. For examples (which could be multiplied), see D. T. Andrew, 'The Secularization of Suicide in England, 1660–1800: A Comment', *Past and Present*, no. 119 (1988), 164 n. 19.

upon a plank on the top of an open cart, in his clothes, and fettered, his face covered with a white cloth'. The corpse was conveyed to the top of Holborn Hill by a procession that included 'the Sheriffs, City Marshalls and near 50 constables'. Finally, it was deposited in a very deep pit and a stake was driven through it. 'The concourse of people assembled on this occasion was very great', remarked *The Times*.[77]

It is tempting to see that retention of the law of self-murder as a deliberate policy. As early as 1760 Edward Umfreville, whose *Lex coronatoria* became the standard guide for the members of his profession, advocated restricting the use of the *felo de se* verdict to the punishment of criminals. Umfreville stressed that 'every Self-killing is not criminal, or to be sentenced in like Manner with what the Law Terms a Self-Murder'. Among those whose suicides 'may admit of a Distinction, even to discriminate and excuse', he listed in addition to lunatics and idiots, persons who had lost their memories through sickness, grief, infirmity, or some other accident, a conception of exculpating insanity that could accommodate a very wide range of emotional disturbances.[78] But he also recalled a case in 1727 that seemed to him to demand special emphasis. Noting that the civil law excused people who killed themselves 'upon any Impatience of [*sic*] Infirmity of Body' and yet still punished those who committed suicide on account of a capital crime, he remembered that a Mr Oneby had slain himself to avoid execution for murder and had been buried at the crossroads in Islington. 'The only Recompence the Law could give' for the crime Oneby had committed, Umfreville observed, 'was that of public Punishment.' In such situations, and when one accused of a crime 'kill'd himself to prevent the Justice of the Law', the 'term [self-murder] may be properly allowed', he concluded.[79]

The practice of ritually burying the bodies of criminal suicides continued well into the early nineteenth century. By that time the very rarity with which the rites of desecration were used added to their dramatic value as a method of defaming notorious malefactors. The burial of John Williams, who committed suicide while awaiting trial for a series of brutal murders that had terrorized London in 1811, was organized as a macabre entertainment. The authorities gave a great deal of thought to the details and aims of the ritual. Soon after Williams's suicide, the magistrate in charge of the murder case repaired to the Home Secretary, Robert Ryder, to ask how the 'usual practice' of burial at a crossroads might be elaborated 'in this extraordinary instance of self-murder'. He

[77] *The Times*, no. 2855 (10 Dec. 1793), 3; no. 2858 (13 Dec. 1793), 3.
[78] Umfreville, *Lex coronatoria*, 1809 edn., 4.
[79] Ibid. 2–3.

suggested interring the body near the scene of the murders, rather than of the suicide, and exhibiting the corpse beforehand. Others wrote to Ryder, recommending other embellishments—Sir John Carr's detailed plan for a procession that would set a 'salutary example' for the 'lower orders' was very like the ceremony Ryder authorized. Williams's body was exhibited to the public on a large board, mounted on a cart. His countenance was 'ghastly in the extreme'; the bloodstained maul and ripping-chisel with which he had killed his victims were displayed beside him. The burial took place in daylight, doubtless to ensure greater attendance. Soon after 9.00 a.m. on 31 December 1811, a procession led by important citizens and, it was said, by several hundred constables proceeded slowly from Coldbath Prison, where Williams had died, to the site of his grave, stopping at the houses of the families he had murdered. The cart that drew his exposed body was followed by a crowd of ten thousand, who brought him at last to a crossroads, where a grave deliberately too small to allow the body to repose in an attitude of sleep awaited. The corpse was crammed into the ground, and a stake was driven through its heart with the same bloody maul that had killed Williams's victims. 'As the blood-stained maul thudded on the stake the silence of the crowd was at last broken and the air became hideous with shouts and execrations.'[80] The grave-diggers sold small bits of wood cut from the stake to spectators as souvenirs. Williams's crimes and his punishment were highly publicized at the time and were the subject later of De Quincey's essay 'On Murder considered as one of the Fine Arts' and a number of less notable literary efforts.[81] Williams's interment was the most famous ritual burial of the nineteenth century, but it was not the last, and other criminal suicides were occasionally desecrated in similar ceremonies until the 1820s.[82]

## THE JURY, THE LAW, AND CULTURAL CHANGE

Unfortunately, we cannot know precisely why juries finally embraced the medical interpretation of suicides uncomplicated by criminal or

[80] P. D. James and T. A. Critchley, *The Maul and the Pear Tree: The Ratcliffe Highway Murders 1811* (New York, 1971), 160.

[81] For fuller accounts, see J. Fairburn, *Fairburn's Account of the Life, Death and Interment of John Williams* (London, [1812]); James and Critchley, *The Maul and the Pear Tree*; Radzinowicz, *History of English Criminal Law*, i. 198; *Notes and Queries*, 7th ser., iii (1887), 237–8. James and Critchley argue, incidentally, that Williams was innocent.

[82] The last such burial seems to have been in June 1823, *Notes and Queries*, 1st ser., vii (1853), 617.

antisocial behaviour. The records are too laconic to reveal arguments that may have been used to justify a lunacy verdict. Two possibilities can be ruled out. As the eighteenth century progressed, men who were medically qualified began to be elected as coroners for the first time. It might be conjectured that they urged the laymen on their juries to regard suicide as the outcome of insanity. But the scanty evidence that has come to light so far suggests otherwise. In two jurisdictions for which good records survive, Norwich and Wiltshire, medically qualified coroners appear to have been more willing to bring in *felo do se* verdicts than their lay colleagues. In later eighteenth-century Wiltshire, where all the coroners were medical men, there were more such verdicts than in Cumberland or Westminster, where they were not. Almost one in six Wiltshire suicides were condemned as self-murderers after 1751; just three of 187 Cumberland suicides and 15 of 1,085 London suicides were.[83] In Norwich the coronership was a stepping-stone to higher municipal office, held mostly by rich clothiers, weavers, and merchants, until about 1737 when the barber-surgeon Ambrose Gedge was elected as one of the two coroners for the city. Gedge remained in office throughout the 1740s and 1750s, acting as the principal coroner, holding almost all of the inquests. It was under Gedge that the proportion of *non compos mentis* verdicts actually fell to its lowest point during the eighteenth century. Almost one-third of all the suicides whose inquests he conducted were judged self-murderers. As soon as he left office lunacy verdicts soared, and after 1770 they became invariable.[84] (See Table 4.3.)

If medical men were not driving the engine of change, at least they had seats near the front of the train; the lawyers rode in the brake-van. The leading legal authorities of the day protested against the lenient interpretation of psychiatric evidence. 'It is not every melancholy or hypochondriacal distemper', wrote the great jurist Matthew Hale, 'that denominates a man *non compos*, for there are few, who commit this offense, but are under such infirmities, but it must be such an alienation of mind, that renders them to be madmen or frantic, or destitute of the use of reason.' His words were repeated almost verbatim in the most widely read eighteenth-century handbook for Justices of the Peace and by Black-

[83] Hunnisett, *Wiltshire Coroners' Bills*; Cumbria RO, D/Lec/CR I; Cumbria RO, Q 11; Westminster Inquisitions; London Inquisitions; Greater London Record Office, MJ/SPC.W; MJ/SPC.E.

[84] Norwich Inquisitions. For information about Gedge's background we are indebted to Margaret Pelling.

stone in his *Commentaries*.[85] The lawyers were worried that juries' disregard for the rules of law would undermine the rule of law. But as they admitted, the punishments for self-murder seemed to juries to be too severe, and so they ignored the authorities' pleas. The point is an important one. For juries in this crime (and in cases involving deodands) were defying a powerful trend in legal thought and opinion. Throughout the later seventeenth and eighteenth centuries, trial juries placed greater and greater emphasis on proving the guilt of the offender. Rules of evidence became much stricter, a development that Barbara Shapiro claims in an important book was 'the leading edge of a new world view' based on philosophical empiricism. She and Keith Thomas have attributed the decline in successful witchcraft prosecutions to greater emphasis on material proofs, and John Beattie has added infanticide to the list of crimes for which convictions became more difficult.[86]

Juries' suspension of the law of suicide would seem at first glance to be another instance in which empiricism and humanitarianism went hand in hand with secularization and mercy. Like witchcraft, self-murder was a supernatural crime, and like infanticide, it was an act that appeared to many to be irrational. Thomas Hobbes pointed to the impossibility of demonstrating conclusively that suicide had been a sane and premeditated act, as the law required. The Law Student in his *Dialogue of the Common Laws* points out that a man cannot be judged *felo de se* unless he is first proved to have been *compos mentis*. 'But how can that be proved of a man dead?' wonders the Philosopher. 'This is a hard place; and before you take it for common-law, it had need to be cleared.'[87] As we have seen, juries prior to about 1640 simply ignored the necessity to prove sanity and presumed it instead. But their behaviour in the eighteenth century did not display greater attention to the rules of evidence. The most penetrating discussion of this matter appears in an anonymous work on the practices of coroners and their juries, published in 1776. Its author, echoing Hobbes, complains that on the occasions when juries brought in *felo de se* verdicts, they did so without regard to the evidence.

85 M. Hale, *Historia Placitorum Coronae: The History of Pleas of the Crown*, ed. S. Emlyn, G. Wilson, and T. Dogherty, new edn. (London, 1800), i. 412; R. Burn, *The Justice of the Peace, and Parish Officer*, ed. C. Durnford and J. King, 21st edn. (London, 1810), s.v. 'homicide'; Blackstone, *Commentaries on the Laws of England*, iv. 189. See also, Foster, *Report of Some Proceedings*, 266; Umfreville, *Lex coronatoria*, 127–8.

86 B. J. Shapiro, *Probability and Certainty in Seventeenth-Century England* (Princeton, 1983), esp. chs. 1–3, 6; Thomas, *Religion and Magic*, chs. 18–22; Beattie, *Crime and the Courts*, 122–4, 362–76.

87 T. Hobbes, *The English Works of Thomas Hobbes*, vi, ed. W. Molesworth (London, 1840), 88–9.

For the suicide's 'state of mind, his mode of thinking and judging, by which he is governed at the *time*, are matters incapable of proof'.[88] But juries were equally ignorant of the truth when they returned *non compos mentis* verdicts:

As Coroners and their Juries do oftentimes return the unhappy *Suicide* to be *Felo de se*, without any justifiable ground or evidence; so do they more frequently return Inquisitions of *Lunacy*, without having even a shadow or presumption of Proof to support them in such Judgment, other than what they infer from their own whimsical reasonings.[89]

They simply came to presume insanity instead of sanity. Some judgements might indeed be described as whimsical. *The Times* reported in 1790 that a body had been found dangling in a bedroom in Bath. 'From some circumstances the Jury hesitated whether or not they should bring in a verdict of lunacy, when one of them (a tailor) declared "he must have been mad, for that yesterday the deceased paid him the amount of a bill which had been due only three months".' A lunacy verdict was duly returned.[90] Even if this story is apocryphal or embellished in the retelling (as it probably was), it illustrates an indisputable truth. No matter how important legal empiricism was in the decline of prosecutions for witchcraft and infanticide, it played no part at all in the decline of *felo de se*. In this instance, juries of middling-class men gradually changed their minds about the crime itself.

There was one important change in the nature of the coroner's jury during the eighteenth century that may well have been a precondition for the shift in jurors' attitudes: their level of literacy increased dramatically. Signatures were rather rare on sixteenth-century inquisitions, but by the reign of George III jurors usually signed their own names to them.[91] This change meant that although they were drawn from much the same social group as they had been a century or two earlier, jurors had become cultural amphibians, equipped to inhabit both the literate realm of the educated élite and the oral domain of folk tradition. At the same time both the governing classes' opinions about suicide and the media that

[88] *Considerations on the Coroner*, 44.

[89] Ibid. 45.

[90] *The Times*, no. 1651 (9 Apr. 1790), 2.

[91] This assertion is based on our reading of all of the sets of inquisitions listed in the Bibliography. We did not, unfortunately, do the systematic counting that would permit one to date this change and to measure its magnitude. For a sample and an analysis that includes coroners' juries and arrives at the same conclusion, see J. S. Cockburn, 'Twelve Silly Men? The Trial Jury at Assizes, 1560–1670', in Cockburn and Green, *Twelve Good Men*, 162–3.

publicized them also changed. Tolerant and even sentimental interpretations of self-killing gradually prevailed over abhorrence and condemnation. Older opinions did not disappear, but they were heard as a counterpoint to a theme of increasing leniency. Changing attitudes to suicide were conveyed to the public by new kinds of publications: broadsides and, most important, magazines and newspapers. Cheap and readily available, the popular papers carried news about suicides and articles debating its legitimacy. To understand the cultural context within which juries changed their interpretation of suicide, we need therefore to examine both the trends in attitudes to suicide and also the role of the press in popular culture.

# 5

# *The Invention of Suicide*

USED more and more commonly, the *non compos mentis* verdict was the most important manifestation of the secularization of suicide. Whatever their private beliefs may have been, jurors acted on the medical interpretation of suicide and so sanctioned the popular rituals punishing the crime less and less often. This change in the responses of juries to suicide effectively transformed its meaning. Most such deaths were no longer treated as diabolical crimes that visited spiritual peril on the village community. The secularization of suicide at the level of the local community was prompted in part by resentment of the crown's right to the goods of felons of themselves. But it was also a response to wider shifts in attitudes to self-destruction, and its relationship to these broader currents of thought is characteristic of other social and cultural changes that occurred in late seventeenth- and eighteenth-century England. Swiftly moving currents that originated among the ruling élite pulled it along, and an undertow of popular traditionalism held it back. Coroners' juries were eventually caught up in the tide of scepticism about supernatural phenomena, but for almost a century, contrary to the charge of their critics, they lagged a little behind progressive opinion. It was not until the reign of George III that juries entirely abandoned the belief that self-murder was a diabolical crime.

Fashionable opinion naturally changed faster than the outlook of coroners' juries or the attitudes of the common people. Polite society —the country house set and the London literati—began to display more tolerant and secular attitudes to suicide within a generation or so after the Restoration. Medical and philosophical ideas that had been the property of a handful of avant-garde thinkers became the common coin of genteel conversation. William Ramesey in *The Gentlemans Companion* (1672) observed conventionally (and incorrectly) that suicide is forbidden by scripture, but he counselled that those who killed themselves ought to be regarded with compassion, for they were frequently the victims of mental illnesses:

> They should rather be objects of our greatest pity than condemnation as murtherers, damn'd Creatures and the like. For, tis possible even for Gods elect, having their Judgments and Reasons depraved by madness, deep melancholly, or [some]how otherwise affected by Diseases of some sorts, to be their own executioners. . . . Wherefore, lets be slow to censure in such cases.[1]

Writing some time after his retirement from the Bar in 1690, Roger North remarked: 'I am of the opinion that men judg too severely of it, in Reputing it cannot be lawfull in any Case.'[2]

It is unlikely that such opinions were very widespread outside polite circles, but liberal attitudes were certainly becoming more conspicuous and more acceptable. They were promoted by the new intellectual movements of the eighteenth century: deism, scientism, humanitarianism, neoclassicism, and romanticism. Philosophers defended people's right to kill themselves; scientific writers blamed mental illnesses for suicide; reformers denounced the laws against self-killing; playwrights and poets praised classical suicides; the Romantics sentimentalized self-destruction. By the reign of George III, secular interpretations were no longer an undertow. The tide of élite opinion about suicide had crested and begun to ebb strongly away from supernaturalism and intolerance toward secular interpretations and liberal attitudes.

The changing temper of the ruling élite's thinking about suicide is epitomized in the history of the word itself. Credit for coining 'suicide' probably belongs to Sir Thomas Browne, who anathematized self-killing. Protesting indignantly against preachers so befuddled with Stoic philosophy that they extolled 'the end and suicide of Cato', Browne employed the neologism precisely to distinguish the neoclassical conception of suicide from the religious and folkloric belief that it was a crime.[3]

[1] W. Ramesey [or Ramesay], *The Gentlemans Companion; or, A Character of True Nobility and Gentility* (London, 1672), 240–1. See also, T. Philipot, *Self-Homicide Murther* (London, 1674), 8.

[2] BL, Additional MS. 32526, fo. 125ᵛ. A longer and somewhat more moderate version of this reflection appears in North's autobiography: R. North, *The Lives of the Norths*, ed. A. Jessopp (Westmead, Farnborough, Hants., 1972 edn.), iii. 151–4. A cousin of North's, Sir Henry North, committed suicide in 1671, his habitual melancholia having been exacerbated by the death of his wife. He was judged *non compos mentis* by the coroner's jury: B. D. Henning, *The House of Commons, 1660–1690* (London, 1983), iii. 152–4.

[3] Sir Thomas Browne, *Selected Writings*, ed. G. Keynes (Chicago, 1968), 50. Browne uses the word in *Religio Medici*, which was composed about 1636 but not published until 1642 (first authorized edn., 1643): A. Alvarez, *The Savage God* (New York, 1973), 48–9. See also, *The Compact Edition of the Oxford English Dictionary* (Oxford, 1971); Wymer, *Suicide and Despair*, 2, 161 n. 4. Alexander Murray thinks that the word 'suicide' may well have been coined earlier, presumably in the Middle Ages: personal communication, 16 Oct. 1987.

Beginning in the later seventeenth century, 'suicide' appeared more and more frequently in tracts and literary works. Walter Charleton, the editor of Epicurus, and Thomas Blount, the lexicographer, used it as early as the 1650s. A host of their early eighteenth-century antagonists used it much as Browne had, as a synonym for self-murder that implied approval of the act—or if not approval, at least tolerance of it.[4] By the second half of the century, 'suicide' had become the usual term to designate self-killing in works of every kind, including those deploring it. In 1771 Thomas Warton wrote the best of several poems titled simply 'Suicide'; learned polemicists such as John Herries, Richard Hey, and Charles Moore preferred it to 'self-murder'.[5] The English lent the word first to the French then to the Spanish, Italians, and Portuguese.[6] Like the trend toward tolerance itself, the word 'suicide' aroused the irritation of some conservatives. Edward Phillips, in his *New World of Words* (1662) grumbled that suicide really means pig-killing: '*Suicide* . . . should be derived from *sus*, a sow, than from the pronoun *sui*, . . . as if it were a swinish part for a man to kill himself.'[7]

## FREE-THINKERS AND *PHILOSOPHES*

The most controversial advocates of new attitudes to suicide were Enlightenment philosophers and men of letters. Deists at home and *philosophes* abroad attacked ideas condemning self-killing and called for repeal of the laws punishing it. The apologists for suicide included some of the most prominent writers of the age as well as lesser libertines and free-thinkers. Montesquieu, Voltaire, d'Holbach, and Hume all refuted the traditional arguments condemning suicide; Beccaria advocated its decriminalization in his celebrated call for penal reform.[8] Grub Street

[4] These sources are conveniently listed, with illustrative quotations, in the *OED*. See also, H. R. Fedden, *Suicide: A Social and Historical Study* (New York, 1972), 29.

[5] J. Herries, *An Address to the Public on the Frequent and Enormous Crime of Suicide* (London, 1774); R. Hey, *A Dissertation on Suicide* (Cambridge, 1785); Moore, *Full Inquiry into Suicide.*

[6] D. Daube, 'The Linguistics of Suicide', *Philosophy and Public Affairs*, i (1972), 387–437 surveys the terms used in various languages to describe suicide.

[7] Quoted in Fedden, *Suicide*, 29. Actually, he was right: M. Griffin, 'Philosophy, Cato and Roman Suicide: I', *Greece and Rome*, xxxiii (1986), 68.

[8] Montesquieu, *The Persian Letters*, trans. C. J. Betts (Harmondsworth, 1973), 152–4; id., *Œuvres complètes*, ii, ed. R. Caillois (Paris, 1951), 135–6, 486, 870–1, 880, 1134; Voltaire, *The Works*, ed. T. Smollett, vii (New York, 1901), 19–33; P. T. d'Holbach, *The System of Nature*, trans. H. D. Robinson, (Boston, 1889), 136–9; D. Hume, 'On Suicide', in his *Of the Standard of Taste and Other Essays*, ed. J. W. Lenz (Indianapolis, Ind., 1965), 151–60; C. Beccaria-Bonesana, *An Essay of Crimes and Punishments*, trans. E. D. Ingraham (Stanford, 1953), 122–7. The outstanding commentaries on these works are L. G. Crocker, 'The Discussion of Suicide in the Eighteenth Century', *Journal of the History of Ideas*, xiii (1952), 47–72; R. Favre, *La Mort dans la littérature et la pensée françaises au siècle des lumières* (Paris, 1978), ch. 11. Less sound, but focused exclusively on England, is S. E. Sprott, *The English Debate on Suicide* (La Salle, Ill., 1961).

*philosophes*, the intellectual foot-soldiers of the Enlightenment, supported these commanding figures. Charles Gildon published a philosophical defence of the suicide of his friend and fellow deist, Charles Blount.[9] Two exiles living in London, the French libertine André-François Boreau Deslandes and the Piedmontese aristocrat Alberto Radicati, count of Passerano, wrote radical Epicurean apologies for suicide that attracted attention in England and abroad.[10] In 1735, a Swede named Johann Robeck composed a Latin treatise justifying self-destruction. As soon as his book was finished, he went to Bremen, dressed neatly, hired a little boat, and rowed out on to the North Sea. His body later washed up on shore. His dissertation was not much read, but his death made its arguments famous. Rousseau mentioned Robeck in the *Nouvelle Héloïse*, and the story was told in England in places as diverse as the *Grand Magazine* (1758), which summarized the contents of his book, and *The Principles of Penal Law* (1771).[11]

The free-thinkers were counter-attacked by battalions of clerical irregulars; a small number of notable philosophers tried to stay neutral or deserted the free-thinking cause.[12] Churchmen all over Europe fired fusillades of sermons at the defenders of suicide and occasionally throughout the eighteenth century they lobbed longer treatises in the direction of the enemy. By now most of these have lost their explosive power, but John Adams's 1700 tract was impressive in its time, and Charles Moore's 1790 treatise is still a marvel of erudition.[13] The clergy's opposition to views that were based on deism or even (as in the case of d'Holbach) outright atheism was predictable enough. And yet not all of the *philosophes* lined up on the other side. Some failed to declare their allegiances; one or two defected to the army of the clerks. Hobbes and Locke had both opposed suicide.[14] Montesquieu published a letter

[9] C. Blount, *The Miscellaneous Works*, ed. Lindamour [C. Gildon] (London, 1696), sigs. A6$^r$–A12$^r$.

[10] A.-F. Boreau Deslandes, *A Philological Essay; or, Reflections on the Death of Free-Thinkers* (London, 1713), 119–21; id., *Dying Merrily; or, Historical and Critical Reflexions on the Conduct of Great Men in All Ages, Who, In Their Last Moments, Mock'd Death, and Died Facetiously*, trans. T.W. (London, 1745), 115–19; A. Radicati, count of Passerano, *A Philosophical Dissertation upon Death* (London, 1732), 86.

[11] J.-J. Rousseau, *Julie: ou la Nouvelle Héloïse*, ed. M. Launay (Paris, 1967), 285; Moore, *Full Inquiry into Suicide*, ii. 74–7, summarizes the book's argument and notices these earlier references. See also, Hey, *Dissertation on Suicide*, 63–7.

[12] The forces on both sides are named and analysed in Crocker, 'Discussion of Suicide'.

[13] J. Adams, *An Essay Concerning Self-Murther* (London, 1700); Moore, *Full Inquiry*.

[14] T. Hobbes, *Leviathan*, ed. C. B. Macpherson (Harmondsworth, 1968), 189; id., *The English Works*, ed. W. Molesworth, vi (London, 1840), 88–9; J. Locke, *Two Treatises of Government*, ed. P. Laslett (New York, 1965), 311, 325, 402.

condoning self-killing in the *Persian Letters* in 1721; but he balanced it in the final editions of the novel with a short reply condemning self-killing. Elsewhere, he reiterated his tolerant views.[15] Diderot did a better job of keeping his head down, concealing his own position in his article on suicide in the *Encyclopédie* and exercising similar caution in his other writings. Rousseau followed the example of the last editions of the *Persian Letters*, debating the case for and against suicide in the *Nouvelle Héloïse*.[16] No one could tell which side he was on; the partisans of both positions were sure he was one of them. Among the leading philosophers of the eighteenth century, Kant alone was an unyielding opponent of tolerant views, who went beyond the usual arguments to formulate a new basis for rejecting self-destruction.[17]

The debate over suicide was one campaign in the war between the champions of 'modern paganism' and traditional Christianity.[18] It raged throughout most of the century and ranged all over Europe. The philosophers seized the initiative. With a couple of exceptions, they abandoned the defensive tactic of defending suicide as 'mere philosophers' and condemning it as Christians, the gambit that Walter Charleton and Henry Dodwell had used in their expositions of the Epicurean and Stoic doctrines of suicide.[19] Some of them were frankly anti-religious. 'One considerable advantage that arises from philosophy', David Hume began his essay on suicide, 'consists in the sovereign antidote which it offers to superstition and false religion.'[20] The free-thinkers were interested in suicide partly because it raised important issues of human freedom and moral obligation. But they also saw attitudes and laws condemning it as the epitome of the errors and superstitious customs that had enthralled past ages. Hume continued his prolegomena: 'Let us here endeavor, to restore men to their natural liberty, by examining all the common arguments against suicide, and showing that that action may be free from every imputation of guilt or blame, according to the sentiments of all the ancient philosophers.'[21]

[15] Montesquieu, *Persian Letters*, 152–4, 316; id., *Œuvres complètes*, ii. 135–6, 486, 870–1, 880, 1134.

[16] Rousseau, *La Nouvelle Héloïse*, 278–91.

[17] M. J. Seidler, 'Kant and the Stoics on Suicide', *Journal of the History of Ideas*, xliv (1983), 429–53.

[18] Crocker, 'Discussion of Suicide'; P. Gay, *The Enlightenment: An Interpretation* (New York, 1966–9).

[19] *Epicurus's Morals*, ed. W. Charleton (London, 1656), sign. d1$^{v}$; H. Dodwell, 'An Apology for the Philosophical Writings of Cicero', in his *Tully's Five Books de Finibus*, trans. S.P. (London, 1702), sec. 22.

[20] Hume, 'On Suicide', 151.

[21] Ibid. 152.

On one level, then, apologies for suicide were intended as a radical challenge to traditional Christian ethics, part of the *philosophes*' attempt to separate moral philosophy from theology. This was a formidable goal, and although they succeeded to a surprising degree, there was little hope that the most iconoclastic arguments that the free-thinkers advanced would command the whole-hearted assent of the literate classes, at least in England. The age of reason, we have forcefully been reminded, remained an age of faith. Atheism and deism failed to rout religion; the church continued to command the loyalty of men and women of every class.[22] On another level, however, the free-thinkers had a more modest and more obtainable objective. By questioning the traditional reasoning behind the condemnation of suicide and criticizing the laws against it, they aimed to encourage greater toleration of suicide in certain circumstances—especially when it was motivated by infirmity or age—and to secure the abolition of the laws punishing it. 'In Europe the law treats suicides with the utmost ferocity', Montesquieu began his discussion of the legitimacy of suicide in the *Persian Letters*. After describing the penalties for self-murder, his Persian traveller, Uzbeck, protests: 'It seems to me, Ibben, that these laws are very unjust. When I am overcome by anguish, poverty, or humiliation, why must I be prevented from putting an end to my troubles, and harshly deprived of the remedy which lies in my power?'[23]

The debate over suicide was an international affray. There are, however, good reasons for concentrating on its ramifications in England. The English were perceived as more tolerant of suicide and more prone to commit it than other nations. Throughout the eighteenth century, critics at home and abroad accused Britons of being a gloomy, suicidal race. Whether or not this perception was correct will occupy us later. The important point in this context is that when they wrote about suicide and its punishment, writers everywhere tended to think of England. Ruminating on the life of Cato, Voltaire could not resist wondering whether the inhabitants of Britain slew themselves 'as deliberately as they do now' when suicide was in fashion in ancient Rome. It seems likely, he muses, that Rome and England have switched roles in this respect. 'Now, English citizens are philosophers and Roman citizens are nothing.' The English kill themselves proudly; the Romans have to have an *indulgentia in articulo mortis* to do so. They are, in other

[22] See, e.g., J. C. D. Clark, *English Society, 1688–1832* (Cambridge, 1985); J. Sambrook, *The Eighteenth Century* (London, 1986), ch. 2.

[23] Montesquieu, *Persian Letters*, 152–3.

words, as enchained by superstition as the barbarian Britons were in Caesar's day.[24] Voltaire went on to retell stories of English suicides, and recalled that he had once received a circular letter from an Englishman offering a prize 'to anyone who should most satisfactorily prove that there are occasions on which a man might kill himself'.[25] The English, rightly or wrongly, were thought to be especially receptive to philosophical arguments in favour of suicide. Rousseau was setting up an ironic reversal of his readers' expectations when in the *Nouvelle Héloïse* he made the proponent of self-destruction a Frenchman and its opponent an English lord.[26] Reformers complaining that the laws against self-murder were unjust tended to think that they were particularly offensive in England. In a famous passage in the *Spirit of the Laws* Montesquieu, noting that the English killed themselves frequently because of the country's dismal climate and its natives' racial predisposition to gloominess, declared that punishing suicide there was absurd: 'It is evident that the civil laws of some countries may have reasons for branding suicide with infamy: but in England it cannot be punished without punishing the effects of madness'.[27]

The first English man of letters to enter the lists on the side of the free-thinkers was Charles Gildon. Embarrassed, perhaps, by the suicide of his friend, Charles Blount, Gildon took up his pen in 1695 to defend him. It was no easy task. After his wife's death, Blount had fallen in love with her sister. He sued for her hand in marriage, but she refused—the precedent of Henry VIII notwithstanding, such matches were regarded as incestuous. Desolated, Blount shot himself. 'In the midst of despair', explains Gildon, he 'found life would be but a perpetual *Evil* without *Astrea*.'[28] Gildon tries in his apology to transform his friend posthumously into a Stoic sage. His passion, argues the free-thinker, had been a mature love, well grounded in reason. His death was 'nothing unworthy of a *Philosopher*', for it was consistent with 'the precepts of Nature and Reason'. Human nature cannot desire the continuance of evil, reasons Gildon, and a life of unremitting pain is unquestionably evil. To end one's life in such circumstances is therefore a greater good than self-

[24] Voltaire, *Philosophical Dictionary*, in his *The Works of Voltaire*, ed. T. Smollett (New York, 1901), vii. 23.

[25] Voltaire, *Works*, vii. 27.

[26] Rousseau, *La Nouvelle Héloïse*, 278–91.

[27] Montesquieu, *Œuvres complètes*, ii. 486; translation from Montesquieu, *The Spirit of the Laws*, trans. T. Nugent, Great Books of the Western World, xxxviii (Chicago, 1952), 107.

[28] Blount, *Miscellaneous Works*, sig. A7$^{v}$.

preservation and is not contrary to natural law. This was Gildon's most substantial argument. It had no exact classical precedents of which we are aware, but it follows from both the Epicurean and Stoic conceptions of nature and closely parallels Epicurus' views. Gildon also dismisses the Pythagorean argument that providence had stationed men on earth like soldiers at their post, and so it was a kind of desertion to commit suicide. He rightly observes that a simile is not an argument, and he complains that the analogy is inexact anyway. Soldiers enlist in an army and so place themselves willingly under their commander's order; human beings do not choose to be born. Finally, he denies that society could rightfully restrain a man from exiting this life, any more than it could rightfully prevent him from emigrating. 'Now if I can leave any one particular Body Politick, I have the same right to leave another, and so on through all those of the World, and then by consequence I offend not, if by my Death I take my self away from all.'[29]

Hard as it is to imagine a love-struck libertine as the exemplar of Stoic mettle, Gildon's defence of Blount seems, as Sprott remarks, to have signalled a new and more vigorous phase in the debate over suicide in England.[30] Self-killing was discussed and defended more openly than ever before. According to alarmed critics, *Biathanatos* was widely read and discussed in the later seventeenth century. Thomas Philipot justified his treatise against suicide, published in 1674, by pointing to the evil influence of Donne's book.[31] On the other side, *Biathanatos* had won terse praise from Blount in 1680, and it was reissued twenty years later.[32] New translations of Montaigne appeared in 1685 and of Charron in 1697.[33] The *Occasional Paper* complained in 1697 that suicide was a practice that some people 'go about to support with false shows of wit, under the Notion of Gallantry and Courage'. Its author reiterated his complaint a year later, charging that some apologists for suicide had committed the deed and declared that they killed themselves on principle.[34] He was thinking of Blount and of another, unidentified libertine.

[29] Ibid., sigs. A6$^r$–A12$^r$.

[30] Sprott, *English Debate*, 73.

[31] Philipot, *Self-homicide-Murther*, sig. $A_2$. For other attacks written about this time, see A. Tuckney, *Praelectiones theologicae nec non determinationes quaestionem varium insignium in scholis academicis Cantabridgiensibus habitae* (Amsterdam, 1679), 159–60; Bodl., MS Rawlinson C. 522, fos. 9–17.

[32] C. Blount, *Philostratus* (London, 1680), 154, quoted in Sprott, *English Debate*, 71.

[33] Sprott, *English Debate*, 82–3. Sprott remarks that the translator of the latter silently inserted some passages questioning his author's views.

[34] Ibid. 73–4.

Charles Leslie, in the 1699 edition of his famous *Short Method with the Deists*, likewise asserted that the 'Theistical Club' had set up self-killing 'as a Principle'.[35] The suicide a year later of Thomas Creech, the editor and translator of Lucretius, seemed to confirm Leslie's view. Creech actually rejected many of the Epicurean arguments his poet expounded, including those seeming to favour suicide. That did not, however, diminish the public's conviction that he had justified his suicide to himself philosophically. Creech 'died as he had lived, like a true Atheist', a critic sneered. One rumour going around was that before his suicide Creech had read *Biathanatos*, fingering a rope as he turned the pages. Voltaire reported another that Creech had written on the manuscript of his commentary on Lucretius 'N.B. Must hang myself when I have finished'. Ever the droll wit, he attributed Creech's death to a desire to follow his author's example and remarked that had Creech 'undertaken a commentary upon Ovid he would have lived longer'.[36]

The clerical establishment was certainly alarmed. Its spokesmen struck back with reason and ridicule. A rising young Etonian named John Adams sprang forward in the same year to refute both Donne and Gildon with a learned treatise that sought to show by natural reason alone that suicide was illicit. His work helped him to become a chaplain to King William and Queen Anne and paved his way ultimately to the provost's lodge at King's College, Cambridge.[37] Other clergymen quickly followed his example, shoring up the traditional conception of self-murder with arguments drawn from ancient and medieval philosophy.[38] Gildon himself was thoroughly vanquished by his clerical enemies. A note Leslie added to his *Short Method* in 1699 abused Blount and blamed Gildon for promoting self-slaughter. The book supposedly shook Gildon's faith in deism; it certainly put him on the spot.[39] In 1705 the Arian Samuel Clarke paused in his famous Boyle lectures on natural

[35] C. Leslie, *A Short and Easy Method with the Deists*, 9th edn. (London, 1745), 41–2; Sprott, *English Debate*, 73.

[36] *DNB*, s.v. 'Creech, Thomas'; T. Hearne, *The Remains of Thomas Hearne*, ed. J. Buchanan-Brown (London, 1966), 298–9; *A Step to Oxford; or, A Mad Essay on the Reverend Mr. Thomas Creech's Hanging Himself, (As 'Tis Said) for Love* (London, 1700); T. F. Mayo, *Epicurus in England (1650–1725)* (n.pl., 1934), 102–4; Voltaire, *Works*, vii. 23. Had Voltaire known that Creech most likely died for love, disappointed at his failure to win the hand of Miss Philadelphia Playdell, he might have reconsidered. Lucretius denounces sexual passion; Ovid celebrates it. The whole story is recounted below, Chapter 8.

[37] Adams, *Essay Concerning Self-Murther*, 1–2; *DNB*.

[38] W. Fleetwood, *The Relative Duties of Parents and Children, Husbands and Wives, Masters and Servants Consider'd in Sixteen Sermons: With Three More Upon the Case of Self-Murther* (London, 1705), 417–95.

[39] Leslie, *Short Method with Deists*, 41–2.

religion to mock Gildon's reasoning as 'weak and childish'. He defended the sentinel simile, quoting passages in which Plato, Cicero, and (of course) Arius had used it, and declared that it was a man's duty to regulate his passions, as Blount so conspicuously had failed to do.[40] By this time, Gildon had already surrendered. Disturbed by the controversy over his preface, he had recanted a few months earlier, announcing that he was now 'perfectly convinc'd, that *Suicide* is not Lawful'.[41] The controversy did not end with Gildon's volte-face. An obscure Devonshire vicar named John Prince issued a belated blast against Donne and Gildon (whom he confused with Blount) in 1709.[42]

Despite his cowardly behaviour in the heat of combat, Gildon established the battle plan that later defenders of suicide followed. All of them were concerned mainly to refute philosophical arguments condemning self-killing that had been advanced or anticipated by ancient philosophers. There was no shortage of these. The Greeks had been deeply ambivalent about the question; and even the Romans had been less favourable than most eighteenth-century thinkers realized.[43] Pythagoras and Socrates had argued that suicide violated one's obligations to God. In the *Phaedo* Socrates repeats Pythagoras' famous simile, and offers another argument to prove that suicide is an offence against God. He asserts that people are God's property, and they consequently have no right to kill themselves without his permission.[44] Plato and Aristotle maintained that governments could rightfully outlaw suicide. Aristotle argued that self-killing injured the state, and that it was illicit even when no decree specifically forbade it.[45] The only philosophical argument against suicide commonly repeated in the eighteenth century that had not been anticipated by the Greeks was Aquinas's contention that it violated natural law. God, he declared, had instilled in human beings an instinctual desire to preserve their own lives, and that desire had the force of law.[46]

[40] S. Clarke, *A Discourse Concerning the Unchangeable Obligations of Natural Religion* (London, 1706), 101–2.

[41] Sprott, *English Debate*, 84–5, 91; C. Gildon, *The Deists Manual* (London, 1705), sigs. A7$^{v}$–B2$^{v}$.

[42] J. Prince, *Self-Murder Asserted to be a Very Heinous Crime* (London, 1709), 12–17.

[43] Griffin, 'Philosophy, Cato, and Roman Suicide: I', 72; J. M. Rist, *Stoic Philosophy* (Cambridge, 1969), 470–516.

[44] Plato, *Phaedo*, 62 B–C, in *The Dialogues of Plato*, ed. E. Hamilton and H. Cairns (New York, 1964), 45.

[45] Aristotle, *Nichomachean Ethics*, 1138$^{a}$11, in *The Basic Works*, ed. R. McKeon (New York, 1941), 1020–1.

[46] T. Aquinas, *Summa theologiae*, xxxviii (New York, 1975), 2a, 2ae, Q64, 5, 31–7.

The sentinel simile, the argument from divine ownership, the law of self-preservation, and the claims of society comprised virtually the whole armoury of the philosophical opponents of suicide. These weapons were wielded repeatedly, and sometimes dexterously, by Anglican clergymen from John Adams to Charles Moore. The free-thinkers counter-attacked with verbal pistols and grapeshot, narrow arguments suitable to philosophical duelling and bold assertions more appropriate to full-scale battle. On the English front, the fiercest champions of suicide were Montesquieu, Radicati, and Hume—at least to judge by the cries they aroused in the orthodox camp. D'Holbach's *System of Nature* and the letter favouring suicide in Rousseau's *Nouvelle Héloïse* had a somewhat smaller impact on opinion. The far less distinguished works of the libertine Boreau Deslandes caused brief sensations. The title of one of them, *Dying Merrily; or, Historical and Critical Reflexions on the Conduct of Great Men in All Ages, Who, In Their Last Moments, Mock'd Death, and Died Facetiously*, nicely conveys their tone. They were iconoclastic, insubstantial works, designed more to shock than to persuade.

Montesquieu's *Persian Letters* was translated into English in 1722, a year after its first French edition, and it instantly became a best-seller, as it had been in France. An epistolary novel, it is composed largely of letters that Uzbeck, a Persian despot travelling in Europe, sends to his wives, eunuchs, and friends at home, reporting his impressions and adventures. One of Uzbeck's letters, addressed to his pious Muslim friend, Ibben, complains of the harshness of European sanctions against suicide and briefly disputes the usual arguments against it.[47] Uzbeck's most important argument is that suicide does not 'disturb the providential order of things', because when a man kills himself, he merely exercises his right to alter the effects of a natural process. Self-destruction no more violates the laws of nature, which Montesquieu identifies with providence, than making a round ball square does. Alluding to the Epicurean belief that matter is immortal and death is merely a change in the 'mode of matter', he depicts suicide as nothing more than the fulfilment of the natural process of dissolution and recreation. It separates body and soul and the former is recycled to form new beings and things. Human beings are quite incapable of affecting the design of a universe governed by impersonal laws of matter and motion. 'We do not realize our littleness', Uzbeck lectures, 'and in spite of everything we want to count for something in the universe, play a part, be a person of importance.' He also rejects the notion that a person's obligations to

[47] Montesquieu, *Persian Letters*, 152–4.

society preclude suicide, arguing that society is founded on mutual advantage, and so when it becomes onerous, one should be free to renounce it.

These arguments condoning suicide establish the moral context of Roxanna's tragic death at the close of the book. As the poison slowly weakens her, she reveals to Uzbeck, her tyrannical husband, that she has never really been his slave. Pretending to obey his capricious command that she remain a virgin, she has secretly taken a lover and transformed the seraglio from a terrible prison into a place of love and pleasure. 'I have lived in servitude', she writes, 'but I have always been free. I have amended your laws according to the laws of nature, and my mind has always remained independent.' Discovered, her lover slain by Uzbeck's eunuchs, suicide is her last gesture of freedom. She even wonders if Uzbeck might admire the bravery of her defiance and her death. She dies justified by the principles of natural law and social beneficence that Uzbeck has earlier used to condemn European laws against self-killing.[48]

For over thirty years, Montesquieu allowed Uzbeck's defence of suicide and Roxanna's death to stand as the only perspective on self-killing in the *Persian Letters*. Then in 1754, attempting to mollify some of his clerical critics, he paired Uzbeck's letter with a very short reply from Ibben, urging the necessity to submit to God's will. The letter ignores the substance of Uzbeck's arguments. 'For a true Muslim', he pontificates, repeating Christian platitudes, 'misfortune is less a punishment than a threat. Those days which encourage us to expiate our wrongs are precious indeed.' One must be patient.[49] Some commentators feel that even recast as a debate, the discussion of suicide is obviously weighted in favour of toleration.[50] Judith Shklar, on the other hand, has argued that the *Persian Letters* in its final form neither unambiguously condones nor condemns suicide. Instead, Montesquieu reclaims self-destruction as an ethical problem, rejecting old prejudices and customs without erecting a new standard by which self-killing is to be judged.[51] Shklar's reading is sensitive and perceptive, but it should be remembered that until 1754 the *Persian Letters* was rightly regarded as a defence of self-killing. And even after the appearance of the new letter dissenting from Uzbeck's view, many readers would have had little doubt as to Montesquieu's own opinion. He had written sympathetically about

48 Ibid. 280–1.
49 Ibid. 154.
50 Ibid. 316; Crocker, 'Discussion of Suicide', 61.
51 J. N. Shklar, *Montesquieu* (Oxford, 1987), 40–1.

suicide and attacked laws punishing it in other works, and his critics had drawn attention to the heterodoxy of his religious and social ideas.[52] It is fair to conclude that Montesquieu was offended by the injustice of traditional laws that punished suicide as such and felt that the morality of the act had to be assessed situationally, depending on the circumstances in which persons took their lives. Thus he distinguishes several motives that precipitated suicides in Rome, some of them admirable, some of them not. He praises Cato, whose death was the tragic climax of the republic, and blames Brutus and Cassius, whose suicides were the first act in a still greater tragedy for the nation.[53] Like other *philosophes*, Montesquieu was partly an ethical relativist, who was profoundly offended by the overarching claims of traditional religious conceptions of sin and virtue.

Radicati's *Philosophical Dissertation upon Death*, published in London in 1732, displays none of the intellectual chiaroscuro of the *Persian Letters*. The exiled Piedmontese aristocrat was a philosophical Epicurean, and his book is a vigorous exposition of the cosmological and ethical doctrines of that school as they were understood during the eighteenth century. Radicati argues that the world is governed solely by the 'general laws of matter and motion'. Matter, which in its elementary forms is imperishable, is ceaselessly formed and reformed into new shapes and beings as things change and creatures die and are born. In this materialist view of the cosmos, death is merely a transition from one form of being to another. It follows that how and when a person dies is unimportant: 'The eternal Laws of Motion cannot, in any wise, be varied, or altered, on account of a Creature's living a longer or shorter Space of Time, that is, its changing sooner or later the Modifications of its Matter.'[54] Despite his materialism, Radicati, like other Epicureans, maintains that Nature is benevolent and promotes human happiness. She would not require people to suffer pointlessly, and she has given them the power to escape pain when pleasure is no longer obtainable. 'Nature's scope in the creation of Animals', he asserts, 'is their felicity.' Like all other animals, therefore, men have 'an intire Liberty to quit Life when it is become troublesome to them'.[55]

[52] Montesquieu, *Œuvres complètes*, ii. 135–6, 486, 870–1, 880, 1134; id., *Persian Letters*, 19; Crocker, 'Discussion of Suicide', 61. Readers of the English translation of the *Persian Letters* would have justly retained the impression that Montesquieu was an apologist for suicide after 1754; Ibben's letter does not appear in the 1760 edn., the last 18th-cent. translation listed in the British Library catalogue.

[53] Montesquieu, *Œuvres complètes*, ii. 135–6.

[54] Radicati, *Philosophical Dissertation*, 92.

[55] Ibid. 85–6.

Radicati's book was neither profound nor original. Nor was it particularly well written. And yet because its arguments allegedly precipitated the most famous suicides of the century, it became the most controversial apology for self-killing published in England prior to 1783, when Hume's 'On Suicide' became widely available. In April 1732, shortly after the appearance of the *Philosophical Dissertation*, a London bookbinder named Richard Smith and his wife Bridget shot their toddler in the head and hanged themselves in their squalid rooms near King's Bench prison. The crime's violence would have been enough to make it newsworthy, but one of the three suicide notes that the Smiths left behind made it sensational. In it they explained that they were under arrest for debt and saw no hope that they would be released from the burden of poverty. They were confined to the 'rules' of King's Bench, and like many other debtors had been unable to satisfy their creditors and regain their freedom. Seeing nothing but a life of degradation ahead of them and their child, they decided to die. The Smiths were bookish, enquiring people, and they justified their suicide and (less convincingly) the murder of their child philosophically. They expound a sort of scientistic deism that absolves them of sin and removes any terror that the traditional penalties for self-murder might have held. Proclaiming their faith in God, they declare that their piety is not 'implicit Faith', but a rational belief, 'deduced from the Nature and Reason of Things'. They have contemplated the order of the heavens and viewed 'those wonders which are to be seen in the minute Part of the World' through a microscope. The wonderful order and harmony of the things that they have seen have convinced them not merely that God exists but that he is benevolent, 'not taking Delight in the Miseries of his Creatures'. They therefore feel free to resign their souls to him 'without any terrible Apprehensions', confident in the knowledge of his goodness.

Having disposed of the eschatological terrors that theologians said awaited self-murderers, they turn to the superstitions of folk religion. Popular religious beliefs placed great emphasis on proper disposal of the corpse after death and its inviolability. The rites of desecration, as we have already seen, were partly intended to terrify potential suicides by inverting the usual rituals of burial and violating the self-murderer's cadaver. The Smiths leave the disposal of their bodies to the authorities, 'the Thing being indifferent to us, where our Bodies are laid'. They reject the whole basis for fearing desecration with a materialist argument, derived ultimately from Epicurean atomism. 'It is the Opinion of Naturalists', they declare, that the bodies of men are constantly changing.

New matter replaces the old, and 'a great many poor Men have new Bodies oftener than new Cloathes'. It follows for them that since divines could not possibly say which of 'those several bodies' we inhabit during our lifetimes will be resurrected, 'it is very probable that the deceased Body may be fore ever silent as well as any other'.[56]

The Smiths' deaths were very widely publicized. The story was told in all the important London papers, which were doubtless plagiarized by the provincial rags; it was elaborated in the leading monthly periodicals, such as the *Gentleman's Magazine*.[57] Nor were they soon forgotten. Tobias Smollett, writing in his *History of England*, asserted that the incident had been the most remarkable occurrence of 1732.[58] It was alluded to by poets, journalists, philosophers, and theological writers throughout the century.[59] The Smiths and their apology for suicide became famous all over Europe, noticed by some of the most eminent writers of the age. Voltaire discussed their deed in his *Philosophical Dictionary*, and Diderot mentioned them briefly in the *Encyclopédie*.[60] Almost a century after their deaths, Solomon Piggott still felt that it was necessary to recount the tale and renounce their views in his book on suicide.[61]

In the short run, the effect of their deaths was to create an almost hysterical fear among conservatives that Radicati's ideas were infecting the lower orders of society, with murderous effects. As long as philosophical suicide was confined to the free-thinking club, Alexander Pope implied, it was a matter for sarcasm; when it spread to artisans, it was a social emergency:

> If *Blount* dispatch'd himself, he play'd the man,
> And so mays't Thou, Illustrious *Passeran*!
> But shall a *Printer*, weary of his life,
> Learn from their Books to hang himself and Wife?

[56] *Gentleman's Magazine*, ii (1732), 723.

[57] See e.g. *London Evening Post*, no. 685 (18–20 Apr. 1732); *Daily Post*, no. 3927 (18 Apr. 1732); ibid., no. 3930 (21 Apr. 1732); *Universal Spectator and Weekly Journal*, no. 185 (22 Apr. 1732); *Country Journal; or, the Craftsman*, no. 303 (22 Apr. 1732); *Fog's Weekly Journal*, no. 181 (22 Apr. 1732); *London Evening Post*, no. 686 (20–2 Apr. 1732); *Historical Register*, xvii (1732), 151–4; *Gentleman's Magazine*, ii (1732), 722–3. For a fuller discussion of the press coverage of the Smiths' suicides, see below, Chapter 9.

[58] T. Smollett, *The History of England, from the Revolution in 1688 to the Death of George II*, new edn. (Philadelphia, 1822), i. 641–2.

[59] See, in addition to the works cited below, Moore, *Full Inquiry into Suicide*, i. 165–7.

[60] Voltaire, *Works*, vii. 24–5; *Encyclopédie*, repr. edn. (Elmsford, NY, [1969]), s.v. 'suicide', iii [iv]. 641.

[61] S. Piggott, *Suicide and its Antidotes* (London, 1824), 153–4.

This, this, my friend, I cannot, must not bear;
Vice thus abus'd, demands a Nation's care.[62]

Radicati, whom Pope referred to by his title, count of Passerano, was certainly not entirely responsible for the Smiths' ideas, although there are strong parallels between the *Philosophical Dissertation* and their suicide note. Views similar to those of the Smiths had been expressed elsewhere. In the *Persian Letters*, for example, Uzbeck asserts that God is too benevolent to want his creatures to go on suffering and alludes to Epicurean ideas about the constant recycling of imperishable matter.[63] James Bramston indicted Matthew Tindal and Bernard Mandeville for having undermined the Smiths' faith and morals. Here is how he imagined Richard Smith recounting his philosophical development:

T'improve in Morals *Mandevil* I read,
And *Tyndal's* Scruples are my settled Creed.
I travell'd early, and I soon saw through
Religion all, e'er I was twenty-two.
Shame, Pain, or Poverty shall I endure,
When ropes or opium can my ease procure?
When money's gone, and I no debts can pay,
Self-murder is an honourable way.
As *Pasaran* directs I'd end my life,
And kill myself, my daughter, and my wife.
Burn but that *Bible* which the Parson quotes,
And men of spirit all shall cut their throats.[64]

The deists, in other words, had laid the foundation on which Radicati merely built the gibbet. There is, in fact, little reason to question the Smiths' assertion that they had invented their own arguments, influenced not only by free-thinkers like Radicati but also by their own scientific observations and studies. It was beyond the vision of contemporary commentators to see men of lowly rank as capable of independent thought. The Smiths' suicides were blamed on the deists, and their note ensured Radicati's tract a notoriety it surely would not otherwise have enjoyed.

62 A. Pope, *Epistle to the Satires*, in his *The Poems of Alexander Pope*, ed. J. Butt (New Haven, 1963), 693–3, ll. 122–7.

63 Montesquieu, *Persian Letters*, 153.

64 J. Bramston [1694–1744], *The Man of Taste (1733)*, ed. F. P. Lock, Augustan Reprint Society, no. 171 (Los Angeles, 1975), 9.

David Hume's appetite for notoriety was almost boundless: he loved to provoke his clerical enemies. Disappointed when his first great work, the *Treatise on Human Nature*, failed 'to excite a Murmur among the Zealots', he complained in a famous phrase that it had 'fallen dead-born from the press'.[65] 'On Suicide', which Hume wrote some time in the early 1750s, was as radical as any of the previous apologies for self-killing, and it aroused the zealots even before it had been published. Hume included it with four other controversial pieces in his *Five Dissertations*, which was printed in 1756. A prepublication copy of the book somehow came into the hands of William Warburton, one of the most vigorous champions of Anglican orthodoxy and a future bishop. Warburton was scandalized by both 'On Suicide' and the essay on the natural history of religion. He threatened prosecution, and enlisted the help of the powerful legal officials and the bishop of London, demanding the suppression of the volume in which the essay was to appear. The bookseller may have been intimidated, and Hume was urged to withdraw the essay by a friend (most likely Adam Smith); he agreed to destroy the print run of *Five Dissertations*, delete 'On Suicide' and revise slightly 'On the Natural History of Religion'. Hume's capitulation to pressure was out of character, and it has provoked a minor scholarly controversy. Tom Beauchamp, the author of one of the few modern commentaries on Hume's essay, rejects the opinion that he yielded to pressure and suggests that he may have recognized the weaknesses in some of the essay's arguments.[66] Given the repetitive, tendentious argumentation that characterized most of the previous philosophizing on the question one wonders instead if Hume did not simply conclude that suicide was a subject that aroused greater passions than the points to be scored were worth.

Whatever Hume's motives may have been, he certainly tried hard to suppress the essay during his lifetime. A few, fugitive copies of *Five Dissertations* somehow escaped the flames, and he attempted persistently to track them down and recover them. The rumour that he lent a copy to a friend who, after reading it, complimented the author on his performance, then promptly shot himself is a baseless slander.[67] Despite his efforts, some copies of the essay circulated clandestinely, selling for high prices.[68] How widely the essay was read, it is impossible to tell. A

65 E. C. Mossner, *The Life of David Hume* (Austin, Tex., 1954), 116.

66 T. L. Beauchamp, 'An Analysis of Hume's "On Suicide"', *Review of Metaphysics*, xxx (1976–7), 92–5.

67 Moore, *Full Inquiry into Suicide*, ii. 66.

68 *Gentleman's Magazine*, liv (1784), 607; *Monthly Review*, lxx (1784), 427–8.

few people obviously knew that Hume had written it and what it said; many others, to judge from the reviews of later editions, knew that he had written and suppressed a defence of self-killing. Controversy over the essay did not reach a high pitch until a year after Hume's death, when a privateering printer brought out the first English edition. (An unauthorized French edition in 1770 seems to have attracted little attention.) By 1777, everyone knew who the essay's author had been, and since Hume was in his grave, deaf to their abuse, his critics assailed Adam Smith, merely because he had been the philosopher's friend.[69] When the first version bearing Hume's name appeared in 1783, the essay was already infamous. The printer (yet another pirate), included a preface disavowing the author's sentiments and translations of Rousseau's letters on suicide: no one believed the editor's retraction was sincere.[70]

Hume's essay, in its several incarnations, supplanted earlier apologies for suicide. It was the most influential argument for the legitimacy of suicide, and indeed it is the only contribution to the debate that philosophers still read. Beauchamp is nevertheless right in believing that it is not one of Hume's most impressive performances.[71] His arguments cannot be said to constitute a coherent defence of suicide. They are instead a series of answers to objections that were commonplace in the early eighteenth century. To counter his opponents' contention that self-destruction violates both God's prerogatives and natural law, Hume seeks to prove that men are incapable of either offence. Like other deists Hume insists that 'the providence of the Deity appears not immediately in any operation, but governs every thing by those general and immutable laws which have been established from the beginning of time'. Human life and death therefore depend not on God but on 'the general laws of matter and motion'. Neither the argument of divine ownership nor the sentinel simile is valid, since it is not God who creates individual men, but rather the natural and social process of reproduction. 'For my own part', reflects Hume, 'I find that I owe my birth to a long chain of

[69] G. Horne, *A Letter to Adam Smith* (Oxford, 1777), 28–9. See also the reply by S. J. Pratt, *An Apology for the Life and Writings of David Hume* (London, 1777), 151, which treats the essay with embarrassment, claiming falsely that Hume had abandoned and 'in some measure reprobated' it, and Horne's *Letters on Infidelity*, reviewed in *Gentleman's Magazine*, liv (1784), 607.

[70] *Gentleman's Magazine*, liv (1784), 607.

[71] Beauchamp, 'Hume's Essay "On Suicide"'. The burden of Beauchamp's argument, that Hume was attempting to refute Aquinas's objections to suicide, seems to us to be overstated. Beauchamp is unaware of the provenance of some of the ideas Hume was refuting and the plethora of tracts restating them.

causes, of which many depended upon voluntary actions of men.'[72] God has no greater claim to be our commander or our owner, he implies, than our parents do. Suicides likewise cannot break the general laws of nature. All the powers and faculties we possess are natural and thus 'from the Creator'. Employing them, no one 'can encroach upon the plan of his providence, or disorder the universe'. It makes no difference in the divine scheme of nature whether people die by the sword, a fatal accident, or a disease. By inflicting a mortal wound on himself a person merely anticipates 'the effects of blind causes'. The suicide uses his natural, God-given powers to 'produce some innovation in the course of nature', but he does not and cannot transgress any natural law. Montesquieu likened suicide to making a round ball square; Hume compares it with diverting the course of the Danube. Unlike Montesquieu or Radicati, Hume grants that men display a 'natural horror of death', but as this is not one of the 'general laws of matter and motion', it does not enjoy the coercive authority that natural law theorists imputed to it. It simply explains why suicide is not more frequent than it is.

Hume's conception of the natural world and human beings' place in it was strongly influenced by Epicureanism. Like Montesquieu and Radicati, Hume supposes that the elemental stuff of human life is imperishable and so endures beyond death:

> When I shall be dead, the principles of which I am composed will still perform their part in the universe, and will still be equally useful in the grand fabric, as when they compose this individual creature. The difference to the whole will be no greater than betwixt my being in a chamber and in the open air. The one change is of more importance to me than the other; but not more so to the universe.[73]

This is an anthropology that at once reduces individual human beings to insignificance and at the same time frees them to die if their deaths promote their own personal benefit. The neo-Epicureans actually stressed the freedom to die more vigorously than their ancient counterparts had done. The ancient Epicureans had granted, despite strong reservations, that suicide was permissible when 'the balance of pain over pleasure became intolerable'.[74] Contemporary translations of Epicurean texts tended to turn this exception into the rule, making Epicurus and

[72] Hume, 'On Suicide', 157.
[73] Ibid. 157–8.
[74] Griffin, 'Philosophy, Cato, and Roman Suicide: I', 72.

his disciples seem more in love with death than they actually had been. 'There is no Necessity for us to live in Necessity', Charleton englished Epicurus, 'since Nature hath been so Kind as to give us, though but one door into the World, yet many doors out of it.'[75] Lucretius' opinions about suicide are not fully spelled out, but his celebrated passage against the fear of death was read as an apology for suicide. This is Dryden's version of it:

> If Life be grown a load, a real ill,
> And I woul'd all thy cares and labours end,
> Lay down thy burden fool, and know thy friend.[76]

Readers reflecting on these lines would inevitably recall the allegation that the poet had himself committed suicide.[77]

Hume's most original contributions to the debate over suicide were in his handling of the problem of the citizen's obligations to society. The central project of eighteenth-century ethical philosophy had been to base moral behaviour on social imperatives rather than on divine commands. Hume's predecessors from Blount to Radicati had argued that society was formed for the benefit of the individual. When a person was no longer capable of benefiting from it, he was therefore free to leave. Gildon had compared committing suicide with emigration, and the analogy was developed by Beccaria, who commented that it actually harmed society less, since the suicide did not transfer the benefit of his property and person to another nation.[78] Hume's approach to the problem was more moderate and more convincing. He insists that 'a man who retires from life does no harm to society; he only ceases to do good; which, if it is an injury, is of the lowest kind'. Like the other apologists for suicide, he stresses that social obligations 'seem to imply something reciprocal'. Those who benefit from society have a duty to promote its interests. But what if misery and infirmity render a person incapable of benefiting from society or contributing to it? Weighing the small benefit to society against the 'great harm' the suffering person sustains by continued living, it is unreasonable to suppose that he may not kill himself. Hume pursues this argument further than Montesquieu, who

[75] *Epicurus's Morals*, 127.

[76] Quoted in J. A. Winn, *John Dryden and His World* (New Haven, 1987), 404. Cf. Lucretius, *On the Nature of the Universe*, trans. R. Lathum (Baltimore, 1963), 122, 124–5.

[77] St Jerome's story of Lucretius' suicide has often been doubted, but it was accepted in the 18th century and is repeated by some authorities today: Y. Grisé, *Le Suicide dans la Rome antique* (Paris, 1982), 177.

[78] Beccaria-Bonesana, *Essay on Crimes and Punishments*, 122–3.

had anticipated it. He declares that when a person has become so infirm that he has become a burden to society, suicide is the only service he may perform that benefits it. In such cases, 'resignation of life must not only be innocent, but laudable'. He thus concludes on utilitarian grounds that suicide may actually be a duty.[79]

## THE ENEMIES OF TOLERATION

The free-thinkers were attacked by an army of conservatives, mismatched battalions of professionals and volunteers, clergy and pious laymen of every sect. At first they fought back with the old weapons—the tested arguments from scripture and medieval theology condemning suicide and the traditional belief that the devil instigated self-murder. But as the century progressed, there was a growing divergence in tactics among the various groupings on the conservative side. The main body of the anti-deistical forces, the Anglican regulars, displayed a marked tendency to meet the free-thinking attack with philosophical arguments. They determined to fight the enemy with his own chosen weapons. John Adams set the tone in 1700 when he declared that he would argue the case against suicide using natural reason alone: 'They who undertake to define the Lawfulness of Self-Murther, (of which there are many in this Age) proceed *chiefly upon Natural Principles*, and will not hearken to any Thing from *Revelation* till these are answered: Wherefore my Design at present is, to consider this Action, according to the *Principles of Natural Reason only*.'[80] His example was followed by the majority of his Anglican co-religionists.[81] Even men like Francis Ayscough and John Cockburn, who conjured with the name and shape of Satan, relied heavily on philosophical arguments in their sermons.[82]

The aims and arguments that the Establishment opponents of suicide used did not change much over the century, and they can best be presented in a brief examination of their earliest and—until Charles Moore—ablest champion, John Adams. Adams's objective was to prove that suicide violated man's obligations to God, to nature, and to

[79] Hume, 'On Suicide', 159–60.

[80] Adams, *Essay Concerning Self-Murther*, 1–2.

[81] The Anglicans' tendency to marshal philosophical arguments against suicide may be noticed, for example, in Z. Pearce, *A Sermon of Self-Murder* (London, 1736); Herries, *Address on Suicide*; Hey, *Dissertation on Suicide*; and Moore, *Full Inquiry into Suicide*.

[82] J. Cockburn, *A Discourse of Self-Murder* (London, 1716).

the state, precisely the propositions that Gildon had questioned. His plan of attack was to choose ancient and medieval arguments against suicide, and then to modernize them with supporting arguments that were consistent with contemporary moral and political philosophy. His task was at once made simpler and more complex by the fact that the two greatest philosophers of the seventeenth century, Locke and Hobbes, had supported his side: Locke had renounced suicide as an infringement on the rights of God; Hobbes had rejected it as a violation of the law of nature. The pedigree of Locke's argument and the prestige of the philosopher ensured its popularity; the origins of Hobbes's claim and the notoriety of its author guaranteed its controversiality.

Adams begins with the claim his enemies would admit less willingly than any other: that self-killing violated man's obligations to God. The challenge Adams faced was to show that even the God acknowledged by the deists, the architect of nature, had a claim on men's lives. Ignoring Pythagoras' famous sentinel simile, Adams bases his case instead on Socrates' contention that men are the property of God and so cannot kill themselves until he permits them to do so by sending them some compelling reason to die.[83] The Socratic argument had two advantages: it avoided the assumption of providential care implicit in the Pythagorean figure, and it had been the basis for Locke's rejection of suicide. Locke had declared that men were not free to kill themselves, even in the state of nature, because they do not enjoy an absolute propriety in their own lives, 'for Men being all the Workmanship of one Omnipotent, and infinitely wise Maker . . . are his Property'. Locke's theory of property supplied a missing term in Socrates' argument, which had not explained why God owned the lives of men, and it connected the prohibition against self-killing with the fundamental elements of his political theory.[84] Property rights, Locke had maintained, were established ultimately by the act of making something—mixing one's labour with it—and if men were not the property of God, who had created them, then how could any other private property be justified? Adams recast the Lockean argument, putting it in terms that an élite dominated by landowners could not fail to understand. Man has a right over his life in some sense, he concluded, '*a Right of Use*, but *not a Right of absolute Propriety*'.[85] The appeal of this claim is easy to see. It was repeated frequently by the opponents of suicide throughout the century, and only

[83] Plato, *Phaedo*, 62b–c, 45.
[84] Locke, *Two Treatises of Government*, 311, 325, 402.
[85] Adams, *Essay Concerning Self-Murther*, 10.

Hume challenged it directly.[86] Adams did not refer directly to Locke, whose authorship of the *Two Treatises* was still a secret in 1700—at least officially—but later writers appealed to his immense and growing authority.

Adams faced a greater challenge in defending the proposition that suicide violated natural law. This may seem at first surprising. The notion that self-preservation was a fundamental law of nature was very widely held throughout the seventeenth and eighteenth centuries. 'The law of self-preservation being infringed', wrote a correspondent to the *Annual Register* in 1764, 'the foundation of other laws is shaken.'[87] The predicament confronting the champions of orthodoxy was that the most compelling English advocate of the primacy of self-preservation was Thomas Hobbes, a thinker they hated more passionately than any of the deists. Hobbes had, moreover, stated the idea in a way that clearly linked it with the prohibition of suicide. 'A Law of Nature (*Lex Naturalis*)', he wrote in *Leviathan*, 'is a Precept, or generall Rule, found out by Reason, by which a man is forbidden to do, that, which is destructive of his life.'[88] An argument so near to the heart of the Hobbesian reactor was contaminated by lethal levels of radioactivity. Not even Locke's declaration that self-preservation was 'the first and strongest desire God Planted in Men, and wrought into the very Principles of their Nature' made it entirely safe.[89] To his credit, Adams confronts the problem directly, rejecting Hobbes's use of the idea on the grounds that 'it opens a very wide door to the worst consequences of Knavery or Cowardice'. His alternative was to propose that the instinct of self-preservation is only the means to a greater end. Natural law does not authorize selfishness, for it requires people to seek the end common to their species, 'the following of Reason by Virtue'.[90] Adams's attempt to show that natural law precludes suicide without endorsing Hobbesian political theory is notable mainly because it was one of several such efforts. Samuel Pufendorf, a philosopher vastly more influential than Adams, made a very similar argument, concluding that people who killed themselves for whatever reason were to be 'reputed as *Sinners against the Law of Nature*'.[91] Throughout the eighteenth

[86] For repetitions of the argument, see, e.g., J. Henley, *Cato Condemn'd; or, The Case and History of Self-Murder* (London, 1730), 2–3; Pearce, *Sermon on Self-Murder*, 12–24; Hey, *Dissertation on Suicide*, 67–8.

[87] *Annual Register*, vii (1764), 194.

[88] Hobbes, *Leviathan*, 189.

[89] Locke, *Two Treatises*, 244. See also, Windstrup, 'Locke on Suicide', 170–1.

[90] Adams, *Essay Concerning Self-Murther*, 31–3.

century, despite their nervousness about Hobbes, the opponents of suicide appealed to natural law and, more specifically, to the instinct of self-preservation.

The proposition that self-killing was contrary to one's obligation to society also required more philosophical ingenuity to prove than might be supposed. The classic authority for the belief that suicide injured the state was Aristotle, but his contention rested on dubious and dangerous arguments. He simply assumes that suicide is an unjust act and declares that since a man cannot commit an injustice against himself, suicide must be an injustice to the state. Moreover, he adds that not only is the state therefore justified in outlawing it but that it is illegal even when no specific injunction forbids it. For, he asserts, what the law does not explicitly permit it forbids.[92] This is not a doctrine that Englishmen jealous of their liberties were likely to find attractive. Haunted once again by the spectre of Hobbes, Adams argues that suicide violates the citizen's obligation to society because it fails to promote the public good. According to Adams, the true end of civil society was the promotion of the public good, and all its members were enjoined to pursue that end.[93] This assertion closely resembles the proto-utilitarianism of Richard Cumberland, a prolix writer and vague thinker, whose *De legibus naturae* (1672) nevertheless greatly influenced moral philosophers.[94] Cumberland himself remarked that the civil laws usually judged 'a *Self-Murderer* injurious, not to *himself alone*, but to the *Publick* also, which he robs of a *Subject*; and that Fact is justly reckon'd among the greatest Crimes'.[95] Adams pursues the notion that men are bound to promote the general good even to the point of denying that idiots and lunatics might legitimately kill themselves: 'There is scarce any Wretch but may be some way or another beneficial to the Publick, even by *his being alive alone*'.[96]

[91] S. Pufendorf, *The Whole Duty of Man According to the Law of Nature*, 2nd edn. (London, 1698), 67–9. Grotius may also have been perceived as an authority for this line of argument, although, as Richard Tuck points out, his statements on suicide are ambiguous, saying that no one had a natural right to injure oneself in one place and that prohibitions against suicide were based on civil, not natural, law in another: R. Tuck, *Natural Rights Theories* (Cambridge, 1979), 70–1.

[92] Aristotle, *Nicomachean Ethics*, 1138$^a$11, 1020–1.

[93] Adams, *Essay Concerning Self-Murther*, 98.

[94] R. Cumberland, *A Treatise of the Laws of Nature*, trans. J. Maxwell (London, 1727), esp. pp. 16, 65, 189. For brief discussions of Cumberland, see *DNB*; F. Copleston, *A History of Philosophy*, v: *Hobbes to Hume* (Garden City, NY, 1959), 64–6.

[95] Cumberland, *Laws of Nature*, 337.

[96] Adams, *Essay Concerning Self-Murther*, 108, 293.

In a more practical vein, Adams stresses the effect that suicide had on public security and the suffering it inflicted on families and heirs, the members of society with the greatest claim on the potential self-killer's care. To allow self-murder, Adams asserts, 'would utterly destroy *the force of Humane Laws*' because the greatest punishment that human laws can threaten is death. If men are taught to despise death, 'they will not be oblig'd to do any Duty, by the fear of this, much less by the fear of anything else; but wou'd Rob, Ravish, Murther, &c'.[97] Moreover, giving people the right to commit suicide would subvert all civil authority, since there is no way to stipulate precisely the circumstances in which self-killing would be allowable. The private judgement of the individual would therefore take precedence over the interests of the state.[98] Adams vigorously protests against the growing leniency that coroners' juries displayed toward suicide. No matter that coroners and their jurors act out of compassion in sparing self-murderers and their families:

> Whatever the *Motive* is, through which the Design of any Law is Eluded; the Consequence will be much the *same*; If a Law be made to restrain a dreadful Sin . . . and such or such a Punishment is appointed to this End; if this Law becomes of *no force* by the very Persons *Preventing* the Punishment, who is [*sic*] *intrusted* by his County to see the Law *Executed*, . . . all the increase of the *Sin forbidden*, . . . *he* will have a share in.[99]

It is not just society in general that would suffer from this subversion of proper authority. The most immediate victims of suicide are and would be the self-murderer's own family and friends. They are disgraced by the 'horrid sense which such an Act imprints upon the best Mens Minds [and] the general Aversion which it causes'. Their shame, and often the 'Confusion and Desolation' of widows and orphans, necessarily harms the state.[100]

These arguments were the core of the conservative case against liberalizing the law of suicide. The threat to public order if the fear of death as a punishment were removed was often stressed in the eighteenth century. The author of a jeremiad against suicide and duelling published in 1728 worried that juries' neglect of the law impeached 'the Wisdom of former Parliaments, and of the present likewise, who have left the old Laws in relation to *Self-Murther* unrepeal'd'.[101] Caleb Fleming declared

[97] Ibid. 26.
[98] Ibid. 27–8.
[99] Ibid. 129.
[100] Ibid. 28.
[101] *Self-Murther and Duelling the Effects of Cowardice and Atheism* (London, 1728), 5.

in 1773 that suicide 'destroys the very foundation of social virtue, and of all moral obligation', and worried that if the practice were approved it would lead to the depopulation of the nation.[102] Richard Hey also feared that tolerating self-killing promoted other crimes and encouraged moral laxity.[103] Manifestly, however, the fear of death was not enough to restrain self-murderers themselves. The opponents of toleration therefore stressed that the posthumous punishments were essential to deterring suicide. The law against self-murder, explained an anonymous author in 1728, was intended to 'deter others from the like inhuman and detestable Practices' by shifting the penalty 'he hath put himself out of the reach of' on to his posterity.[104] William Fleetwood explained the logic behind forfeiture and profane burial, as eighteenth-century conservatives viewed them:

> Such is the Natural Affection a Man bears to his Wife, and Children, Family and Dependents, such is the respect he has to his own Fame, such the kindness he bears even to his own dead Body, that, were he sure, his Estate would be forfeited, and his Effects carried from his family; were he sure he would be buried in the High-way, and with a Stake driven through him . . . he would give way to calmer Councils.[105]

This was a theme to which the opponents of reform returned repeatedly. Fifty years after Fleetwood's sermons were published, for example, Francis Ayscough urged that 'before a Man commits this last rash Action he should think on the afflicted Friend, the mournful Widow, and the fatherless Family; the Tears, the Anguish, and misery of all those who had a Right to his Love and Protection'.[106] A correspondent to the *Annual Register* in 1764 attempted to bring familial duty into line with contemporary political theory, arguing that the obligation that the would-be suicide owed to his family and friends was based on a free compact, rather than on patriarchal relations.[107]

## PHILOSOPHY AND PUBLIC OPINION

It is impossible to gauge how influential philosophical apologies for suicide were. A fellow of Lincoln College who wrote a short work

[102] C. Fleming, *A Dissertation upon the Unnatural Crime of Self-Murder* (London, 1773), 9.

[103] Hey, *Dissertation on Suicide*, 33–45.

[104] *Self-Murther and Duelling*, 5–6.

[105] Fleetwood, *Relative Duties*, 486.

[106] F. Ayscough, *A Discourse against Self-Murder* (London, 1755), 12.

[107] *Annual Register*, vii (1864), 194.

refuting *Biathanatos* around 1705 could not get it published and was mocked in the senior common room because, according to Thomas Hearne, his colleagues thought that there was no occasion for such a book.[108] Only a few libertines blew their brains out like Blount or strung themselves up like Creech: a character in Bishop Berkeley's *Alciphron* complains churlishly that not enough of them have had the courage to act on their principles.[109] And yet there can be little doubt that in the two or three decades following the Glorious Revolution radical views were being voiced more loudly and heard more sympathetically than ever before. Epicureanism was in vogue in the late seventeenth and early eighteenth centuries. Epicurus' disciple, Lucretius, was admired extravagantly. John Evelyn and John Dryden translated parts of *De rerum natura*, and Thomas Creech published a full version with a commentary in 1684. Reissued repeatedly in the eighteenth century, it outsold Pope's Homer. The glamorous French exile, Charles de Marguetel de St Denis, Sieur de Saint Evremond, attracted the noble libertines, a candle in a cloud of butterflies. Bedazzled perhaps by the figures associated with Saint Evremond, Thomas Mayo, the historian of Epicureanism in England, declares that Epicurus' influence waned after Creech's death in 1700, but this is wrong.[110] A new edition of *Epicurus's Morals* appeared 1712, with a commentary wrongly ascribed to Saint Evremond. It included a disclaimer regarding the philosopher's approval of suicide but granted that it might be excused in the most extreme circumstances and provided a catalogue of suicides justified in antiquity.[111] Mediated by Gassendi, Epicurean atomism continued to influence contemporary scientists and virtuosi. Epicurus was used and praised by d'Holbach, Voltaire, Diderot, and Condillac; Hume included a long defence of the Epicurean philosophy in his *Enquiries Concerning Human Understanding* (1777).[112]

Many conservatives believed that the apologists had succeeded in persuading a large segment of fashionable society that suicide was

[108] T. Hearne, *Remarks and Collections*, ed. C. E. Doble, Oxford Historical Society Pubs., ii (Oxford, 1885), i. 73.

[109] G. Berkeley, *Alciphron*, in *The Works*, ed. A. A. Luce and T. E. Jessop, iii (London, 1950), 92. See also, Pearce, *Sermon on Self-Murder*, 16.

[110] Mayo, *Epicurus in England*, 103.

[111] *Epicurus's Morals . . . To Which is Added, An Essay on Epicurus' Morals, Written by Monsieur St. Evremont and Made English by Mr. Johnson*, trans. J. Digby (London, 1712), 195–200.

[112] Gay, *Enlightenment*, ii. 304–8; D. Hume, *Enquiries Concerning Human Understanding*, ed. L. A. Selby-Bigge, 3rd edn., ed. H. Nidditch (Oxford, 1979), 132–48.

legitimate. Bishop Berkeley, for instance, complained shrilly that 'atheistical men', devoid of either natural or revealed religion, 'are an increasing number, and this too among people of no despicable rank'. He held up Radicati's *Philosophical Dissertation* as the culmination of the 'minute philosophers'' whole programme.[113] Clerical polemicists charged repeatedly that the deists had caused an epidemic of suicide. The author of a tract on the 'supposed suicide of Samson', for example, lamented that he lived 'in an *Age* and *Country*, wherein few *Weeks* together do rarely pass; that do not afford the Instances of that execrable Wickedness; to the great Reproach and Scandal of the *Nation*; Which doubtless is much owing, to those licentious *Writers*, that have impudently pretended to justify it'.[114] Some pious laymen shared this estimate of the free-thinkers' deadly infuence. The famous physician George Cheyne thought that suicide was more frequent than ever before because of the English predisposition to melancholia and 'the *blasphemous* and *frantick Apologies* [for self-killing] grafted on the Principles of the *Infidels*, and propagated by their *Disciples*'.[115]

These alarums were symptoms of the clerical establishment's anxiety that their influence over lay society was waning. They should not be taken too literally. But the defenders of suicide did win a partial victory over their conservative opponents. They forced the clergy to justify the prohibition of suicide on philosophical grounds, and they proved that the question of its legitimacy was debatable, at the very least. Adams's strategy of fighting the free-thinkers with their own weapons was flawed, despite its attractiveness to other Anglican polemicists. In the first place, it yielded the point that arguments from revelation were no longer convincing to many members of polite society. Moreover, it committed the orthodox to a battle that they simply could not win: the philosophical arguments against suicide were all answerable. Neither side possessed plainly superior authority. There was consequently a growing recognition that suicide could not simply be condemned as invariably wrong. 'Orator' Henley conceded the point in 1730, beginning his refutation of the free-thinkers' arguments with the observation that there was a fierce controversy over the right to commit suicide.[116] An anonymous reviewer evaluating Jean Dumas's treatise against

[113] Berkeley, *Works*, i. 253.

[114] *Two Dissertations: The First on the Supposed Suicide of Samson* . . . (London, 1754), 11–12, 43. See also, *Self-Murther and Duelling*, 45–55.

[115] G. Cheyne, *The English Malady*, 3rd edn. (London, 1734), p. iii.

[116] Henley, *Cato Condemn'd*, 2.

suicide in 1774 also admitted that the public was divided into irreconcilable factions over the question. Granting that Dumas's book was on the whole well intended and scored some debating points, he concluded wearily that 'it is not likely to be much read by the admirers of the *Lettres Persannes*, the *System de la Nature*, or the *Nouvelle Heloise*'.[117]

As the century progressed, more and more of the public concluded that the legitimacy of suicide was an arguable question. Liberal opinion seems to have been especially strong in London. A letter in the *London Journal* in 1724 contrasted Aristides, who manfully endured poverty and disappointment, with Philander, who slew himself in the midst of luxury and (improbably) happiness. 'I approve, I applaud *Aristides*', the letter's author declares, 'but at the same Time, I think my self at Liberty to pity *Philander*.'[118] Recounting his suicidal crisis in the 1760s, William Cowper recalled that his father had asked him to read a defence of suicide when the poet was just eleven years old. The lad argued against it and found, to his surprise, that his father seemed to side with the author. The changing climate of opinion, in fact, contributed to Cowper's morbid distress in later life. Living in London as a young barrister, he began to be tormented by temptations to kill himself. He kept meeting people casually in the city's chop-houses and pubs who thought that it was perfectly legitimate to do so:

> I fell into company, at a chop-house, with an elderly, well-looking gentleman. . . . At length self-murder became the topic; and in the result, we agreed, that the only reason why some men were content to drag on their sorrows with them to the grave, and others were not, was, that the latter were endued with a certain indignant fortitude of spirit. . . . Another person, whom I met at a tavern, told me, that he had made up his mind about that matter, and had no doubt of his liberty to die as he saw convenient.[119]

In the 1780s and 1790s public debates about the morality of suicide were staged in London. In 1786, the 'New Westminster Forum', a school for elocution, announced that it was sponsoring a debate on the question, 'Is Suicide an Act of Courage', for which ladies and gentlemen were charged sixpence admittance.[120] Three years later, following the spectacular suicide of a Frenchman in Greenwich Park, a clergyman called for another debate on the same question to be held at Coach-Makers' Hall

[117] *Monthly Review*, 1 [50] (1774), 152.

[118] Quoted in Sprott, *English Debate*, 109–10.

[119] W. Cowper, *Memoir of the Early Life of William Cowper* (London, 1816), 27–9. Roy Porter identifies the vindication of suicide Cowper's father asked him to read as the *Persian Letters: A Social History of Madness* (London, 1987), 94.

[120] *The Times*, no. 367 (27 Feb. 1786), 1.

in Cheapside. *The Times* reported that suicide was 'at present a general subject of conversation among all ranks of people', and the debate, crowded and protracted, had to be reconvened for a second session.[121]

The free-thinkers thus forced their opponents to fight on their own turf and battled them to a draw. The deadlock permitted the reading public to judge suicide according to the circumstances that had motivated them. Sympathy was potentially greatest for those people who were driven by pain and misery to take their own lives. The apologists for suicide realized this, and they were careful to appeal to their readers' compassion. Uzbeck in the *Persian Letters* pleads for persons 'overcome by anguish, poverty, or humiliation'. The editor of the 1712 edition of *Epicurus's Morals*, although embarrassed by the philosopher's views, nevertheless stressed that he had allowed suicide in cases of extreme necessity.[122] Radicati emphasized the right of those who were wretched and sick to kill themselves. A man is not an enemy to himself, he stresses, when 'quite tired and oppressed, either with Poverty, or Contempt, or Sickness, or Bondage, he shall voluntarily cease to live'.[123] And Hume laid it down as a virtue that those who have become so infirm that they are a burden to others should remove themselves from society.[124] Even the opponents of suicide conceded that it might be permissible in such a situation. Rousseau's letter condemning self-destruction granted that 'the acute pains of the body, when they are incurable, may justify a man's destroying himself', and Adam Smith also thought that infirmity and settled misery might pardon suicide.[125] It was these 'easy' cases that were most likely to be granted by readers who, like Roger North, had little fondness for deism or Epicureanism. He strongly believed that it was no sin to commit suicide rationally to escape afflictions, particularly wretched old age, chronic diseases, and tormenting maladies. 'The condition of a man may be such that his paine is beyond support, and life desperate; and it were a charity to dispatch him.' Murder is forbidden by the Sixth Commandment but not suicide, which in such cases 'is a curtesie to himself and injury to no man'. Developing this thought in his autobiography, North claimed that it cannot be right to extend the doctrine of providence to forbid the 'most rational and innocent means

121 Ibid., no. 1302 (26 Feb. 1789), 3; no. 1312 (5 Mar. 1789), 3.

122 Montesquieu, *Persian Letters*, 153; *Epicurus's Morals*, 196–7.

123 Radicati, *Philosophical Dissertation*, 90.

124 Hume, 'On Suicide', 159.

125 Rousseau, *La Nouvelle Héloïse*, quoted in Moore, *Full Inquiry into Suicide*, 2: 101; A. Smith, *The Theory of Moral Sentiments*, ed. D. D. Raphael and A. L. Macfie (Oxford, 1976), 281–8.

for relief and ending torment'.[126] Expressions of pity for men and women who killed themselves to escape age or infirmity can be found in many eighteenth-century diaries and newspapers, as we shall see in a later chapter, and the mood of sympathy for the sufferings of suicidal people was consistent with a broad movement in moral philosophy that elevated 'irresistible compassion' to a principle of human nature.[127]

The free-thinkers also reinforced the growing conviction that the laws punishing self-murder were unfair and obsolete. One did not have to accept Montesquieu's arguments that self-killing might be justified to agree with him that the existing penalties should be abolished or changed.[128] The *philosophes* called attention to the discrepancy between the treatment of suicide in Roman law and the rituals of desecration. 'No Roman law condemned self-murder', Voltaire declared flatly (and wrongly). 'Notwithstanding this humane law of our masters, we still drag on a sledge and drive a stake through the body of a man who has died a voluntary death.'[129] The philosophers were, in effect, calling attention to the fact that the customs for disgracing suicides were neither Roman nor Christian. They were superstitions pure and simple, worthy of Horace Walpole's scornful dismissal, as 'the absurd stake and highway of our ancestors'.[130] More persuasively, the free-thinkers emphasized the unfairness of punishing the suicide's heirs. 'We punish the son for having lost the father', continued Voltaire, 'and the widow for being deprived of her husband.'[131] This is the main theme of Beccaria's attack on the law of suicide:

> Suicide is a crime which seems not to admit of punishment, properly speaking; for it cannot be inflicted but on the innocent, or upon an insensible dead body. In the first case, it is unjust and tyrannical, for political liberty supposes all punishments entirely personal; in the second, it has the same effect, by way of example, as the scourging a statue.[132]

[126] BL, Add. MS 32526, fo. 125$^{v}$; North, *Lives of the Norths*, iii. 151–4.

[127] N. S. Fiering, 'Irresistible Compassion: An Aspect of Eighteenth-Century Sympathy and Humanitarianism', *Journal of the History of Ideas*, xxxvii (1976), 195–218; J. B. Radner, 'The Art of Sympathy in Eighteenth-Century British Moral Thought', in R. Runte (ed.), *Studies in Eighteenth-Century Culture*, ix (Madison, Wis., 1979), 189–210.

[128] Montesquieu, *Persian Letters*, 129–30.

[129] Voltaire, *Works*, vii. 33.

[130] H. Walpole, *The Yale Edition of Horace Walpole's Correspondence*, ed. W. S. Lewis (New Haven, 1937–83), xxxi. 267 (s.n. 'Hesse, George').

[131] Voltaire, *Works*, vii. 33.

[132] Beccaria-Bonesana, *Essay on Crimes and Punishments*, 122.

Beccaria's essay, published in England in 1767, was immensely influential. It did not, as we shall see, lead to the repeal of the law of suicide, but it certainly helped to create a climate of opinion in which juries' failure to enforce its penalties was widely condoned.

# 6

# *Élite Opinions, Plebeian Beliefs*

THE philosophical debate over suicide has claimed the largest share of attention in historians' accounts of attitudes to self-killing. And yet changing opinion was characterized less by growing assent to the arguments of the free-thinkers than it was by an increasingly sympathetic and even sentimental outlook. This shift in the educated élite's feelings about suicide was expressed in a wide range of literary genres and public statements. Perhaps the most important vehicle for the new sympathy was the periodical press, and we shall devote a full chapter to the depiction of suicide in the newspapers. First, though, we shall examine the broad intellectual movements that promoted more lenient views and social and religious beliefs that militated against them. Many scholars now complain that the venerable division of the eighteenth century into an Augustan age, when the tone of intellectual life was set by neoclassicism, and a Romantic period, when it was increasingly dominated by sentimentalism, is too crude, or even wrong altogether.[1] Yet again, however, revisionism has clarified the complexities of the past at a cost of obscuring our ability to see the broad trajectory of change. Attitudes to suicide were strongly influenced by neoclassicism, particularly in the first half of the eighteenth century, and they were also powerfully shaped by the emergence of romanticism in its later decades. Roman heroes who had killed themselves were extravagantly admired, and their example was one of the bases of a new fashion for honourable suicides among real and aspiring gentlemen. Towards the end of the century, the publication of Goethe's *Sorrows of Young Werther* and other romantic tales made

[1] J. Sambrook, *The Eighteenth Century: The Intellectual and Cultural Context of English Literature, 1700–1789* (London, 1984), 207–9, states the case strongly and reviews the relevant scholarship concisely.

sentimental suicides, especially deaths for love, occasions for maudlin lamentation, rather than shocked condemnation.

Moreover, the whole context of thought about suicide was determined by attitudes to religion that originated in the seventeenth century and continued to flow strongly through élite opinion, like a tidal wave after an earthquake. The rivalry between Catholics and Protestants and within Protestantism between Anglicans and Puritans that had climaxed in the English Revolution and the Revolution of 1688 left the ruling élite with an enduring hatred and fear of papists and Protestant enthusiasts. For over a century and a half after 1660 Establishment propagandists assailed Catholics and sectarians, reinvoking horrified memories of civil war and revolution. One that that both the papists and Protestant fanatics had in common—at least in the eyes of Anglican zealots—was their claim to possess special powers to interact with supernatural beings. Jesuit priests exorcised people possessed by the devil and healed diseases miraculously. Dissenters and sectarians—Presbyterians in the late seventeenth century and French Prophets and Methodists in the next century—also cast out devils and cured the sick, using prayer and fasting, as their Puritan forebears had. The most pious Protestant sectarians claimed to experience immediate intercourse with both divine and diabolical spirits. Anglicans charged repeatedly that they laid claim to divine inspiration, as the religious radicals of the Interregnum had.[2]

These enduring hatreds and fears encouraged scepticism about supernatural intervention in the natural world. They coincided with the scientific revolution and fostered scientism and rational religion among the Anglican élite. Even the clergy were committed to denouncing supernaturalist zeal and showing that natural philosophy and Christianity were reconcilable.[3] A number of historians have recently insisted that the old view of the eighteenth-century church as a moribund institution

[2] G. Williamson, 'The Restoration Revolt against Enthusiasm', *Studies in Philology*, ii (1933), 571–603 is the classic treatment of this theme. See also, M. Heyd, 'The Reaction to Enthusiasm in the Seventeenth Century: Toward an Integrative Approach', *Journal of Modern History*, liii (1981), 258–80; H. Schwartz, *Knaves, Fools, Madmen, and that Subtile Effluvium: A Study in the Opposition to the French Prophets in England, 1706–1710* (Gainesville, Fla., 1978), a more far-ranging work than the title and dates suggest; M. MacDonald, 'Religion, Social Change, and Psychological Healing in England', in W. J. Sheils (ed.), *The Church and Healing*, Studies in Church History, xix (Oxford, 1982), 101–25; A. M. Lytes, *Methodism Mocked* (London, 1960).

[3] M. C. Jacob, *The Newtonians and the English Revolution, 1689–1720* (Ithaca, NY, 1976); id., *The Cultural Meaning of the Scientific Revolution* (Philadelphia, 1988), chs. 3–5; C. E. Raven, *Natural Religion and Christian Theology* (Cambridge, 1953); J. Spurr, '"Rational Religion" in Restoration England', *Journal of the History of Ideas*, xlix (1988), 563–85.

in a cynically secular age is a caricature. In place of the slumbering congregation depicted in Hogarth's famous etching, *The Sleeping Congregation*, we are now supposed to imagine a lively scene of devoted divines and devout worshippers.[4] In this case, too, the pendulum of historical argument seems to have swung too far. For although the church retained a good deal more vitality than its contemporary critics and many modern historians have recognized, the Anglican élite's faith in the immanent potency of the supernatural waned noticeably in the eighteenth century. Fashionable religion was rational religion: the most influential defence of the faith was Butler's *The Analogy of Religion, Natural and Revealed, to the Constitution and Course of Nature* (1736), which purported to prove that Christianity was as reasonable as the natural religion espoused by the deists. The French Prophets and the Methodists were assailed as madmen, mentally ill fanatics whose religious enthusiasm was both a cause and a type of lunacy.[5]

In these circumstances the traditional belief that Satan was the author of suicide could not survive. It became as obsolete in Establishment circles as beliefs in witches, ghosts, and diabolical possession. If it was insane to believe that one could converse with God or his angels, then it could hardly be rational to hear the devil or feel his promptings. There were, of course, many who were reluctant to banish God and Satan from the world. The clergy—who were, after all, specialists in the supernatural—generally agreed that the age of miracles had passed, but there was no agreement about when it had ended or where the boundary between nature and the supernatural should be drawn. Dissenters and sectarians rejected the new stress on natural causes and rational religion. The Nonconformists clung to their old faith in the supernatural causes of suicide—as they did their belief in diabolical possession and exorcism by prayer and fasting—into the early eighteenth century. And when their confidence in supernatural effects began to wane, these venerable beliefs were seized upon by the Methodists and by some Anglican evangelicals. Their faith in the power of Satan was wholly sincere, but

[4] The most impressive attempt to demonstrate this thesis to date is J. M. Albers, 'Seeds of Contention: Society, Politics and the Church in Lancashire, 1689–1790', Ph.D. thesis (Yale, 1988). See also, Sambrook, *Eighteenth Century*, ch. 2; N. Sykes, *Church and State in England in the XVIIIth Century* (Cambridge, 1934); G. Rupp, *Religion in England, 1688–1791* (Oxford, 1986), ch. 24; J. C. D. Clark, *English Society, 1688–1832* (Cambridge, 1985), which goes so far as to cite Methodism and the evangelical revival as signs of the vitality of orthodox Anglicanism, 235.

[5] M. MacDonald, 'Insanity and the Realities of History', *Psychological Medicine*, xi (1981), 11–25; R. Porter, 'The Rage of Party: A Glorious Revolution in English Psychiatry?', *Medical History*, xxix (1983), 35–50; and the references cited above, n. 2.

it was also an evangelical stratagem. The Methodists were notorious for preaching sermons that proclaimed the dangers posed by the devil and by witches. A vast amount of anecdotal evidence shows that many—perhaps most—of the common people continued firmly to believe in these malevolent forces throughout the eighteenth century. The spiritual world that Tudor and Stuart preachers had invoked remained the domain of plebeian religion long after it had been abandoned by the governing élite. There is, unsurprisingly, some evidence that suggests that old beliefs in the supernatural causes and consequences of self-murder also survived among many people of humble social standing. Thus the main divisions of opinion about the meaning of self-killing followed the same broad divisions of religious belief and cultural outlook that had been laid down in the struggles of the seventeenth century.

## CATO AND THE CODE OF HONOUR

The conviction that self-destruction was permissible and even laudable in certain circumstances was fortified more by the obsession with classical Rome than by philosophical argument. One measure of the force of neoclassical attitudes is the cult of Cato of Utica, the most famous of the Stoic suicides. Cato was a household god to the 'Augustan' upper classes.[6] Writing in the *Tatler* in 1709, Jonathan Swift dreams that he is transported to Elysium, where he witnesses a gathering of all the ancient worthies, including Cato, whom Lucan declares possesses 'more Merit than their whole Assembly' and whom Cicero praises in a vehement discourse.[7] Swift's admiration for Cato was unbounded—he even held him up to Stella as a model to follow in matters of honour:

> In Points of Honour to be try'd
> All Passions must be laid aside:
> Ask no Advice, but think alone,
> Suppose the Question not your own:
> How shall I act? is not the Case,
> But how would *Brutus* in my Place?

[6] J. W. Johnson, *The Formation of English Neoclassical Thought* (Princeton, 1967), 95–105; I. Donaldson, *The Rapes of Lucretia* (Oxford, 1982), 150, 191 n. 11, lists many other sources.

[7] A. Ross (ed.), *Selections from the Tatler and the Spectator* (Harmondsworth, 1982), [No. 81], 118. For the attribution of this essay to Swift, see Johnson, *Formation of Neoclassical Thought*, 279.

In such a Cause would *Cato* bleed?
And how would *Socrates* proceed?[8]

Cato achieved his apotheosis as a hero in England in Joseph Addison's hugely successful tragedy *Cato* (1713), which depicts his suicide as an act of pathetic, surpassing nobility. The play brought tears to Pope's eyes and captured the imagination of the crowd: 'Ministers and Oxford students, Grub Streeters and country rectors, squires and royal physicians, deans and printers—everyone saw something of himself in Cato and a great deal of Cato in himself.'[9] Lesser writers joined in adulating the Utican. Henry Dodwell, the non-juring theologian, had approved Cato's suicide in his defence of Cicero's philosophy, published over a decade before Addison's tragedy.[10] Immediately after *Cato* was performed, Lewis Theobald published a *Life and Character of Marcus Portius Cato Uticensis*, and a generation later he was memorialized in a biography of Cicero that Conyers Middleton wrote and Colley Cibber digested.[11] Nicholas Rowe's translation of Lucan's *Pharsalia*, one of the chief texts of the Cato cult, established Rowe's reputation as a poet.[12] The Whig enemies of Robert Walpole, John Trenchard and Thomas Gordon, employed the Roman martyr's name for the title of their famous *Cato's Letters* (thus by implication equating Walpole with the dictator, Caesar).

Cato's example was used to justify modern suicides from time to time. Most sweeping and extreme was Hume, who declared that: 'In all cases Christians and Heathens are precisely upon the same footing: *Cato* and *Brutus*, *Arrea* and *Portia* acted heroically; those who now imitate their example ought to receive the same praises from posterity.'[13] When the poetaster Eustace Budgell cast himself into the Thames in 1737, he left

[8] J. Swift, *Collected Poems of Jonathan Swift*, ed. J. Horrell (London, 1958), ii. 724, 'To Stella, Visiting Me', 11. 35–42.

[9] Johnson, *Formation of Neoclassical Thought*, 100. Addison's enthusiasm for Cato was long-standing. He had begun the play as an undergraduate, and he defended the Roman as a pattern of virtue in other publications as well: see, e.g., *The Spectator*, ed. D. F. Bond (Oxford, 1965), no. 349, iii. 299–300.

[10] H. Dodwell, 'An Apology of the Philosophical Writings of Cicero', in *Tully's Five Books de Finibus*, trans. S.P. (London, 1701), sects. 13–24. Dodwell doubted that Cato's death would excuse modern suicides, but his arguments and examples were so weighted that many classed this book as a defence of suicide.

[11] L. Theobald, *The Life and Character of Marcus Portius Cato Uticensis* (London, 1713); C. Cibber, *The Character and Conduct of Cicero, Considered, From the History of His Life, by the Reverend Dr. Middleton* (London, 1747), esp. pp. 71–2, 96–7, 131, 198; Johnson, *Formation of Neoclassical Thought*, 276–7 nn. 5, 9.

[12] Lucan, *Pharsalia*, trans. N. Rowe (London, 1721); Johnson, *Formation of Neoclassical Thought*, 98, 278–9 nn. 22, 26.

[13] D. Hume, 'On Suicide', in his *Of the Standard of Taste and Other Essays*, ed. J. W. Lenz (Indianapolis, Ind., 1965), 160.

behind one unfinished couplet to justify his deed:

What Cato did and Addison approved,
Cannot be wrong.[14]

Charles Moore complained in 1790 that this famous bit of doggerel 'has been caught up by many a suicide since the days of Budgell, to justify his own murder'.[15] George Gregory, the evening preacher of the Foundling Hospital, compared Clive of India, who killed himself in 1774, with Brutus and with Cato, whose suicides, he thought, could not be regarded as sinful.[16] *The Fair Suicide*, a dramatic monologue idealizing the death of a young lady deceived by her lover, climaxes with a paean to Cato, whose suicide justifies the speaker's decision to take her own life:

Long, long he strove to prop the sinking State,
And as 'gainst *Cesar*, so he strove 'gainst Fate:
Till with the vain, the glorious Labour tired,
He stabb'd himself Immortal—and expir'd!
Was this a Coward's Act? did this appear
A base inglorious, weak, and abject Fear?
No—'twas a gen'rous godlike great Disdain,
A Sense superior to the Vulgar Strain.[17]

As the poetaster declaims, Cato had killed himself to protest against the imposition of a dictatorial government: his example therefore had connotations that could easily be misconstrued. Alexander Pope opted for a more general reference to ennobling Roman suicides in his 'Elegy to the Memory of an Unfortunate Lady', a poem that may have inspired the vastly inferior *Fair Suicide*. Addressing the suicide's shade, he asks rhetorically:

Is it, in heav'n a crime to love too well?
To bear too tender, or too firm a heart,
To act a Lover's or a *Roman's* part?
Is there no bright reversion in the sky,
For those who greatly think, or bravely die?[18]

[14] *DNB*; *Gentleman's Magazine*, vii (1737), 315.
[15] Moore, *Full Inquiry into Suicide*, ii. 114.
[16] G. Gregory, *Essays Historical and Moral* (London, 1785), 341–2.
[17] *The Fair Suicide* (London, 1733), 9.
[18] A. Pope, *The Poems of Alexander Pope*, ed. J. Butt (New Haven, 1963), 262, ll. 6–10. This poem proved to be among Pope's most popular lyrics; it was set to music by Matthew Greene, and the song was published as a broadside in 1729. It was illustrated by William Blake, in a portrait of Pope: M. Mack, *Alexander Pope: A Life* (New York, 1988), 312–9, 325, 328, 331, 333.

Writing as *The Humourist*, Thomas Gordon was forced to qualify his condemnation of suicide with the admission that it was not forbidden by the Romans, 'nor did they apprehend any mischievous consequences from it to the Community in general'.[19] The greatest historian of the age, Edward Gibbon, not only praised Roman attitudes to suicide, he sneered that 'the precepts of the Gospel or the church have at length imposed a pious servitude on the minds of Christians, and condemn them to expect, without a murmur, the last stroke of disease or the executioner'.[20]

Admiration for Roman heroes and for Cato in particular was buoyed along by the educated élite's enthusiasm for aspects of Stoicism. The career of Stoicism in Georgian England has been somewhat misconstrued. In a famous essay R. S. Crane sought to demonstrate that the origins of the Romantic concept of the man of sentiment may be found in the growing rejection of Stoic beliefs about the dangers of the passions.[21] This is no doubt true, and we shall return to this theme when we discuss the opposition to the palliation of suicide. But Stoicism continued to enjoy great popularity through much, if not all, of the eighteenth century. Joanna Innes has rightly called attention to scholarly neglect of the Stoic tradition: it remained far more vital than has been generally recognized.[22] The Stoic injunction, 'Follow Nature', was, after all, the Enlightenment's motto.[23] Moral philosophers, the most notable of whom was Adam Smith, continued to find in Stoicism a source for their own views.[24] The virtues expounded by the Stoic philosophers —wisdom, justice, courage, and self-control—were immensely attractive to eighteenth-century polite society and had obvious affinities with the aristocratic code of honour.

[19] T. Gordon, *The Humourist: Being Essays upon Several Subjects*, i, 4th edn. (London, 1741), ii, 2nd edn. (London, 1735), ii. 135, 137–8. Mixed editions of this work seem to have been commonplace.

[20] E. Gibbon, *The Decline and Fall of the Roman Empire* (New York, n.d.), ii. 727; Moore, *Full Inquiry into Suicide*, ii. 71.

[21] R. S. Crane, 'Suggestions Toward a Geneaology of the "Man of Feeling"', *English Literary History*, i (1934), 205–30. See also, H. W. Sams, 'Anti-Stoicism in Seventeenth- and Early Eighteenth-Century England', *Studies in Philology*, xli (1944), 65–78.

[22] J. Innes, 'Jonathan Clark, Social History and England's "Ancien Regime"', *Past and Present*, no. 115 (1987), 182.

[23] B. Willey, *The Eighteenth Century Background* (New York, 1965), 14, 70, 85; P. Gay, *The Enlightenment: An Interpretation* (New York, 1966–9), i. 303–4. For the influence of Stoicism on French attitudes to suicide in the late 18th cent., see D. Outram, *The Body and the French Revolution* (Oxford, 1989), ch. 6.

[24] A. Smith, *The Theory of Moral Sentiments*, ed. D. D. Raphael and A. L. Macfie (Oxford, 1976), 5–6. Smith added a section on suicide, mildly objecting to the Stoic doctrine on it, to the 1790 edn.: 281–8.

Cato was the indisputable example of honourable suicide. Extolled with Brutus in Latin texts and translations that were the staple diet of young gentlemen, his death sanctioned the belief that suicide could be an honourable deed. Thanks to the pioneering work of Donna Andrew and subsequent studies by J. C. D. Clark and V. G. Kiernan, it is clear that the aristocratic code of honour continued to authorize violence as a means of preserving or regaining one's reputation throughout the eighteenth century. Although the nobility had been transformed from a military caste into a political élite in the sixteenth and seventeenth centuries, aristocratic values still retained a patina of militaristic chivalry after 1700. Perhaps this was partly the consequence of periodic warfare and of the resulting growth in the officer corps.[25] The militarism of the English élite, however, seems to have been more superficial than that of continental aristocracies, which were called upon frequently to defend their countries. 'A class detached from its original setting', Kiernan remarks astutely, 'is likely to adopt customs that present once serious occupations in a vestigial or emblematic form.' He observes that a fashionable portrait-painter in the late seventeenth century kept a suit of armour in his studio for his clients to don. The accoutrements of war had already become costumes for martial fantasies. Forms of address, the obsession with heraldry, and many other conventions of aristocratic manners mimed a feudal past long vanished. Mark Girouard has shown how these vestigial and slightly ridiculous conventions multiplied and intensified in the nineteenth century, when the English upper classes revived the code of chivalry as they imagined it must have been. Walter Scott's historical novels, extravagantly anachronistic paintings, country houses that mimic castles like movie sets made out of stone are the enduring artefacts of the Camelot craze. In 1839, Lord Eglinton actually staged a tournament at which the cream of the Tory aristocracy played at being medieval knights and ladies in driving rain.[26]

Not all of the survivals of chivalry were harmless absurdities. Honour and violence were still closely linked in the eighteenth century, and the form of violence most intimately connected with the aristocratic code was the duel. Duelling underwent a period of relative decline in the seventeenth century, caused as much by the spread of the rapier—a deadly weapon that made fighting exceedingly dangerous—as by gov-

25 D. T. Andrew, 'The Code of Honor and Its Critics: The Opposition to Duelling in England, 1700–1850', *Social History*, v (1980), 409–34; Clark, *English Society, 1688–1832*, 108–18; V. G. Kiernan, *The Duel in European History* (Oxford, 1988).

26 Kiernan, *The Duel*, 153; M. Girouard, *The Return to Camelot* (New Haven, 1981).

ernment pressure and legal prohibitions. But in the eighteenth century, duelling once more became commonplace; so much so that its finest historian asserts that it then achieved its apogee. The triumph of aristocratic culture, long stretches of peace, and the élite's obsessive desire to distinguish themselves from the mercantile classes and lesser gentry all contributed to the revival of duelling. So did the introduction of duelling pistols, weapons so inaccurate that the odds of either party dying in a fight fell to one in fourteen, the odds of being wounded to one in six.[27] Adherence to the code of honour was one of the signs that set a gentleman apart from the inferior ranks, and it remained the basis of aristocratic manners in the eighteenth century. 'The duel set the gentry class above all others', Kiernan writes, 'as possessing a courage and resolution no other could emulate, and a code of conduct none but it could live up to.'[28] The basic rule of honour, as Bernard Mandeville asserted, was that a gentleman should 'suffer no affront, which is a term of art for every Action designedly done to undervalue him'.[29] The duel served, as Andrew remarks, 'to settle infractions of the code of honour; it dispensed both judgment and execution in a single event'.[30]

Although no one openly advocated the practice, suicide could serve the same function as the duel among men of honour. It could erase the stain of disgrace or forestall further dishonour by proving both the suicide's courage and his commitment to the ethics of his class. Captain James Battersby, a violent and proud man, was so '*Tremblingly alive* to a sense of honour, he could not endure the least surmise of indignity'. He stabbed himself in 1785 after being arrested for fighting a duel, leaving behind a note that read:

> An Apology (if any there can be) for Suicide
> Death before dishonour.[31]

The duel was an elaborate performance, with a strict etiquette, and among men of fashion there was an etiquette for honourable suicide as well.[32] Naturally it was a much less elaborate code. Boreau Deslandes

[27] L. Stone, *The Crisis of the Aristocracy* (Oxford, 1965), 242–50; Kiernan, *The Duel*, 99, 101–2, 141–5.
[28] Kiernan, *The Duel*, 159.
[29] Quoted by Andrew, 'Code of Honour and Its Critics', 411.
[30] Ibid. 413.
[31] *Gentleman's Magazine*, lv (1785), 159.
[32] For the etiquette and psychology of duelling, see Kiernan, *The Duel*, chs. 8–9; Stone, *Crisis of the Aristocracy*. 244–6.

captured its essence when he remarked that 'there may be certain Instances wherein Suicide might be not only pardonable but glorious', provided that it was 'untinctur'd with either Brutality or Despair'.[33] To be honourable, in other words, a suicide had to be an act of cool resolution, a deed of calm reason rather than passionate impulse. A young man who had squandered a fortune that he had made in the East Indies showed that he knew how to die like a gentleman in 1784. After ruminating on his fate for several days, he 'conciliated his mind to that awful and horrible destiny, to which his proud spirit and precipitation had hurried him'. He wrote several letters, then took up a pistol and 'with the greatest composure', shot himself.[34]

In addition to displaying calm resolution, men of honour were supposed to choose a suitable method to kill themselves. The preferred instruments of death were the weapons of the duel, the pistol and the sword, although another kind of lethal implement might have to do in a pinch, such as a razor. Hanging was proscribed, just as it had been for the Romans.[35] Charles Moore heard a story that a 'man of consequence' had criticized another gentleman who had hanged himself: 'What a low-minded wretch, to apply the halter! Had he shot himself, like a gentleman, I could have forgiven him.'[36] The conventions of honourable suicide were observed with a fidelity that seems astonishing in retrospect. Peers, knights, and gentlemen made up less than 10 per cent of the reported suicides between 1660 and 1714, but they accounted for over 70 per cent of the shootings. Conversely, just under 20 per cent of them hanged themselves, but in all other classes two-thirds or more of suicides died by the rope. In 1798 the earl of Buckinghamshire made a list of thirty-five notables who had killed themselves since the mid-century. Sixteen had shot themselves with pistols; a couple had fallen on their swords; eight had used knives or razors. Only five had hanged them-

[33] A. F. Boreau Deslandes, *Dying Merrily; or, Historical and Critical Reflexions on the Conduct of Great Men Who, in Their Last Moments, Mock'd Death and Died Facetiously*, trans. T.W. (London, 1745). The first French edition of this book appeared in 1714. For an earlier English example of this genre, see C. Blount, *The Miscellaneous Works*, ed. Lindamour [C. Gildon](London, 1695), sigs. $A_6$–$A_{12}$. For a later one written in English and printed in London, see A. Radicati, count of Passerano, *A Philosophical Dissertation upon Death* (London, 1732), esp. 85–92.

[34] *Annual Register*, xxvii (1784), Chronicle, 209.

[35] Y. Grisé, *Le Suicide dans la Rome antique* (Montreal, 1982), 141–9. One wonders if in an age immersed in the classics there was not some conscious connection between the Roman proscription and the tastes of the *beau monde*.

[36] Moore, *Full Inquiry into Suicide*, i. 357. The tale was repeated a generation later by S. Piggott, *Suicide and its Antidotes: A Series of Anecdotes and Actual Narratives, with Suggestions on Mental Distress* (London, 1824), 174.

selves, and one of those was a woman, Lady Emma Long.[37] Men of quality, or those who merely pretended to gentility, knew that their failure to carry out the rites of honourable suicide would mean disgrace. Thomas Davers, who poisoned himself in 1767, complained bitterly that his poverty had deprived him of all the dignities of his rank, even the means to die like a gentleman:

> Of laudanum an ample dose,
> Must all my present ills compose:
> But the best laudanum of all
> I want (not resolution) but a ball.[38]

The conviction that there is a right way to kill oneself, depending on one's social status, has vanished from the modern world as class distinctions have gradually replaced status discriminations. The eighteenth century, with its dynamic capitalist economy, nevertheless preserved the traditional social hierarchy by integrating the landed élite, gentry, and merchant gentlemen culturally. To die like a gentleman mattered even to men who repudiated the world and fled expectations they could no longer endure.

The aristocratic code of honour had always disturbed Christian critics, and its use to justify duelling and suicide in the eighteenth century aroused intense criticism. Suicide and duelling were often equated in sermons and pamphlets opposing them both.[39] The connection was irresistible, since both actions involved losing or at least risking one's life for principles that one rated at a higher value than the Christian virtues of patience and hope. Both, moreover, seemed to critics to be clear violations of the Sixth Commandment. As the century progressed, however, attacks on duelling and suicide increasingly reflected bourgeois hostility to aristocratic mores. As Andrew argues persuasively, to middle-class critics duelling, suicide, and gambling formed a 'grand constellation of vice'—an interrelated set of sins that were authorized by the code of honour.[40] In retrospect, this line of attack seems palpably

[37] Buckinghamshire RO, D/MH, Private Papers, A 14. The others killed themselves in a variety of ways: drowning, jumping, swallowing brass nails.

[38] *Annual Register*, x (1767), 59; *Gentleman's Magazine*, xxxvii (1767), 93.

[39] See e.g., *Self-Murther and Duelling the Effects of Cowardice and Atheism* (London, 1728); *Duelling and Suicide Repugnant to Revelation, Reason, and Common Sense* (London, 1774); J. Herries, *An Address to the Public, On the Frequent and Enormous Crime of Suicide* (London, 1774), 29–30.

[40] D. T. Andrew, 'The Secularization of Suicide in England: A Comment', *Past and Present*, no. 119 (1988), 161–4; Clark, *English Society*, 106, 110–11. See also, Andrew, 'The Code of Honour and Its Critics'.

false. Many more poor people killed themselves than aristocrats; poverty was more frequently the motive for suicide than dissipation. Aristocratic suicide was an acute problem only from the perspective of a small and very self-regarding subculture. But it was, after all, a subculture that occupied the very heights of English society. It might be more accurate, though inelegant, to call it a 'superculture'. Critics attacked aristocratic suicide and hardly noticed the self-slaughter of the lower orders because of the contemporary conviction that it was the upper classes whose example determined the mores of the rest of society. In a popular book on the *Importance of the Manners of the Great to General Society*, for instance, Hannah More asserted: '*Their* example is the fountain from whence the vulgar draw their habits, actions and characters.'[41]

Perhaps the most devastating form of criticism that could be aimed at an order obsessed by pride of rank was ridicule. And the satirists wasted no time in mocking the aristocratic code of honour and the etiquette of suicide. William Withers was striving for a Swiftian effect when he proposed in 1711 to write a whole treatise on the '*Art of Suicide*'. 'In a Nation Renown'd as ours is, for such Great and frequent Examples of *Heroic Death*', he declaimed, 'as none of our Neighbours can boast of, no Body should yet have taken into Consideration the Miscarriages that often happen in so *Serious* an Affair, merely for want of a *Conduct*, answerable to our Native *Intrepidity*.' A conduct book for would-be suicides was urgently required; meanwhile the immediate needs of the most desperate may be served by recalling four rules. They ranged from choosing the most effective and least messy means of dying to writing a suicide note, so that your wife might have the pleasure of reading it in future.[42] The cynical satirist, the *Connoisseur*, was well aware that there was an etiquette of suicide, and he used that fact with devastating effectiveness in his criticism of the unequal application of the law: 'The poor sweating wretch, starving in a garret, tucks himself up in his last garters; a second, crossed in love, drowns himself, like a blind puppy, in *Rosamond's Pond*; and a third cuts his throat with his own rasor. But the man of fashion almost always dies by a pistol.'[43] Edward Moore, writing in the *World* a year later in 1756, was still more inventive. He proposed the establishment of a 'Receptacle for Suicides', a luxurious structure in whose 'convenient apartments' men and women of fashion could kill themselves in a manner suitable to their rank. Disappointed

41 Quoted in Clark, *English Society*, 104.
42 W. Withers, *Some Thoughts Concerning Suicide, Or Self-Killing* (London, 1711), 3.
43 [G. Colman and B. Thornton], *Connoisseur* (London, 1755), 297.

ladies could drown themselves in marble baths, fed with the purest spring water, gentlemen gamesters could shoot themselves with pistols charged with loaded dice; actors and actresses could choose to slay themselves with daggers or poison; gentlemen of the army might fall on swords fitted to the floor. And the generality of the middling classes could hang themselves at the Receptacle in a long room in which a range of halters had been placed and tied. The point of the joke was to call attention to pretensions that obscured the real horror of suicidal death: 'The disfiguring pistol, the slow stupefaction of laudanum, the ignominious rope, the uncertain garter, the vulgarity of the new river, and the fetid impurity of Rosamond's pond.'[44]

Other satirists assailed the motives rather than the means that typified aristocratic suicide. Taking his cue from Montesquieu, John Brown sneered at those who justified English suicides with Roman examples: 'The Roman killed himself, because he had been unfortunate in *War*; the *Englishman*, because he hath been unfortunate at Whist: The *old* Hero, because he had *disgraced* his *Country*; the *modern*, because he dare not show his head at *Arthur's*.'[45] The connection between gambling and aristocratic self-killing was not a polemical fiction. As we shall see in a later chapter, members of the governing élite channelled more and more of their competitiveness into the casinos as they became less accustomed to and less suited for the field of battle. All levels of society gambled feverishly in the eighteenth century, and this fuelled the conviction that luxury was one of the chief causes of suicide. The *Connoisseur*, for example, maintained that the true cause of self-destruction was despair 'brought on by wilful extravagance and debauchery'. He drew up a table of more specific causes, which he sardonically proposed should be the basis for a Bill of Suicide that would be issued in addition to the regular Bills of Mortality:

Of Newmarket Races
Of Kept Mistresses
Of Lotteries
Of French Claret, French Lace, French Cooks, and French Disease
Of a Country Seat
Of a Town House
Of Fortune Hunting
Of a Tour thro' France and Italy
Of Lord Bolingbroke
Of an Equipage
Of Covent Garden
Of Plays, Operas, Concerts, Routes, Drums, etc.
Of keeping the best Company[46]

44 [E. Moore], *World*, no. 193 (16 Sept. 1756), 1161–2.

45 J. Brown, *An Estimate of the Manners and Principles of the Times* (London, 1757), 95.

46 [Colman and Thornton], *Connoisseur*, 299–300.

The dissenter Caleb Fleming offered a comprehensive list of the evils that promoted and accompanied self-destruction. 'Levity, luxury, impiety, and enormous vice, have been the guilty cause which has brought upon us these formidable evils:' suicide, unemployment, high prices, emigration, starvation, gambling, a crisis in public credit, and debauchery among the rich.[47] John Herries made the connection between increasing luxury and rising rates of suicide as compellingly as he could: 'As the luxury and depravity of the age seem to be rising to a crisis', he wrote in 1774, 'so *Suicide*, the offspring of hell, the dire attendant of guilt, remorse and despair, begins to infect, by its baleful influence, more unhappy votaries than ever.'[48] On one level such criticisms were indisputable; but they also ignored the fact that the vast majority of people who killed themselves were the victims of circumstances they could not control rather than of the temptations of excessive wealth.

It is easy to see why the *bon ton*'s suicidal habits inspired revulsion among clerics and middle-class moralists. But it is equally important to recognize that they sometimes also aroused pity and sorrow, emotions grounded in admiration and empathy. Thus the fashionable socialite, Fanny Braddock, who killed herself at Bath in 1731, was described as a lady universally mourned, who had been esteemed in her lifetime for her genteel behaviour and good sense. Braddock was at first criticized, albeit mildly, for being 'a great admirer of that hazardous Dependence, Gambling', but the tale of her death was embellished in the retelling until it was eventually transformed into a sort of sentimental melodrama.[49] George Hesse, a friend and companion of the prince of Wales who shot himself in 1788 after sustaining a 'shock of the most momentous nature' at the gaming tables, was not reproached at all. Hesse had met the prince in about 1785 and soon came to share his riotous and ruinous company. In June 1788, after a night of gaming at Philimore's, an establishment the prince himself had recently founded after other casinos objected to the behaviour of some of his entourage, Hesse returned home, wrote five letters, and shot himself with a pistol. The papers were elegiac. Despite *The Times*'s hostility to suicide in general, its reporter recounted his life and death without a critical word. He describes Hesse as a gay, vivacious man, whose 'wonted display of spirits' was eclipsed when he realized the

[47] C. Fleming, *A Dissertation upon the Unnatural Crime of Self-Murder* (London, 1773), sig. A1.

[48] Herries, *An Address on Suicide*, 6.

[49] *Fog's Weekly Journal*, no. 150 (18 Sept. 1731); *Gentleman's Magazine*, i (1731), 396; J. Wood, *A Description of Bath, 1765* (Bath, 1969), 447–53.

magnitude of his financial calamity. His good humour had returned just before his suicide, when his mood was 'as if he were deliberately determined to meet a fate, which every one who knew him must pathetically lament—and those who knew him not, sincerely pity'. His friends and acquaintances, the paper concludes, have been 'touched to the extreme of social sensibility' by his loss, for he 'had the universal testimony of a worthy report'.[50]

## ROMANTIC SUICIDE

The worship of Cato waned after the mid-century, although it did not disappear altogether. A new sensibility that placed a higher value on the passions and imagination than had neoclassical writers made his Stoic fortitude seem less attractive to many members of polite society. Romanticism, however, did not arrest the trend toward sympathetic treatments of suicide: to the contrary, it sentimentalized self-destruction. The supreme example is known to everyone. The huge success of Goethe's *Sorrows of Young Werther* (1774) prompted imitations of the tragic suicide with which it ends in art and life. Writers all over Europe produced cloying scenes of lovelorn youths killing themselves.[51] English poets penned verses transforming an already sentimental story into sheer bathos. Charlotte Smith, aroused perhaps by the fact that she shared the Christian name of Goethe's heroine, produced no fewer than five poems on the subject. Speaking in the voice of doomed Werther in one of them, she exlaims:

> By those, who know the force of hopeless care
> On the worn heart, I sure shall be forgiven,
> If to elude dark guilt and dire despair,
> I go uncall'd—to mercy and to heaven![52]

Many people worried that *Werther* seemed to be a thoroughgoing defence of romantic suicide. But others took the opportunity to amplify that tendency far beyond anything Goethe may have intended. Robert Merry's 'Elegy Written after Having Read The Sorrows of Werther' claimed that there was 'a class distinct' of persons whose emotions were

50 *The Times*, no. 1091 (5 June 1788), 4. See also no. 1090 (4 June 1788), 3.

51 S. P. Atkins, *The Testament of Werther* (Cambridge, Mass., 1949).

52 Quoted in Moore, *Full Inquiry into Suicide*, ii. 151–2. For many other examples, see Atkins, *Testament of Werther*, chs. 2, 5.

so exquisite that their suicides were excused and even pitied by the Lord himself:

> Th'Eternal Pow'r, to whom all thoughts arise,
> Who ev'ry secret sentiment can view,
> Melts at their flowing tears, their swelling sighs,
> Then gives them force to bid the world adieu.[53]

The *Werther* mania spread so rapidly through the reading public that four different English translations were issued between 1779 and 1799, and three more were published in the first decade of the nineteenth century.[54] It was widely alleged that many real men and women were following Werther's example. And perhaps the critics were right about some deaths. According to the *Gentleman's Magazine* for example, a young woman was discovered in November 1784, dead by her own hand, with a copy of *Werther* under her pillow.[55]

The zenith of sentimental suicide in England, however, was the massive effusion of emotion that followed the death of the poet Thomas Chatterton in 1770. A boy of only seventeen when he poisoned himself in squalid poverty, Chatterton's dazzling skills as a poet and the notoriety that surrounded his forgeries of medieval verse made him an irresistible symbol of tragic genius. Within months of Chatterton's death, commemorative verses appeared. But the incident became the stuff of legend after Herbert Croft interpolated Chatterton's story into his epistolary pot-boiler, *Love and Madness* (1780).[56] Croft had purloined the poet's letters to his sister, and he used them to embellish the tale of Martha Reay's murder at the hands of James Hackman, who attempted suicide immediately after shooting her. Croft glosses over Chatterton's actual suicide—'But who can bear to dwell upon, or argue about, the self-destruction of such a being as Chatterton?'—and passes on to pure panegyric, describing in pathetic terms the room in which he died and paralleling his life and poetical gifts with Milton's in a long, incredible passage.[57] *Love and Madness* was a huge best-seller, mostly because Miss Reay's murder and Hackman's trial had created a sensation in London

[53] Quoted in Atkins, *Testament of Werther*, 37.

[54] O. W. Long, 'English Translations of Goethe's Werther', *Journal of English and Germanic Philology*, xiv (1915), 169–203.

[55] Andrew, 'Secularization of Suicide', 159. See also *Gentleman's Magazine*, liv (1784), 964, for the suicide of a Dutch officer committed in 'a similar circumstance'.

[56] H. Croft, *Love and Madness* (London, 1780), 125–244.

[57] Ibid. 197–9, 235–9.

society.[58] By linking the two tales, the *crime passionnel* of the age and the boy genius's suicide, Croft ensured the success of his book. He also planted the seeds of Chatterton's posthumous fame.

Chatterton's legend flourished like a poppy in a hot climate. It was watered by the maudlin tears shed for Werther after Goethe's novel was published. One of its translators, echoing Robert Merry, declared that Werther's 'feelings, like those of our Chatterton, were too fine to support the load of accumulated distress'.[59] Philip Thicknesse erected a monument to him on his estate, complete with an inscription taken from Vicesimus Knox, a saccharine author. Artists represented his wretched life, his final despair, and even his suicide itself. As early, perhaps, as 1775, John Flaxman produced a drawing of *Chatterton Drinking from the Cup of Despair*, an allegory in which a rather plump, Grecian Chatterton accepts a bowl of poison from a grotesque figure armed with knives and ropes. About 1780 Flaxman also drew a design for a monument to Chatterton.[60] But the most amazing image of the suicide is a piece of pure kitsch: an engraving of Chatterton composing in his garret was transferred on to a souvenir handkerchief in 1782. 'Hard indeed', part of its long caption runs, 'was his fate, born to adorn the times in which he lived, yet compelled to fall a victim to pride and poverty! His destiny, cruel as it was, gives a charm to his verses, and ... the recollection of his miseries awakens a tender sympathy and sorrow.'[61] All of the English Romantics celebrated Chatterton's genius and lamented his tragic death; Keats, the boy wonder among them, dedicated *Endymion* to his memory. Coleridge eulogized him in his first major poem, his 'Monody on the Death of Chatterton', and Wordsworth made him immortal as

> Chatterton, the marvellous Boy,
> The sleepless Soul that perished in its pride.[62]

Chatterton mania continued well into the nineteenth century. The

[58] *DNB*, s.v. 'Hackman, James'; *Gentleman's Magazine*, il (1779), 210, 212–3; J. Boswell, *Life of Johnson*, ed. R. W. Chapman and J. D. Fleeman (Oxford, 1980), 1018–19; Croft, *Love and Madness*, 1–125, 244–96.

[59] Quoted in Moore, *Full Inquiry into Suicide*, i. 141–2.

[60] K. Z. Cieszkowski, 'The Legend Makers: Chatterton, Wallis and Meredith', *History Today*, xxxii (Nov. 1982), 35–6.

[61] E. H. W. Meyerstein, *A Life of Thomas Chatterton* (London, 1930), 475–6, plate facing p. 476.

[62] Ibid., chs. 18–20, *passim*; L. Kelly, *The Marvellous Boy: The Life and Myth of Thomas Chatterton* (London, 1971), chs. 8–12; W. Wordsworth, 'Resolution and Independence', ll. 43–4, in S. Gill (ed.), *The Oxford Authors: William Wordsworth* (Oxford, 1984), 262.

glorification of a contemporary suicide could not have been more complete.[63]

The ground had been worked for the romantic stereotype of suicide by the so-called 'graveyard poets' of the mid-century. Their morbid fascination with death and taste for melancholy were immensely popular. Edward Young's relentlessly gloomy *Night Thoughts* was among the most admired poems of the age. Robert Blair, the author of 'The Grave', and Thomas Warton, who wrote 'The Suicide' in 1771, were also greatly esteemed. None of these poets condoned suicide, but the sentimentalization of death inspired pity for self-slayers and eroded the revulsion that suicide had formerly inspired. Warton's poem is an ironic illustration of this trend. In the first part of the ode the poet meditates on the grave of a youth, describing his suicide and attributing it to penury and unrequited love. His fancy magnified his misery, filling 'his soft ingenuous mind | With many a feeling too refin'd'. No matter, Warton concludes this part of the poem, that the youth's death deprived him of funerary rites and monuments, the muses will ensure that his memory is preserved:

> Pity shall woo the weeping nine,
> To build a visionary shrine,
> Hung with unfading flowers, from fairy regions brought.

Having created a mood of sentimental grief, Warton recalls himself to his duty as a clergyman:

> Forbear, fond bard, thy partial praise;
> Nor thus for guilt in specious lays
> The wreath of glory twine.

Several stanzas emphasizing man's divine obligation to live out his allotted time and endure afflictions patiently close the poem. But the opposition of sentiment and moral imperatives is made perfectly plain in this poem; and the power of 'specious lays' to make readers forget that suicide is an irreligious crime is demonstrated even as it is deplored.[64]

A good many other poets neglected the sermon Warton appended to his depiction of sentimental suicide. Anna Seward, 'the Swan of Lichfield', described one of her mawkish lamentations on the death of her beautiful friend Honora Sneyde, as 'written in a summer evening, from

[63] For full treatments of the Chatterton legend, see Meyerstein, *Life of Chatterton*, ch. 20; Kelly, *The Marvellous Boy*, chs. 8–15; Cieszkowski, 'Legend Makers'; L. J Kaplan, *The Family Romance of the Imposter-Poet Thomas Chatterton* (New York, 1988), esp. chs. 1, 9.

[64] T. Warton, 'The Suicide', in *The Works of the British Poets*, ed. Robert Anderson (London, 1794), xi. 1070.

the grave of a suicide'.[65] Eleanor Sickels, surveying eighteenth-century verse, describes the fundamental change in attitudes to melancholy in poetry as a shift 'from intellectual generalization and restrained sentiment to intensely imaginative subjectivity'.[66] This is, of course, merely to say that the decline of neoclassicism and rise of romanticism are reflected in the poetry of gloom. And although no one wished to promote suicide, the elevation of feeling as a primary aesthetic value was essentially at odds with traditional moral judgements. This was especially obvious in works about blighted love-affairs, for love-suicide had always been judged in literature by the ethics of courtly love rather than Christian theology. Sickels comments that not many bereaved lovers killed themselves in eighteenth-century poetry, in spite of Werther's example. But she herself points to a half-dozen instances in which star-crossed lovers kill themselves, the tragic climax of their pathetic stories. She recounts as well a significant anecdote about the popular poet and dramatist Frank Sayers. In the original edition of his 'Moina', the bard kills himself when he learns that his mistress has been sacrificed at her husband's funeral rites. A chorus of praise follows, depicting his death as a noble action. Later, Sayers struck these verses from a new edition of the poem, 'from excessive moral scrupulosity', his editor remarks, 'lest the praise of heroic suicide should perhaps operate dangerously in common life'.[67] The most interesting implication of Sayers's change of heart is the recognition it implies that literary depictions of suicide like the one in his drama encouraged identification and admiration at the expense of moral judgement.

Romantic suicide and suicide for love were not necessarily connected: Werther killed himself for love; Chatterton died for want of recognition. But the most conspicuous effect of the new ideal on attitudes to suicide was a revival of the tradition of tragic love-suicide. The papers abounded in tales of young men and women who had killed themselves because of unrequited love or whose parents had broken off their love-affairs.[68] The supreme love-suicide of the age was a failed attempt: Hackman's murder of Miss Reay and his attempted suicide. The tale was hyped and sentimentalized not merely by Croft but also by a host of even lesser writers and journalists. Admittedly, the story was almost too good to be true. Miss Reay was a star; she had been shot down as she emerged from a

65 Quoted in E. M. Sickels, *The Gloomy Egoist* (New York, 1932), 238.

66 Ibid. 3.

67 Ibid. 228.

68 Many of these are quoted and cited below, Chapters 8 and 9.

performance of (it is claimed) *Love in the Village*. Hackman had attempted to dispatch himself with a second pistol, which had misfired. He was captured by the crowd as he was trying to pulverize his skull with the pistol butt. At his trial, which was presided over by an unsympathetic William Blackstone, Hackman defended himself on the grounds that the pangs of unrequited love had overcome his reason. To prove that he had been insane and had gone to Covent Garden only to kill himself and not Miss Reay, he introduced as evidence a suicide note he had written to his brother-in-law, Frederick Booth:

> You know where my affections were placed; my having by some means or other lost her's (an idea which I could not support) has driven me to madness. The world will condemn me, but your good part will pity me. God bless you, my dear Fred. ... May Almighty God bless you and yours with comfort and happiness, and may you ever be a stranger to the pangs I now feel! May heaven protect my beloved woman, and forgive me this act, which alone could relieve me of the world of misery I have long endured! Oh! if it should ever be in your power to do her any act of friendship, remember your faithful friend, J. Hackman.

The plea did not work: Hackman was condemned and hanged at Tyburn. But his suicide note was printed everywhere, and his tragic devotion to Miss Reay attracted widespread sympathy, some of it from notable observers. Boswell, who attended the trial, seems to have believed Hackman's defence, for he describes him as 'the unfortunate Mr. Hackman' who had acted 'in a fit of frantick jealous love'. Samuel Johnson, who shared Blackstone's severer judgement, got into a verbal brawl with his friend Topham Beauclerk over Hackman's guilt. Croft, of course, presented the tragedy in the most pathetic terms.[69]

A positively Wertherian incident was reported by *The Times* in 1789. It, too, aroused the pity of the town. A beautiful young girl named Eleanor Johnson, just seventeen years old, poisoned herself in her master's house. She had been in love with a black man named, ironically, Thomas Cato. He had, it was learned, sent her a letter, accusing her of deceit; she, in turn, had written to him even as she felt the effects of the poison snuff out her life:

> The letter I received this evening makes me very unhappy, to think you should ... say I am deceitful and forget my fond embraces so soon; no, my dear, I am not deceitful, nor did not intend to be—if I had, I should not have given my company to one not of my own colour. ... Was you the finest man that ever my

[69] *DNB*, s.v. 'Hackman, James'; *Gentleman's Magazine*, il (1779), 210, 212–13; Boswell, *Life of Johnson*, 1018–19; Croft, *Love and Madness*.

eyes beheld, after using me in this manner, I would not make you my husband; but I did intend it, from my heart, even to this hour—but I am sorry to say, I shall never be married, nor ever shall enjoy anything more again. ... I am very sure the hour of immortality is drawing very near—I can feel my heart decay very fast—you could not make me recompence for the hurt you have done me with the words of your cruel letter, was you to die at my feet.—One favour I beg of you is, if not too much trouble, to see me after I am dead, as I shall not live to be married, or even see another day.—Let these few words be printed in your heart, as I am not able to write any more—for my eyes are flowing with tears—and my heart doth ach [*sic*] so, I cannot hold my pen—but am your sincere well-wisher—'till death—E. Johnson.

The paper claimed that when he was examined by the jury, 'the Black appeared so ignorant and illiterate' nothing could be learned from him. He must have had the fatal letter written by a scribe. When he heard Eleanor's epistle read to him he wept bitterly.[70]

This story was almost as sensational as the murder of Miss Reay. The readership of *The Times* could not resist the obvious literary parallel, and one letter-writer used her suicide note to criticize affected sentiment, contrasting her unlearned, and hence natural, expressions of emotion, with the literati's polished, and hence artificial, passion: 'Poor ELEANOR JOHNSON's last dying letter to her OTHELLO Thomas Cato, is replete with all the rudeness of unlettered sensibility—a sensibility infinitely more affecting than all the refining elegance of unfeeling *sentiment*!'[71] *The Times*, forgetting for a moment its campaign to stiffen the laws against suicide, complimented the jury for bringing her in *non compos mentis* 'after a very humane and attentive consideration'.[72] Indeed, the effect of Eleanor Johnson's tale on the London public was so great that it precipitated two public debates on the causes of suicide, and more specifically, whether it proceeded from 'disappointment in the tender passion'. Announcing the second, *The Times* remarked, 'Those who have heard of the late suicide, committed by the unhappy girl, who was in love with the Mulatto, together with other similar cases, ... will allow this subject to have a very high claim to public attention.'[73]

## CAUSES OF CHANGE

It is easier to detect the growth of tolerant attitudes to suicide among the

[70] *The Times*, no. 1268 (28 Sept. 1789), 3.
[71] Ibid., no. 1271 (1 Oct. 1789), 3.
[72] Ibid., no. 1268 (28 Sept. 1789), 3.
[73] Ibid., no. 1300 (4 Nov. 1789), 3; no. 1307 (12 Nov. 1789), 3.

governing classes than it is to explain them. In his excellent study of attitudes to death in eighteenth-century France, John McManners argues that the reluctance of authorities there to enforce the law against suicide was a manifestation of Enlightenment humanitarianism.[74] Although there is no doubt that much of the discussion of suicide in England was suffused with the most advanced philosophical opinions of the day, the secularization of suicide there was a more complex and revealing cultural change than it seems to have been in France. The attitude of the English élite to suicide in the eighteenth century cannot accurately be described as humanitarian. Very few people openly advocated the liberalization of the law against suicide. French lawyers were apparently reluctant to exact the full penalties for self-murder. In England, in contrast, the leading legal authorities of the day protested against the lenient interpretation of psychiatric evidence.[75] Most importantly, the law of suicide remained unchanged throughout the eighteenth century, and a minority of suicides continued to be declared *felones de se* and subjected to all the old punishments. The English élite's attitude to suicide became more tolerant, but toleration had limits that were inconsistent with the humanitarianism of the *philosophes*.

The resistance of English lawmakers to reform is especially notable when one compares them with their counterparts elsewhere. In France, the law of suicide was strengthened in the late seventeenth century, but it was enforced very rarely in the eighteenth. Legal pronouncements made it increasingly difficult to carry out the rites of desecration, and they were abolished in 1770. Suicide was decriminalized altogether in 1791.[76] In Geneva the last example of dragging the corpse of a suicide through the streets occurred in 1732. The old law remained in force until 1792, but the city officials declared in 1735 that all suicides were insane, and so to be spared punishment, except those who killed themselves after they had been sentenced to death. 'La bonne Philosophie', remarked the Procurator General, 'a contribué à adoucir cet usage de rigueur.'[77] But

[74] J. McManners, *Death and the Enlightenment* (Oxford, 1981), ch. 12.

[75] M. Hale, *Historia placitorum coronae: The History of Pleas of the Crown*, ed. S. Emlyn, G. Wilson, and T. Dougherty (London, 1800), i. 412; R. Burn, *The Justice of the Peace, and Parish Officer*, ed. C. Durnford and J. King, 21st edn. (London, 1810), s.v. 'homicide'; Blackstone, *Commentaries on the Laws of England*, iv. 189. See also, Umfreville, *Lex coronatoria*, 127–8 and the discussion in Ch. 4, above.

[76] A Bayet, *Le Suicide et la morale* (Paris, 1922), 666–76, 704. Dorinda Outram points out that the fiscal penalties for suicide were restored briefly, between 1793 and 1795: Outram *The Body and the French Revolution* (New Haven, 1989), 91.

[77] L. Haeberli, 'Le Suicide à Genève au XVIII$^{e}$ siècle', in *Pour une histoire qualitative* (Geneva, 1975), 126–27.

the most pertinent contrast, perhaps, was with America. Most of the colonies initially adopted the traditional English punishments, although some of them restricted forfeiture. Pennsylvania and Delaware effectively abolished forfeiture in 1701, and after the American Revolution, inspired by the writings of the *philosophes*, Maryland and New Jersey decriminalized suicide in their new constitutions. Thomas Jefferson, in an unsuccessful attempt to bring about a sweeping reform of the criminal law of Virginia, cited Beccaria to justify the abolition of forfeiture and went on to provide a philosophical and practical argument against punishing suicide. Noting that the law was seldom applied by juries because 'men in general . . . disapprove of this severity', he declared, 'Let it then be done away.'[78]

In England, therefore, the humanitarian arguments of the *philosophes* had less influence on the men who made laws than they did elsewhere. Medical opinion certainly provided the main rationale for suspending the old penalties for suicide. Adam Smith added a passage to his refutation of philosophical arguments in favour of suicide declaring:

> There is, indeed, a species of melancholy ... which seems to be accompanied with, what one may call, an irresistible appetite for self-destruction. ... The unfortunate persons who perish in this miserable manner, are the proper objects, not of censure, but of commiseration. To attempt to punish them, when they are beyond the reach of human punishment, is not more absurd than it is unjust.[79]

And yet once again the evidence for direct influence is surprisingly sparse. So far as we have been able to discover, only one eighteenth-century medical writer advocated the suspension of the law on the grounds that suicide was an act of lunacy. 'Everyone who commits suicide is indubitably *non compos mentis*', wrote William Rowley in 1788, 'and therefore suicide should ever be considered an act of insanity.'[80]

Rowley's approval of juries' merciful practice was unique; his complete lack of interest in what *kind* of insanity prompted suicide was typical. The physicians made no notable contributions to the understanding of suicide in the late seventeenth and eighteenth centuries. When they mentioned the subject at all, they were content to repeat the Renaissance commonplace that melancholy (sometimes rechristened the

[78] K. Burgess-Jackson, 'The Legal Status of Suicide in Early America: A Comparison with the English Experience', *Wayne Law Review*, xxix (1982), 63–6, 78–9; T. Jefferson, *The Papers of Thomas Jefferson*, ii, ed. J. P. Boyd (Princeton, 1950), 496.

[79] Smith, *Theory of Moral Sentiments*, 287.

[80] W. Rowley, *A Treatise on Female, Nervous, Hysterical, Hypochondriacal, Bilious, Convulsive Diseases ... With Thoughts on Madness, Suicide, &c* (London, 1788), 343.

vapours or the spleen) often led to self-destruction.[81] Richard Blackmore, for instance, remarked in his best-selling *Treatise of the Spleen and Vapours* that when melancholy patients 'through great Despondency and Inquietude, discover Marks of a Design upon their own Lives, their Distemper exceeds its proper Nature and Extent, and has contracted a Degree of Lunacy'.[82] The chief difference between the treatment of the psychiatric causes of suicide before and after the Civil War is that later writers no longer insisted that its medical causes, such as melancholy, might be amplified by supernatural ones, namely Satan and his minions. Except for clerical writers, Georgian authors who discussed the medical psychology of suicide assumed that its causes were entirely physical or psychological. Even very pious doctors like the famous George Cheyne no longer invoked the devil as the author of self-murder after 1700.[83]

It is notable as well that the medical and philosophical arguments for tolerating suicide contradicted one another. Medical apologists presumed that suicide was the action of a demented person; anyone who committed it was therefore innocent of his own murder because he was insane. Philosophical apologists argued that suicide was sometimes permissible because it could be defended as a rational course of action in certain circumstances. Juries acted increasingly on the former assumption while the press and pamphleteers debated the correctness of the latter point of view. The contradiction was apparent to contemporaries. Declaring in 1779 that the practice of excusing suicides as lunatics 'strikes severely against that pretended philosophy which some men have asserted as a justification of suicide', one commentator explained: 'The law, therefore, supported by reason, determines that suicide is an act of lunacy (another term for cowardice) and that he who commits it was [*sic*] void of reason and philosophy at the time.'[84]

The reasons why élite opinion grew more tolerant in the eighteenth century thus cannot be discovered solely by reading philosophical and medical texts. The views that they expounded were not accepted fully, nor were they consistent with each other. And yet the ruling classes certainly did embrace a more tolerant and secularized attitude to suicide

[81] Medical writings on melancholy are usefully discussed in C. A. Moore, *Backgrounds of English Literature, 1700–1760* (Minneapolis, 1953), ch. 5, and J. F. Sena, 'The English Malady: The Idea of Melancholy from 1700 to 1760', Ph.D. thesis (Princeton, 1967).

[82] R. Blackmore, *A Treatise of the Spleen and Vapours* (London, 1725), 163.

[83] G. Cheyne, *The English Malady; or, a Treatise of Nervous Diseases of All Kinds*, 3rd edn. (London, 1734), esp. pp. ii–iii.

[84] *The Case and Memoirs of the Late Rev. Mr. James Hackman ... And Also Some Thoughts on Lunacy and Suicide* (London, 1779), 25–6.

that was a kind of refracted image of contemporary philosophical and medical thought. They were, we believe, conditioned by historical experience to accept ideas that were free from the taint of religious zeal and superstition, even though they did not subscribe whole-heartedly to the sceptical conclusions and the reforming programme of the *philosophes*. All over western Europe in the eighteenth century, governing élites were sick of religious strife and eager to find new and less controversial grounds for intellectual and social discourse. This was particularly true in England, where the events of the Puritan Revolution left a lasting impression on the governing classes. Reflecting in 1790 on the historical origins of 'liberal opinions' about suicide, Charles Moore traced them back to the reaction against the 'affectation of piety and bigotry of puritanism in Cromwell's days', which had led to 'the opposite extreme of licentious and atheistical principles' in the Restoration. The victorious supporters of the crown regarded 'the presence of God anywhere, or his concern at human actions, a mere bugbear and puritanical chimera; and hence in order to get rid of superstition and bigotry, they fell prey to infidelity and practical atheism'. Improvements in 'useful learning' and the establishment of religion on a rational basis subsequently tempered the infidelity of the age: 'the extremes of atheistical licentiousness were equally avoided by the pious and rational believer'. But scepticism and infidelity did not disappear altogether in the eighteenth century. 'Free thinking' and 'liberal principles', which culminated in defences of suicide like David Hume's notorious essay, were in reality 'neither more nor less than freedom from the restraints of virtue and religion'.[85]

Moore's analysis of the cultural changes that fostered new attitudes to suicide is perceptive in spite of its obvious tendentiousness. The ruling élite's horror of religious fanaticism after the Restoration coincided with new developments in philosophy and science and encouraged among educated laymen a 'hankering after the bare Mechanical causes of things'.[86] However violently they quarrelled in the late seventeenth and early eighteenth centuries, the contending parties in church and state were united in their hatred of religious radicals and Catholics.[87] For over a century after 1660 Establishment propagandists denounced 'enthusiasm' and 'superstition' as subversive forces that endangered English

[85] Moore, *Full Inquiry Into Suicide*, ii. 68–70. See also *Spectator*, iv. 117.

[86] H. Halliwell, *Melampronoea; or a Discourse of the Polity and Kingdom of Darkness* (London, 1681), 77–8.

[87] G. Holmes, *Religion and Party in Late Stuart England*, Historical Association Pamphlet G.86 (London, 1975); G. R. Cragg, *From Puritanism to the Age of Reason* (Cambridge, 1950), esp. 64.

society. The enemies of enthusiasm and superstition saw one similarity between the sectarians and the papists: they both claimed miraculous gifts. Enthusiasts believed that they were divinely inspired and felt the motions of God and the devil in their hearts; Catholic priests were bogus conjurers and exorcists. It was therefore essential to discredit the presumption that good and evil spirits intervened directly and frequently in human affairs. Modern claims to inspiration were dismissed as the symptoms of mental or physical illnesses; natural causes were adduced for the pious emotions of the enthusiasts and the spiritual afflictions that they and the papists were supposed to alleviate.[88] The scientific arguments advanced by the champions of orthodoxy were not impressive, but they were lent greater plausibility by the achievements of natural philosophers and the support of the church hierarchy. Despite the anxieties of men such as Joseph Glanvill, who feared that the reaction against enthusiasm had gone too far, scientism and rational religion prevailed and scepticism about spiritual phenomena became more and more commonplace among the governing classes after the Restoration.[89]

Once the equation of suicide and madness had become a ruling-class shibboleth, it was inevitable that religious zealots would be blamed for causing suicide as well as for spreading melancholy and lunacy. The Methodists were the commonest target for such charges. A Tory mouthpiece, the *Norwich Gazette*, reporting the suicide of a poor woman in 1743, added that 'her Brains were turned by Balls the Methodist'.[90] People believed this sort of propaganda. The Anglican controversialist John Jones developed an overpowering hatred for the evangelical, John Berridge. He believed that Berridge was a Methodist, and objected to his

[88] See the works cited above, n. 2.

[89] J. Glanvill, *Saducismus triumphatus; or, Full and Plain Evidence Concerning Witches and Apparitions*, ed. C. O. Parsons (Gainesville, Fla., 1966); M. Hunter, *Science and Society in Restoration England* (Cambridge, 1981), ch. 7. This is obviously a very simplified explanation of an enormously complex change. For alternative views see, in addition to Hunter, Thomas, *Religion and Magic*, chs. 18–22; C. Webster, *From Paracelsus to Newton* Cambridge, 1982); B. J. Shapiro, *Probability and Certainty in Seventeenth-Century England* (Princeton, 1983), esp. chs. 1–3, 6. In a characteristically stimulating article, Christopher Hill has demonstrated that some of the religious radicals later denounced as enthusiasts were, paradoxically, materialists or mortalists: 'Irreligion in the "Puritan" Revolution', in J. F. McGregor and B. Reay (eds.), *Radical Religion and the English Revolution* (Oxford, 1984), 199, 201–4. This current of radical thought was largely ignored by Establishment propagandists after the Restoration, and it is difficult to estimate what influence it may have had on the common people, or indeed how representative it was. Mortalism obviously precluded belief in ghosts, an integral ingredient in traditional ideas about suicide. For the decline of ghost-beliefs, see Thomas, *Religion and Magic*, 587–606.

[90] *Norwich Gazette*, 20–7 Aug. 1743.

'enthusiastical career'—his vigorous campaign of open-air preaching. Jones accused Berridge of driving his auditors to distraction and madness. As his anger rose, so did his charges. 'Within these 8 or 9 weeks', he wrote to a physician friend, 'no fewer than eight of his auditors have on ye account of his doctrines, destroyed themselves', four of them on the same day. He found a ready audience for his slander: the physician responded with stories of two females who 'left this Life by the Help of Water and Hemp', the 'genuine fruits' of enthusiasm.[91] In 1751 the papers published a bizarre story that in order to prove a Methodist couple who hanged themselves were insane their relatives produced a version of the New Testament the man had written out in his own blood. The tale was reprinted in the *Gentleman's Magazine,* polite society's *arbiter elegantiae*.[92]

Charges in the Establishment press that the Methodists were responsible for frequent suicides were redoubled later in the century. They seem to have been especially commonplace in the 1780s and 1790s. Quoting the Right Reverend Bench in 1788, *The Times* remarked that the Methodists had founded no fewer than sixteen 'religious shops' in Lambeth and there were Sunday 'tub orators' in St George's Fields. 'To the doctrines of those places', the article continued, 'are to be attributed the numerous suicides committed in and about London.'[93] Two years later, the *Morning Herald* sarcastically denounced John Wesley's belief that suicide might be reduced if the people who committed it were publicly disgraced: 'The pious John Wesley has proposed a remedy for *suicide*, by *gibbeting* the unhappy victim of despondency. Would not a total extirpation of the gloomy and absurd tenets of Methodism be much more conducive to that purpose?'[94] The press also continued to repeat allegations that specific suicides and attempted suicides had been caused by Methodism or another variety of religious enthusiasm.[95] Accusations

[91] Dr Williams's Library, Jones Papers, 39 B. 24, nos. 15–17, 19, 21. From these papers, it appears that Berridge may have served as Jones's curate at some point. For both, see *DNB*, s.v. 'Berridge, John' and 'Jones, John'; for Berridge, see also Rupp, *Religion in England*, 479–80.

[92] *Gentleman's Magazine*, xxi (1751), 183. See also, ibid., 183; 17 (1747), 398; D. Jarrett, *England in the Age of Hogarth* (London, 1976), 185–6.

[93] *The Times*, no 1063 (3 May 1788), 3. See also, ibid., no. 1092 (6 June 1788), 2; no. 1738 (19 July 1790), 3.

[94] Quoted in L. Radzinowicz, *A History of English Criminal Law and its Administration from 1750* (New York, 1948), i. 217 n. 54.

[95] See e.g. *The Times*, no. 469 (23 June 1786); 2; no. 478 (4 July 1786), 3; no. 1061 (1 May 1788), 3; no. 1118 (8 July 1788), 4; no. 1128 (29 July 1788), 3; no. 1576 (13 Jan. 1790), 3; no. 1760 [misnumbered](29 Dec. 1790), 3.

like these stung. An imperfectly literate lay preacher named J. Hamlin wrote to the *Salisbury Journal* in 1788, complaining that the people of Daverhill 'givs it out that it was oing to I that the womun there hangd herself, because when I preached to the fokes I told um as how they was all dammed as dident foller my way'. Hamlin was afraid that the slanders might cause his congregation to abandon him, 'and by that means they would be eternally lost'.[96] One of the most celebrated mad-doctors of the day, William Pargeter, declared that doctrines of Methodism and the fascination that the faithful had with hell increased suicide, despite the strong natural inclination against it.[97] Another eminent authority on insanity, Alexander Crichton, charged that Methodism caused suicide by fostering melancholia and an overwhelming desire for eternal happiness. The affliction, he remarked, was a common one, 'especially among the lower orders of methodists'.[98]

The reaction against enthusiam did not extinguish the clergy's faith that religion was the sovereign remedy for suicidal gloom. Clerics of every denominational hue urged sufferers to seek the counsel of divines, and they continued to compose prayers and pious meditations to comfort the despairing. But it did prompt both churchmen and laymen to adopt a much more cautious tone. Some writers warned against any action that might transform sadness into religious mania. Writing in 1720, Thomas Gordon doubted that 'a vigorous Application to Religion' was advisable in cases of the spleen, for the disease not only prompted suicide but also gave rise to 'devotional Ravings, wild Visions, and idle Prophesies'.[99] When the neurotically depressed William Cowper found consolation in the religious poetry of George Herbert, a 'near and dear relative' advised him to stop reading it, 'for he thought such an author more likely to nourish my disorder, than to remove it'.[100] Dr Pargeter believed that religious melancholics should be purged, vomited, bled, blistered, and sedated, like other madmen, but he was pessimistic about their chances of recovery:

> It is worthy of remark as regret, that we can scarcely expect *enthusiastic* madness to be relieved, much less to be cured. And what is still more deplorable, the insane, in that case, are more likely to destroy themselves, than any other.[101]

[96] The letter was reprinted verbatim in *The Times*, no. 1038 (4 Apr. 1788), 3.

[97] W. Pargeter, *Observations on Maniacal Disorders* (Reading, 1792), 35–6.

[98] A. Crichton, *An Inquiry into the Nature and Origin of Mental Derangement* (London, 1798), ii. 57–8.

[99] Gordon, *The Humorist*, i. 13. Herries, *Address to the Public*, 32–5.

[100] W. Cowper, *Memoir of the Early Life of William Cowper* (London, 1816), 9–10.

[101] Pargeter, *Observations on Maniacal Disorders*, 135.

## TRADITIONALISTS

Beneath the flowing tide of toleration, there was a strong undertow of conservative opinion. Some critics feared that the uncritical adulation heaped on Cato promoted self-slaughter.[102] Richard Steele, for instance, declared in his first book that Cato had left the world 'by an Action below the Precepts of his Philosophy, and the Constancy of his Life'.[103] The wonderfully eccentric London preacher, 'Orator' Henley, entitled his 1730 harangue against self-murder *Cato Condemn'd*.[104] Other writers, not all of them driven by jealousy, complained about the popularity of Addison's *Cato*. Writing in 1718, Henry Stephens objected that drama should promote the improvement of one's country, and so Addison's representation of Cato was 'therefore very improper (not to say worse) for this Nation and Age, wherein too many shorten their Days after so wicked and dishonourable a Manner'.[105] Noting that Addison's Cato seems at the last instant to regret his act, the poetical wine merchant, Thomas Beach, concluded that Cato's suicide was wrong from a Christian perspective:

> Nor should we dare to antedate his will,
> Whose royal mandate runs, 'Thou shalt not kill'!
> What Cato faintly guess'd, we surely know,
> To hold our hand, and check the fatal blow.[106]

Steele later changed his mind, and so did Beach, who died by his own hand.[107] Reservations about venerating classical suicides did not arrest the trend of élite opinion. But they should not be dismissed as unimportant; they demonstrate the persistent ambivalence that Georgian intellectuals felt toward the pagan past. On the one hand, they admired it more avidly than even their humanist forebears had; on the other, they feared

[102] I. Donaldson, *The Rapes of Lucretia* (Oxford, 1982), 130–53 treats this theme fully.

[103] R. Steele, *Tracts and Pamphlets*, ed. R. Blanchard (New York, 1967), 15.

[104] Henley, *Cato Condemn'd; or, The Case and History of Self-Murder* (London, 1730), 16, 17–18 for Cato.

[105] *The Free-Thinker*, ed. A. Phillips, 3rd edn. (London, 1719), i. 24. See also E. A. Bloom and L. D. Bloom (eds.), *Addison and Steele: The Critical Heritage* (London, 1980), 22, 288; *Self-Murther and Duelling*, 7–17; Fleming, *Dissertation upon the Unnatural Crime of Self-Murder*, 5; J. Boswell, *The Hypochondriack*, ed. M. Bailey (Stanford, 1928), ii. 137–8.

[106] Donaldson, *Rapes of Lucretia*, 154–4. Charles Moore also argued that Addison had not really intended Cato's example to condone suicide: *Full Inquiry into Suicide*, ii. 113–6.

[107] For Steele, see *Spectator*, No. 290, III: 33; R. Steele, *The Englishman*, ed. R. Blanchard (Oxford, 1955), no. 25 (1 Dec. 1713), 105, no. 34 (22 Dec. 1713), 139. For Beach, see *DNB*, *Gentleman's Magazine*, vii (1737), 377; BL, Stowe MS 748, fos. $150^r$–$151^v$.

that too great a dependence on classical models promoted values and behaviour that were irreligious.

Clergymen or pious laymen, assailing atheism, blamed deism and natural religion as the cause of frequent suicide. Dr George Cheyne, whose famous book, *The English Malady*, was published within a year of the Smiths' deaths, attributed the apparently rising suicide rate to melancholy and the '*blasphemous* and *frantick Apologies* grafted on the Principles of the *Infidels*, and propagated by their *Disciples*'.[108] Bishop Berkeley was of the same opinion: 'As the minute philosophy prevails, we daily see more examples of suicide.'[109] The author of a tract on the 'supposed suicide of Samson' lamented similarly that he lived 'in an *Age* and *Country*, wherein few *Weeks* together do rarely pass; that do not afford the Instances of that execrable Wickedness; to the great Reproach and Scandal of the *Nation*; Which doubtless is much owing, to those licentious *Writers*, that have impudently pretended to justify it'.[110] Later in the century, the *Werther* mania inspired similar alarm among conservatives. 'Do you like the *Sorrows of Werther*?', Queen Charlotte asked Fanny Burney:

> 'I—I have not read it, ma'am, only in part.'
>
> 'No? Well, I don't know how it is translated, but it is very finely writ in German, and I can't bear it.'
>
> 'I am happy to hear that, for what I did look over made me determined never to read it. It seemed only writ as a deliberate defence of suicide.'
>
> 'Yes; and what is worse, it is done by a bad man for revenge.'[111]

Some ministers carried their conservatism so far that they balked at burying suicides judged *non compos mentis* with the usual Christian rites. In 1760, for example, the great authority on coronership, Edward Umfreville, wrote that he had heard 'of some Clergy who ... have denied the Whole, or a Part of the Office, to a Lunatic ... who hath laid violent Hands upon himself'.[112] He complained that the clergymen who had drafted the rubric forbidding Christian burial had failed to insert the word 'feloniously' into it; lawyers, he declared, would not have made the same mistake. The strict construction of the rubric, so that it could

[108] Cheyne, *English Malady*, p. iii.

[109] G. Berkeley, *Alciphron*, in *The Works of George Berkeley, Bishop of Cloyne*, ed. T. E. Jessop (London, 1950), iii. 92.

[110] *Two Dissertations: The First on the Supposed Suicide of Samson*... (London, 1754), 11–12, 43. See also, *Self-Murther and Duelling*, 45–55.

[111] Quoted in Atkins, *Testament of Werther*, 39.

[112] Umfreville, *Lex coronatoria*, 8.

exclude all self-killers, was endorsed by an impressive authority, Charles Wheatly. In his standard commentary on the *Book of Common Prayer*, first printed in 1715 and reissued many times afterwards, he maintained that madmen were not excused,

Since neither the rubric nor our old ecclesiastical laws make any exception in favour of those who may kill themselves in distraction, and since the Office is in several parts of it improper in such a case. As to the Coroner's warrant, I take that to be no more than a certificate that the body is not demanded by the law, and therefore the relations may dispose of it as they please. For I cannot apprehend that a Coroner is to determine the sense of a rubric, or to prescribe to the Minister when Christian burial is to be used.[113]

Wheatly's views, however, were vigorously opposed by the leading expert on ecclesiastical law, Richard Burn, who asserted that the rubric 'extendeth not to idiots, lunatics, or persons otherwise of insane mind'.[114] Umfreville argued that the true intent of the legislature had been to assure that persons *non compos mentis* would receive the full ceremonies; the *Monthly Review*, reviewing his book favourably, asserted more baldly that it was wrong for the clergy to withhold Christian burial from lunatics.[115] It is not easy to determine how closely either of these flatly contradictory injunctions was followed. Many suicides were admitted to the churchyard but buried on the north side. On the other hand, many other suicides were interred more or less normally. The Essex coroner who wrote to the minister of Lowlaton in 1706 ordering the admission of Robert Smith's body to the churchyard had no doubt about the supremacy of secular authority in this matter; nor did the rector of Saxton-in-Elmet in Yorkshire, who always wrote in the parish register beside the names of lunatics who killed themselves the phrase, 'who upon the Coroner's Inquisition was thought worthy of Christian burial'.[116]

Opposition to tolerant attitudes differed among the leading religious denominations. However much they may have deplored deism, Establishment churchmen were firm converts to rational religion. They generally preferred philosophical argument to supernaturalist rhetoric in their tracts and sermons opposing suicide, as we have seen. There were

[113] C. Wheatly, *A Rational Illustration of the Book of Common Prayer* (Cambridge, 1858), 568.

[114] R. Burn, *Ecclesiastical Law* (London, 1763), ii. 35.

[115] Umfreville, *Lex coronatoria*, 9–10; *Monthly Review*, xxiii (1760), 446.

[116] BL, MS Lansdowne 825, fo. 57$^{r}$; Yorkshire Archaeological Society, *Parish Registers*, xliii (1932), Register of Saxton-in-Elmet, 113, 117.

exceptions. In 1709 John Prince, an obscure rector, reminded his readers that 'the Devil ... is very often the Author (or chief Agent) of this abominable Sin of Self-murder' and produced proofs of Satan's powers.[117] As late as 1755, Francis Ayscough, a moderately successful clerical careerist and courtier, declared in a sermon that suicidal thoughts were surely suggestions of Satan.[118] But for the most part it was the Nonconformists and Methodists who preserved the old faith that self-murder was literally diabolical. Writing in 1785, Richard Hey, a fellow of Magdalene College, Cambridge, and a barrister of the Middle Temple, remarked that too many of the opponents of suicide had been given to intemperate zeal, and so had seemed suspicious to the audience at which he aimed.[119]

For several generations after the Restoration the Nonconformists strove to arrest the advance of new attitudes to self-destruction. The most important of their works on suicide was Richard Gilpin's *Daemonologia Sacra* (1677). Gilpin claims that 'the accurate searches into the Secrets of Nature', so fashionable among gentlemen, had not revealed the true causes of things, and he has written his book in order to prove that the devil is responsible for phenomena that sceptics regard as purely natural.[120] Concentrating mainly on psychological states, he devotes a great deal of attention to despair and suicide. Satan, he insists, is able to manipulate the thoughts and moods of men, seeking to destroy their bodies as well as their souls. He uses several strategies, urging men directly to kill themselves, magnifying their disappointments, and drawing them into rash and dangerous actions.[121] Writing in 1726, the famous hymnist Isaac Watts reiterated Gilpin's contention that Satan could use natural means to disturb mental tranquillity and drive men to despair. When the humours are 'ruffled' by disease, asserts Watts, 'the great Enemy of the Soul is swift to make his advantage of it. ...These hurrying, wicked Thoughts may arise from the Disorders of the Body, or from *Satan*.'[122] The author of the anonymous *Discourse upon Self-Murder* commends the Nonconformist practice of prayer and fasting, and declares emphatically that sin, 'in conjunction with the Devil, is the Root

[117] J. Prince, *Self-Murder Asserted to be a Very Heinous Crime; in Opposition to all the Arguments Brought by the Deists, to the Contrary* (London, 1709), 18.

[118] F. Ayscough, *A Discourse Against Self-Murder* (London, 1755), 15, 17.

[119] Hey, *Dissertation on Suicide*, 1–2.

[120] R. Gilpin, *Daemonologia Sacra; or, A Treatise of Satan's Temptations* (London, 1677), Pt. 1, sig. B1$^r$, 29–31.

[121] Ibid., Pt. 2, 280, Pt. 3, 108–16.

[122] I. Watts, *A Defense against the Temptation to Self-Murder* (London, 1726), 75.

and Parent of *Self-Murder*'.[123] Dissenters often counselled despairing men and women, and sometimes they organized fasts to ward off the devil's assaults. For example, when Thomas Burridge, an apprentice bodice-maker, 'was seized with extraordinary and violent Temptations of Satan' so that he tried to kill himself in 1712, a group of nearly fifty of the faithful gathered to pray and fast for his deliverance. Their meeting was a success, and he was healed in the midst of a fit.[124]

By the middle of the eighteenth century, as their evangelical energy waned, the Nonconformists grew almost as hesitant to blame Satan for self-murder as were their Establishment adversaries.[125] The Methodists and some Anglican evangelicals, however, took up traditionalist beliefs and rhetoric. The Methodists whole-heartedly embraced the older assumptions about the forces that were active in the world. Their pneumatology was unabashedly anachronistic and demotic. It was designed at once to oppose the fashion for rational religion and to appeal to men and women of humble rank. Both George Whitefield and John Wesley rejected the notion that miraculous events were a thing of the past. Both accepted the 'superstitions' of the people and tried to set them in a theological framework. In this sense they were the heirs of the Elizabethan and Jacobean Puritans. Wesley was notorious for defending popular beliefs in witches and diabolical possession, and he declared that nervous disorders were often exacerbated by Satan and his minions. Both in his journals and in the *Arminian Magazine* Wesley printed many accounts of people who were tempted by Satan to kill themselves. Richard Rodda, for instance, recalled in his autobiography that when he was about twenty, in around 1763, the devil spoke to him, urging him to commit suicide: 'The devil likewise tempted me to destroy myself. One day, when I had a razor in my hand, he told me that [it] was a fit instrument for the purpose. He likewise added, if I did, I should be happy for ever. But something within answered, No murderer hath eternal life abiding in him.... At length I threw the razor on the ground, and fell on my knees. God soon heard me, and rebuked the destroyer'.[126] Rodda's narrative, like the speeches of humble believers more than a century earlier, attributes his despairing and self-destructive urges to

[123] *A Discourse upon Self-Murder*, 2nd edn. (London, 1754), 7–8, 15, 17–18, 20.

[124] T. Aldridge, *The Prevalency of Prayer* (London, 1717), 34–6. For an earlier example, see J. Barrow, *The Lord's Arm Stretched Out in an Answer of Prayer* (London, 1664), esp. p. 13.

[125] See e.g., the arguments against suicide in P. Doddridge, *A Course of Lectures On the Principal Subjects of Pneumatology, Ethics, and Divinity* (London, 1763), 186–9.

[126] *Arminian Magazine*, iv (1784), 356.

Satan and his hopeful and self-preserving desires to God. Other early lay preachers and followers described their own suicidal temptations in the same way. The lives of John Wrolley, Benjamin Rhodes, John Haine, John Prickard, George Shadford, Mary Sharp, Christina Malenoir, and W. Grimshaw, all printed in the *Arminian Magazine*, include similar passages, and so do the narratives of Thomas Mitchell, Thomas Payne, Sampson Stainford, and Robert Wilkinson, which appeared elsewhere. The manuscript autobiographies and diaries that have survived add Samuel Hodgson and Thomas Rankin to the list of the faithful tempted by Satan.[127]

None of the Methodist autobiographers used the imagery of traditional religious psychology more vividly than John Valton. The son of French immigrants and a former Roman Catholic, Valton became a very influential Methodist preacher. He kept diaries that recounted his turbulent emotions for many years and wrote at least two versions of his autobiography. Like Bunyan, whose *Grace Abounding* he had read, Valton weaves Satan into the pattern of his spiritual life, as a figure who appears to him almost daily at times, suggesting evil thoughts and prompting dismal moods. 'A Day of sore trial and temptation', he noted in a brief but typical diary entry in 1775, 'suicide was frequently suggested to me'.[128] And like Bunyan, Valton depicted his struggles with the devil as a violent combat that continued without respite for much of his adult life. Upset in 1767 because some people he knew had fallen ill, Valton himself became more and more miserable. His agony grew until he was, in his own words, 'only fit for Bethlehem'. At the very height of his suffering, the devil intrudes, urging him to kill himself: 'O I am damned, damned', he cries. 'I am fairly over come. I yield, I yield....O Spira, Spira, I remember thy Fate and Tremble. I envy the Damned! O what shall I do? "Hang your self". No Devil, I dare not do that.'[129] The other side of diabolical temptations were divine transports, and Valton

[127] *Arminian Magazine*, ii (1779), 147, 420–1; iii (1780), 209; vii (1784), 356; viii (1785), 413–14; xi (1788), 573; xiii (1790), 69; xiv (1791), 494–6; xv (1792), 478–9; xviii (1795), 6; *The Lives of the Early Methodist Preachers*, ed. T. Jackson, 3rd edn. (London, 1865–6), i. 242, 271, 292; ii. 285, 304; iv. 117, 179; v. 248; vi. 141, 213; Methodist Archives, John Rylands Library, Manchester: Untitled MS autobiographies and diaries of Samuel Hodgson, 126–7; John Valton, i. 103, iv. 11–12, 25, vii. 47, 56; Thomas Rankin, 39–40. Many other passages in these sources and in the other autobiographies and diaries in the Methodist Archives demonstrate the continuity of Methodist religious psychology with 17th-cent. popular Protestantism. The figures of Satan and his demons are frequently invoked as the causes of anguish and despair.

[128] Valton, Autobiography and Diaries, vii. 56.

[129] Ibid. iv. 11–12.

had his days when the power of God triumphed over the motions of the Enemy. As he grew older and his emotions became less turbulent, he had fewer occasions to wonder, as he once had, 'what comes from Thee, from Satan, and from Nature'.[130]

The poet William Cowper, an evangelical, suffered horribly from diabolical temptations to kill himself. Recalling his first spell of suicidal madness during a period of tranquillity, he depicted his several suicide attempts in the 1760s in terms of a supernatural struggle, easily as vivid and as violent as those Valton experienced. He concluded that two men who asserted the legitimacy of suicide in conversation with him were 'emissaries of the throne of darkness let loose upon me'. He was not entirely persuaded by their reasoning and postponed killing himself, although 'Satan was impatient of delay', he recalled later.[131] Eventually, Cowper made several attempts on his life which God prevented from succeeding, saving him once by sending 'the convincing Spirit' to dissuade him from poisoning himself and again by causing the garter from which he had hanged himself to break, just as the strangling youth heard voices telling him ' 'Tis over' and saw visions of hell. Languishing in despair afterward, he can be thankful only that 'the capital engine in all the artillery of Satan had not yet been employed against me'.[132] Alarmed relatives committed Cowper to the madhouse of the pious Dr Nathaniel Cotton, where he was converted to a passionate religious faith, which sustained him in pious sanity for a few years.[133]

## PLEBEIAN BELIEFS

It is difficult to know how widely the outlook of the Methodists and evangelicals was shared. Many of the preachers whose autobiographies John Wesley preserved were men and women of humble origins. About three-fourths of the preachers whose autobiographies he collected were

[130] Ibid. iv. 38.
[131] Cowper, *Memoir*, 27–30.
[132] Ibid. 32–7, 40–3, 50.
[133] R. Porter, *A Social History of Madness* (London, 1987), 93–102, analyses Cowper's suicidal moods sensitively and points out that when he suffered a relapse in later life, he was no longer able to understand his feelings in terms of conventional religious psychology.

artisans.[134] Richard Rodda, a miner, was perhaps typical; John Valton, a clerk, was unusual because of his extensive education. Their world-view was characteristic of an old-fashioned popular piety—the religion that regarded *The Pilgrim's Progress* practically as the fifth gospel—and it undoubtedly appealed to many ordinary people who were not Methodists, helping to validate and sustain traditional ideas about self-murder. On the other hand, it would be a grave error simply to equate Methodist beliefs with popular religion. The Methodists were widely reviled, and although the sect grew explosively, it never in the eighteenth century attracted more than a small minority of the working population to join it. In this instance, however, Methodist piety and plebeian cosmology overlapped. Historians have shown that ordinary men and women were reluctant to abandon beliefs that reinforced their view of the universe as a theatre of spiritual warfare between the forces of good and evil, and they continued to fear the power of Satan and malign spirits throughout the century.[135]

Although we shall never be able to gauge their numbers or determine their economic and social backgrounds with precision, there can be no doubt that many people who were not Methodists or evangelicals continued to believe that Satan instigated suicide and that self-murder was spiritually perilous. Eighteenth-century chapbooks and broadsides still depicted the devil tempting real people to kill themselves.[136] When the notorious murderer Francis David Stirn poisoned himself in 1760, the authorities found that he had written in red ochre on a prison wall, 'O Lucifer, Son of the Morning! How art thou brought down to Hell,

[134] M. Watts, *The Dissenters: From the Reformation to the French Revolution* (Oxford, 1978), 407–8. Watts's analysis is based on T. Jackson's *Lives of the Early Methodist Preachers*, which was compiled from the biographies and autobiographies published originally in the *Arminian Magazine*. Jackson's collection is quite comprehensive, but it is bowdlerized here and there.

[135] Thomas, *Religion and the Decline of Magic*, 582–3, 666–7; R. W. Malcolmson, *Life and Labour in England, 1700–1780* (London, 1981), 83–93; J. F. C. Harrison, *The Second Coming: Popular Millenarianism, 1780–1850* (New Brunswick, NJ, 1979), 40–9, 52, 104–5, 125, 127, 235 n. 58, 253. Such beliefs persisted, at least in some rural areas, into the 19th century: W. R. Ward, *Religion and Society in England, 1790–1850* (London, 1972), 47, 78–9; J. Obelkevich, *Religion and Rural Society: South Lindsey, 1825–1875* (Oxford, 1976), ch. 6. Cf. F. B. Smith, *The People's Health, 1830–1910* (New York, 1979), 334–8.

[136] P. M. Swanson, 'Popular Literature in the Eighteenth Century: The Dicey Chapbooks', Ph.D. thesis (Northwestern, 1985), 94–102, 132–3, 153, detects increasing scepticism in accounts of supernatural intervention in this world. On the other hand, the devil and evil spirits still appear in some of the broadsides, mostly from the early 19th century, printed in the British Library's collection of *Broadsides Printed in Bristol* (Catalogue No. 1880 c. 20), nos. 309–11, 314–15, for example.

to the side of this pit.'[137] Dissatisfied with this brief allusion, the newspapers also printed a German poem, falsely attributed to Stirn, in which, as the *Annual Register* later reported, 'as is usual with such criminals, he charges the devil with prompting him to his crime'.[138] In the last half of the century, suicides still alluded to Satan in their last speeches and notes. A drunken coachman warned in his 1765 suicide note 'never let the Devil get the upper hand of you', and a destitute woman who drowned herself in 1783 wrote that she had been 'strouglen with the Devel sence Saturday morning'.[139] Before he poisoned himself in 1792, John Abbott was heard to rise in the night, crying and muttering, saying 'Oh, here is the Devil [who] has got hold of me; pray for me, pray for me.' Asked as he lay dying what had made him take the poisonous stuff, he responded, 'The Devil.... There is the Devil; let me go!'[140] Belief in the spiritual perils caused by self-murder also survived the turn of the century. *Mist's Weekly Journal* reported in 1726 that an account of 'a Spectrum, in the Shape of a Weaver of Crediton, who kill'd himself' was circulating in Exeter.[141] At about the same time the poet James Thomson, recounting the quaint superstitions of shepherds and milkmaids, rustics of 'witless heart', explained that villagers avoided haunted towers and wandered far to avoid the grave

> Of him, whom his ungentle fortune urged
> Against his own sad breast to lift the hand
> Of impious violence.[142]

An eighteenth-century chapbook reprinted in 1807 described the noisy apparition of John Fox of King's Lynn, who had hanged himself and been buried at a crossroads. Fox's spectre returned, noisily crying out that he was undergoing the torments of hell.[143]

137 *London Evening Post*, no. 5127 (11–13 Sept. 1760), 3.

138 *Annual Register*, iii (1760), 130.

139 Westminster Inquests, William Bold (2 Apr. 1765); E.H. (10 Dec. 1783).

140 London Inquests, John Abbott (12 Feb. 1792). Samuel Berg told friends that he had seen the devil four times before he killed himself: ibid., Samuel Berg (4 Dec. 1798).

141 *Mist's Weekly Journal*, no. 81 (5 Nov. 1726).

142 *The Works of Mr. James Thomson* (London, 1803), i. 91–2. The quote is from the 'Summer' segment of Thomson's famous 'Seasons', which was published in its final form in 1746. In 1726 ten inhabitants of a Lancashire parish complained to the justices when the body of a suicide was buried in the highway near their homes, although they did not explain in their petition why they found its presence so offensive: Lancashire County RO, QSP 1248/15.

143 *A Dreadful Example for Wicked Husbands* (n.pl., 1807), 4.

The ritual burials of the dwindling number of condemned self-murders were accordingly carried out punctiliously. When juries returned verdicts of *felo de se*, eighteenth-century coroners issued warrants directing the churchwardens to bury the bodies of suicides in a public highway.[144] The newspapers mentioned ritual burials from time to time throughout the eighteenth century. A bank-robber who shot himself in 1722, for instance, was reported to have been 'wrapp'd in an old Blanket, and buried upon Blackheath, with a Stake drove through him'. And in 1779 the *Annual Register* noted that an embezzler had been interred in the traditional way.[145] The crowds that sometimes attended self-murderers to their graves were undoubtedly attracted by the horror and the spectacle, but their presence also testifies to their continuing acceptance of the ritual itself.[146] Evasions of the custom were not lightly permitted. The night after a Shropshire shoemaker who had hanged himself in 1731 was declared a *felo de se*, his family buried him hugger-mugger in his own back garden. The parish authorities, however, would not tolerate this irregularity, and a few days later they dug up the body and reinterred it in the public highway.[147] Suicides who were not judged *felo de se* were interred in the north side of churchyards, along with executed felons, excommunicates, and unbaptized infants. Popular abhorrence of these polluted grounds was so strong that late eighteenth-century clergymen, distressed by popular superstitions and running out of space to bury bodies, could not easily persuade families to inter their relatives there. Gilbert White was hopeful that the example set by 'two or three families of best repute' in Selborne, who decided to be buried in the north side of his churchyard, would cause 'the prejudice to wear out by degrees'. But Sir John Cullum reported in 1784 that his success in persuading a few families to bury their dead in the north side when he became rector of Hawstead twenty years earlier had not won favour.

[144] Umfreville, *Lex coronatoria*, 8. Examples of such warrants may be found scattered in the Westminster Inquests; a rare example of a certificate that the coroner's order had been carried out is printed in T. R. Forbes, *Crowner's Quest*, Transactions of the American Philosophical Society, lxviii (Philadelphia, 1978), 38.

[145] *Weekly Journal*, no. 201 (22 Sept. 1722); *Annual Register*, xxii (1779), 207. See also, *London Journal*, no. 317 (21 Aug. 1725); *Fog's Weekly Journal*, no. 130 (20 Mar. 1731); *London Evening Post*, no. 1945 (29 Apr. 1740); *Whitehall Evening-Post*, no. 2251 (19 Aug. 1760). *The Times* reported at least ten profane burials between 1785 and 1799.

[146] Radzinowicz, *History of English Criminal Law*, i. 196–8.

[147] *Fog's Weekly Journal*, no. 130 (20 Mar. 1731). Jarrett, *England in the Age of Hogarth*, 186, gives a 1755 example.

His parishioners continued to put bodies in the south side, even though they had to dig up the bones of their ancestors to do so.[148]

## CONCLUSION

During the century and a half after the English Revolution the belief that suicide was a diabolical crime was gradually abandoned by the ruling élite. Supernaturalist explanations for all kinds of behaviour lost their appeal to educated laymen, and even churchmen, locked in a propaganda battle to discredit enthusiasm and superstition, rejected the notion that God and his angels, or Satan and his demons, intervened frequently in the lives of ordinary people. The rise of science and secular psychology provided alternative ways to understand physical and mental phenomena that had previously been viewed as supernatural effects. The growth of scepticism about the powers of mystical forces had begun before the Civil War, and it was at once more complex and limited than any brief generalization can convey. But it is, we believe, evident that the reaction against religious zealotry greatly accelerated the governing classes' adoption of a more secular and scientistic outlook. This shift in perspective eroded the foundation of the Christianized concept of suicide that medieval and Tudor preachers had striven to create. In its most extreme forms it encouraged Stoic and Epicurean defences of self-killing. Churchmen and pious laymen still regarded self-murder as a sin in the eighteenth century and opposed it on religious grounds. But the clerical establishment no longer presumed that suicide was instigated by Satan, and they paid increasing attention to the philosophical and moral implications of the act. Adamant in their opposition to deist philosophers, they nevertheless permitted them to set much of the agenda in the argument over the legitimacy of self-destruction.

The general trend toward a more tolerant and secular attitude to suicide did not extend to evangelical groups or to many of the common people. Supernatural beliefs about suicide survived among the lower orders well into the eighteenth century. They were aspects of a world-view that was profoundly symbolizing and habitually eclectic. Misfortunes of all kinds were regularly attributed to evil spirits; wonderful

148 Both White and Cullum are quoted in J. Brand, *Observations on the Popular Antiquities of Great Britain*, iii (1849; repr. Detroit, 1969), 292. The problem persisted into the 19th cent.: see, G. L. Gomme (ed.), *The Gentleman's Magazine Library: Popular Superstitions* (London, 1884), 135, 205–6.

deliveries were less regularly credited to God. The natural and supernatural realms were believed to be overlapping. Any event might have natural or supernatural causes or both. This outlook seems to have been little affected by the changing opinions of the educated classes in the late seventeenth and early eighteenth centuries. It is more difficult to tell how widespread it remained in the age of George III. Studies of popular religion in the early nineteenth century have discovered evidence of the vigorous survival of supernaturalism. We have seen that some people continued to attribute self-murders to diabolical temptation, and that the ghost beliefs that underlay the rites of desecration endured. But it will never be possible to know with certainty how vigorous these notions remained beyond the circle of the pious minority who have left diaries and other evidence of their attachment to the old cosmology. Nevertheless, the fragments of testimony that remain show that the belief that suicide was a diabolical act decayed more slowly among the lower orders of society than it did among the educated élite.

So many historians have asserted that there was a growing polarization between élite and popular culture in the early modern period that the idea has become trite.[149] Like other such assertions, it is both true and misleading. The growing divergence between élite and plebeian attitudes to self-destruction and its significance—at least in the period from about 1660 to 1780 or so—partially validates it. But a stark dichotomy does not convey the true complexity of the cultural changes that fostered new attitudes to suicide any better than two-class models explain how and why punishment of it declined. In the first place, the decisions of coroners' juries over a very long period mediated between the attitudes of the élite and those of the common people. The gradual pace of the change, selective enforcement, and the preservation of the rites of desecration as an instrument of social control for a long time after they had ceased to express the prevailing interpretation of suicide minimized the potential for public clashes over the elimination of ritual burials, such as those that occurred elsewhere in Europe.[150] Furthermore, just as the consensus of the Elizabethan age concealed strong differences of outlook and interest, so the fragmentation of the succeeding era did not merely result in two opposing views, neatly arrayed by social rank. Sectarians and evangelicals of high and middling status had

149 A somewhat fuller discussion of this idea, from a slightly different angle, is provided below in the Epilogue. The historians we have in mind are cited there.

150 *Annual Register*, xix (1776), 173; Henri Brunschwig, *La Crise de l'état prussien* (Paris, 1947), 79.

their own reasons for clinging to supernaturalism that placed them at odds with the trend of thinking among the educated élite generally. The press, which was resolutely middle-class in its prejudices, generally embraced the secularism of the ruling élite, but it was also the vehicle for the opinions of worried traditionalists. That there was a growing divergence between the world-view of the upper and middle classes and the beliefs of the common people seems irrefutable. Polarization, however, was only one of the motions that gradually pulled apart the constellation of attitudes and practices that had created the Tudor and Stuart attitude to self-murder. And it was only one aspect of the much more varied set of beliefs about suicide in the cultural firmament of Georgian England.

# III

# THE HERMENEUTICS OF SUICIDE

a Doue to all the world, the lost E.H.

Anonymous suicide note (1783)

# 7

# *The Identification of Suicides*

SOCIOLOGISTS have in recent years challenged Durkheimian approaches to the study of suicide. The attack has been mounted on two fronts. Critics have assailed the 'positivists'' reliance on official statistics. They have shown that suicide rates are generally inaccurate, and that they do not reflect the actual rate at which suicide is committed. More specifically, they have demonstrated that the ratio between recorded suicides and the 'real' suicide rate is not constant but varies from time to time as the personnel and procedures of certifying agencies change. They have argued that the classification of a death as a suicide is a complex social event. A suicide verdict is arrived at only after the coroner, witnesses, family, and others have analysed the circumstances surrounding the death and the background of the deceased in light of prevailing definitions of and attitudes to suicide and what one scholar calls 'folk theories' about the states of mind, motives, and personal history of people who kill themselves.[1] On a broader front, the critics have attacked the theories underlying statistical studies. They have called for approaches and methods that owe more to phenomenology and symbolic interactionism than to positivism and functionalism. The ethnomethodologists emphasize the labelling process and focus their attention on the agencies that classify deaths and the attitudes and procedures that influence their choices. The phenomenologists call for a broader approach that regards suicidal acts and gestures as 'socially

[1] The classic challenges are J. D. Douglas, *The Social Meanings of Suicide* (Princeton, 1967); H. Garfinkel, *Studies in Ethnomethodology* (Englewood Cliffs, NJ, 1967). The most searching discussion of suicide statistics is S. Taylor, *Durkheim and the Study of Suicide* (London, 1982), which is excellent on 'folk theories' as well. See also, J. M. Atkinson, *Discovering Suicide* (London, 1978).

meaningful actions'.[2] In both camps, the stress is on the analysis of meanings—of beliefs, attitudes, patterns of behaviour, and their interpretation.

This trend in the sociology of suicide parallels the rising preoccupation with intepretation in the social sciences and literary theory. Symbolic anthropologists have developed dazzling techniques for deciphering cultural codes; sociologists have advocated analysing society as if it were a text, written and read by its participants according to a grammar of motives and conventions of expression; literary theorists have propounded a range of new approaches to textual analysis, often very radical, that emphasize the polysemous and dynamic qualities of language.[3] These approaches to society and to literature have strong affinities with Michel Foucault's conception of discourse, although there are important distinctions between the various disciplines and schools involved and between them and Foucault's own highly personal and variable philosophy.[4] All of these new directions have their roots ultimately in European philosophical traditions that reject empiricism. And for that reason above all they have had little appeal for British and American historians. There is in English-speaking countries a powerful reluctance to abandon the notion that the 'real world' is reflected more or less accurately in texts and in language itself. There is much more to be said for this conviction than its critics allow, but there is no gainsaying the fact that the conventional assumptions of social scientists, literary scholars, and historians have been very strongly challenged.

For the historian of suicide, particularly of suicide in early modern Europe, the challenge is especially unsettling. Like most other kinds of early modern documents, records of suicides present formidable problems to would-be statisticians. No legal tribunal kept documents for statistical purposes, and one eminent historian has gone so far as to pronounce the most important set of English criminal court records—the indictments tried at the assizes—to be worthless for social

[2] Douglas, *Social Meanings*, chs. 13–9. See also, Taylor, *Durkheim and Suicide*, chs. 6–8.

[3] For lucid and influential commentaries, see C. Geertz, *The Interpretation of Cultures* (New York, 1973); J. B. Thompson *Critical Hermeneutics: A Study in the Thought of Paul Ricoeur and Jürgen Habermas* (Cambridge, 1981); J. Culler, *The Pursuit of Signs: Semiotics, Literature, Deconstruction* (London, 1981); T. Eagleton, *Literary Theory: An Introduction* (Minneapolis, 1983).

[4] M. Foucault, *The Order of Things*, trans. anon. (New York, 1970); id., *The Archaeology of Knowledge*, trans. A. Sheridan (New York, 1972); id., *Discipline and Punish*, trans. A. Sheridan (New York, 1977) are perhaps the most important texts. For an illuminating exposition of the concept of discourse and its relation to 'power', see A. Megill, *Prophets of Extremity* (Berkeley, 1985), 237–52.

analyses. The clerks of the assizes were concerned only that indictments fulfil the legal requirements for the trial to go forward, not that the information in them on matters such as the occupations of the accused be accurate.[5] Coroners' inquisitions were prepared much more hastily than indictments, and inaccuracies in them had less serious legal consequences. Moreover, the rules and procedures that regulated the way that suicides were identified and recorded changed over time. Shifts in attitudes to suicide itself also changed the way in which juries went about their work. Faced with all these difficulties, a historian who simply assumed that statistics derived from inquisitions reflect the realities of suicide and proceeded to analyse the patterns in them from a Durkheimian perspective would be naïve to the point of folly.

Another approach to the social history of suicide is therefore necessary. Taking some cues from the critics of Durkheimianism and from scholars with similar views in other fields, these last three chapters will focus on the interpretation of suicide. Their premiss will be that there has been in every era a hermeneutics of suicide, a set of institutions, procedures, and beliefs that identified suicidal deaths and assigned them meanings. The key institutions and conventions in this process are parts of a constellation of means of creating and communicating meanings that might be called the mode of communication. Our argument will be that the secularization of suicide coincided with the emergence of a new mode of communication that changed the ways in which people learned about suicides and interpreted their significance. In this, the final phase of the print revolution, reading at last displaced ritual, writing eclipsed symbolic action, in the communicative behaviour of ordinary men and women. England entered for the first time the age of mass media. We shall begin by looking at the way deaths were classified as suicides in the Tudor and Stuart period, concentrating on the social dynamics of the inquest. Then we shall turn to prevailing convictions about the psychology of suicide. After a pause to assess the reliability of evidence based on inquest verdicts, we shall discuss in the next chapter the range of motives to which suicide was attributed. Finally, because the rise of the periodical press in the eighteenth century radically transformed the mode of communication, we shall examine in the last chapter the ways in which suicides were represented in newspapers and what the consequences of publicity were.

[5] J. S. Cockburn, 'Early Modern Assize Records as Historical Evidence', *Journal of the Society of Archivists*, v (1975), 215–31.

## THE RITUALS OF INTERPRETATION

Suicide is easier to define than it is to identify. The western definition of suicide has remained much the same for thousands of years. John Sym stated it concisely in 1637 when he declared that self-murder was 'the voluntary destroying of a mans owne life, by his owne meanes and procurement'.[6] It is the deliberate destruction of one's own life. But as Sym also recognized, not all self-killing is self-murder. Neither martrys who died rather than recant their faith, nor soldiers who rushed to certain death in battle, nor sportsmen who were killed risking their lives in dangerous games were generally considered self-murderers in early modern England. Children, idiots, and lunatics, who were incapable of reasonable volition, were also exempted. The very existence of the *non compos mentis* verdict displays a certain inability to decide whether or not idiots and lunatics were really suicides. They killed themselves willingly but not wittingly. Sym spent several pages of his treatise considering the sorts of self-killing that were not self-murder.[7] Theologians flung ink at one another, debating whether or not the death of Samson might be defined as a suicide. Strict moralists tried to widen the definition to include all kinds of risky, sinful, and self-destructive behaviour.

Still, despite these complicating matters, the problem of defining suicide is simpler than the task of deciding when a suicide has occurred. The classification of a death as a suicide is complex and contingent. It is the outcome of a series of judgements and actions taken by laymen and officials. Coroners act on their own notions about the state of mind, circumstances, and medical history that suicides typically have. Juries have their own theories about how suicides happen. Families or occasionally officials may pressure coroners to find that a death was or was not a suicide. And there is often plenty of room for debate. Forensic evidence is seldom conclusive—despite the impression left by television shows and mystery novels. Few people leave notes, and even when they do, coroners in England today do not regard them as conclusive proof that a suicide has occurred.[8] Many persons threaten to kill themselves, write notes hoping to call attention to their deed, and then accidentally succeed where they had hoped to fail. In the absence of a note, however, it is extremely difficult to be sure that a dead person actually intended to kill himself.

6 Sym, *Lifes Preservative*, 2.
7 Ibid., esp. 172–4.
8 Taylor, *Durkheim and Suicide*, ch. 4.

The coroner's inquest and the burial of the deceased's body were rituals of interpretation. The inquest was a public drama, in which a large number of people met to consider the significance of the words and actions of a dead person. At least twenty-four men were summoned from the immediate vicinity of the death, and not less than twelve of them were chosen to serve on the jury. Anyone who had information about the death or the deceased was ordered to appear as a witness. Bystanders assembled to watch the proceedings. The fact that the coroner's inquest, unlike other kinds of inquests, was open to everyone and participated in by many of the neighbourhood was, the Elizabethan diplomat Sir Thomas Smith implied, its defining characteristic. In his description of English government, he felt obliged to correct the common misapprehension that the world 'coroner' was derived from *corona populi*, a circle or assembly of people. The false etymology had gained currency, Smith believed, because the inquest 'is commonly in the streete in an open place, and in *Corona populi*'.[9] Like other sorts of ritual, the inquest was a patterned public performance, played out according to a script, laid down by the legal handbooks, lent a certain sacral character by the oaths administered to jurymen and witnesses. The burial of the body was even more obviously a ritual of interpretation. The body of a *felo de se* was interred profanely; the corpse of a person who had been *non compos mentis* was interred more or less normally. In either case burials might be attended by crowds of neighbours. A laconic description of the burial in 1573 of Thomas Maule, a Derbyshire man, recounts that he was interred at midnight 'at the nighest crosse roades with a stake yn him—manie peopple from Manesfeild'.[10] Interments broadcast symbolically the jury's verdict to the whole community. That was one of their most important functions.

An inquest verdict usually represented the community's collective 'reading' of the physical evidence, the events that preceded the death, and the words and actions of the dead. This may seem at first an implausible claim. Jurors, after all, withdrew at the conclusion of the inquest to deliberate on the testimony that they had heard, and it was they who found the verdict. But in fact from the moment of the

[9] T. Smith, *De Republica Anglorum*, ed. M. Dewar (Cambridge, 1982), 108.

[10] J. C. Cox, *The Parish Registers of England* (London, 1910), 114. Hundreds of people were allegedly involved in a town–gown riot that broke out near Oxford after Frideswide Taylor hanged herself in 1555: PRO, STAC 4/7/14; KB 9/588/2, m. 237; KB 29/189/2d; T. R. Murphy, '"Woful Childe of Parents Rage": Suicide of Children and Adolescents in Early Modern England, 1507–1710', *Sixteenth Century Journal*, xvii (1986), 269 n. 34.

discovery of a dead body, the relatives, friends, and neighbours of the deceased played a key role in determining whether or not a death had been a suicide. Surprisingly few suicides were open and shut cases. Physical evidence was even less conclusive than it can be today. Juries often displayed considerable forensic ingenuity, and experienced coroners no doubt became skilled detectives. As early as 1514, for example, a jury investigating the hanging death of the Lollard Richard Hunne in the Tower of London discovered evidence that proved Hunne had been murdered and was not, as the ecclesiastical authorities claimed, a suicide. The inquisition they returned shows that they made a minute examination of the body and found that both its positioning and appearance were inconsistent with death by hanging.[11] Coroners and juries were familiar with the signs of violent death—rare must have been the adult in early modern England who had not seen an execution, a drowned body, or even a person killed by a gun or a knife. Juries looked carefully for signs inconsistent with self-inflicted injury and occasionally their findings determined their verdict. They also examined minutely the scene of the death, and sometimes they found clues that pointed strongly to suicide or that ruled it out. The standards of detection that they were expected to maintain are hinted at in the Star Chamber bills challenging the verdicts of juries. A case accusing a coroner of complicity with the family in 1597 asked how the jury could have ruled the death of Henry Carant an accident when his gown had been found beside the well in which he drowned. The crown concluded that he had removed it so that his body would fit into the narrow shaft.[12] In other cases, the crown on the attack or juries in their own defence called attention to clues, such as suspicious marks on the ground or floor indicating a fall or a struggle. Answering the almoner's charge that they had conspired to return a bogus verdict of misadventure, the family of John Stoner and the jury who found his death an accident were defiant. There was, they asserted, 'no direct evidence at all' to prove that he had drowned himself, and they pointed out that the river bank where he was found had been undermined by the current.[13] A thorough and alert investigation of the death scene was required in every case, and juries seem generally to have satisfied the requirement.[14]

[11] T. R. Forbes, *Surgeons at the Bailey: English Forensic Medicine to 1878* (New Haven, 1985), 75–82.

[12] PRO, STAC 5/A6/3.

[13] PRO, STAC 8/7/42.

[14] For good descriptions of a jury investigating and puzzling out the cause of a death, see *The Diary of Thomas Turner*, ed. D. Vaisey (Oxford, 1984), 307–8.

However conscientious they may have been, juries could seldom prove conclusively that a death had been a suicide from the physical evidence alone. Lawrence Braddon demonstrated this all too well in his long campaign to keep alive the theory that the earl of Essex had been murdered. The transcript of the coroner's inquisition, which was published by the government, was unusually detailed. It showed that Essex had been found dead in a locked room, lying in his own gore, a razor beside his body. Braddon and his Whig confederates produced witnesses who disputed the official version of the facts, notably challenging the jury's assertion about the position of the razor. They exploited the medical evidence against the jury as well. Disputing the conclusion of the surgeons who had testified at the inquest, Braddon declared that every doctor and surgeon he had discussed the matter with had told him that no one could inflict such an injury upon himself as they had described.[15] A contemporary ballad called 'Rome's Cruelty' took up the refrain:

> His Throat was cut from Ear to Ear,
> The Iug'lar Veins and Gullet too,
> The which this worthy Noble Peer,
> Could not have life nor strength to do.[16]

In *Innocency and Truth Vindicated* Braddon generalized his findings to question the reliability of coroners' verdicts not just in this case, but in every case: 'You can't but be so much a lawyer and historian, as to know that a coroner's inquest is not conclusive and final, but may be contradicted, and almost daily is.' Citing the murder of Sir Thomas Overbury, he points out that 'sometimes the coroner's inquest finds men to have died of a natural distemper, which after appear to have been barbarously murdered'.[17]

Very rarely, coroners sought the help of medical experts to evaluate the physical evidence. When they were called, they were seldom very

[15] BL, Sloane MS 78, fos. $20^v$–$21^r$; BL, Harleian MS 1221, fos. 295–7; [L. Braddon], *Murder Will Out; or, a Clear and Full Discovery that the Earl of Essex did not Murder himself, but was Murdered by Others* (London, 1689); id., *Innocency and Truth Vindicated* (London, 1689), reprinted in *A Collection of Scarce and Valuable Tracts ... of the Late Lord Somers*, ed. W. Scott, 2nd edn. (London, 1813), x. 72–174.

[16] H. E. Rollins (ed.), *The Pepys Ballads*, vol. iii: 1666–88 (Cambridge, Mass., 1930), no. 108, p. 97.

[17] *Somers' Tracts*, x. 146. For other suicides that looked like murders or vice versa, see BL, Add. MS 4460, fos. 76–7; J. P. Kenyon, *The Popish Plot* (Harmondsworth, 1974), Appendix A; S. Knight, *The Killing of Justice Godfrey* (London, 1984), pt. v, chs. 4, 5.

much more reliable than lay witnesses, although their testimony frequently swayed the jury. Forensic medicine was poorly understood, and throughout the early modern period England lagged far behind continental nations in the field. The most famous and embarrassing demonstration of the weakness of contemporary forensic pathology was the investigation of the suicide of Miles Sindercombe, the would-be assassin of Oliver Cromwell. Although his guards in the Tower of London had heard Sindercombe ask for poison and had seen him wiping his face and hands after his family left him, eminent medical men could not prove that he had poisoned himself. The attending surgeons opened Sindercombe's body, but they found none of the symptoms they associated with death by poison. The Lieutenant of the Tower therefore summoned Sir Richard Napier, MD, and Christopher Fern, the Reader of Anatomy at Gresham College, who examined Sindercombe's brain. These distinguished experts were also baffled. They found the brain bloody and swollen, 'which must be the effect of some violent and preternatural cause'. Yet, they lamely confessed, 'are we not able positively to determine what that is'. The lesions were greater than those caused by apoplexies and other such diseases and compatible only with contusion or some severe external injury. This was not a conclusion the government could have welcomed, and so three more surgeons were summoned, two wardens of the college of surgeons, Mr Charles Stamford and Mr Nicholas Brethers, and a Mr Lawrence Loe. They at least considered the possibility of poison, only to confess that they could not discover 'the usual or common symptoms or effects accompanying the taking of known and sharp poisons causing sudden death'.[18] A *felo de se* verdict could be justified only because of the fortuitous discovery of Sindercombe's suicide note.

Poisoning filled contemporaries with superstitious terror. There was a sinister, magical quality to it: in medieval Latin, poisoning and sorcery were described with the same word, *veneficium*. Both were women's crimes; poisoning was a kind of deadly kitchen craft. A special penalty, boiling alive, was devised to execute poisoners during Henry VIII's reign after a disgruntled scullery lad named Richard Roose tried to kill Bishop John Fisher and members of his household by lacing their porridge with arsenic. Poisoning remained treason punishable by boiling

[18] W. Cobbett, T. Howell, *et al.* (eds.), *Cobbett's Collection of State Trials*, v (London, 1811), cols. 856–8.

until the end of Henry VIII's reign.[19] Vestiges of this superstitious fear may be detected in the way that suicides who had poisoned themselves were treated by coroners' juries. Among the inquisitions returned to King's Bench, over twice as many women as men were found to have poisoned themselves, even though the overall ratio of men to women among recorded suicides was almost two to one. When the use of the *felo de se* verdict began to decline in the later seventeenth and eighteenth centuries, juries were slower to find poisoners insane than they were people who chose other methods of suicide. Between 1660 and 1714, for instance, over 85 per cent of poisoners were convicted as self-murderers. Eight of the ten suicides who poisoned themselves in eighteenth-century Norwich were judged *felo de se*, about four times the rate of conviction that one would expect.[20] A more or less reliable test for arsenic, the poison most commonly used by identified suicides in the sixteenth and seventeenth centuries, was not developed until 1836; a method of detecting opium, the poison of choice in the later eighteenth century, was not available until much later.[21]

Poisoning was, admittedly, the most difficult cause of death to determine. And it was evidently uncommon—slightly more than 3 per cent of the identified suicides between 1485 and 1714 died by poison. But enough has been said to show that Braddon was right, despite his tendentious hyperbole. A verdict based on forensic evidence was a conjecture. Furthermore, given the frequency of drowning, such conjectures were required fairly often. S. J. Stevenson may exaggerate slightly when he claims that about one half of suicides by drowning and accidental drownings in the Elizabethan period might be reclassified one way or the other, but he is certainly correct to suggest that what might be called the 'uncertainty figure' was very high.[22]

## THE SIGNS OF SELF-MURDER

To build a case that a suicide had occurred, juries were forced to rely on

[19] Forbes, *Surgeons at the Bailey*, 123–4; W. R. Stacy, 'Richard Roose and the Use of Parliamentary Attainder in the Reign of Henry VIII', *Historical Journal*, xxix (1986), 1–15 is the best account. See also, his 'The Bill of Attainder in English History', Ph.D. thesis (Wisconsin-Madison, 1986), 87–93.

[20] Norwich Inquisitions. The rate of *felo de se* verdicts overall was around 20%.

[21] Forbes, *Surgeons at the Bailey*, 136–7, 151–4.

[22] S. J. Stevenson, 'The Rise of Suicide Verdicts in South-East England, 1530–1590: The Legal Process', *Continuity and Change*, ii (1987), 63–5.

intangible evidence. They examined witnesses who had spoken to the deceased or observed his behaviour before his death, looking for what John Sym called felicitously 'the signs of self-murder'. Sym's list of them includes solitariness, 'a strange change in outward behaviour', a 'mindlessness and close dumpishness' and speeches and actions implying that something important was about to happen.[23] Once more, for the period prior to the eighteenth century, Star Chamber challenges to juries' verdicts provide the best evidence about how they were supposed to evaluate evidence. The crown's case against the family of John Stoner and the jury of his inquest (the defiant response to which we mentioned above) rested entirely on circumstantial psychological evidence of the kind Sym mentioned. The king's almoner asserted that he had been 'desperately minded and having, as it seemed by the sequel, a purpose and full resolution ... to destroy and make himself away'. The day before his death, the crown claimed, Stoner said that he could not sleep and 'doubted he should go beside himself'. He had become reclusive, avoiding a visitor who came to the house and dressing to leave home only to change his mind and lie down on his bed. He also told someone that 'he was growing into such a humour as that he doubted he should make them all afraid shortly'.[24] Examining Star Chamber cases like this one and depositions given at inquests where they are available, it is possible to reconstruct crudely the popular psychology of suicide. The subject is an elusive one, mainly because juries had to decide not only whether the deceased was in a suicidal state of mind but whether or not he was sane. Juries, it should be emphasized, looked for a motive in cases of putative suicide as well as the tokens of mental and social alienation. We shall discuss suicide motives in detail in the next chapter.

Some people signalled their desperate urges unmistakably, writing notes, threatening suicide, or making unsuccessful attempts on their lives. Suicide notes were very rare prior to about 1700. Sir Walter Ralegh wrote a letter to his wife before he stabbed himself in an unsuccessful suicide attempt in the Tower in 1603.[25] The rich London merchant, William Doddington, left a bitter note behind, blaming his ruin on a business rival, when he jumped to his death in 1600, and Lancelot Johnson was alleged to have left his wife a note before he disappeared

[23] Sym, *Lifes Preservative*, 159–61.

[24] PRO, STAC 8/3/10.

[25] Wymer, *Suicide and Despair*, 20; S. J. Greenblatt, *Sir Walter Ralegh: The Renaissance Man and His Roles* (New Haven, 1973), 114–17 is the best discussion of Ralegh's suicide attempt and note.

in 1617.[26] But there are precious few such examples. After the turn of the century, notes became more common, although they still figured in only a small minority of inquests into suicides.[27] Announcing that one intended to kill oneself invited intervention, but it happened more often than one might have supposed. Dozens of patients told Richard Napier that they were going to kill themselves. One of them, a woman named Joan Kent from the nearby village of Padbury, returned to him at least nine times in November 1618. She drowned herself in January.[28] Ploughing a field in about 1717, Robert Lowthian turned to his son and said suddenly that he would put an end to himself were it not for the sake of his family. A year later the young man found his father hanging in his barn.[29] In 1771, the miserable Thomas Norman told a friend: 'I am a strange horrible Wretch. I shall certainly Hang Myself, Drown Myself or Cut my Throat.' The next week he shot himself.[30] Dinah Holmes, who was accounted a 'silly Massling body', not quite right in the head, had said again and again that she would hang herself before she finally did so in 1781.[31]

Contemporaries regarded previous suicide attempts as conclusive evidence that persons had killed themselves. They could also prove premeditation, and so before 1700 they were usually cited to justify a *felo de se* verdict. Prosecuting the coroner in the Henry Carant case, the almoner added to his charge of careless detective work the assertion that he had refused to hear witnesses who would have testified to his previous attempts to kill himself. A famous law case in the 1650s turned on just the same assertion.[32] Reporting the suicide of one of his parishioners in 1572, an Essex rector noted that before he was found hanging in his oak-tree, John Brand had attacked himself with a knife, drunk ratsbane, and, in his most elaborate failure, put a five-bushel sack over his head and jumped into a pond.[33] According to his political enemy, Sir John Bramston, John Lemot Honeywood was a paragon of determination. Realizing that his wife had tricked him out of a fortune, he seized a turkey rump from the dinner table and tried to choke himself to death. When that attempt failed, he tried again, flinging himself down a flight

26 BL, Lansdowne MS 99, no. 32, fos. 88$^{r}$–89$^{v}$; PRO, STAC 8/3/10.
27 18th cent. suicide notes are discussed below, Ch. 9.
28 Bodl., Ashmole MS 230, fos. 85$^{v}$, 86$^{v}$, 93$^{v}$, 99$^{v}$, 158$^{v}$–159$^{r}$.
29 Cumbria RO, D/Lec/CR I, 27/4.
30 Westminster Inquisitions, Thomas Norman (24 May 1771).
31 Cumbria RO, D/Lec/CR I, 90/1.
32 PRO, STAC 5/A5/3; Barclay's Case (1658). See also STAC 5/A6/35; STAC 5/A15/12.
33 Essex County RO, D/P 27/1/2, 9.

of stairs. Again unsuccessful, he at last hanged himself with his garters, defeating the vigilance of the guards his wife had hired to prevent his suicide.[34] The coroner holding the inquest into the death of Robert Ravell in 1717 departed from the usual formula in the inquisition, charging that Ravell had been 'severall years melancholly and [had] made frequent attempts to destroy himself'.[35]

The clues that preceded suicide in most cases were more subtle than these examples. They were words or gestures that implied depressed moods, more extreme forms of mental illness, or an expectation that death was imminent. The almoner charged, for example, that Francis Marshall had killed himself. He reported that Marshall's neighbours heard him make 'diverse and sundry discontentful speeches', saying that he was a reproach to them and weary of living. He said he would sell his goods. But they knew he was suicidal not only by these hints but 'also by his countenance and behaviour', the almoner alleged.[36] Sym thought that many of 'the signs of self-murder' were at least in part symptoms of melancholy. Among those most prone to suicide he numbered in first place, '*melancholic* people; *because* they are most *cogitabundi & tristes*, *given to musing and sadnesse*, on whom Satan works most; *and* they are most subject to discontentment, and apt thereupon to entertaine impressions and resolutions of *self-murder*'.[37] This was a common conviction among laymen and doctors throughout the early modern period. Laymen had no difficulty in recognizing the symptoms of melancholy—they were enshrined in characters and literary stereotypes. Describing melancholy in his *Art of Memory*, John Willis personified it succinctly: 'a man very sad, who having his arms wreathed up, and his hat pulled downe in his eyes, goeth up and down in a discontented manner'.[38] People gripped by pathological gloom were solitary and taciturn. An obscure Elizabethan playwright, Edward Guilpin, made these traits the marks of malcontent melancholy:

> But see yonder,
> One like the unfrequented Theater
> Walkes in dark silence, and vast solitude,
> Suited to those black fancies which intrude,
> Upon possession of his troubled breast.[39]

[34] J. Bramston, *The Autobiography of Sir John Bramston*, ed. T. W. Bramston, Camden Society, Orig. Ser., no. 32 (London, 1845), 377–8.
[35] Cumbria RO, D/Lec/CR I, 26/1. Ravell was found *felo de se*.
[36] PRO, STAC 8/3/4.
[37] Sym, *Lifes Preservative*, 254.
[38] Quoted in B. G. Lyons, *Voices of Melancholy* (London, 1971), 22.
[39] Quoted ibid. 23.

In retrospect, witnesses and journalists described suicides in much the same language. Someone told the almoner that he had seen Lancelot Johnson beside the Thames before he drowned, walking 'in a very sad, deep melancholy and discontented manner'.[40] A pamphleteer's account of Robert Long's suicide in Newgate in 1685 called attention to his gestures and movements, which made him the very emblem of melancholy: 'He became very Melancholly, his Countenance, at the same time, shewing a kind of Wildness, not being in the least free in speech, but of a Reserved temper, being often observed to Sigh and Groan to himself, little regarding either Eating or Drinking.'[41] Almost a century later, after John Coker drowned in 1781, a friend explained to the inquest jury that he had 'appeared to be very Melancholy and spoke very little'.[42] Susanna Spring, who was found drowned two years later, was ruled a suicide because just before her death she had 'looked very Melancholy and low Spirited, and hanged down her Head', as a passer-by testified.[43]

Examples such as these could be multiplied into the hundreds. Laymen were sometimes surprisingly exact in the terminology that they used to describe suicidal melancholy. In 1711, for example, a poor and pathetically deluded Cumberland woman named Ann Garnett killed herself. She invoked the devil to explain her state of mind, but her neighbours seem to have placed more emphasis on her melancholia, and they demonstrated an informed awareness of the traditional scientific explanations for the disease and its symptoms. One of them testified that when she assured Garnett that her hallucinations were not real, Garnett herself 'told this deponent that the same proceeded from a Melancholy humour'. Other witnesses in the case used technical language with equal ease.[44] Just as often, however, witnesses simply referred to people they believed to have killed themselves as 'low-spirited'. A friend recalled that Elizabeth Kitching had been dull and low-spirited for about three weeks before her suicide in 1772. She had remained in bed a lot, and once the witness had come upon her in the posture of despair, holding a rope like

[40] PRO, STAC 8/3/10.

[41] *A Sad and Dreadful Account of the Self-Murther of Robert Long, alias Baker* (London, 1685).

[42] Westminster Inquisitions, John Coker (10 Dec. 1781).

[43] Westminster Inquisitions, Susanna Spring (18 Apr. 1783). See also, ibid., William Robertson (9 Oct. 1771); Edward Smith (7 Feb. 1780).

[44] Cumbria RO, D/Lec/CR I, 22/2.

an actor in a morality: she was 'upon a Hay Mow laying in a very Dejected Way and Lamenting and had a Rope with her'.[45]

Outright madness was also considered prima-facie evidence that a suicide had occurred. Prior to the Restoration, this often led to a *felo de se* verdict when a *non compos mentis* finding ought to have been recorded, as we have seen. Logically, lunatics should not have been regarded as suicides at all. Some medical men and many laymen nevertheless believed that the utterly insane were particularly liable to kill themselves. The medieval encyclopaedist, Bartholomeus Anglicus, whose book continued to be popular until 1550 or so, warned that some madmen 'cryen, and lepe, and hurt and wounde them selfe and other men'.[46] It was this fear—that madmen were likely to harm or kill themselves or others—that justified their incarceration or restraint in the sixteenth and early seventeenth centuries.[47] Later in the seventeenth century, as attitudes began to change, the contradiction or paradox implied in earlier decades disappeared—it was perfectly reasonable to regard madmen as potential suicides, since suicide was increasingly considered an act of madness. The signs of madness were as well known to laymen as those of melancholy. They included raving, extreme rage, violent agitation, incoherent and rapid speech, and (especially in the eighteenth century) extravagant delusions. After an old man called Thomas Cooke hanged himself in Norwich in 1717, witnesses recalled that they had 'perceived some actions in the deceased which looked as if he was disordered in his head'. A friend elaborated, saying that when he came to visit Cooke, he realized he was disordered in his head 'by severall Actions he made, as throwing his hands and clapping his sides and puffing with his mouth and stamping with his ffoot'.[48] A fellow soldier recounted at the inquest on Thomas Arless in 1769 that he had heard Arless start up in the night in bed and cry aloud, 'They are coming! They'll tear me to pieces, there are a thousand Bullocks and Horses and they will have me.' He looked 'very wild' the day he was found hanged.[49] Charles Arbuckle was one of many who was deemed suicidal in retrospect partly because he had given 'wild, distracted looks'.[50]

[45] Cumbria RO, D/Lec/CR I, 81/5.

[46] R. Hunter and I. Macalpine (comps.), *Three Hundred Years of Psychiatry, 1535–1860* (London, 1963), 4. See also, P. B. R. Doob, *Nebuchadnezzar's Children: Conventions of Madness in Middle English Literature* (New Haven, 1974), 113.

[47] MacDonald, *Mystical Bedlam*, 141. See also 132–8 for a fuller discussion of the relationship between madness and suicide in this period.

[48] Norwich Inquisitions, Thomas Cooke (20 Dec. 1717).

[49] Westminster Inquisitions, Thomas Arless (17 Oct. 1769).

[50] Westminster Inquisitions, Charles Arbuckle (7 Jan. 1773); Martha Macarty (20 Nov. 1773).

After 1700 or so, as asylums and mad-doctors began to proliferate, evidence that a dead person had been confined to a madhouse or had been treated by a specialist in mental disease began to be heard at inquests as proof of suicide. Such testimony effectively immunized the deceased from a *felo de so* verdict, but it also virtually assured that he would be judged a suicide, no matter how frail the other evidence was. Because of the growing numbers of private madhouses, particularly in the London suburbs, and the expansion of public asylums, a substantial number of London and Westminster suicides were former patients. Others had been confined to workhouses, probably because they were too poor to afford a private madhouse and were ineligible for a public asylum. Isabella Brown committed suicide in a workhouse, where she had been confined for about ten days. She had been examined there by a surgeon, who testified at the inquest that he had decided she was insane from the answers she gave to his questions and treated her 'as a Lunatick by administering proper Medicines for a Person in that Condition'.[51] At least sixteen other Westminster suicides had been treated as lunatics between 1760 and 1790. In a couple of other instances a physician and an apothecary testified that they had recommended confinement just before their patients' suicides.[52] In the later eighteenth century raging lunatics were clapped in gaols, workhouses, and asylums much more often than ever before, because there were more and bigger institutions in which to confine them. William Black reckoned that about half of the inmates admitted to Bedlam between 1772 and 1785 were violent, and that around 15 per cent of them had already attempted suicide at least once.[53]

Often witnesses who thought that a person had committed suicide mentioned physical illnesses that they supposed had unbalanced the dead person's mind. A jury in Cockermouth, for instance, decided that Margaret Pearson, who had been found drowned, had killed herself after they heard Peter Peile say that she had suffered a fever that had made her delirious and left her dull and low-spirited.[54] Rich men blew out their

[51] Westminster Inquisitions, Isabella Brown (8 July 1762). See also, John Sergeant (28 Nov. 1767).

[52] Westminster Inquisitions, Edward Stockdale (12 Apr. 1790); John Dyne (31 Oct. 1788). For other suicides who had been treated for madness, see London Inquisitions, John Warner (7 Sept. 1791); Ann Moore (16 Sept. 1791); Ann Kell (30 Mar. 1795); Ann Marsh (13 Jan. 1796); William Rand (11 Aug. 1797); Theodosia Onder, *alias* Ross (6 Nov. 1797); William Moor [*sic*](17 Feb. 1798); Samuel Berg (4 Sept. 1798); John Hall (3 Nov. 1798); Greater London RO, MJ/SPC.W/309.

[53] W. Black, *A Dissertation on Insanity*, 2nd edn. (London, 1811), 13–14; see also the comments on 17–18.

[54] Cumbria RO, D/Lec/CR I, 88/7.

brains because their gouty joints gave them intolerable pain. Horace Walpole announced matter-of-factly to a correspondent that John Crowley, a man who had inherited £400,000 a year earlier, 'had a fit of the gout last week, and shot himself'.[55] At the other end of the social scale, a pauper named Richard Raine killed himself because he could not stand the sensations caused by the worms teeming in his gut.[56] When Abraham Wood, a poor pensioner, cut his throat in 1744, a Cumberland witness testified that he had been sound in his mind but long ill in body.[57]

Walpole was convinced that madness and suicide were hereditary diseases; he attributed one nobleman's suicide to 'madness of the blood'.[58] This belief was widely shared throughout the period. Medical writers made little of hereditary propensities to self-destruction, but they blamed bad breeding for mental disorders generally. 'It comes to pass that our generation is corrupt', railed Burton, 'we have ... many feral diseases raging among us, crazed families, *parentes paremptores* [our parents are our ruin], our fathers bad, and we are like to be worse.'[59] Ordinary people had no doubts on the score. Joan Kent told Napier before she drowned herself that she was afraid she would 'kill herself as her father did drown himself'.[60] To some observers, the suicide of the earl of Bath in 1701 just two weeks after his father had killed himself seemed to confirm that insanity galloped in the family.[61] Walpole (again) recalled when he learned of the death of Hans Stanley in 1780 that his father had also cut his throat and attributed his suicide to 'A sudden fit of frenzy'.[62]

It would be unwise to look for any very coherent psychology of suicide in these popular stereotypes about the causes of self-slaughter. No very coherent psychology of suicide exists today, despite the strident claims of rival sects of psychologists, psychiatrists, psychoanalysts, and psychobiologists. Both experts and laymen agree, for instance, that many people who kill themselves are depressed when they do so. And yet

55 H. Walpole, *The Yale Edition of Horace Walpole's Correspondence*, ed. W. S. Lewis (New Haven, 1937–83), xxxv. 236.

56 Westminster Inquisitions, Richard Raine (12 Oct. 1768).

57 Cumbria RO, D/Lec/CR I, 53/2. See also, Westminster Inquisitions, Hester Heerlin (27 June 1766).

58 Westminster Inquisitions, The Duke of Bolton (5 July 1765); Walpole, *Correspondence, Letters*, xiii. 147.

59 R. Burton, *The Anatomy of Melancholy*, ed. H. Jackson (London, 1972), i. 211–16.

60 Bodl., Ashmole MS 230, fo. 93$^{v}$.

61 J. Evelyn, *The Diary of John Evelyn*, ed. E. S. de Beer (Oxford, 1955), v. 475–6; Hertfordshire RO, Diary of Lady Sara Cowper, Pensanger MSS, D/EP F 29, i. 133; Narcissus Luttrell, *A Brief Relation of Affairs of State* (Oxford, 1857), v. 86.

62 Walpole, *Correspondence*, xxix. 5. See also ibid., vii. 201, 422; xxxiii. 161.

studies plainly show that many also manifest no discernible sign of depression other than their suicides. A very wide range of mental and emotional disturbances can precede a suicide.[63] But it is possible to analyse the behaviour that seemed in retrospect to presage suicide in a slightly different way, looking at the actions people described from the perspective of their own unconscious expectations about social conduct rather than from the perspective of modern psychology. Almost all of the signs of suicide implied what might be called 'temporal shallowness'. They violated the observer's expectation that other people will behave pretty much as they have in the past and that they, like him, normally presume a personal future that, while finite, is indeterminate. Thus an unwanted reclusiveness was deemed significant not only because it was a sign of melancholy but also because it marked a departure from the deceased's past behaviour.

Sometimes the changes people noticed were very striking. Friends and fellow workers recalled, for instance, that Richard Wade had been 'out of his senses' for three weeks before he died, drunken and incoherent, full of wild looks. He told a fellow worker that 'he could not stay here or bear it', and he came to a friend's shop and cried out to her, 'You do not know my Distress!'.[64] Relatively slight shifts in habitual demeanour might also be cited in retrospect as signs of a suicidal state of mind. People often mentioned that suicides had grown taciturn and passive. Other suicides signalled their intentions by behaving in ways that were inconsistent with the future rather than the past. John Stoner had had a conversation about making over some tithes to his children and warned he might do something that would upset his family.[65] Elizabeth Mobbs gave a solitary hint that she intended to kill herself. She told her husband in March 1774 that she had pawned her dress because she would not need it again. Only after she was found drowned did he realize the true significance of her remark.[66] Thus although witnesses sometimes read the actions of suicides as the signs of specific stereotypes of disease, such as melancholy, they also stressed the importance of gestures and remarks that they did not link with a particular illness. These could be

[63] Convenient reviews of the literature are, D. Lester, *Why People Kill Themselves: A Summary of Research Findings on Suicidal Behavior* (Springfield, Ill., 1972); id., *Why People Kill Themselves: A 1980s Summary of Research Findings on Suicidal Behavior* (Springfield, Ill., 1983); M. P. Battin, *Ethical Issues in Suicide* (Englewood Cliffs, NJ, 1982), 3–7.

[64] Westminster Inquisitions, Richard Wade (9 Apr. 1776).

[65] PRO, STAC 8/3/10.

[66] Westminster Inquisitions, Elizabeth Mobbs (1 Mar. 1774). See also, ibid., Daniel Miller (9 Mar. 1774); John Ryley (3 June 1762); Thomas Bull (6 June 1767).

operatic expressions or very subtle variations in everyday behaviour. The semiotics of suicide on which its popular psychology rested was not simply an aspect of lay medical discourse. It involved a broader and more elusive set of assumptions about the relationship between emotion and action and between inner mental states and behaviour over time.

The shock that a suicide caused was inextricably linked to people's conception of the relationship between time and identity. We all assume a continuity of the self, in ourselves and in the other people we know, and suicide is stunning because it cuts life short and repudiates identity. Thinking back on the behaviour of dead persons whom they suspect have killed themselves, observers naturally look for changes of mood that signalled the disintegration of the self, a preparation for death. And they also look for signs that the suicide anticipated the extinction of his identity. Potential suicides share the same assumptions of continuity and when they try to ask for help, warning others of their self-destructive moods, they hint—broadly or subtly—that they do not any longer think that the future is indeterminate. Anthropologists, historians, and sociologists have argued recently that notions of the self (one's conception of one's own and other people's identities) are socially constructed.[67] Anthony Giddens emphasizes that establishing and maintaining one's identity involves managing the impression one makes on other people over time, a process he calls positioning. 'Positioning here', he explains, 'involves many subtle modalities of bodily movement and gesture, as well as the more general motion of the body through the regional sectors of daily routines.'[68] We monitor ourselves, playing out the roles that we ourselves and others have fashioned for us, drawing on a common 'script' understood by the members of our culture. The signs of suicide in early modern England were expressions, gestures, and actions that seemed to imply a foreshortening of time and discontinuity of identity.

In the eighteenth century, as the *non compos mentis* verdict came to be used more routinely, almost any vague disturbance—some evidence of

[67] T. C. Heller *et al.* (eds.), *Reconstructing Individualism: Autonomy, Individuality, and the Self in Western Thought* (Stanford, 1986), 53–63; D. W. Sabean, *Power in the Blood: Popular Culture and Village Discourse in Early Modern Germany* (Cambridge, 1984), esp. pp. 30–6, 206–12; M. Z. Rosaldo, *Knowledge and Passion: Ilongot Notions of Self and Social Life* (Cambridge, 1980); M. Carrithers *et al.* (eds.), *The Category of the Person* (Cambridge, 1985).

[68] A. Giddens, *The Constitution of Society* (Cambridge and Oxford, 1984), 84. For an excellent brief discussion of this perspective, see ibid., 78–84. Its most effective recent advocate has been E. Goffman: see, esp. *The Presentation of the Self in Everyday Life* (Garden City, NY, 1959); *Interaction Ritual* (Garden City, 1967); *Frame Analysis* (New York, 1974).

anxiety or distress—might be put forward as a reason to believe that a person had killed himself and also as an excuse for his supposed suicide. The mother of John Taylor, a Norwich apprentice, asserted at the inquest on his body merely that he had been 'much disordered in his Senses', and his master and mistress agreed that he had been 'disordered'. The jury declared that he had committed suicide while he was *non compos mentis*, even though he had been missing for months before he was found drowned.[69] A fellow lodger told a Westminster inquest that Hannah Bignell, whose master described her as dull, stupid, and apprehensive, had been disordered in her senses ever since she hit her head on a saucepan.[70] Physical pain seems also to have been mentioned more frequently as a reason for believing that a death had been a suicide.

In general, however, there was a great deal of continuity in the medical conditions and significant actions that were associated with self-killing. Melancholy, the spleen or vapours, and low spirits led the van throughout the period. Madness perhaps became a little more prominent. The most noticeable shift was the disappearance of testimony about religious behaviour. Prior to the English Revolution, observers often stressed the failure to perform religious duties as a proof that a death had been a suicide. A number of examples were discussed in Chapter 2, when we showed how even the language of legal documents came to reflect the antithesis of God/life and Satan/suicide.[71] Eighteenth-century coroners' records and court cases seldom contain any mention of religion, except for occasional remarks attributed to the dead person or his relatives. Neither the juries nor the officials measured the intentions or the mental health of the dead by trying to guess what their relationship with God might have been.

The decline in references to religious behaviour in inquest evidence was, of course, a reflection of the gradual secularization of suicide—indeed, of the whole mental world of early modern English people. A second change, still more significant methodologically, was a growing arbitrariness in the interpretation of moods and actions as the pressure on juries to classify deaths as self-murders declined. Subjected to less and less supervision by royal authorities, eighteenth-century juries grew lax

69 Norwich Inquisitions, John Taylor (28 Jan. 1755).

70 Westminster Inquisitions, Hannah Bignell (28 June 1768).

71 PRO, STAC 5/A22/1; STAC 8/3/10; Barclay's Case, *English Reports*, lxxxii. 1273; J. Miller and K. H. Rogers, 'The Strange Death of Edward Langford', *Wiltshire Archaeological and Natural History Magazine*, lxii (1967), 108; S. J. Stevenson, 'Social and Economic Contributions to the Pattern of "Suicide" in South-East England, 1530–1590', *Continuity and Change*, ii (1987), 232–3.

about investigating suicides, and in general preferred to treat ambiguous cases as accidents or natural deaths. The jury deliberating on the body of William Hutchon of Norwich in 1762, for example, was persuaded that he had cut his own throat because he had 'diverse Cronical Diseases', including an ulcerated leg, but they nevertheless brought in a verdict of natural death, blaming the maladies for his action.[72] Juries' handling of deaths by drowning suggests just how much less rigorous they became than they had been in the Tudor and Stuart period. Drownings that were returned as suicides dropped off dramatically in some jurisdictions and virtually disappeared in others. In late eighteenth-century London, drownings accounted for 17 per cent of suicides in Westminster and Middlesex. In the City of London and Southwark, only *one* such verdict was returned in the last two decades of the century. Wiltshire's diligent coroners found 27 per cent of suicides had died by drowning.[73] Even this high figure is, however, as much as 10 per cent lower than it had been in the later sixteenth and early seventeenth centuries. It was, moreover, not unusual for juries to return the non-verdict of 'found drowned' on bodies or to classify obvious suicides as natural deaths in the later eighteenth century. An extreme case occurred in 1773 when an anonymous man who had been seen to jump into a pond at Westminster was returned as 'found drowned'.[74] Juries in the eighteenth century were responding to the concerns of their communities and the families of suicides, avoiding verdicts that would shame the dead and his survivors, just as their predecessors had been influenced by government pressure.

## THE SUICIDE RATE

The sensitivity of the coroner's inquest to the administrative and social context in which it worked makes it an unusually interesting institution. But it also reduces the value of many of the statistics that one can compile—at the expense of vast effort—from the inquisitions it produced. The overall suicide rate is particularly suspect; it is a rope of sand that slips through the hands of historians who try to secure it to

[72] Norwich Inquisitions, William Hutchon (14 Feb. 1762).

[73] R. F. Hunnisett, 'The Importance of Eighteenth-Century Coroners' Bills', in E. W. Ives and A. H. Manchester (eds., *Law, Litigants and the Legal Profession* (London, 1983), 129.

[74] Westminster Inquisitions, Unknown Man (14 Dec. 1773).

other factors, such as prices or wages. Contemporary observers had no doubts about the trajectory of the suicide rate; they complained throughout the period that it was higher than ever before and rising rapidly. Writing in the preface to Sym's *Lifes Preservative*, the Puritan divine William Gouge declared: 'I suppose, that scarce an age since the beginning of the World hath afforded more examples of this desperate inhumanity than this our present age.'[75] Before the end of the seventeenth century, such assertions were uncommon, and they were made mostly by clergymen, eager to inveigh against the immorality of the age or the pernicious influence of rival confessions. After about 1690, however, commentators began to deplore the frequency of suicide with greater urgency. John Evelyn confided to his diary in 1694 his concern that several persons had lately slain themselves; by 1705 he was persuaded that 'never was it known that so many made themselves away as of these late years among us, among both men of quality and others'.[76] The playwright William Congreve defended theatrical diversions in 1698 with the improbable argument that they were a necessary preventative against suicide, which he believed was more frequent in England than anywhere else: 'Are there not more Self-murders, and melancholick Lunaticks in *England*, heard of in one Year, than in a greater part of *Europe* besides?'[77] In the next century, Congreve's rhetorical question became a shibboleth, repeated and discussed all over Europe.[78]

There have been numerous attempts to calculate a suicide rate for early modern England, and scholars have advanced bold and baseless generalizations about the figures that they have arrived at. These exercises have been driven by the conviction that suicide rates are a direct measure of the health (or sickness) of the social organism at a given time. Peter Laslett, for instance, declares: 'Suicide is the most usual index of social demoralization, of *anomie* as the sociologists call it. If ever we could get to know anything reliable about it in these earlier times, it would probably be an even more sensitive index than it is now, marking

[75] Sym, *Lifes Preservative*, Preface, sig. A4$^{v}$. Cf. Sym's own observation that his tract is 'too necessary and usefull' because nowadays 'so many doe most wretchedly and unnaturally *kill* themselves', sig. a1$^{v}$. See also, J. Bradford, *The Writings of John Bradford*, ed. A. Townshend, Parker Society (Cambridge, 1848), 61.

[76] Evelyn, *Diary*, v. 165, 593. See also, Thomas James, *Spira's Despair Revived* (London, 1694), sigs. A5$^{v}$–A6$^{r}$.

[77] W. Congreve, *The Complete Works*, ed. M. Summers, iii (London, 1923), 206.

[78] R. Bartel, 'Suicide in Eighteenth-Century England: The Myth of a Reputation', *Huntington Library Quarterly*, xxiii (1960), 145–58.

the relationship between personal discipline and social survival.'[79] In a pioneering set of articles, P. E. H. Hair estimates yearly suicide rates for Nottinghamshire and Essex in the sixteenth century that ranged from around 3.4 to 4.0 per hundred thousand population. Noting that no suicides were recorded on a thirteenth-century Bedfordshire coroner's roll, he concludes that hostility to suicide had kept the rate at which it was committed low in the Middle Ages but that attitudes had become more permissive in the sixteenth century.[80] Hair is cautious about blaming the Reformation for sky-rocketing rates of self-slaughter, but S. E. Sprott shows no such restraint. Using the London bills of mortality, he produces a set of suicide statistics, calculated meaninglessly as ratios of the overall mortality figures in the bills, and proclaims that the rise of militant Puritanism had caused an epidemic of suicide in the metropolis.[81] More recently, Michael Zell found that the rate of recorded suicide in late sixteenth-century Kent was about 10.0 per 100,000, a figure that closely matches modern rates.[82] Still other historians, comparing Tudor suicide rates from various localities with modern figures, have concluded that the sixteenth-century rate was not high but low. The latest assay of this kind is J. A. Sharpe's tentative suggestion that the suicide rate was between 4 and 6 per 100,000 or higher, which he says is half or a third of the suicide rate in Britain today. 'This figure provides ammunition', he remarks, 'for those arguing that the early modern world was a less stressful and more idyllic place than the modern industrial state.'[83]

[79] P. Laslett, *The World We have Lost*, 2nd edn. (London, 1971), 145. The point is made more briefly in the latest edition of *The World We have Lost*, 3rd edn. (New York, 1984), 173.

[80] P. E. H. Hair, 'A Note on the Incidence of Tudor Suicide', *Local Population Studies*, v (1970), 36–43; id., 'Deaths from Violence in Britain: A Tentative Secular Survey', *Population Studies*, xxv (1971), 5–24. M. MacDonald, 'The Inner Side of Wisdom: Suicide in Early Modern England', *Psychological Medicine*, vii (1977), 565–82, argues that the statistics are unreliable but that suicide was not rare in the Tudor and Stuart period.

[81] S. E. Sprott, *The English Debate on Suicide: From Donne to Hume* (La Salle, Ill., 1961). For criticism of Sprott's unconventional methods, see Hair, 'Note on the Incidence', 37–8.

[82] M. Zell, 'Suicide in Pre-Industrial England', *Social History*, xi (1986), 309–10.

[83] J. A. Sharpe, *Early Modern England: A Social History, 1550–1760* (London, 1987), 112. Arguing against Lawrence Stone's contention that violence was endemic in early modern society, however, Sharpe also concluded that the suicide rate was low: J. A. Sharpe, 'The History of Violence in England: Some Observations', *Past and Present*, no. 108 (1985), 209–11. In both of these places, Sharpe qualifies his suggestions with wise remarks about the problems raised by the evidence. He overstates, however, the prevalence of suicide today, at least as measured by the comparable set of statistics. The rate of reported suicide for England and Wales for 1975–84 rose from about 7.5 to 8.5 per 100,000: G. M. G. McClure, 'Suicide in England and Wales, 1975–1984', *British Journal of Psychiatry*, cl (1987), 309–14. See also, United Nations, *Demographic Yearbook, 1985* (New York, 1987), 786–7; *Home Office Statistical Bulletin*, Coroners' Statistics: England and Wales, 1981 (9 Nov. 1982), Table 2; M. Alderson, *International Mortality Statistics* (London, 1981), Table 170.

It is understandable that scholars should wish to draw conclusions after all the hours they have spent gathering and tabulating the data. But D. M. Palliser rightly points out that attempts to pursue Laslett's suggestion and compute a suicide rate for the Tudor and Stuart era continue to be frustrated by problems that beset the measurement of other crimes, missing records and a demonstrable but incalculable discrepancy between recorded suicides and the higher 'real' rate at which the offence was committed.[84] S. J. Stevenson, in the most searching discussion of the problem, shows why we are unlikely ever to discover that 'real' rate. He concludes that record loss, inadequate numbers of coroners or their poor performance on the job, the absence of records for most boroughs and many liberties, and the vagaries of classification all reduce the value of the inquisition evidence.[85] From the perspective of a nation-wide study like this one, perhaps the most serious problem is that we cannot know how many inquests were held in liberties that did not have to return inquisitions to the central courts, nor can we even be certain that the numbers of such liberties remained constant. The most conspicuous of the places whose coroners did not report to the central courts was the most important of all, London and Middlesex. And except for a single roll for the year 1590, all of the London coroners' records prior to about 1760 have been lost.

The rates of suicide that can be calculated from the inquisitions in King's Bench records are undoubtedly much lower than they would be if all the missing records could be found. The preposterously low figures, never rising above 4.22 and averaging around 2 per 100,000, can tell us nothing at all about the health or sickness of Tudor and Stuart society. Even the long-term rise and fall in deaths reported to the central government over the centuries was determined mainly by the vigilance and laxity of the Crown's efforts to supervise coroners and by cultural change, as we have seen. These are painful conclusions, arrived at after thousands of hours of effort. They demonstrate why a Durkheimian history of suicide in early modern England will probably never be written. Total scepticism, however, raises some problems as well. In some years blighted by harvest failure and low wages—1574, 1587, and 1597–1600, for example—the suicide rate shot up. It would be mulish not to believe that there was a connection between the hardship that the poor were experiencing and the rise in the number of suicides. On the

[84] D. M. Palliser, *The Age of Elizabeth* (London, 1983), 314.
[85] Stevenson, 'Rise of Suicide Verdicts', 37–75.

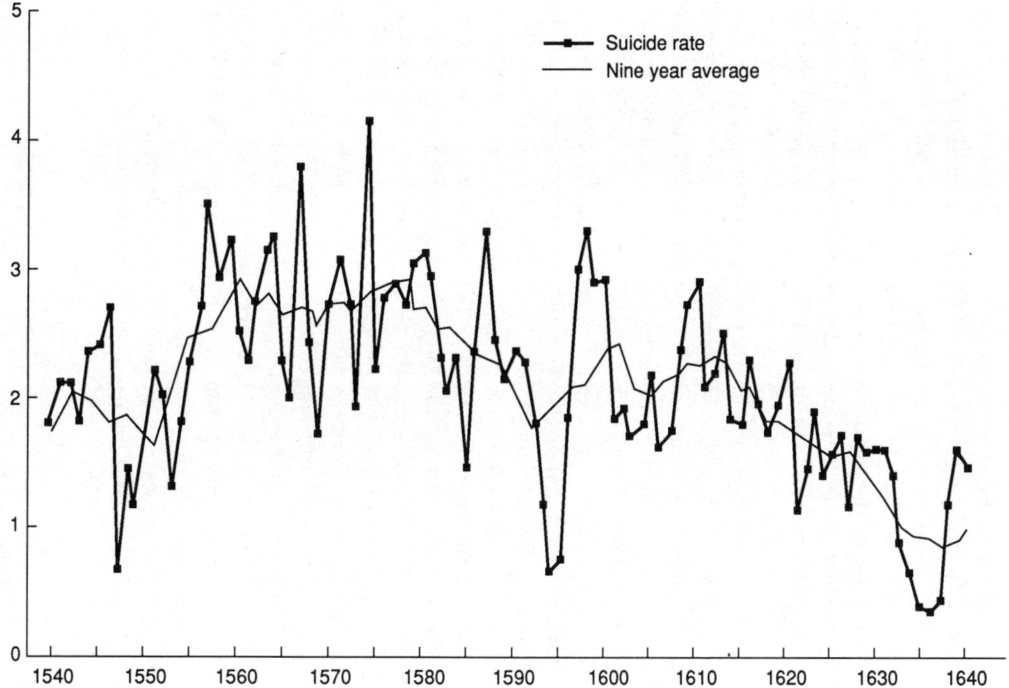


FIG. 7.1. Suicide rate, 1540–1640

*Source*: PRO, KB 9, 10, 11, 140; PL 26; HCA 1.

other hand, even when enforcement was at its height, between about 1560 and 1640, there was no overall correlation between prices and the suicide rate. And when economic and social conditions were at their very worst, in the mid-1590s and the 1620s, there was no jump in the average suicide rate, either.[86]

After 1640 the reporting of suicides to the central government declined and finally stopped almost altogether. It is impossible to construct a meaningful suicide rate for any part of England in the early eighteenth century, let alone the whole country. The London bills of mortality would seem to offer the greatest opportunities for compiling an index of gloom that would span the century. They were undoubtedly the chief source of a growing conviction that suicide was rapidly increasing after 1660. The fact that the bills themselves were printed and circulated is mildly surprising. They do not make exciting reading. Nevertheless, the bald list of persons who died 'within the bills' was printed weekly from the early seventeenth century; a yearly summary was also issued in mid-December. The practice of circulating printed versions of the bills has received little attention, but it is in itself significant. As Paul Slack has shown in a brilliant study of the impact of the plague in Tudor and Stuart England, information about the spread of the disease was crucial to local governments and to individuals all over England, and its dissemination helped prompt improvements in quarantining that eventually controlled the infection.[87] Fear made the rhythms of dying in London and the methods that death used to claim his victims the concern of the whole kingdom. The bills were not, however, limited to plague. They also featured a listing of 'casualties', including suicides. The weekly bills gave the number of people who had killed themselves, listing them by parish and indicating lunacy verdicts and occupations now and then; the yearly summaries reported the total number of persons in the parishes encompassed by the bills who had 'murdered themselves' or 'made themselves away'. The bills not only

[86] Two other years in which the suicide rate rose, 1638 and 1639, also followed bad harvests. For price and wage data, see C. J. Harrison, 'Grain Price Analysis and Harvest Qualities, 1465–1634', *Agricultural History Review*, xix (1971), 135–55; W. G. Hoskins, 'Harvest Fluctuations in English Economic History, 1480–1619', *Agricultural History Review*, xii (1964), 28–46; id., 'Harvest Fluctuations in English Economic History, 1620–1759', *Agricultural History Review*, xvi (1968), 15–31; J. Thirsk (ed.), *The Agrarian History of England and Wales*, vol. iv: *1500–1640* (Cambridge, 1967), ch. 9, Statistical Appendix; and especially the useful discussion in Palliser, *Age of Elizabeth*, 48–50.

[87] P. Slack, *The Impact of Plague in Tudor and Stuart England* (London, 1985), 148–9, 240–1, 244–5, 252–4.

circulated beyond the metropolis, they were also reprinted in the London and provincial newspapers, and so reached a much larger audience. Papers as remote from London as the *Gloucester Journal*, the *Kentish Post*, the *Derby Mercury*, and the *Northampton Mercury* published them.[88]

Taken at face value, the figures in the bills told a simple and striking tale. Almost every year from 1660 to 1735, the number of suicides increased. The eleven-year moving average of reported suicides rose from about fifteen per year in the 1660s to about fifty per year in the 1730s. The average incidence then declined gradually to about twenty-five per year in the last decade of the eighteenth century. Contemporaries would, of course, have noticed the trends in the weekly and yearly figures that were widely published, and very high figures—those that exceeded or nearly equalled the highest number reported previously—undoubtedly captured their attention more strongly than low or average ones. They were aware of the rapid growth that London was experiencing; we now estimate that the population of the metropolis more than doubled between 1650 and 1800. But the size of the city at any given time in that period was unknown and few newspaper readers could have guessed the suicide rate when they read the mortality figures. The raw numbers were what commentators remarked upon, and so no doubt did the rest of the reading public.

Some readers recognized that the figures in the bills were bogus. The early demographers used the bills extensively, and they remarked on some of their defects. John Graunt, who criticized their accuracy on several points, remarked that the number of people listed in them as having died of lunacy was too low and may have meant to imply the same thing about suicides. Writing in 1662, he was just about the only observer who remarked that suicide was comparatively infrequent. In a discussion of stillbirths, he pointed to one source of inaccuracy that applied to suicides as well—persons buried outside the churchyard were not necessarily noticed in the bills.[89] Isaac Watts also displayed an acute awareness of their imprecision, and his comments on them are highly interesting. The number of suicides listed in the bills was, in Watts's opinion, a minimum figure: many of those who were entered as

[88] G. A. Cranfield, *The Development of the Provincial Newspaper, 1700–1760* (Oxford, 1962), 95–6.

[89] J. Graunt, *Natural and Political Observations Mentioned in a Following Index, and Made Upon the Bills of Mortality*, in *The Economic Writings of Sir William Petty*, ed. C. H. Hull (New York, 1964), ii. 355, 360.

'drowned' and 'found drowned' must also have brought about their own deaths, 'tho' surviving Relatives might conceal it from the Notice of the Public'.[90] His reservation was undoubtedly right. Many of the persons listed in contemporary inquests as 'found drowned' were almost certainly suicides.[91] There were other reasons why the figures in the bills are suspect. Reporting of deaths by parish clerks was voluntary, and they often failed in their duty. 'For some large parishes no account is sent for weeks together', complained a commentator in 1759, 'and the account for several is sometimes inserted in one weekly bill. If this was done without any omissions the account would come right at the end of the year; but omissions in many, there is good reason to believe, are never supplied or corrected.'[92] The bill for 10 December 1793, for example, notes that the anomalously high numbers of deaths reported for the week were due to several clerks, who belatedly filed their returns for the whole year then. Finally, as writers who use the bills for historical study are aware, the boundaries of the part of the metropolis 'within the bills' were altered from time to time, so that the deaths recorded were from an area that was expanding geographically as well as demographically.[93]

Nevertheless, it is doubtful if the public had any awareness of just how little the figures in the bills were worth. And it is easy to see how contemporaries who read them in the late seventeenth and early eighteenth centuries got the impression that suicide was increasing inexorably to levels that were previously unknown. There were many years between 1661 and 1740 when the incidence of suicide was very much higher than normal. The high figures, moreover, increased in magnitude by stages. Leaving aside the anomalously large number of suicides reported for 1660, the worst years in the later seventeenth century saw 20–30 such deaths. The peak numbers between 1700 and 1720 were in the range of 35–40. The peak years in the 1720s and 1730s produced figures between 59 and 65. It is also easy to guess one reason why the decline in reported suicides after about 1740 attracted no notice. Until about 1780, the years

[90] I. Watts, *A Defense Against the Temptation to Self-Murder* (London, 1726), p. iv.

[91] G. I. Greenwald, 'Medicolegal Progress in Inquests of Felonious Deaths: Westminster, 1761–1866', MD thesis (Yale, 1980), 51. Cf. M. L. White, 'Westminster Inquests', MD thesis (Yale, 1980), 82. Our own examination of the inquests confirms the judgement of Greenwald and White. The weekly bills usually listed up to a dozen persons 'found drowned' per year in the early 18th cent.; the category was dropped later on, perhaps because its uselessness was recognized.

[92] Quoted in W. Ogle, 'An Inquiry into the Trustworthiness of the Old Bills of Mortality', *Journal of the Royal Statistical Society*, lv (1892), 442.

[93] These changes are conveniently summarized ibid., Appendix B.

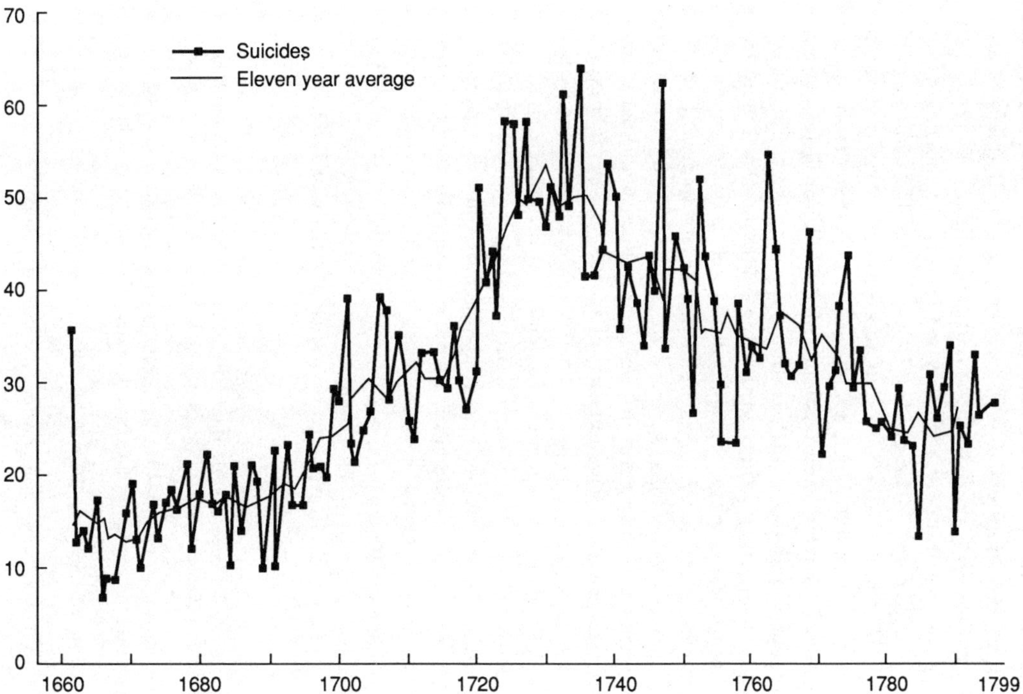


Fɪɢ. 7.2. Suicides in the London bills of mortality, 1660–1799

*Source*: yearly bills of mortality, 1660–1714; weekly bills of mortality, 1715–99

in which suicides were much higher than average—for example, 1749, 1755, 1765, 1772, and 1778—equalled the numbers reported in the deadliest decades, the 1720s and 1730s. In other words, if people paid most attention to figures that were shockingly bad, as they surely did, then the decline in the average figure would be less noticeable than the fact that the worst years were as bad as ever.

## THE IDENTITIES OF SUICIDES

The suicide rate thus cannot tell us very much about early modern society. Its history is the history of illusions. Nor can an examination of the incidence of suicide among specific social groups reveal as much as we would wish. Like the overall suicide rate, the figures showing what kinds of people killed themselves display the real incidence of suicide among different groups only through the distorting lens of official procedures and contemporary preconceptions. They will not sustain bold hypotheses about the relative propensity to commit suicide among men and women, rich and poor, old and young. But they highlight some notable variations and reveal how the interplay of actual events, administrative procedures, and attitudes toward gender, class, and age affected the classification of suicides. Before we explore social attitudes, the angles of distortion in the figures, however, we must first take a brief look at the patterns in the glass.

Men were returned as suicides twice as often as women in almost every sample of inquisitions that survive as well as in the notices of suicide in the weekly bills of mortality for London. The sex ratio in the King's Bench data for 1485–1714 was 1.8 men for every one woman; for Norwich in the eighteenth century, it was 2.3 to 1; and for greater London it was 2 to 1. Only in Cumberland—for reasons that are unknown—did the ratio approach equality: it was just 1.2 to 1. Completed suicide was almost certainly a masculine act; similar findings without quite the same defects have been produced for other times and places. No one has really produced a satisfying explanation for the imbalance of sexes among suicides. Men's greater propensity for violence seems to be one cause; they have apparently always chosen more lethal methods when they attempt suicide.[94] In the early modern period

[94] Epidemiological research, however, suggests that men act with more determination than women when they select less violent methods: D. Lester, *Why People Kill Themselves: A Summary of Research Findings on Suicidal Behavior* (Springfield, Ill., 1972), ch. 6. Cf. McClure, 'Suicide in England and Wales, 1975–1984'.

men were much less likely to try to drown or poison themselves than women, and far more likely to hang or shoot themselves. Even these findings cannot be trusted too far, however, and certainly not far enough to justify ambitious theories about gender and suicide. For juries were naturally more likely to discover a suicide that was violent than one that was passive and covert, and so more likely to classify the deaths of males as suicides. In fact, the ratio of men to women in all kinds of deaths by violence was high—higher, in fact, than for suicides. Moreover, men had far more personal property to seize than women did. The chattels of wives were technically the property of their husbands. The deaths of men were therefore much more likely to have been given close attention by juries and by the almoners than those of women.[95] The precise ratio of men to women who were judged suicides in early modern England was thus the result of administrative and cultural factors as well as the actual inclination of each sex to kill themselves. Consider the ratio of men to women among suicides in various status groups (Table 7.1). It is extremely unlikely that labourers' wives were a lot happier than their more prosperous sisters, and yet they had far the lowest rate of suicide relative to men of their class. Labourers' wives were very near the bottom of the hierarchies of status and gender; their suicides were of little consequence legally and financially. It is probable that coroners and their juries were simply less assiduous in classifying them as suicides, and in noting their status when they did, than they were when they investigated men and women of greater importance and wealth.

Table 7.1. *Sex Ratio of Selected Status Groups, 1485–1714*

| Status | Men | Women | Ratio |
|---|---|---|---|
| Peers/Knights | 4 | 1 | 4.0:1 |
| Gentlemen | 151 | 35 | 4.3:1 |
| Yeomen | 344 | 103 | 3.3:1 |
| Husbandmen | 703 | 156 | 4.5:1 |
| Craftsmen | 874 | 187 | 4.7:1 |
| Labourers | 1,335 | 179 | 7.5:1 |
| Totals | 3,411 | 661 | 5.2:1 |

*Note*: Reported statuses only. Does not include children.
*Source*: PRO, KB 9, 10, 11, 140; PL 26; MCA 1.

95 Hunnisett, 'Importance of Eighteenth-Century Coroners' Bills', 128–9.

Data on status and occupation—always problematic for this period, anyway—are similarly suspect and similarly revealing. They show plainly how reverence for social rank affected the judgements of coroners' juries. Inquisitions recorded rank fitfully and inconsistently. Among the almost 13,000 inquisitions returned to King's Bench between 1485 and 1714, a status or occupation was listed about 60 per cent of the time. Many of the categories juries used are useless for sociological analysis; they were noted only to identify the individual. There were, for example, 826 women described simply as wives, 513 as widows, and 1,167 as spinsters. But despite the fact that all adult women had to fall into one or another of these categories, the marital status of thousands of them was stated in terms of their husband's rank or (more often) ignored altogether. Furthermore, the category of spinsters included both unmarried women and married women who really were wool spinners—ninety-seven of them were described as married, and there were probably many more. Early modern juries were confronted by a society in which many people of both sexes played overlapping roles. It was perhaps relatively simple to know how to fit male landowners and farmers into the status hierarchy. But it was notoriously difficult to classify people who were artisans, craftsmen, hawkers, and paupers. Men and women of humble rank did what they could to make a living. Many—perhaps most—plied more than one trade, and coroners seem mainly to have chosen to record the job for which the person was best known at the time of his death. They certainly made no effort to reduce the profusion of labels to broad categories. Hundreds of different trades are listed in the inquisitions on suicides returned to King's Bench. In a large sample of over a thousand inquisitions from the later sixteenth century there were (not counting gentlemen, husbandmen, yeomen, and labourers) 61 servants, 13 clerics, 12 tailors, 11 shepherds, 8 weavers, 8 vagabonds, 7 smiths, 5 apprentices, 4 bakers, 4 cobblers, 3 millers, 3 milliners, 3 butchers, 2 tile-makers, 2 thatchers, 2 sawyers, and 2 minstrels. Thirty-one other occupations were listed as callings of solitary suicides. They ranged in status from a cowherd to a judge and in skill from an armourer to a groom. Juries' vision of the social and economic structure of their society was like a painter's panorama of some great congregation of humanity, such as Hogarth's *Southwark Fair*, in which hundreds of people at various levels of an imagined scene are performing a bewildering array of actions, linked by their common presence in a structured space but not by similarities between the things that they are doing. The social hierarchy was a collectively imagined space, stable and divided into clearly recognized planes, teeming with people whose position on it was variable and shifting.

The place of the people near the top of the hierarchy was more fixed and more conspicuous than those of the masses at the base of the structure. And they exercised a powerful influence over their social inferiors even in death. Consider the fact that peers, knights, gentlemen, and their families accounted for just 1.6 per cent of all recorded suicides between 1485 and 1714. Experts' estimates of the numbers of the nobility and gentry vary, but they formed a proportion of the population several times that size. If one considers just those categories that are social ranks, then the sum rises to a more plausible 4.6 per cent. But this was a group of people whose status was very unlikely to escape the notice of coroners and go unreported, whereas men and women of lower rank were often described in terms of alternative occupational labels or marital status, or simply by name. The nobility and gentry were also the group most likely to be given the benefit of the doubt by juries or even to be protected by bogus verdicts. Complaints about this were voiced through the centuries, and there was substance to such charges. We have already seen that men and women of quality were more likely to be found *non compos mentis* than their social inferiors. Many more were certainly spared the indignity of a suicide verdict. Gossips knew that the earl of Bath, who shot himself in 1701 a fortnight after his father's death, had committed suicide, but the coroner's jury returned a verdict of misadventure. The *Flying Post* reported to the world at large that he had been 'unfortunately killed by the casual going off of a Pistol', and that a verdict of *per infortuniam* had been returned after the inquest had heard that his lordship was 'under no manner of Discontent'.[96] For obvious reasons, it is rarely possible to detect successful cover-ups, and so their frequency cannot be determined.

Even the ages that coroners recorded, and only a few of the most conscientious of them did so, manifest both procedural habits and real social problems. It is very likely that the ages of young adults were reported less often than those of the very young and the very old, for whom they were an identifying characteristic. The surviving evidence over the period 1485–1714 nevertheless suggests strongly that children and the elderly were over-represented among recorded suicides. (See

[96] Evelyn, *Diary*, v. 475–6; Luttrell, *A Brief Relation*, v. 86; Hertfordshire RO, Diary of Lady Sara Cowper, Pensanger MSS, D/EP F 29, i. 1, 133; *The Flying Post* (4–6 Sept. 1701); *DNB*, s.v. 'Grenville, Charles'.

Table 7.2 *Age Structure of Reported Suicides*

| Age | England, 1485–1714 | | Norwich | |
|---|---|---|---|---|
| | N | % | N | % |
| 0–4 | | | | |
| 5–9 | 10 | 1.0 | | |
| 10–14 | 159 | 15.9 | 9 | 3.5 |
| 15–19 | 150 | 15.0 | 24 | 9.2 |
| 20–24 | 121 | 12.1 | 22 | 8.5 |
| 25–29 | 40 | 4.0 | 15 | 5.8 |
| 30–34 | 93 | 9.3 | 20 | 7.7 |
| 35–39 | 31 | 3.1 | 10 | 3.8 |
| 40–44 | 92 | 9.2 | 27 | 10.4 |
| 45–49 | 19 | 1.9 | 27 | 10.4 |
| 50–54 | 82 | 8.2 | 17 | 6.5 |
| 55–59 | 24 | 2.4 | 18 | 6.9 |
| 60–64 | 100 | 10.0 | 41 | 15.8 |
| 65+ | 80 | 8.0 | 30 | 11.5 |
| TOTALS | 1,001 | 100.0 | 260 | 100.0 |

*Source*: PRO, KB 9, 10, 11, 140; PL 26, HCA 1; Norwich Inquisitions.

Table 7.2.) Like idiots and lunatics, the very young were not supposed to have been mentally capable of committing *felo de se*. Legal authorities were more or less agreed, at least by the mid-seventeenth century, that persons under the age of fourteen could not be guilty of self-murder. In practice, children were returned as *felones de se* at much younger ages, and teenagers were very numerous among suicides.[97] Indeed, more suicides were recorded among children than in any other age group. Child suicides were at least proportional to their numbers in the population among boys and girls 10–14 and markedly higher than proportional among youths 15–24. The age group 15–19, for which comparative statistics are not readily available, was certainly greatly over-represented. Moreover, adults in the prime of life were, by comparison, somewhat under-represented. (See Table 7.3.)

The finding that children in early modern England slew themselves with unusual frequency is very striking. Suicide by children is very rare in all modern societies for which we have statistics, regardless of the

[97] It is worth noting as well that the property of young people, while it was usually of small value, was all chattels and hence forfeitable.

Table 7.3 *Age Structures of Suicides and the General Population*

| Age | Suicides, 1485–1714 % | Norwich Suicides % | England, 1541–1799 % |
|---|---|---|---|
| 0–4 | 0 | 0 | 12.9 |
| 5–14 | 16.9 | 3.5 | 20.1 |
| 15–24 | 27.1 | 17.7 | 17.7 |
| 25–50 | 38.0 | 51.5 | 41.0 |
| 60+ | 18.0 | 27.3 | 8.3 |
| TOTALS | 100.0 | 100.0 | 100.0 |

*Sources*: PRO, KB 9, 10, 11, 140; PL 26, HCA 1; Norwich Inquisitions; E. A. Wrigley and R. S. Schofield, *The Population History of England, 1541–1871* (Cambridge, Mass., 1981), Appendix 3, 528–9.

publicity and research that occasional rashes of teenage suicide in the United States have provoked. Less than one-half of 1 per cent of suicides certified by English coroners in 1983 were boys and girls younger than fifteen.[98] Almost 7 per cent of Tudor and Stuart suicides fell into that age group, and self-killing by young men and women in their early twenties was also much more common proportionally than it is today. Contemporaries recognized that youthful suicide was a danger, and most of them who commented on the problem agreed that abusive parents and masters were its main cause, particularly among young children and teenagers. (Frustrated love affairs were also blamed for the deaths of young adults, as we shall see in Chapter 8.) Sir William Denny warned 'the Frighted Childe'—a type in his didactic poem, *Pelicanicidium* (1653)—not to kill himself.

> Who's there? The woful Childe of Parents Rage.
> Whither art [thou] going to prevent thine Age?
>
> . . . . . . . .
>
> Storms last not Alwayes. Have a Care, mad Childe!
> Thou thinkest to scape the Worst, and art beguil'd.

[98] Great Britain, Office of Population, Censuses and Surveys, *Mortality Statistics—Area Review of the Registrar General on Deaths by Area of Usual Residence in England and Wales, 1983*, Series DH 5, no. 10 (London, 1984), Table 5, 20. The statistical validity of the inquisition data presented in this chapter is discussed in Murphy, '"Woful Childe of Parents Rage"', 261–2, which offers a more wide-ranging discussion of some of the data and examples discussed below.

Thy Parents Wrath may sooner be appeas'd,
Than everlasting Torments can be eas'd.[99]

Historians now agree that most Tudor and Stuart parents did not brutalize their children. But the social customs that regulated physical violence and sent boys and girls out of the parents' homes to work for other adults in their teens (or younger) permitted a wide latitude for abuse. The family was the foundation stone of the social order, and fathers and masters had unquestioned authority to discipline their dependents. Indeed, curbing the passionate actions of youth was one of their most important duties: family discipline was the most important type of social control and the model for all other kinds of regulation and punishment.[100] Understandably, neither the authorities nor the relatives of mistreated children were anxious to intervene on their behalf. Terrified and brutalized boys and girls had nowhere to turn and killed themselves to escape their elders' wrath, as Denny's doggerel warned. For instance, the twelve-year-old Agnes Addam went horse-riding with a girlfriend in 1565 and dirtied her clothes. She started to return home, but then, seized with terror over what her father would do when he saw her spoiled outfit, she rushed into a pond and drowned herself.[101] A boy who threw a piece of glass at his brother in 1729 was so frightened of the beating he knew he would receive from his father that he hanged himself in the outhouse.[102] A few years later the son of a Hackney tradesman, a boy of thirteen, fell victim to a cruel practical joke. He had lost his hat, and his father had threatened to beat him within an inch of his life if he lost his new one. Overhearing the threat, the boy's sister hid the hat, and when he realized that it was missing, he hanged himself 'for fear of being chastised by his Father'.[103] Step-parents were notoriously brutal by reputation. 'What Stepmother has frighted thee to do | That'?

[99] W. Denny, *Pelicanicidium, or The Christian Adviser against Self-Murder* (London, 1653), 4.

[100] Good discussions of family discipline are C. Hill, *Society and Puritanism*, 2nd edn. (New York, 1967), ch. 13; S. D. Amussen, *An Ordered Society: Gender and Class in Early Modern England* (Oxford, 1988), chs. 2, 4. For evidence of parental benevolence that provides an antidote to the poisonous examples below, see L. A. Pollock, *Forgotten Children: Parent–Child Relations from 1500 to 1900* (Cambridge, 1983), ch. 5. For more poison, see L. Stone, *The Family, Sex and Marriage in England, 1500–1800* (London, 1977), 161–74.

[101] PRO, KB 9/613/2, m. 219; KB 29/200/2d. The jury described her motives as '*timor parentium correctionis* and '*metus castigationis*'.

[102] *Fog's Weekly Journal*, no. 41 (5 July 1729).

[103] *Weekly Miscellany*, no. 264 13 Jan. 1737/8).

Denny asked his 'woful Childe'.[104] And occasionally the stereotype was true. Elizabeth Smith was admittedly a difficult girl. By the time she was twelve, she had a history of truancy and had run away from home five times. She was the only one of her mother's children who lived with her new husband. Elizabeth's step-father admitted that he had beaten her at least twice in the past year, claiming that 'she was a very untoward girl'. When she disappeared in February 1786, her step-father and mother did not even bother to look for her, thinking that she had 'got into a bad House'. She had in fact drowned herself in the New River, 'thro the dread fear of some corporal punishment', in the jury's opinion.[105]

Violence was not the only form of abuse that drove children to suicidal despair. Will Rogers visited Richard Napier twice in 1598, complaining of Satan's temptations. He had no money and Napier had to supply medicines for him gratis. 'His father is so worldly and wretched that he will give him nothing to help him', the astrologer explained.[106] More pathetic still, the nine-year-old Thomas Travell tried to drown himself in 1612 because he no longer wanted to live in poverty and misery.[107] How widespread these subtler forms of mistreatment were cannot be determined: no one ever prosecuted them, and no one willingly admitted depriving a dead child of necessities at an inquest. The possibility is never raised in the surviving depositions for the late seventeenth and eighteenth centuries.

Young people left home to work as servants or apprentices in the houses of strangers in their early teens. Law and custom forbade them to flee the homes of masters and mistresses who made them miserable or who abused them. Only the most flagrant brutality was regarded as sufficient grounds for leaving a master. Boys and girls who ran away and returned home could normally expect little sympathy from their parents. Miserable as an apprentice to a weaver, the twelve-year-old Daniel Rose returned home and complained to his family. They must have admonished him to go back to his master, for he left the house that evening and was found dead the next morning, hanging in his master's garden.[108]

104 Denny, *Pelicanicidium*, 4.

105 Middlesex Coroners' Inquisitions, MJ/SPC.W, 325. For a much earlier parallel, see PRO, KB 9/769/1, m. 91.

106 Bodl., Ashmole MS 228, fos. 139$^{v}$, 142$^{v}$ (Rogers). Another of Napier's patients, the 20-year-old Richard Sanders, went stark mad after his father 'checked' him and was also 'tempted': Ashm. 201, fos. 160$^{r}$, 167$^{v}$, 186$^{r}$, 230$^{r}$; 230, fo. 5$^{r}$ (Sanders).

107 Bodl., Ashmole MS 409, fo. 35$^{r}$ (Travell).

108 PRO, KB 11/18/7, m. 9. For other suicides identified as runaway servants, see KB 9/629/2, mm. 254–5; KB 9/665/2, m. 620. Stevenson, 'Social and Economic Contribution to Suicide', 229–31, anticipates the remarks here and provides more evidence in support of them. Some 273 persons were identified as servants.

The plight of unhappy children was dire. Stories of mauled and mutilated apprentices and servants were commonplace. The terror beatings might inspire was a plausible motive for suicide. In 1519 a cobbler's servant in Stoke next Winchester in Hampshire ate a leg of mutton when his master was away. Knowing what the penalty for his gluttony was likely to be, he hanged himself rather than face the cobbler's wrath.[109] Riding his master's horse from St Faith's fair to his house in Norwich in 1730, Thomas Riley lost the animal somehow. His employer, Mr Luck, was furious, and threatened him. 'Being but a young lad', the coroner's jury deduced, Riley 'was terrified by the fear of punishment', and while his master and mistress were away, he hanged himself on their loom.[110] A Holborn woman locked her serving boy in a room because he had brought fewer potatoes home from market than he was supposed to have done. The lad tried to kill himself.[111]

Juries were reluctant to erode the right to discipline servants by finding masters culpable, except in the most compelling cases. Elizabeth Skinner beat her husband's nine-year-old servant to death in 1595, but the jury who investigated his death refused to find her culpable of any crime.[112] Servants who died trying to escape their master's brutality were sometimes excused as the victims of illness or accident and sometimes they were condemned as self-murderers. Nine-year-old Katherine Cok died from exposure, hiding from her master in a hedgerow in 1520. The jury returned her *felo de se*.[113] Whether the death was judged a suicide or a misfortune, juries *never* presented masters for causing a servant to die like this.[114] Their attitude reflected the outlook of most adults. Testifying before the inquest on Thomas Empson, a Westminster apprentice who hanged himself in 1779, his mistress admitted that her husband had 'corrected' the boy with a leather strap. The jury found that the lad had slain himself while insane.[115] Girls had another reason to fear their masters. Mary McClure was a London servant who drifted from job to job and displeased her parents by living out of wedlock with a man for five months. She grew melancholy and then finally drowned herself, however, when she discovered that she was pregnant, 'having submitted

109 PRO, KB 9/477, m. 118. See also, KB 9/598/1, mm. 87, 87a (1556); KB 9/1073/2, m. 121 (1561). MacDonald, *Mystical Bedlam*, 87–8, gives other examples of servants and apprentices whose mental disorders were attributed to mistreatment by their masters or the fear of it.

110 Norwich Inquisitions, Thomas Riley (8 Oct. 1730).

111 *Annual Register*, xxi (1778), 172.

112 PRO, KB 9/690/2, m. 225.

113 PRO, KB 9/482, m. 101.

114 Murphy, '"Woful Childe of Parents Rage"', 267.

115 Westminster Inquisitions, Thomas Empson (7 May 1779).

to her Master's will'.[116] Whether Mary had been seduced or raped, no one knew, but her dilemma was disturbingly common.

The data available for Norwich in the eighteenth century show a much smaller number of children than one would expect from the statistics on the Tudor and Stuart period. Young people in the stage of life at which they would be in service, between fifteen and twenty-four, on the other hand, were very numerous, as they had been in previous centuries. It is not clear how representative the Norwich data may be in this respect: the sample is a small one. But it is possible that the increasing conviction that children were innocent creatures and greater sensitivity to the feelings of parents may have influenced Georgian juries.[117] We have already seen that one Norwich teenager who hanged himself was counted as an accident.

Old people, like children, were unusually numerous among Tudor and Stuart suicides, although the figures are more ambiguous. Contemporaries were particularly bad at remembering the ages of people over forty, and they typically rounded off to the most plausible decade—persons allegedly fifty, sixty, seventy, and eighty accounted for over 70 per cent of the reported suicides over forty-nine. If half the people whose ages were guessed at sixty were actually still in their fifties, then the over-representation of the aged would look much less dramatic than it does. Moreover, the propertyless state of many old people may have made juries more willing to bring in verdicts of *felo de se* than they were in the case of young people with families that might be impoverished by the loss of their goods. And yet even if the figures were deflated and the predisposition of juries were granted, suicides by the elderly would nevertheless still exceed their proportions in the population at large and far exceed such deaths among people in the prime of life. The Norwich data show an even more striking preponderance of people over sixty than the earlier evidence. It is impossible to tell if this represents a real change in the welfare of the old, since the sample is small and complementary data are unavailable. But at the very least, these figures fortify the conclusion that the elderly in early modern England were unusually suicidal.

It is easy to understand why. Early modern society revered age but despised the old. For many people—particularly men of property—advancing age brought wealth, power, and honour. But for others—

[116] Middlesex Inquisitions, MJ/SPC.W, 346. For earlier examples, see MacDonald, *Mystical Bedlam*, 87–8.

[117] Stone, *Family, Sex and Marriage*, ch. 9.

especially propertyless men and poor widows—it brought destitution. Nothing then could alleviate the miseries of bodily decay or the horrifying erosion of one's mental powers. Contemporary literature, in fact, exaggerated and mocked the disintegration caused by advancing age: the old, like Lear, were thought liable to end their lives sans everything.[118] Just like Lear, the humble husbandman Edmund Belshere gave over his goods to his daughters and lived with them in his old age. After his wife died, however, he repented of the arrangement, casting the deed of conveyance he had signed into a neighbour's fireplace. He was unable to resume his work and found no remedy for his discontent afterwards; in 1599 he killed himself. His defiant destruction of the deed had not undone his dependence on his daughters, but it did bring them trouble after his death, for they were unable to produce it to defend themselves against the greed of the manorial lord, who seized Belshere's goods.[119] Men and women who became too old and impotent to perform their usual tasks were liable to fall into degrading poverty. It was with some surprise, therefore, that the *Weekly Journal* reported that 'an antient [*sic*] Seaman' had killed himself after his friends had secured for him a pension for his subsistence as long as he lived. He had, the paper commented, 'taken Care to save the Government that charge'.[120] John Lythe's suicide in 1524 was easier to understand, and much more familiar. 'Languishing in poverty and filled with profound sadness', Lythe, a man of seventy years and more, hanged himself in a barn.[121] Over two centuries later, Cuthbert Cousins died for the same reason. Found with his throat slashed but still alive, he was asked 'how he came to do that Act, to which [he] ... answered that being an old man and out of work, he did it for want'.[122] Many old people were supposed to have committed suicide because their waning mental powers robbed them of their reason. Just before he shot himself, the papers related in 1796, an

[118] K. Thomas, *Age and Authority in Early Modern England*, repr. from *The Proceedings of the British Academy*, lxvii (London, 1976), 31–46. Margaret Pelling has shown that in 16th-cent. Norwich, one-third to one-half of the men and women over sixty needed poor relief, and one-fourth of them were severely disabled: M. Pelling, 'Illness Among the Poor in an Early Modern Town: The Norwich Census of 1570', *Continuity and Change*, iii (1988), 282.

[119] PRO, STAC 5/A28/8.

[120] *Weekly Journal*, no. 29 (1719). He shot himself on his ship, and it is possible that he simply could not endure the loss of the livelihood that had been the basis of his social identity.

[121] 'in paupertate existens et gravi tristicia [*sic*] repletus ... languens': PRO, KB 9/529, m. 144.

[122] Westminster Inquisitions, Cuthbert Cousins (4 Apr. 1772). The jury, in an act of pity, returned a verdict of natural death.

elderly man complained of his bodily ailments and said that 'the horrours he experienced when asleep ... cannot be equalled by any human distress.... He was a prey to the most frightful apprehensions.' He had, it was said, taken increasingly large doses of laudanum to dull his disordered senses—the actual cause, no doubt, of his terrifying dreams.[123] There seem to have been no significant changes in the prestige or security of the old in the early modern period. And indeed, if the Norwich data are representative, their condition may have grown a good deal worse in the eighteenth century.

123 *Annual Register*, xxxviii (1796), 32.

# 8

# *Motives for Suicide*

CONTEMPORARIES had clear notions about the kinds of behaviour and moods that preceded suicide and the sorts of people who were more or less likely to commit it, however broad and imprecise the folk psychology of suicide may have been. They also had definite ideas about the motives that moved men and women to slay themselves. And just as juries were unlikely to find an ambiguous death a suicide without evidence that it fitted the psychological profile they associated with self-slayers, so they were highly unlikely to return a suicide verdict without evidence of a plausible motive. When they tried to explain why people killed themselves, observers typically mentioned calamities that might befall anyone. Their conception of the stresses that shattered the psychological well-being of men and women was grounded on their own frustrations and disappointments and on widely held beliefs about the sources of unhappiness. It was the mirror image of the vision of an ideal life in early modern society. To sustain their social positions and navigate through the uncertainties they encountered, people relied on a shared set of beliefs about security and danger, about the actions and events that promoted their well-being or destroyed it. The commonly accepted motives for suicide marked out dangerous passages in the social world, like the legends on old maps warning of hostile peoples and perilous seas.

The folk sociology of suicide was rooted in the fundamental institutions and values of early modern society. It grew out of a universal recognition of the importance of the nuclear family, of the uncertainties of economic life, of the need to win and keep a good reputation, and of the difficulties in reconciling romantic love and family interests. Commentators provided inventories of the calamities that might cause people who were psychologically or spiritually frail to kill themselves. John Sym, for example, listed economic failure, dishonour, the death or suffering of friends and relatives, unrequited love, and family strife.[1] A generation later, Thomas Philipot pointed to some of the same sorts of distressing events as the causes of suicide: financial loss, poverty, and dishonour.[2] Isaac Watts, writing in 1726, also recognized that self-destruction had its immediate origins in the 'frequent Crosses and Calamities of this Life', which were compounded by moral weaknesses: wild lust, secret criminal practices, impatience of mind, horror of poverty, and jealousy.[3] The Nonconformist Caleb Fleming divided the motives for suicide by sex, declaring that women killed themselves for sexual shame, romantic passion, infidelity, and mistreatment by their husbands whereas men slew themselves because of worldly ruin, bad luck at gambling, criminal waste of money, and chagrin over some very sudden provocation.[4]

Examining these lists, it quickly becomes apparent that two kinds of distressing events are confounded together in them. Some, such as family strife, bereavement, and economic failure threatened the psychological security and physical survival of the individual. They were breakdowns in his relationship to the institutions that were his chief sources of emotional support and supplied his most basic needs. They determined his identity: in his own eyes and in the perceptions of society at large. Others, such as dishonour and sexual disgrace, arose out of the individual's relationship with the wider society. They were failures to maintain one's social standing or to negotiate successfully the difficult transition from the single to the married state, the most crucial shift in social positioning that occurred during one's life. There is in these lists an implicit recognition that emotional security depended on maintaining good relationships in the family and the workplace and also on preserving a persona, an image in the eyes of others that influenced the ways that one was treated.

## THE PERILS OF EVERYDAY LIFE

The family was the atom of English society, and sentiment was the force that bound its particles together. Its nucleus was a married couple;

1 Sym, *Lifes Preservative*, 214–21.

2 T. Philipot, *Self-Homicide Murther* (London, 1674), 15–20.

3 I. Watts, *A Defense Against the Temptation to Self-Murther* (London, 1726), pp. v–vi.

4 C. Fleming, *A Dissertation Upon the Unnatural Crime of Self-Murder* (London, 1773), 13–14.

around this core relationship orbited children and servants, parents and siblings, and more distant kin.[5] Village communities and, above them, the county and national communities of the gentry and aristocracy, were composed of many such atoms, arranged in patterned hierarchies, like the building-blocks of complex molecules. The family defined the individual's social identity to a much greater extent than it does today. Its members provided not only psychological and economic support, they also were, to a degree, inseparable from each other. Historians have recently suggested that the very concept of the person had a different meaning for early modern people from what it has for us. They argue that the person was conceived of in terms of his relationship with others in his family and in his community, rather than as a psychologically unique and independent being.[6] This may overstate the extent to which early modern people were different from us, but there is no doubt that their sense of the connection between the individual and the nuclear family had a distinctive character that is difficult for us fully to grasp. A person without a family was in a sense not a person; one's status and role in the community followed from one's role in a family. The stages of the life cycle were understood more in terms of a progression away from the nucleus of the family than in terms of phases in one's emotional development. Infants were seen as extensions of their parents for the first few months and years of life; young children remained at home, close to their parents as they grew up; adolescents moved out of the nuclear family and joined another household, where they lived and worked at its outer valences, outside the circle of parents and children; finally, young men and women joined together in marriage, established a new household, and started the whole process over again.

Marital breakdown was the most dangerous kind of social fission that

[5] L. Stone, *The Family, Sex and Marriage in England, 1500–1800* (New York, 1977); A. Macfarlane, *Marriage and Love in England, 1300–1840* (Oxford, 1986); K. Wrightson, *English Society, 1580–1680* (London, 1982), chs. 2–3; R. Houlbrooke, *The English Family, 1450–1700* (London, 1984); S. D. Amussen, *An Ordered Society: Gender and Class in Early Modern England* (Oxford, 1988); M. Ingram, *Church Courts, Sex and Marriage in England, 1570–1640* (Cambridge, 1987), chs. 5–6. D. Cressy, 'Kinship and Kin Interaction in Early Modern England', *Past and Present*, no. 113 (1986), 38–96, modifies earlier exaggerated statements about the insignificance of wider kinship ties. The evidence presented below on the stresses of family life from the notebooks of Richard Napier is amplified in MacDonald, *Mystical Bedlam*, ch. 3.

[6] N. Z. Davis, 'Boundaries and the Sense of Self in Sixteenth-Century France', in T. C. Heller *et al.*, *Reconstructing Individualism: Autonomy, Individuality, and the Self in Western Thought* (Stanford, 1986), 53–63; S. Greenblatt, 'Fiction and Friction', ibid., 30–52; D. W. Sabean, *Power in the Blood: Popular Culture and Village Discourse in Early Modern Germany* (Cambridge, 1984), esp. 30–6, 206–12.

could occur, and marital problems naturally ranked high among the motives observers attributed to suicides. Many people were supposed to have killed themselves because their spouses had been unfaithful or had died, or because they did not love them and abused them with words or blows. Scores of suicidal men and women trudged to Great Linford in the early seventeenth century, seeking the help of Richard Napier. Some of them told him tales of unfaithful wives and of brutal, improvident, or indifferent husbands.[7] So pervasive was the assumption that marital misery was a prime cause of suicide that Charles Hammond, in a ballad blaming the Devil for the death of George Gibbs, felt it necessary to absolve his wife:

> His Wife and he liv'd lovingly,
> 'twixt them no discontent,
> A very good report hath she,
> her case most do lament.[8]

Witnesses at inquests also regarded affection as an essential part of marriage and the loss of it as a sufficient explanation for suicide. Blaming Mary Little's suicide on her grief over the death of her son. Margaret Mackareth told a Cockermouth jury that she could not think of 'any other Motive that could Induce the Deceased to lay Violent hands upon herself, as her Husband always behaved to her tenderly and with great Affection'.[9]

Most of the victims of bad marriages among Napier's clients were wives. This is not to say, however, that observers thought that marital problems were less important as a cause of suicide for men than they were for women. Completed suicide, after all, was a predominantly male act. What contemporaries did recognize clearly was that men and women had different expectations from marriage, and that the frustrations that might lead them to kill themselves were therefore somewhat different as well. The suicides of men were often blamed on their inability to maintain their position as the rulers of the household. Female insubordination and, above all, sexual infidelity were humiliating affronts that threatened the self-worth and, indeed, the sexual identity of men.[10]

[7] MacDonald, *Mystical Bedlam*, 75, 98–105. Cf. Ingram, *Church Courts, Sex and Marriage*, 183–4.

[8] H. E. Rollins, *The Pack of Autolycus* (Cambridge, Mass., 1927), 123.

[9] Cumbria RO, D/Lec/CR I, 85/4.

[10] For the example of John Lemot Honeywood, recounted in Chapter 7, see J. Bramston, *The Autobiography of Sir John Bramston*, ed. T. W. Bramston, Camden Society, os, xxxii (1845).

Richard Simpson, who cut his throat in 1763, was a miserable, violent man. He accused his wife of sleeping with another man and beat her often. Before he killed himself, he threatened to kill her and swore that his own suicide was her fault.[11] Typical newspaper stories reported in 1729 that during an argument with his wife a schoolmaster at Westminster School leaped out of a window and ran into the Thames up to his neck and in 1766 that a Mr Pernell of Holborn committed suicide on his wedding day after a row with his young bride.[12]

In return for their subordination, women expected to be treated with respect and affection. At the very least, husbands were supposed to fulfil the role of patriarch responsibly. A man who brutalized his wife and squandered the family's resources not only imperilled her life; he also degraded her socially by ruining the family's standing and its reputation with its neighbours. Being married to such a man was sufficient explanation for suicidal feelings and actions. Poor Katherine Wells, one of Napier's patients, found herself yoked with a helpmeet who was a monster. He squandered the forty-pound dowry she had brought to the marriage and treated her with contempt. 'Worse for that her husband maketh small reckoning of her', she explained to Napier several times in several ways. Helpless to change him or her situation, she turned her anger and her fear inward. She declared that she was vexed by an 'ill spirit' that tempted her to kill herself or her child. Whenever she saw a knife, she flung it down, lest she yield to those temptations.[13] An eighteenth-century chapbook entitled *A Dreadful Example for Wicked Husbands* gave a moralizing twist to the familiar litany of female victimization. It told the story of John Fox, who was as irresponsible as Katherine Wells's husband. Deeply in debt and faced with ruin and poverty, he falls into despair and hangs himself. Later his ghost returns, advising loose youths to behave more carefully and lovingly than he had.[14] A less fantastic tale of masculine remorse appeared in the *Annual Register* in 1766. It reported that in August a labouring man on the Isle

[11] Westminster Inquisitions, Richard Simpson (26 Aug. 1791).

[12] *British Journal; or, the Censor*, no. 70 (3 May 1729); *Annual Register*, ix (1766), 126.

[13] Bodl., Ashmole MS 228, fos. 228$^r$, 240$^v$, 241$^r$ (Wells). For another client, who blamed her suicidal depressions on a husband who became progressively more drunken and irresponsible over a period of fifteen years, see Bodl., Ashmole MSS 199, fo. 132$^v$; 237, fos. 9$^r$, 41$^r$; 196, fo. 22$^r$; 227, fos. 57$^r$, 218$^v$; 405, fo. 217$^v$ (Neale). For similar examples, all of them women, driven to suicidal despair by their husbands, see Ashm. MS 228, fo. 183$^v$ (Howe); 202, fo. 130$^r$ (Howe); 408, fo. 109$^r$ (Robarts); 413, fo. 148$^r$; 406, fos. 370$^r$, 372$^r$ (Bateson). To be fair, men occasionally made the same complaint; see, e.g., Ashmole Ms 238, fo. 76$^v$ (Harrys).

[14] *A Dreadful Example for Wicked Husbands* (repr. n.pl., 1807).

of Wight had hanged himself because he had refused his wife a little wine just before she died. 'The thought of denying her, what he since thought reasonable, urged him to this rash action.'[15]

Although contemporary conceptions of gender plainly structured the peril men and women perceived in married life, it is impossible to dispel the impression that throughout the early modern period both sexes also hoped that their spouses would love them. Suicides and the people who explained their deaths afterwards frequently cited simple quarrels or conjugal indifference as causes of self-destruction. A newspaper story in 1718, for example, reported that a London woman 'having had some Words with her Husband, went up Stairs in a Passion, and hanged herself'.[16] Almost a half-century later, a friend of Barbara Gray told a Westminster inquest that before she hanged herself, Barbara had complained of a disagreement with her husband and exclaimed, 'she had rather be hanged than lead that life'.[17] More telling than such tales, of which there are hundreds, are the many stories of men and women who fell into suicidal moods after their spouses died. Margaret Lancton, for instance, repaired to Napier in 1621, utterly miserable because of her husband's death five weeks earlier. Four years later, she was back again, still lamenting his death and complaining of suicidal urges.[18] At the 1762 inquest on the body of an Essex woman named Hannah Baldwin, all of the witnesses agreed that she had hanged herself with a skein of worsted yarn because of her grief over her husband's death some months earlier. He had left her pregnant, penniless, and alone, they testified; for weeks on end 'she used to cry excessively' and said just before she died that 'she might as well be hanged as starve to death'.[19] Ann Tiffin had been spared poverty when she was widowed, but she was no less devastated by her loss. Ever since the death of her husband Jeremiah, testified a friend of many years, she had 'laboured under great Afflictions of Mind and has since that time made some former attempts to kill herself'. Her lunacy, he said, grew by degrees, so that she was incoherent at times and 'Complained heavily on the Burthen she had upon her Mind' at others.

15 *Annual Register*, ix (1766), 124.

16 *Weekly Journal*, no. 72 (26 Apr. 1718). See also *London Journal*, no. 318 (28 Aug. 1725); no. 360 (18 June 1726); *Annual Register*, ix (1766), 126; *Norwich Mercury* (14–21 Apr. 1739).

17 Westminster Inquisitions, Barbara Gray (23 Sept. 1767).

18 Bodl., Ashmole MSS 220, fo. 40$^{r}$; 233, fo. 143$^{v}$ (Lancton).

19 Essex County RO D/DHt T 140/100. For other examples, see *Weekly Journal*, no. 231 (30 Mar. 1723); *Mist's Weekly Journal*, no. 11 (10 July 1725).

She hanged herself, he concluded, because of the disorder of mind her husband's death had caused.[20]

Parents and children were held together as a family in distinctive, gendered configurations by powerful social and psychological forces. Both men and women felt the strength of affection for their children, but its intensity differed for fathers and mothers and varied according to the age (and probably the sex) of the child. The bonds between parents and children were strongest when the latter were young, but they tied mothers to children more powerfully than they did fathers. Among Napier's suicidal patients, for instance, it was not unusual for women to identify so completely with their children that in the grips of despair they were tempted either to kill themselves *or* their children. This terrible urge plumbed the deepest depths of a mother's alienation from ordinary happiness. Her children were her greatest source of emotional satisfaction and the fulfilment of her chief social duty. Eleanor Byrge was terrified to pick up a knife, she told Napier in 1617, lest she slay herself or, still more terrible, her child. She 'cannot abide her child', she lamented, 'though she love it'.[21] When her child was accidentally poisoned in 1608, Margaret Whippan became suicidal, and her maid, who felt responsible for the accident, actually drowned herself in a frozen pond.[22] A dozen of Ann Garnett's neighbours testified at the inquest on her body in 1711 that she had been overcome with melancholy, 'and the reason thereof', one related, 'was at first Chiefly occasioned by the death of her Two Children, being all she then had, a little before'.[23] Men were not immune from suicidal grief when their children died, but it seems to have been rarer and to have been prompted by deaths that

[20] Cumbria RO, D/Lec/CR I, 72/4. In a precarious world where the family was the basis for economic security, remarriages often followed quickly on the funerals of husbands and wives. But remarriage did not necessarily mean the end of grief and suicidal gloom: Bodl., Ashmole MSS 402, fo. 9$^{r}$ (Watley or Wasley); 227, fos. 80$^{r}$, 139$^{r}$ (Clark); Cumbria RO, D/Lec/CR I, 59/1.

[21] Bodl., Ashmole MS 220, fos. 21$^{v}$, 80$^{r}$ (Byrge). For some other examples of maternal temptations to suicide/murder, see Ashmole MSS 201, between fos. 20 and 21 (Cox); 203, fo. 86$^{r}$ (Auburne); 218, fo. 210$^{v}$ (Davys); 220, fos. 2$^{v}$ (Ogles), 34$^{r}$ (Croutche), 41$^{v}$, 47$^{r}$, 57$^{r}$ (Musgrove), 180$^{r}$, 181$^{r}$ (Turnell); 231, fo. 39$^{r}$ (Woodland); 211, fo. 196$^{r}$ (Whitesyde); 212, fo. 89$^{v}$ (Neuman); 224, fo. 168$^{v}$ (Tyrle); 231, fo. 9$^{r}$ (Allyson); 237, fo. 20$^{r}$ (Barton); 239, fo. 179$^{r}$ (Savill); 409, fo. 65$^{r}$ (Edwards), 79$^{r}$ (Colman). For three examples of men who were tempted to kill themselves or their children, see Ashmole MSS 224, fo. 114$^{v}$ (Maddison); 231, fo. 74$^{r}$ (Morice); 414, fo. 74$^{r}$ (Lyne).

[22] Bodl., Ashmole MS 229, fo. 97$^{v}$ (Whippan).

[23] Cumbria RO, D/Lec/CR I, 20/2. See also, ibid. 85/4 Mary Little (1 June 1776); 97/4 William Hartley (5 Aug. 1788); London Inquisitions, Maria Stevens (2 July 1796).

occurred in more shocking circumstances. The *Weekly Journal* related a macabre calamity that befell a Wiltshire farmer in 1718. Disgusted with his son, who was doing a lazy job of ploughing a field next to their house, he took up a clod of earth and hurled it at the boy, knocking him down. 'Art thou sullen?' shouted the enraged father when his son did not leap back to his feet. Running over and kicking the boy, he realized with horror that he had killed him. Told of the accident, his wife ran out of the house, leaving their eighteen-month-old baby sitting on the end of the table. The baby fell off and broke its neck. 'After which', reported the *Weekly Journal*, 'the miserable Man went away and hang'd himself.'[24] Desperate men and women sometimes attributed their suicidal urges to grief over the deaths of other relatives, besides children and spouses, but on the whole, it seems obvious that the strongest ties of affection were between husbands and wives, parents and young children. And it was those relationships people naturally examined most intensely after a suicide had occurred.

It was not merely the quality of the interpersonal relationships within the family that enhanced or destroyed the well-being of its members. The family was a workshop as well as a domestic unit in early modern England, and the status or even the very survival of individuals depended upon its fortunes. Prosperity was the foundation of domestic tranquillity; poverty was a main cause of misery. Men and women of all ranks were vulnerable to ruin. After the death of her husband in 1622, creditors descended on the home of Anne Lockwood. They turned her out and sealed up the house; 'his whole personal estate was in danger to have been consumed and creditors unsatisfied'. Eleven days later, Anne killed herself. Her entire estate consisted of the clothes she was wearing when she died.[25] Farming families had to cope with the abiding perils of bad weather and animal diseases, as well as the continual changes in land tenure that reduced the numbers of small farmers in long waves of enclosure from the fifteenth through to the nineteenth centuries. Thomas Birchmore's sheep 'grew rotten' in the abysmal spring of 1623. Unable to pay a debt of £8, he strung himself up, only to be rescued by his brother.[26] Mary Hill grew anxious and 'tempted' when her landlord —a minister—threatened to throw her and her family out of their

24 *Weekly Journal*, no. 64 (1 Mar. 1718).

25 PRO, STAC 8/3/18.

26 Bodl., Ashmole MS, 218, fo. 82$^{v}$ (Birchmore). Two years later, he was still in debt, railing against his mother and wife, infected with smallpox, and evidently frenzied by some mental illness: Ashmole MS 402, fo. 170$^{r}$.

house.[27] Nor were the more affluent immune from financial despair. A scrivener named Frith, who had once been worth four or five hundred pounds a year, shot himself in King's Bench prison in 1619 after he had been arrested for debt.[28] In the sixteenth and early seventeenth centuries, the almoner sometimes cited 'losses and crosses' as a good reason to believe that suspicious deaths had been suicides.[29]

The opportunities for gain in the eighteenth century were vastly greater than they had been in the Tudor period, but the teeming capitalist economy also afforded little leeway for the unlucky and incapable. 'The dominating impression of life in eighteenth-century London, from the standpoint of the individual', observed Dorothy George over fifty years ago, 'is one of uncertainty and insecurity.'[30] Harvest fluctuations, depressions in trade, fiscal crises, and war made business and employment exceedingly risky. There were at least thirteen periods of financial crisis in the eighteenth century. Some of these, including the most famous of them all, the bursting of the South Sea Bubble, had a smaller impact on private business than contemporaries believed or historians have assumed.[31] But the precise scope of nation-wide financial disasters is less important in this context than the way in which economic uncertainty affected people's lives. Although the crisis of 1720 and 1721 may not have destroyed the economy, the fall of South Sea stocks produced widespread panic and set off a small wave of suicides. The number of people recorded in the London bills of mortality as having 'made themselves away' almost doubled the year after the crash, rising from 27 to 52; the climacteric of 1721 inaugurated a long period of generally high rates of reported suicide in London that lasted for the next two decades.[32] There were six suicides in a single week in January 1721, an unprecedented figure, and in that same week *Applebee* published a

[27] Bodl., Ashmole MS 221, fo. 46$^{v}$ (Hill).

[28] *The Letters of John Chamberlain*, ed. N. E. McClure, American Philosophical Society, Memoirs 12, Pts. I–II (Philadelphia, 1939), ii. 223; S. J. Stevenson, 'Social and Economic Contributions to the Pattern of "Suicide" in South-East England, 1530–1590', *Continuity and Change*, ii (1987), 234. For other examples, see Bodl., Ashmole MS 223, fo. 31$^{v}$ (Wynterton); BL, Lansdowne MS 99, no. 32, fos. 88$^{r}$–89$^{v}$; *The Correspondence of Henry Hyde, Earl of Clarendon*, (London, 1828), i. 303, and BL, Add. MS 4460, fo. 42.

[29] See e.g., PRO, STAC 8/3/4; STAC 8/3/10.

[30] M. D. George, *London Life in the Eighteenth Century* (1935; repr. New York, 1965), 269.

[31] J. Hoppit, 'Financial Crises in Eighteenth-Century England', *Economic History Review*, 2nd ser., xxxix (1986), 39–58.

[32] General bills of mortality, 1660–1800; weekly bills of mortality for 1715–1800. We have tabulated suicides from the bills preserved in the Guildhall Library, London.

parody of South Sea suicides, written by Daniel Defoe.[33] Although he had himself published reports of suicides attributed to the Bubble's bursting, Defoe complained that the South Sea catastrophe was being blamed for every delict and disaster that occurred. It is used, he claimed, 'to cover the Misfortunes of all the Gentlemen and Ladies, who either for Love or worse Occasions, take the liberty to give themselves a Pass to another World, on their own Authority. And if any Man is *Felo de Se*, and falls upon himself with Sword, Gun, or String; or ingulphs himself by a Leap over-board into the Thames, and the like; the usual Parenthesis of (*being Lunatick*) which was formerly used in his Favour, is left out, and that of (*South Sea*) more to the Advantage of his Character, is placed in its Room.' He concluded with a satirical proposal to lend official sanction to the new euphemism by altering the language of coroners' inquisitions and the bills of mortality.[34]

We cannot know how many people killed themselves as a result of the Bubble. But some certainly did, and the press was in no doubt about the fatal effects of the crash. James Milner, a very prominent London merchant, shot himself in November 1721 after having mounted a furious attack in the House of Commons on the directors of the South Sea Company.[35] The *Weekly Journal* reported in April 1721 that an anonymous gentlewoman had flung herself out of a window to her death and commented that her 'great Losses by the South-Sea are said to have distracted her'. A few weeks later the same paper noted the suicide of a tradesman, 'who by the Severity of the Times was reduced to very great Straights in his business . . . [and] was grown melancholy on the near Approach to Poverty'.[36] The Bubble was merely the most notorious financial catastrophe; periodic business crises brought with them new waves of suicides attributed to financial ruin. In 1729, for instance, a year when bankruptcy was even more common than it had been in 1720 and 1721, the press reported that a publican who had lost his business and been 'much reduced' hanged himself in Worcester.[37] In 1772 in the midst

[33] Weekly Bill (1721), no. 5 (17 Jan. 1720/1).

[34] W. Lee, *Daniel Defoe: His Life and Recently Discovered Writings* (repr., Hildesheim, 1968), ii. 323–5. See also, P. Rogers, '"This Calamitous Year": *A Journal of the Plague Year* and the South Sea Bubble', in his *Eighteenth Century Encounters: Studies in Literature and Society in the Age of Walpole* (Brighton, 1985), 167, n. 8.

[35] R. Sedgwick, *The House of Commons, 1715–1754* (Oxford, 1970), ii. 259–60.

[36] *Weekly Journal*, no. 125 (22 Apr. 1721); 129 (20 May 1721). For other examples and a pertinent discussion of contemporary reactions to the crisis, see Rogers, '"This Calamitous Year"', esp. 154–5.

[37] *Fog's Weekly Journal*, no. 24 (8 Mar. 1729). For other examples, see ibid., no. 151 (25 Sept. 1731); *Weekly Journal*, no. 218 (29 Dec. 1723).

of perhaps the worst concatenation of public and private financial failures of the century, Horace Walpole noted that two men ruined by bank failures had killed themselves and the *London Chronicle* attributed the suicide of 'an eminent Jew merchant' to the same cause.[38]

So closely associated were wealth and happiness in the minds of early modern Englishmen, that they found it difficult to believe that anyone would kill himself while in possession of an adequate living, let alone a large fortune. Again and again, diarists and newspaper writers expressed their amazement at the suicides of the rich. Richard Smyth, an official of the Poultry Compter in London, recorded that Auditor Beale had flung himself to his death from a window in 1674. Beale, Smyth noted, 'died worth a great estate in lands and monies'. No one knew what might have caused him to kill himself, and the coroner's jury finally decided that he had been insane: 'Some pretend it was by accident, others through frenzy . . . whereof the coroner's inquest found that he perished by throwing himself down in his frantick fit.'[39] John Evelyn was the most prominent of several contemporaries who wondered at the suicide of Francis Godolphin. He remarked that no motive was known; Godolphin had had a large estate. A broadside enumerated the advantages the Treasurer's cousin had enjoyed more fully: 'He was related to a Right Honourable Family, blest with a Plentiful Estate, a Good Wife, and Several Children.' The author concluded that Godolphin had been mad.[40] Newspaper stories about suicides typically noted when they were finely dressed or sums of money were found on their bodies. The *Weekly Journal* reported, for instance, in 1718 that an anonymous man had been found hanged on Hampstead Heath with 'ten Pounds . . . in his pocket'.[41] That same year the same paper recorded that Squire Farrendon had killed himself even though he was worth £1,500 a year and that a Mr Bowyer had taken his life just fifteen months after inheriting an estate valued at £2,000 per annum.[42] When most people were experiencing hard times in the early 1720s, the London papers were especially atten-

38 H. Walpole, *The Yale Edition of Horace Walpole's Correspondence*, ed. W. S. Lewis (New Haven, 1937–83), xxiii. 420.

39 *The Obituary of Richard Smyth*, ed. H. Ellis, Camden Society, os xliv (1849), 102.

40 J. Evelyn, *The Diary of John Evelyn*, ed. E. S. de Beer, (Oxford, 1955), v. 505–6; *A Full and True Account, How Francis Godolphin . . . Cut His Own Throat* (London, 1702). For a later parallel, see 'The Diary of George Sloper, 1753–1810', in *Some Annals of the Borough of Devizes* (Devizes, 1925–6), ii. 259.

41 *Weekly Journal*, no. 71 (19 Apr. 1718).

42 Ibid., no. 74 (10 May 1718); no. 100 (8 Nov. 1718).

tive to persons who committed suicide in spite of comfortable incomes.[43] In the months after the South Sea Bubble burst, they reported with astonishment that an unnamed merchant purportedly worth £60,000 had hanged himself in a 'Fit of Discontent'.[44] A half-century later, such stories still struck readers as remarkable. Parson Woodforde copied into his diary a newspaper account of the bloody suicide of a Captain Bruce, who had recently married a woman worth £3,000 per year. 'No reason assigned for it', he noted.[45]

These were spectacular exceptions. Contemporaries rightly believed that suicides much more often killed themselves because they had lost their fortunes or had sunk into desperate and irredeemable poverty. Poverty and suicide were linked in the practices of coroners' juries and the comments of contemporaries. 'A poore man', remarked Richard Smyth, describing the suicide of Thomas Hardesty, a London bookseller, in 1658.[46] Almost half of the persons judged *felo de se* before 1640 were supposed to have had no goods at all, and although undervaluation was widespread, it is equally clear that large numbers of reported suicides were poor labourers, servants, and workers in menial trades. About one-fourth of suicides whose ranks or jobs were recorded by coroners between 1485 and 1714 fell into one of those categories or were servants, apprentices, paupers, or 'single men', who appear mostly to have been solitary wanderers. The vulnerability of the poor to hardship probably explains why the suicide rate occasionally soared in periods of poor harvests. But at the same time, there was no long-term correlation between prices and the suicide rate, as we have seen, and after about 1600, it would be fruitless to expect one. English agriculture became increasingly productive, and nation-wide famines vanished.[47] The establishment of a regular system of poor relief at that time and the subsequent publication of Books of Orders—rules for distributing relief when hardship was acute—also lessened somewhat the impact of harvest and

[43] Ibid., no. 66 (5 Mar. 1720); no. 21 (?) (21 May 1720); no. 85 (16 July 1720); no. 110 (7 Jan. 1721); 129 (20 May 1721); no. 133 (17 June 1721); no. 230 (23 Mar. 1723).

[44] *Weekly Journal*, no. 111 (14 Jan. 1721).

[45] J. Woodforde, *The Diary of a Country Parson*, ed. J. Beresford (Oxford, 1981), i. 250.

[46] Smyth, *Obituary*, 46–7. For examples of suicides identified by juries as destitute, see KB 9/670/2, m. 262; KB 9/676/2, m. 175; KB 9/684/1, m. 6; KB 9/710/1, m. 45; KB 9/1073/1, m. 66. Forty-five inquisitions in the King's Bench series described suicides as paupers. These seem often to have been residents of almshouses.

[47] A. Appleby, *Famine in Tudor and Stuart England* (Stanford, 1978); C. G. A. Clay, *Economic Expansion and Social Change: England 1500–1700* (Cambridge, 1984), i. 8–9, 16–19, 103–4. For an explanation of why the occasional spikes in the suicide rate are meaningful, when the rate is otherwise highly suspect, see above, Chapter 7.

trade fluctuations on the poor.[48] Individuals nevertheless still killed themselves to escape destitution, and although their numbers may not have been sufficient to result in statistically significant fluctuations in the suicide rate, their suicides demonstrated the continuing precariousness of subsistence in the sixteenth and seventeenth centuries.

There is no reason to believe that the situation changed after 1700 although the inquest data are even harder to interpret and poor relief was perhaps administered more effectively, at least in rural areas. Newspaper reports and annotations in coroners' records in the late seventeenth and eighteenth centuries often describe suicides as 'poor'. In Norwich, for instance, stray remarks in coroners' records and the local newspapers make it clear that the many weavers and artisans who killed themselves were mostly paupers and not the grandees of the worsted trade. An annotation on the inquest of Phillip Letree, who was brought in *felo de se* in 1727, explained, 'as to his goods & chattells, there is nothing to make any seizer of', and given the practices of city officials, this has the ring of truth about it. Just three years later a jury reported that Anne Letree, perhaps Phillip's sister or even his wife, was so 'very poor there is nothing whereby any Distress can be made'.[49] References to pauper suicides are very frequent in the London inquests and newspapers throughout the eighteenth century. In June of 1725, for example, when the weather had ruined crops in the region, the *London Journal* reported: 'Two of the poor Haymakers that were come to work in these Parts finding themselves in the utmost Necessity and unable to beg, hang'd themselves to put an end to their Want.' Two issues later the same paper remarked that there had been more self-murders in the preceding week than for many weeks before.[50] Some people fell into destitution because

[48] A. L. Beier, *Masterless Men: The Vagrancy Problem in England* (London, 1985); P. Slack, *Poverty and Policy in Tudor and Stuart England* (London, 1988).

[49] Norwich Inquisitions, Phillip Letree (28 Feb. 1727); Ann Letree (4 May 1730). See also, ibid., John Brightmore (7 Apr. 1750), who died in the 'Lukeham dwelling house'. For the prevalence of weavers and more menial occupations, see the Norwich Inquisitions generally and the newspapers mentioned below. (Note how many persons hanged themselves from looms with yarn and had no possessions or only a couple of skeins of wool. The city collected deodands at least through the 1760s, so most of these were probably propertyless or had no goods of any significant value.) For economic and social conditions in the city, see P. J. Corfield, 'The Social and Economic History of Norwich, 1650–1850', Ph.D. thesis (London, 1976). Poor people's suicides are mentioned explicitly in the *Norwich Mercury* (14–21 Apr. 1739); ibid. (15–22 Aug. 1747), *Norwich Gazette* (15–22 Aug. 1747), and Norwich Inquisitions, Robert Atkins (18 Aug. 1747); *Norwich Mercury*, no. 329 (31 July 1756); no. 409 (18 Feb. 1758); *Norwich Gazette* (19–26 Feb. 1743); (5–12 Nov. 1743).

[50] *London Journal*, no. 309 (26 June 1725); no. 311 (10 July 1725); and, for a report on the effects of the weather on crops, no. 310 (3 July 1725).

they could not get work; others were incompetent and failed at their trades. A despairing carpenter explained to a friend in his suicide note, 'my Work did not sute me and poverty overtook me.'[51]

The plight of men and women without any means of subsistence was almost unimaginably terrible. The Georgian social safety net was woven with a wide mesh. People who did not qualify for relief under the settlement laws or who were denied adequate support by their parish had no other recourse. The newspapers reported in 1717 the story of a poor woman with two children who applied to the authorities at Clerkenwell for a rise in her allowance. The parish gave her a shilling, but refused a weekly increase. She pleaded hard for more, but could not obtain it, whereupon she told a churchwarden that she would drown one of her children. 'He let her go, taking little Notice of what she threatened, and the next Morning she drowned the biggest Child . . . and afterwards drowned herself and an Infant at her Breast. The poor Child was found clinging to her when dead.'[52] A very similar fate befell another woman thirteen years later. In 1730 someone travelling along the road from Greenwich to Woolwich noticed a woman hanging from a tree. A child was sitting on the ground nearby. Bystanders rushed to cut her down and revive her. She told them 'that Fear of Starving had reduced her to that Act'. Within a week, she was found dead, hanged once more in an orchard in the neighbourhood.[53]

The state of the London poor was especially desperate in the early and mid-eighteenth century, when all the measures of social degradation peaked. Drunkenness, infanticide, child and infant mortality, and petty crime burgeoned as the city expanded faster than its economy or its amenities could readily bear.[54] So did suicides listed in the bills of mortality—which is probably significant in spite of the massive inaccuracies that they contained. At the very least the soaring numbers of self-killings listed in the bills strengthened the contemporary conviction that there was a connection between immiseration and suicide. The most famous visual depiction of London poverty, *Gin Lane*, expresses the idea

[51] London Inquisitions, George Davis (21 Jan. 1796).

[52] *Weekly Journal*, no. 23 (18 May 1717).

[53] *Fog's Weekly Journal*, no. 101 (29 Aug. 1730). For two persons who said that destitution had driven them to suicide, see London Inquisitions, Anne Bearer (13 Dec. 1788); John Crocker (22 June 1789). Perhaps the most affecting tale of all was related in the suicide note of a woman who signed herself as E.H.; it is discussed below, Chapter 9.

[54] George, *London Life in the Eighteenth Century*; George Rudé, *Hanoverian London, 1714–1808* (Berkeley, 1971); P. J. Corfield, *The Impact of English Towns, 1700–1800* (Oxford, 1982), ch. 5.

with characteristic narrative economy. Hogarth's horrifying satire, issued in February 1750, has become so familiar that we seldom look closely at it any more. We see the drunken woman, oblivious as her child falls to its death, the skeletal man, dead or about to die in the foreground. But we are apt to overlook the figure of a suicide hanging in a ruined apartment over Kilman Distiller. He is a barber, ruined perhaps by lack of business and alcoholism. His body is on the same level as the steeple of St George's Bloomsbury in the background, and it has turned away from this symbol of church and state to face the distiller's shop—and the viewer.[55] Conditions in London improved in the later eighteenth century, but they worsened elsewhere and ruin and poverty remained prominent among the causes of suicide. '*The rich oppress the poor, and my distresses are fully come*!' Richard Moth, a Surrey man, had written in his notebook before he hanged himself in 1786. Formerly a master wheelwright, he had, *The Times* remarked, 'shewn some obvious marks of insanity, which no doubt originated from a reflection of his indigent circumstances'.[56] Less than two months later the same paper reported that an old man of nearly eighty had hanged himself at Reading because a new rule there made paupers wear badges with the initial letters of the parish to which they belonged.[57]

Poverty was, in fact, so obvious a motive for suicide that witnesses at inquests and journalists seldom elaborated on it. For those who had not slipped into the ranks of the destitute, the peril that seems to have been most feared was arrest for debt. When debtors were apprehended, they often fought violently to escape.[58] Prisoners who did not manage to avoid arrest or use the law to their own advantage had ample reason to be enraged, hopeless and ashamed. Their chances of regaining their freedom and their credit were small. Suicides by debtors were not new in the eighteenth century, but concern about the law probably helped give them greater prominence in the papers and in the eyes of the public. A news story in 1721 struck a familiar chord. A tailor who had been arrested by his landlord, 'having lain sometime in Confinement . . . and finding no likelihood of being discharged', hanged himself.[59] Although they were famous for their deistical suicide note, the principal motive for the suicides of Richard and Bridget Smith had been their imprisonment

[55] R. Paulson, *Hogarth's Graphic Works*, rev. edn. (London, 1989), 147–8, 370.
[56] *The Times*, no. 407 (13 Apr. 1786), 3.
[57] Ibid. no. 457 (9 June 1786), 3.
[58] George, *London Life in the Eighteenth Century*, 310; P. H. Haagen, 'Imprisonment for Debt in England and Wales', Ph.D. thesis (Princeton, 1986), 127–33.
[59] *Weekly Journal*, no. 139 (29 July 1721).

for debt. 'I am informed', Richard wrote bitterly to his cousin Brindley, that a certain anonymous person 'has taken some Pains to make the World believe he has done me some Services. I wish that said Person had never troubled his Head about my Affairs, . . . for it is entirely owing to his meddling, that I came Penniless into this Place.'[60] Nor was it only artisans who suffered arrest for debt. The *Weekly Journal* reported in 1720 that, 'having sheltered himself from his Creditors for some Time in the Mint', a gentleman managed to recoup his fortune by playing the exchange market and honourably discharged his debts, only to find himself suddenly ruined again by the fall of the South Sea stocks. Utterly dejected, he hanged himself.[61] Ironically, creditors were vulnerable to ruin because of the law as well. A widow who kept an alehouse was distraught when a man to whom she had lent £40 was cleared under the 1729 Insolvency Act. He taunted her with his luck, and she drowned herself in angry despair.[62] But nobody had much sympathy for prosperous lenders who found that they could not recover their loans. Two money-lenders killed themselves in 1730 and 1731, one in Cumberland and one in Shropshire. The Shropshire man was found *felo de se*, and 'the proper Officers thereupon seized all his Effects, besides a considerable Sum of Money', the press reported with satisfaction.[63]

## HONOUR AND SHAME

Family breakdown and financial ruin were readily comprehensible reasons for despair. They deprived individuals of the relationships and material goods that defined their identifies and sustained their survival. Another set of motives for suicide that contemporaries recognized involved dishonour and shame, the social and emotional consequences of violating the cultural rules. Despite the manifest importance of cultural 'control mechanisms'—as Clifford Geertz calls them—historians have as yet made little progress toward constructing a typology of them or showing how they changed over time.[64] Norbert Elias's massive

[60] *Historical Register*, lxiv (1732), 151–4. For another bitter suicide note addressed to a creditor, see Westminster Inquisitions, John Bawcutt (25 Mar. 1783).
[61] *Weekly Journal*, no. 100 (29 Oct. 1720).
[62] *Fog's Weekly Journal*, no. 104 (19 Sept. 1730).
[63] Ibid., no. 74 (21 Feb. 1730); no. 130 (20 Mar. 1731).
[64] C. Geertz, *The Interpretation of Cultures* (New York, 1973), esp. ch. 2.

trilogy on manners in medieval and Renaissance history has shown how rich and how revealing the project is, and a growing body of scholarship about conduct books aimed at the upper and middle classes exists.[65] But we still know little about the variations between the mores of those groups and the lower orders, or between genders. A study of suicide motives cannot provide the basis for a typology and history of English codes of conduct. But it can help to identify some of the ideals that were most strongly held in the early modern period.

Early modern people believed that dishonoured men and women slew themselves to escape or to erase shame. Shame, as Elias has observed, is an emotion of extreme anxiety that stems from our fear of social degradation. It is aroused when one does something that transgresses rules of behaviour that are held both by people whose wrath or ridicule one fears and by oneself. In other words, it is aroused both by fear of external restraints and by a sense of having violated one's own ideals. The shamed person dreads the loss of respect of others whose values he has adopted. They are his reference group, as the social psychologists say, and his internal mechanisms of self-restraint, his superego as Freudians say. Elias sums up this dual quality of shame neatly:

> Shame takes on its particular coloration from the fact that the person feeling it has done or is about to do something through which he comes into contradiction with people to whom he is bound in one form or another, and with himself, with the sector of his consciousness by which he controls himself.[66]

People who killed themselves because of dishonour or shame were believed to accomplish various things, depending on their class, their sex, and the circumstances of their disgrace. Gentlemen believed they could redeem their honour by suicide; a brave death compensated, in some measure, for a bad life. Men of lower social standing could escape shame by killing themselves. They were not supposed to gain admiration

[65] N. Elias, *The Civilizing Process*, trans. E. Jephcott (Oxford, 1978); id., *Power and Civility: The Civilizing Process, Volume II*, trans. E. Jephcott (New York, 1982); id., *The Court Society*, trans. E. Jephcott (New York, 1983). A lucid commentary is R. Chartier, *Cultural History*, trans. L. G. Cochrane (Ithaca, 1988), ch. 3. Much pertinent information and insightful comment may now be found in P. Borsay, *The English Urban Renaissance* (Oxford, 1989), chs. 9–10; M. B. Becker, *Civil Society in Western Europe, 1300–1600* (Bloomington, 1988). Recently completed Oxford D.Phil. theses by A. Bryson and F. A. Childs, which we have been unable to consult, analyse conduct books for our period. Keith Thomas's as yet unpublished research on fashion and manners will greatly advance the project: paper on fashion presented to the Department of Psychology, Oxford University, 1982.

[66] Elias, *Power and Civility*, 292–3.

by their deaths, but they did at least put a period to their suffering. Finally, women could either redeem their honour—as Lucretia had—or they could like men escape their disgrace, gaining a measure of posthumous revenge on the rakes who had betrayed them.

Each stratum of society and both sexes possessed strong notions about what kinds of behaviour were honourable and what actions were shameful. Indeed, these shared codes were the basis of cultural distinctions between them. We should begin with men of fashion, members of the aristocracy and gentry, and of those sectors of the middle class that aped the behaviour of their betters. It was this group, with its elaborate and archaic code of honour, that contemporaries identified with suicide because of disgrace. Gentlemen slew themselves and each other in the name of honour throughout the early modern period. Suicide and duelling were closely linked, as we have seen, and one sort of suicide for honour might be best regarded as a kind of substitute for combat: it occurred when satisfaction could not be obtained by fighting.[67]

In other cases, suicide was not so much a substitute for combat as a means of redemption. The clearest picture of the terrible shame a gentleman might experience and the boon a courageous death might seem to offer is the letter Sir Walter Raleigh wrote to his wife just before he stabbed himself in the Tower.

> I am nowe made an enemie and traytor by the word of an unworthie man. . . . Oh intollerable infamie. Oh god I cannot resiste theis thoughtes, I cannot live to thinke how I am deryded. . . . O death hasten the[e] unto me, that thowe maiste destroye the memorie of theis and laye me up in darke forgetfullnes. O death destroye my memorie which is my Tormentor; my thoughts and my life cannot dwell in one body.[68]

Suicides that were motivated by patriotism were especially noble. The death of the Florentine republican Filippo Strozzi was the most celebrated case: imprisoned after the assassination of his enemy Alessandro de' Medici, he poisoned himself and left behind a note, equating his death with that of Cato of Utica.[69] There were no modern Catos among

[67] Perhaps the best example is the suicide of the earl of Berkshire, which has been mentioned several times already: *The Letters of John Chamberlain*, ed. N. E. McClure, American Philosophical Society Memoirs 12, Parts I–II (Philadelphia, 1939), ii. 423; S. D'Ewes, *The Diary of Sir Simonds D'Ewes (1622–1624)*, ed. E. Bourcier (Paris, n.d.), 74, 159–60; *DNB*, s.v. 'Norris, Francis'.

[68] S. J. Greenblatt, *Sir Walter Ralegh* (New Haven, 1973), 114–7 discusses this letter and Ralegh's views about honourable suicide. See also John Aubrey's account of the death of Lord Falkland: *Aubrey's Brief Lives*, ed. O. L. Dick (Harmondsworth, 1982), 154.

[69] E. Cochrane, *Florence in the Forgotten Centuries, 1527–1800* (Chicago, 1973), 38; Wymer, *Suicide and Despair*, 16. For an interesting discussion of political suicides in France, see D. Outram, *The Body and the French Revolution* (New Haven, 1989), ch. 6.

English suicides, but some gentlemen did kill themselves because they had failed at their public duties and could not endure the knowledge that they had injured their nation or their sovereign. Easily the most affecting example was the death of John Temple, the son of Sir William Temple, the statesman and man of letters. Appointed William III's secretary of war in 1689, the younger Temple's first act was a disastrous attempt to end the Irish rebellion by diplomatic legerdemain. Not for the last time, English disingenuousness was no match for Irish cunning, and Temple was betrayed and humiliated. Ashamed and distraught, Temple wrote his family a moving note absolving them of any part in his despair and leaped off London bridge. Another paper was found in his pocket that read: 'My folly in undertaking what I could not execute has done the king great prejudice, which cannot be stop'd no easier way for me than this: may his undertaking prosper, may he have a blessing.'[70]

The number of aristocrats and gentlemen who slew themselves in the name of honour increased greatly after 1700. The sheer frequency of suicide among the aristocracy made it seem as though premeditated self-slaughter were customary in the highest ranks of English society. The earl of Bath caused a sensation when he shot himself in September 1701 within a fortnight of his father's suicide, passing on the cursed title to his own son. Three earls of Bath were present at the funeral of the father and grandfather, scandalmongers quipped.[71] The shooting deaths of the earl of Scarborough (1740), Lord Montfort (1755), the duke of Bolton (1765), Lord Saye and Sele (1788), the earl of Caithness (1789), and Viscount Mountmorres (1797) were widely publicized.[72] These patricians were joined by foreign noblemen, some of whom journeyed to England expressly to kill themselves. A younger son of the French chancellor shot himself in 1789, immediately after his arrival at Brighton. He had with him a great deal of money, jewels, and insignia of honour,

[70] *DNB*, s.v. 'Temple, Sir William'; *The Early Essays and Romances of Sir William Temple*, ed. G. C. M. Smith (Oxford, 1930), pp. xii, 25, 193–4 n. 60; D. Nokes, *Jonathan Swift: A Hypocrite Reversed* (Oxford, 1985), 17; N. Luttrell, *A Brief Historical Relation of State Affairs*, (Oxford, 1857), i. 524. A similar motive precipitated the suicide of Dr George Butts, the vice-chancellor of Cambridge University, who hanged himself in 1632 after he had allegedly insulted the king during a royal visit by mounting a performance of Peter Hausted's *The Rival Friends*, which was deemed offensive, and by mishandling the promotion of a score of scholars to be granted higher degrees on the occasion. There are several versions of the story: PRO, C 115/M 35/XC 1172 (We are grateful to Cynthia B. Herrup for this citation.); *CSPD, 1631–1633*, 297, 302; D. Masson, *The Life of John Milton* (Gloucester, Mass., 1965), i. 252–7; L. J. Mills, *Peter Hausted: Playwright, Poet, and Preacher* (Bloomington, Ind., n.d.), 17–25.

[71] *Complete Peerage*, ii. 22 n.

[72] Ibid., s.v. the titles listed.

and no one could explain his suicide note: 'Je meurs innocent; J'en atteste le Ciel.' The prince of Wales intervened immediately with local officials, apparently in an attempt to ensure that the chevalier's remains would be returned home 'to mingle with their native dust', but the French preferred that he be interred in the fatal soil of England.[73] The very same month the son of a German general had shot himself in Hyde Park.[74] Frederick, the son of the king of Corsica, shot himself in Westminster Abbey in 1797 and received an honourable burial (not in the Abbey, though) and a suitable epitaph.[75] Another long-time London resident, the Sicilian nobleman the duke of Sorentino, did the same thing in Lowthorpe's coffee-house, a more conventional setting, eighteen months later.[76] Commentators reinforced the impression that men of fashion frequently died by their own hand, the victims of a false code of honour. Brought down by his own extravagances, 'Sir Foppington falls into Despair, and dies in Suicide', sneered the author of *Hell upon Earth*.[77]

Critics and satirists complained loudly that the motives that drove men of fashion to slay themselves were base and frivolous, and it is difficult not to agree. They charged that the chief cause of suicides for honour was gambling. The *Connoisseur* announced in 1755 that the final member of the Last Guinea Club, a band of gentlemen who had sworn to kill themselves when they had cantered through their fortunes, had at last fulfilled his vow.[78] The *Gentleman's Magazine* published an essay in 1787 linking duelling and suicide as the progeny of gambling, and Charles Moore included in his great treatise on suicide shorter tracts attacking the other vices. These three crimes were, he thought, intimately connected, impious, and reckless: gambling was a chief cause of suicide; duelling, based on the same code as honourable suicide, was a way of hazarding one's life.[79] However exaggerated the critics' claims were, the connection between gambling and suicide was undoubtedly a strong one. The fashionable casinos of London and Bath were social blast furnaces, where aristocratic gold, gentry silver, and merchant steel were

73 *The Times*, no. 1261 (19 Sept. 1789), 2; no. 1262 (21 Sept. 1789), 2; no. 1263 (22 Sept. 1789), 2; no. 1269 (29 Sept. 1789), 2; no. 1275 (6 Oct. 1789), 3.

74 Ibid., no. 1265 (24 Sept. 1789), 3; no. 1267 (26 Sept. 1789), 3. A French gentleman had done precisely the same thing at Greenwich seven months before: *Annual Register*, xxxi (1789), 200.

75 *Annual Register*, xxxix (1797), 11.

76 Ibid., xli (1799), 23–4; *The Times*, no. 4507 (12 June 1799), 3.

77 *Hell upon Earth; or, the Town in an Uproar* (London, 1729), 36.

78 [G. Colman and B. Thornton], *Connoisseur* (London, 1755), i. 295–6.

79 Moore, *Full Inquiry into Suicide*, sig. C2$^{v}$ and *passim*.

fused into a tough alloy of common values. At Arthur's, Boodles's, or White's in London, at the many casinos in Beau Nash's Bath and other provincial spas, the English élite participated in a shared culture, a central ritual of which was gambling.[80] The elaborate rules of contemporary card games mirrored the intricate rules of manners; the unbreakable conventions of honour demanded that violations of decorum be satisfied by violence. In 1741 a gamester named Nourse fell into a violent argument with Lord Windsor at a fashionable London casino, and challenged the peer to a duel. Windsor refused, and Nourse, knowing that he could not have refused to fight an equal, was so enraged and humiliated by the insult that he went home and cut his throat.[81] When Sir John Bland was arrested for giving worthless bills to cover losses of £32,000 that he had run up in a single evening, his banker had to advance him £500 'to save him from the affront, and prevent him from killing himself on the spot'. The banker cunningly engaged Bland's honour not to seek satisfaction in a duel with the man who had arrested him, but the ruse left Bland with no alternative except suicide, which he committed soon afterwards.[82]

Gambling was a Georgian equivalent of the tournament. And like the tournament, gaming could be dangerous. Fortunes were lost in a matter of hours. Men who entered Arthur's with the carriage of nobility left it ruined and dishonoured. Horace Walpole blamed the suicides of Bland, Lord Montfort (1755), and William Skrine (1783), all of them Members of Parliament, on huge gambling losses. Skrine, whose enemies sneered at his origins because he was the son of a rich Bath apothecary, was famous for risky play at high stakes. When one night he lost his claims to gentility at Brooks's, he repaired to a tavern and blew his brains out. Bland was also notorious for playing for high stakes, and Montfort, who died indebted for £30,000, was reputed to have had 'the sharpest genius at the time' on the turf and at the table.[83] Honour could be won at gaming as well as lost, although it was a kind of honour that was a

[80] J. C. D. Clark, *English Society, 1688–1832* (Cambridge, 1985), 106–7; Borsay, *English Urban Renaissance*, 248–50, 272–3.

[81] Walpole, *Correspondence*, i. 145.

[82] Sedgwick, *House of Commons, 1715–1754*, i. 98–9 (Bland).

[83] Ibid., i. 492–3 (Bromley, Lord Montfort); L. B. Namier and J. Brooke, *The House of Commons, 1754–1790* (London, 1964), i. 98–9 (Bland); iii. 443 (Skrine); Westminster Inquisitions, William Skrine (8 Mar. 1783). Henry Bromley, Lord Montfort: Walpole, *Correspondence*, xx. 461. For another famous case, the suicide of the socialite Fanny Braddock at Bath in 1731, see *Gentleman's Magazine*, i (1731), 396–7, and the discussion below, Ch. 9.

bubble—marvellous to behold and easily burst. Jenison Shafto compounded his fabulous luck as a gambler into a seat in parliament and a place in the highest political and social circles. His eminence was due entirely to his success as a gamester among men whose chief recreation was wagering, and when his fortunes suffered a sudden reverse in 1771, he shot himself.[84]

Some of the nobs who chose the honourable death had lost their substance through sheer improvidence, rather than in the dangerous rites of gaming. John Damer, who attracted the attention of the whole nation when he shot himself, was easily the most spectacular of these. The son of Lord Milton, Damer was married to Anne Seymour-Conway, a notable sculptor, whom Walpole admired and patronized. The young couple were the most fashionable pair of the age, and one of the most profligate. They spent their way through an enormous fortune without the help of an addiction to gambling, according to Walpole. He estimated Damer's worth at £5,000 per year with £22,000 in reversion. The papers were full of bolder speculations. According to William Cole's notes on the *Cambridge Chronicle*, for instance, Damer enjoyed an annual income of £37,000, but could not pay his bills. He seems to have owed at least £10,000 outright and, more ominously, to have guaranteed a bond worth £91,000. Some time before his death, his father had become disgusted with his son and his wife and refused to save him from his creditors again. Casting a '*distracted Eye* on his *Situation*', Damer began dropping hints that he would kill himself. Thanks to the intervention of a friend, Lord Milton relented, it was said, and set off to London with £30,000. Before he could arrive, Damer threw himself a last, extravagant party. He rented rooms in the Bedford Arms in Covent Garden, where he was entertained until three in the morning by a blind fiddler named Burnet and four ladies of the night, including 'Little Miss Richmond that sings'. At the end of the festivities, he clapped his hat on the fiddler's head, went up to his room and shot himself dead.[85]

Sheer greed or foolishness hurled other gentlemen into disgrace. Some abused their official positions—or were accused of doing so. It hardly mattered whether or not the charges were true. Political passions ran high in the eighteenth century, and the partisan pack showed no pity

[84] Namier and Brooke, *House of Commons, 1754–1790*, ii. 426–7.

[85] BL, Add. MS 5824, fos. 97$^{v}$–98$^{v}$. Horace Walpole believed that Damer and his two brothers were at least £70,000 in debt: Walpole, *Correspondence*, xxxix. 202–3. See also, *Gentleman's Magazine*, x (1766), 383; Westminster Inquisitions, Hon. John Damer (15 Aug. 1776); *DNB*, s.v. 'Anne Seymour Damer'; Namier and Brooke, *House of Commons, 1754–1790*, i. 297.

when they were in full chase. Hounded by his enemies because of his alleged mismanagement of the East India Company, Lord Clive killed himself in 1774.[86] John Powell, an official in the Pay Office, was accused of malversation in a case that attracted enormous publicity. The charges may have been wrong or exaggerated, and they were certainly politically motivated. Powell was supported by Edmund Burke, the new paymaster, who reinstated him and defended him in a parliamentary shouting-match that ended only when the playwright and MP Richard Brinsley Sheridan pulled Burke back into his seat. Burke's loyalty was a matter of legal principle, not a conviction that Powell was entirely blameless. He wrote to Powell, explaining that his actions on his behalf were undertaken to secure him a fair hearing; Burke himself had not formed an opinion as to his guilt or innocence. Powell grew more and more despairing, and according to his servant, 'irresolute, timid, jealous and suspicious of every Body'. On 25 May he cut his throat. Burke testified at the inquest the next day, and in a last gesture of generosity, swore that since his actions had been debated in the House of Commons, Powell had been badly disturbed. His testimony helped to persuade the jury to bring in a lunacy verdict, but it did not dispel the general conviction that Powell's suicide had been an admission of guilt.[87] A surprisingly high number of Members of Parliament committed suicide in the eighteenth century, twenty-one at least, which may partly reflect the uncertainties of political life and the psychological consequences of disgrace and ruin.[88] The game of high politics was a blood sport.

Contemporary writers supposed honour to be the possession exclusively of gentlemen, an attribute of rank, symbolized by the swords that they alone were authorized by tradition to wear. Men of humbler station and women of all ranks nevertheless cherished their reputations and sometimes took their lives when they were disgraced. For although the

86 *DNB*, s.v. 'Clive, Robert'; *Complete Peerage*, s.v. 'Clive'.

87 E. Burke, *The Correspondence of Edmund Burke*, ed. H. Furber (Cambridge, 1965), v. 87–8, 90–1; Westminster Inquisitions, John Powell (26 May 1784). The politician Richard Rigby, who had when he was a paymaster defended Powell, also testified at the inquest that Powell had been destroyed mentally by the accusations against him. For similar cases involving eminent men, see *Annual Register*, xxii (1779), 207; Sedgwick, *House of Commons, 1715–1754*, ii. 277 (Humphry Morice [d. 1731], MP and director of the Bank of England, which he defrauded of more than £29,000); Namier and Brooke, *House of Commons, 1754–1790*, ii. 124 (Robert Mayne, MP [d. 1782], who defrauded people to cover stock losses).

88 B. D. Henning, *History of Parliament: The Commons, 1660–1689* (London, 1983), i. 676–7, iii. 114; Sedgwick, *House of Commons, 1715–1754*, i. 155; Namier and Brooke, *House of Commons, 1754–1790*, i. 176. The biographical dictionary of MPs in parliament 1689–1714 has not yet been published; it will surely supply more cases.

mores that guided their behaviour were less formalized than the aristocratic code of honour, they were no less compelling. Mandeville, indeed, held the opinion that shame was the only reason why people killed themselves. 'Nobody would kill himself wilfully but to avoid something', he reasoned; and that something must be worse than death itself.[89] An anonymous man who drowned himself in 1719 had a slate in his pocket scratched with the legend, ''Tis better to die than be exposed.'[90] A virtually illiterate servant who hanged herself fifty years later blamed her employers for giving her a 'bad Carracter' (*sic*) and so ruining her life.[91]

No matter how poor they were, men and women knew that it was vital to be 'of a good character'. Those words occur frequently in contemporary documents and distinguished the favoured, who might receive assistance and compassion, from the damned, who could expect no help or mercy in life or in death. Establishing and maintaining a good reputation were essential both in business affairs and social life. The English were a mobile folk who lived out their adult lives in towns and villages other than where they were born. Kinship ties, while not as insignificant as we once thought, were relatively weak, and people were compelled to develop close working relationships with persons to whom they were not related. Credit, employment, poor relief, and social advancement were all impossible without the goodwill of one's neighbours and the village or town élite.[92] There were expressions of surprise when men and women with spotless reputations killed themselves, partly because suicide was still considered by many to be incompatible with godly behaviour and partly because it was unclear why a person still in possession of his honour would kill himself unless he were mad. Reporting that a lunacy verdict had been returned after the suicide of Thomas Frogget in 1731, for instance, *Fog's Weekly Journal* remarked that he had been 'a Person of a Good Character, lying under some Discontent'.[93] The *Norwich Mercury* explained in 1744 that Lydia Royce had been found insane by the coroner's jury. Her body 'very decently dress'd' had been

[89] B. Mandeville, *The Fable of the Bees*, ed. F. B. Kaye (Oxford, 1924–9), i. 209. See also, i. 209–10; ii. 136.

[90] *Weekly Journal*, no. 26 (8 Aug. 1719).

[91] Westminster Inquisitions, Mary Banks (27 Feb. 1769).

[92] The best discussion of this subject is now Amussen, *An Ordered Society*, 98–104. See also Cressy, 'Kinship and Kin Interaction'.

[93] *Fog's Weekly Journal*, no. 154 (16 Oct. 1731). See also, *Weekly Journal*, no. 230 (23 Mar. 1723).

discovered in the river, and witnesses had testified that she had 'lived as a Servant in several Families of Reputation in this City and with a very good Character'.[94]

The worst and most shameful offences were naturally those that had the most terrible consequences—public humiliation and the loss of one's life or livelihood. But humiliation could be deadly in itself: again and again in accounts of suicides, disgrace was invoked as the principal motive for self-destruction. Brought before the mayor of Gloucester in 1605 and accused of stealing 30*s*. from his master, John Ashley ran away and drowned himself.[95] Elizabeth Beck, a widow who stole a quilt and some other items of small value from her landlady, was a woman whose death in 1762, like her life, was of no public consequence at all. Her offence and her fate were more typical of people who killed themselves for shame, most of whom were poor and some of whom were convicted as self-murderers. Recognizing that 'her Circumstances were very bad', the drummer's wife from whom she had stolen did not arrest her but merely demanded notes for their value. The discovery of Elizabeth's crime stripped her of her last shred of self-respect; she walked wordlessly to her room and hanged herself. It cost her a Christian burial as well, for the jury found her *felo de se* in spite of testimony that she had been melancholy and not 'right in her Mind' for a month because of gloom and gin.[96] This is a tale that could be matched by many others. Necessity drove some people to steal from their masters; simple temptation overcame others. The vast differences in wealth between rich and poor were starkly evident, because the wealthy lived in close proximity to the poor. They employed servants and labourers at low wages; prosperous merchants and craftsmen shared lodgings in London and other cities with families of much lower circumstances.

Almost every crime imaginable prompted people to kill themselves in remorse and despair. Accused witches, schoolboy arsonists, highway robbers, horse thieves, murderers, and sex maniacs sometimes reached

[94] *Norwich Mercury* (1–8 Dec. 1744). See also, Norwich Inquisitions, Lydia Royce (5 Dec. 1744).

[95] PRO, KB 9/1073/1, m. 64; T. R. Murphy, ' "Woful Childe of Parents Rage": Suicide of Children and Adolescents in Early Modern England', *Sixteenth Century Journal*, xvii (1986), 266.

[96] Westminster Inquisitions, Elizabeth Beck (13 Apr. 1762). For an early case of a man who killed himself after he was arrested for stealing a staff worth just 6*d*., see KB 9/593/2, m. 154.

for the knife or noose when they were exposed.[97] Sir William Denny included 'A Desperate Malefactor' among his gallery of suicidal types.[98] Hardly a desperate malefactor, Will Porter galloped off with someone else's horse on a drunken escapade in 1617. The horse's owner was enraged; he arrested Porter and had him clapped into the Northampton gaol, where he languished for five weeks. After he was freed, Porter came to Napier for help, explaining that when he had been in prison he had been tempted to kill himself and that his suicidal urges had not abated since his release. He thought he was 'haunted with an ill spirit'.[99] The spirit haunting Will Porter was shame and embarrassment. Other lawbreakers faced execution; and yet even while awaiting punishment, it was often their reputations that concerned them as much as the certainty of suffering. Nothing was more painful than the traitor's death; the offender's body was dismembered in a ritual that exacted symbolic retribution for his crime and protracted his pain as long as possible. Two days after he had been sentenced to be drawn and quartered in 1654, Simon Bourne poisoned himself in Worcester Castle. Miles Sindercombe did the same thing three years later in the Tower, and in his suicide note he tried to explain his feelings: 'I take this course, because I would not have all the open shame of the World executed upon my Body.'[100] Lesser criminals, facing the ordinary rites of execution, also recoiled from public disgrace. A soldier who hanged himself at Plymouth in 1765 left a note to his master explaining that he could not restrain his propensity to thievery, and 'chose that method of putting a period to his life rather than the more public one of dying on the gallows'.[101] Suicides by condemned prisoners were commonplace; the notorious criminals Mary Compton and Francis David Stirn poisoned themselves at their trials.[102] Shame tormented criminals' families, too; it drove the father of two men

[97] For examples of the crimes mentioned, see C. L'E. Ewen, *Witchcraft and Demonianism* (London, 1933), 406, 453; *Wiltshire Coroners' Bills*, no. 1680; J. S. Cockburn (ed.), *Western Circuit Assize Orders, 1629–1648*, Camden Society, 4th ser., xvii (London, 1976), no. 939; KB 11/22/2, m. 14; and the other citations to this paragraph.

[98] W. Denny, *Pelicanicidium, Or the Christian Adviser against Self-Murder* (London, 1653).

[99] Bodl., Ashmole MS 201, fo. 144$^r$ (Porter). For examples of Tudor and Stuart suicides to escape arrest, trial, or punishment, see KB 9/588/1, m. 103; KB 9/588/2, mm. 188, 191.

[100] KB 9/865/2, m. 115; *The Whole Business of Sindercome* (London, 1657), 14, 19. See also, KB 9/661/1, m. 252.

[101] *Gentleman's Magazine*, xxxv (1765), 536.

[102] *An Account of the Seizing, Apprehending, Behaviour, Confession, and Commitment to Newgate of Mary St. Dunstan* (London, 1693); *Annual Register*, iii (1760), 130. Eighty-five persons whose suicides are recorded in the King's Bench data were identified as prisoners. For interesting examples, see PRO, KB 9/588/2, m. 188; KB 9/757/3, mm. 103, 384–5; KB 9/598/2, m. 191. See also, *Fog's Weekly Journal*, no. 86 (16 May 1730); no. 97 (1730).

who were hanged for horse theft in 1766 to attempt suicide.[103] Because they were almost certain to be judged *felo de se*, prisoners who took their own lives rather than submit to public execution demonstrated that they dreaded that disgrace more than the desecration of their cadavers.

Susan Amussen has shown in a subtle analysis that proper behaviour in early modern England was determined by gender. Sexual reputation was always more important to women than it was to men, and it became more so as the period progressed. '"Honesty"', she writes, 'had one meaning for women and another for men. Women's honesty was determined and judged by their sexual behaviour; men's honesty was judged by their neighbours in a wide variety of contexts, and bore a closer relation to our notion of honesty as "truthful".' Men played a wider set of roles outside the family than women, and so the standards by which their behaviour was measured were more various.[104] And yet the English people valued chastity less highly than the classic European 'honour and shame societies' in the Mediterranean and North Africa have in the past or do today. Greek and Spanish codes of honourable behaviour, for instance, make an absolute distinction between masculine honour and feminine shame. Among Greek and Spanish pastoralists, women are always tainted with shame, even when they are chaste, and they are utterly dishonoured by fornication, adultery, or rape. Those crimes require vengeance on the offending male and his family as well as punishment of the woman.[105] The English, in contrast, had a comparatively relaxed attitude to women's sexual delicta. Premarital sex and adultery were commonplace, and they were lightly punished.[106] When the Puritan regime experimented with making bastardy and adultery capital crimes in the 1650s, prosecutors, local officials, and juries simply refused to enforce the law.[107] Rape was rarely prosecuted successfully

103 *Annual Register*, ix (1766), Chronicle, 94.

104 Amussen, *An Ordered Society*, 99–104. For more evidence supporting Amussen's arguments, see, J. A. Sharpe, *Defamation and Sexual Slander in Early Modern England*, Borthwick Papers, lviii (York, 1980); Ingram, *Church Courts, Sex and Marriage*, ch. 10.

105 J. K. Campbell, *Honour, Family and Patronage* (Oxford, 1964), 200–1, 268–74; J. A. Pitt-Rivers, *The People of the Sierra*, 2nd edn. (Chicago, 1971), ch. 8.

106 Macfarlane, *Marriage and Love*, 239–44. It should be emphasized that the comparison implicit in this judgement is with the classic honour and shame societies and that there were important shifts in attitudes to and punishments of sexual transgressions in this period: Ingram, *Church Courts, Sex and Marriage*, chs. 7–8.

107 K. Wrightson, 'The Nadir of Illegitimacy in Seventeenth-Century England', in P. Laslett, K. Oosterveen, and R. M. Smith, *Bastardy and Its Comparative History* (London, 1980), 176–91; K. Thomas, 'The Puritans and Adultery: The 1650 Act Reconsidered', in K. Thomas and D. Pennington (eds.), *Puritans and Revolutionaries* (Oxford, 1978).

throughout the period. Juries evidently believed that the prescribed punishment, death, was too severe, and they simply would not convict. In the eighteenth century, rape was tried more successfully as attempted rape, because that offence carried a lesser penalty.[108] Sexual crimes by women and against women were treated less severely in England than in some other societies partly because they were less important in forging links between networks of kin and more important as members of the household economy. Alan Macfarlane has rightly stressed that a comparatively lax attitude toward sexual offences was a corollary of a marriage system based on small, independent households that promoted late marriage and romantic love.[109] The freedom women were allowed permitted some slight latitude for sexual experimentation; paradoxically, it also made it more difficult to avenge rape. The comparatively light punishments for sexual crimes should not, however, lead one to conclude that women could break sexual rules with impunity. Fornication and adultery, if discovered, were matters for public humiliation. Bearing a bastard compounded the offence and could result in whipping and in imprisonment for a year. Illicit pregnancy was regarded as a strong motive to suicide by unmarried women throughout the period. Another of Sir William Denny's suicidal stereotypes was 'A Wench with Childe'.[110] Testifying to his belief that Elizabeth Gore's death in 1614 had not been accidental, Robert Negus told the court of Star Chamber that the wretchedly poor creature, 'a little before her death, being unmarried, was delivered of a bastard girl, and thereupon this defendant verily believeth, drowned herself'.[111] The suspicion that a young woman who drowned after a quarrel with her boyfriend in 1672 had been pregnant convinced Oliver Heywood and his neighbours that she had probably cast herself into the river. 'The Crowner and his Jury sate on Wednesday [and] found it chance medley', he admitted, 'but tis vehemently suspected that the young woman was with child, and that they might have [had] some angry words, and that she in a discontent

[108] J. A. Sharpe, *Crime in Seventeenth Century England: A County Study* (Cambridge, 1983), 63–5; J. M. Beattie, *Crime and the Courts in England, 1660–1800* (Princeton, 1986), 124–31.
[109] Macfarlane, *Marriage and Love*, 242–4.
[110] Denny, *Pelicanicidium*, 9.
[111] PRO, STAC 8/2/41.

might doe that.'[112] Some young women panicked after they gave birth to illegitimate children and killed them, compounding their shame. A Welsh girl hanged herself in 1729 after her stepmother 'threatened to discover that she murdered her Bastard Child about two Months old'.[113]

Young women were more vulnerable to seduction and betrayal than their counterparts in the modern Mediterranean world because of the comparative freedom of courtship and the rules that governed it. Young men and women normally sought out their own mates and then secured their parents' permission to marry. Long-standing custom permitted young people who were betrothed to have sexual relations. Adverse economic conditions forced many couples to postpone marriage and made it more difficult to plan weddings, for the capital necessary to establish a new household was more difficult to obtain. This explains the rise in bastardy in the late sixteenth and early seventeenth centuries. Economic change contributed to illegitimacy in the next century somewhat differently, by providing new opportunities for young people to earn their own living and forcing more and more of them into jobs in the cities or in rural industry. The role of elders in determining when marriage was possible was reduced. Couples in these circumstances married earlier and engaged in premarital sex more frequently, and the result was an increase in both legitimate and illegitimate births. The latter naturally attracted far more attention, for it led to infanticide and the abandonment of children.

Popular wisdom declared that pregnancy was the surest way to the altar, and some girls probably let themselves be seduced in spite of the

[112] O. Heywood, *His Autobiography, Diaries, Anecdote and Event Books*, ed. J. Horsfall Turner (Bingley and Brighouse, 1881–5), iii. 197. For other examples of suicides because of illicit pregnancy, see PRO, KB 9/588/2, m. 214; KB 9/755, m. 247; KB 11/16/1 (unnumbered); KB 11/22/8, m. 7; PRO, CHES 18/3 (Sarah Brown); J. Aubrey, 'Observations', in his *Three Prose Works*, ed. J. Buchanan-Brown (Carbondale, Ill., 1972), 352. Because autopsies were rare and inquisitions formulaic, it is certain that there were a great many such cases that are not identified in the surviving inquisitions. For the prevalence of young women, often identified as spinsters or servants, among recorded suicides, see above, Chapter 7. For an interesting example of a pregnant servant suspected of committing suicide when she went missing, see *The Diary of Thomas Turner, 1754–1765*, ed. D. Vaisey (Oxford, 1984), 203, 205, 206.

[113] *Fog's Weekly Journal*, no. 48 (23 Aug. 1729). Very occasionally men also killed themselves after murdering their bastard children: KB 9/584, m. 99; KB 9/725/3, m. 499. Attempted abortions that resulted in the deaths of mothers were technically *felonia de se*: for examples, see KB 9/871/2, m. 160; KB 11/1/2, m. 28.

risks. More often—to judge from the complaints of wronged women—men abused the conventions of courtship. Stories of women like Elizabeth Umpleby, who killed herself in 1733, were familiar *exempla*. Pregnant by John Addinell, Elizabeth 'demanded to him to perform his Promise of Marrying her', showing him a paper packet of poison that she said she would take if he refused. He denied her anyway.[114] Respectable people were outraged by masculine duplicity, partly because the bastards that lying males bred became the parish's charge, but also because of a genuine sympathy for the young women who had been seduced and betrayed. *Fog's Weekly Journal* reported a story that a pregnant servant had hanged herself after the father of her child renounced his promise and absconded; 'which if true', sputtered the angry author of the piece, 'he deserves to be hanged on the same Tree'.[115] Over fifty years later *The Times* published a melodramatic account of male perfidy and female suicide. Opening with a cloying elegy to Miss Lynch, the daughter of a genteel family in the West Country, the story told of her love for a gentleman of high standing in a learned profession. Their courtship was sanctioned by her parents, who looked forward to their marriage happily. But at length she proved with child, either through the gentleman's 'system of seduction' or some 'accident' or 'unlooked-for-opportunity', and the family tried to arrange a wedding immediately. The gentleman, however, lay low and did not acknowledge her plight until three days after her child was born, when he presented himself at her bedside and offered to marry her. The betrayed woman was indignant. 'You are come too late!' she cried, 'Had you married me before I became the mother of a bastard, and before my dishonour was divulged to the world, a whole life of grateful and submissive love should have repaid you; as it is, I refuse not only to be your wife, but I refuse to live.' Resolutely rejecting any food, she carried out her pledge by starving herself to death.[116]

Adulterous wives were in less danger of discovery than unmarried young women, but they, too, bore the consequences of their infidelity more heavily than their lovers. A gentlewoman who drowned herself at Deal after the catastrophic end to her affair with a naval officer wrote that she could not bear to face her husband and family, adding bitterly that her lover could 'wish and swear, and forswear, to screen himself from

[114] *Fog's Weekly Journal*, no. 234 (28 Apr. 1733). See also, *The Times*, no. 949 (11 Jan. 1788).

[115] *Fog's Weekly Journal*, no. 206 (14 Oct. 1732).

[116] *The Times*, no. 543 (30 Sept. 1786), 1. See also, ibid., no. 578 (9 Nov. 1786), 2.

shame' as she, big with his child, could not.[117] How much rape dishonoured women is unclear. After Lovelace violates her, Clarissa is plunged into despair and guilt and contemplates suicide, and there was a good deal of discussion of the legitimacy of suicide to escape ravishment, most of it by clergymen denouncing the example of Lucretia.[118] But it is very difficult to find examples of actual suicides by rape victims. Despite the rarity of convictions for rape, some men nevertheless killed themselves out of shame when their sexual offences were exposed. In 1717, the newspapers reported that a Southwark milkman stabbed and hanged himself, 'being struck with Remorse, for having deflowered his Wives Daughter upon the Bed where her Mother lay dead'.[119] A London horner who raped a teenage girl took the same course to escape conviction in 1729.[120] These were exceptional incidents. The code of masculine honour plainly precluded violent rape, particularly when it involved young girls, but at the same time the courts were unable to find a very satisfactory way of punishing offenders. The fear of dishonour may have constrained some and disgrace prompted the suicides of a few men, but contemporaries' attitudes to sexual exploitation were far too ambivalent to compensate for the law's failure to protect women from men who ignored the constraints that honour and shame were supposed to impose on them.

[117] *London Journal*, no. 359 (11 June 1726). The pain and humiliation that homosexuals must have endured has left few traces in the records of 18th century suicides. Men were regularly tried for sodomy at the Old Bailey and often exposed to public disgrace in the pillory when they were convicted. But homosexuality was so shameful in itself that nobody was likely to mention it at an inquest lest the jury bring in a verdict of *felo de se*. One remarkable case of sexual deviance that led to a suicide attempt occurred in Bristol in 1760. A young man who pretended to be a nobleman stabbed himself and cut his throat. His rescuers discovered that he was in fact a hermaphrodite, and the authorities had to summon a board of midwives to determine which sex he was. Labelled a male after a humiliating examination and debate, he was consigned to the House of Correction. The habits of dissimulation by which he had concealed his sexual ambivalence perhaps made him misrepresent his social standing as well. In a society where hierarchies of gender and status determined one's social identity, he had no fixed position at all. It is easy to guess why he would have felt desperately alienated. *Annual Register*, iii (1760), 161.

[118] I. Donaldson, *The Rapes of Lucretia* (Oxford, 1982), esp. chs. 2, 4, 8.

[119] *Weekly Journal; or, Saturday's Poet*, no. 43 (5 Oct. 1717). A suicide who killed himself 'because of his guilt' in 1553 compounded the sin of incest by killing his daughter's baby: KB 9/584, m. 99.

[120] *Fog's Weekly Journal*, no. 47 (16 Aug. 1729); For the rarity of convictions for rape, see [J. Applebee, (ed.)], *Select Trials at the Sessions House in the Old Bailey* (1742; repr. New York, 1985) and n. 108 above.

## AFFLICTIONS OF THE HEART

Historians have recently emphasized the importance of romantic love in English courtship.[121] England's economic system promoted high levels of geographic mobility, and its family structure and cultural values were perfectly adapted to its increasingly capitalistic practices. Marriage was possible only when enough money could be got together to form a new household, separate from that of either set of parents. Young people therefore married at a relatively late age, in their mid-twenties or later, and they normally spent a decade or so living away from home and working as servants or serving apprenticeships. Except among the upper classes, few parents chose spouses for their children. Young men and women had plenty of opportunities to meet potential wives and husbands in the homes where they worked, at alehouses, or at church rituals and festivals. Frequently they formed attachments and then sought their parents' permission to marry. Ideally, the selection of a spouse was a joint decision, in which both children and parents weighed affection and economic considerations equally. In practice, young people tended to be more swayed by their hearts, and their parents to be more concerned about their purses. Despite the freedom normally allowed children and the stress placed on love, parents continued to exercise considerable authority. Marriage without their blessing and their financial assistance was seldom possible and never advisable. This meant that young people confronted the difficult task of finding a mate who was attractive to them, economically and socially appropriate, and acceptable to their parents. The potential pitfalls were many; the emotional pain they caused could be unendurable.

There were some notable changes in courtship among the mass of people in the early modern period. Old forms of customary marriage slowly declined in the eighteenth century, and the Marriage Act of 1753

[121] The two paragraphs that follow summarize a large and highly contentious literature. The fundamental works are J. R. Gillis, *For Better, For Worse* (New York, 1985), chs. 1–2; Stone, *The Family, Sex and Marriage*; Macfarlane, *Marriage and Love*; Wrightson, *English Society*, chs. 2–3; Houlbrooke, *English Family*, ch. 4; Ingram, *Church Courts, Sex and Marriage*, chs. 6–7. J. R. Gillis, 'From Ritual to Romance: Toward an Alternative History of Love', in C. Z. Stearns and P. N. Stearns (eds.), *Emotion and Social Change* (New York, 1988), 87–122, by far the most challenging treatment of courtship so far, appeared after this chapter had been substantially completed. A new study of marriage and marital breakdown by Lawrence Stone should appear shortly; some of its conclusions were presented in Stone's Curti Lectures at the University of Wisconsin-Madison in 1986 and have been drawn on here. The evidence presented below from the notebooks of Richard Napier is amplified in MacDonald, *Mystical Bedlam*, ch. 3.

made it more difficult and expensive to marry formally. Consensual unions probably became more frequent. But ordinary men and women's desire to achieve both emotional satisfaction and economic security remained more or less the same, as far as we can tell. Among the landed élite, however, there was an increasing emphasis on romatic love after about 1650. Aristocratic parents had always arranged marriages for their children. The stakes in prestige and in property were too great to permit a boy or girl besotted by physical passion to make an inappropriate choice. Examples of love matches and of parents who took their children's happiness into consideration when selecting a spouse in the early seventeenth century can nevertheless be found.[122] And after the Restoration, parents began to permit their sons and daughters to play a greater part in selecting their wives and husbands. Members of the Georgian aristocracy and greater gentry began to believe that love ought to be as important to them as it was to their servants when they courted. The reasons for this change are controversial; some were economic and some were cultural. They almost certainly included the spread of the strict settlement and the influence of middle-class values on the élite. In this context, the significant issue, however, is that as romantic love and free choice became more commonplace among the aristocracy, they too were exposed to the pangs and perils of premarital romance. Misunderstandings and manipulations of the customs of courting were very common, and suicides were very frequently blamed on them. Young men and women slew themselves because of the pain of unrequited love, infidelity, or lovers' quarrels. Next to financial ruin and destitution, tragic love-affairs were probably the most commonly mentioned motive for suicides. Thomas May declared to Richard Napier in 1629 that he would hang himself if he could not have a wench whom he loved; Dorothy Geary carried out the threat, but failed; Richard Malins succeeded.[123] Many others, like Elizabeth Church, fell into a suicidal funk when they discovered that their suitors had been unfaithful.[124] Forty years after Napier's death, in 1675, John Evelyn witnessed a lovesick servant's suicide attempt. He described the episode with an irony that bordered on sarcasm: 'This was a journey of Adventure and knight errantry, one of the Ladys servants being as desperately in love with Mrs.

[122] L. Stone, *The Crisis of the Aristocracy* (Oxford, 1965), 609–10; S. H. Mendelson, 'The Weightiest Business: Marriage in An Upper-Gentry Family in Seventeenth-Century England: Comment', *Past and Present*, no. 85 (1979), 126–35.

[123] Bodl., Ashmole MS 406, fo. 21 (May); 222, fo. 96$^{r}$ (Geary); 182, fo. 77$^{r}$ (Malins).

[124] Bodl., Ashmole MS 214, fo. 143$^{r}$ (Church); 227, fo. 129$^{r}$ (Walson).

*Howards* Woman, who riding on horseback behind his *Rival*, the amorous and jealous Youth . . . had certainly here killed himself, had he not been prevented; for alighting from his horse and drawing his sword, he endeavoured to fall upon it twice or thrice.' Several days after the party arrived in London, the young man succeeded in poisoning himself.[125] Examples of suicides attributed to unrequited love during the next century might be multiplied until their individual tragedies became intolerably tedious. A story that may stand for many others appeared in the *Weekly Journal* in 1719. A body, the paper reported, of an anonymous man had been hauled from the New River: 'He had his Pocket filled with Stones, and nine Pence in Money, and a love Letter when he was taken out of the water.'[126]

Despite the importance that the English placed on romantic love, they remained deeply ambivalent about it throughout the early modern period, and that ambivalence is reflected in reports of love-suicides. On the one hand, it was recognized that love was an inevitable and desirable part of courtship; on the other, it was feared that love might lead young people to contract unsuitable matches that imperilled their own futures and the social standing of their families. Moreover, everyone knew that the passage from adolescence to marriage was emotionally risky, and that reconciling desire with practical imperatives could be painful. All of these themes were developed in imaginative literature about love; they were also implicit in scientific theories about it. Renaissance physicians and popular writers, like their medieval forebears, declared that love was a disease, called melancholy, that overcame its victims' judgement and reason. It drove them mad and made them miserable. After she dived into a pond and was pulled out, Napier diagnosed Elizabeth Lawrence as a woman 'mad with love and melancholy'.[127] Robert Burton provided an elaborate pathology to explain the causes and effects of love melancholy, and although the explanations for the malady's physiology changed with fashions in medical theory, later physicans clung to the notion that love might cause mental and physical aberrations.[128] There was more emphasis on the dangers of love in the sixteenth and early seventeenth centuries than there was after the Restoration, but even in

125 Evelyn, *Diary*, iv. 71.

126 *Weekly Journal*, no. 23 (9 May 1719). See also, ibid., no. 28 (13 June 1719); *Fog's Weekly Journal*, no. 9 (23 Nov. 1728); no. 44 (26 July 1729); no. 140 (10 July 1731); Westminster Inquisitions, Thomas Holman (28 Aug. 1782).

127 Bodl., Ashmole MS, 415, fo. 210$^r$ (Lawrence).

128 R. Burton, *Anatomy of Melancholy*, ed. H. Jackson (London, 1978), iii. 40–257. See also L. Babb, *The Elizabethan Malady* (East Lansing, 1951), chs. 6–7.

the eighteenth century social commentators stressed that passion easily exceeded reasonable bounds. Reflecting on the suicide of a beautiful girl in 1790, *The Times* blamed disappointed love for her death and exclaimed, 'How frequent is the commission of suicide!'[129]

Reports of suicide for love oscillate between pure tragedy and farce. Although their authors recognize the real pain that drove some young people to kill themselves for love, they frequently slip into a sardonic, satirical tone that sabotages the seriousness of the report. A 1729 story in *Fog's Weekly Journal* told of a young woman who in her anxiety to die first hanged herself and then, immediately after being rescued, poisoned herself. She had committed these desperate acts 'on Account of her Spark's being marry'd to another', the newspaper writer comments flippantly.[130] Love-suicides were embarrassing. They displayed at once the nobility and power of human passion and the inability of its victims to control their own feelings and actions. They revealed, in other words, the human spirit simultaneously at its most exalted and at its most debased. Unable to resolve the contradictory significance of love-suicide, observers often distanced themselves and their readers from the act itself with irony and even humour.

Love-suicide was a staple of great literature and pulp entertainments. The antithesis of love and death heightened the power of the lovers' story, which in turn served to call attention to a central problem in western European societies—the need to balance the desires and the happiness of the individual against the interests of family and society. English literature in the sixteenth and seventeenth centuries includes some of the greatest works about romantic love. The tradition that produced *Romeo and Juliet* and *Antony and Cleopatra* was perpetuated by Dryden and Rowe after the Restoration. *All for Love* drove its model, *Antony and Cleopatra*, from the boards in the eighteenth century.[131] The practitioners of the new genre, the novel, rapidly made romantic love a central theme of their works, and they extended their attention to a realistic depiction of the feelings and problems that confronted middle-class characters. It would be critical folly to generalize about the complex and changing treatment of love in early modern literature. But it is useful in this context to keep in mind the banal truth that the main theme in romantic tragedies—and in comic works as well—is the conflict between love and duty. However transcendent or ridiculous their treatments of

129 *The Times*, no. 1609 (20 Feb. 1790), 3.

130 *Fog's Weekly Journal*, no. 41 (5 July 1729).

131 G. H. Nettleton, A. E. Case, and G. W. Stone, Jr. (eds.), *British Dramatists from Dryden to Sheridan*, 2nd edn. (New York, 1969), 72.

it were, contemporary works of literature pointed again and again to the problems that their characters confronted in resolving that dilemma. In this context, suicide was permissible and even noble, for it expressed a recognition that individuals might be called upon to sacrifice their happiness and freedom of choice for the good of some wider imperative.

Romantic catastrophe was a staple commodity in chapbooks and ballads as well. And crude though their plots and characters were, they touched on dilemmas and emotions that many people had themselves experienced. In some ways, they presented romantic love and its complications more accessibly than great tragedies did. They certainly conveyed clearly popular attitudes to courting and courtship customs. Like their more sophisticated counterparts, the ballads frequently depicted love and duty as irreconcilable and ended in tragic suicides. A favourite theme was the difficulty in matching true love with social and economic advantage. The suicidal lover who had been dumped by a socially ambitious woman was a stock type in the ballads. 'The Two Unfortunate Lovers', published in 1684, tells of a mercer's daughter who haughtily rejects the suit of a merchant, confident that she has won the heart of a gentleman: 'no Merchant my Person shall ever imbrace; While a Rich noble Gallant young Squire's in place.' The merchant pines and dies; the squire thinks better of a marriage to a tradesman's daughter and turns the tables on her. The ballad ends with the heroine's suicide. She repents her cruelty and drinks poison so that she may join in death the suitor she had rejected in life: 'Then she took up the draught, and did trembling cry, I am coming my Love, for thy sake will I dye.'[132] Precisely the same sentiment was sung in a lower social key in 'The Faithful Lover's Farewell', which tells of proud Betty, a cook who rejects the advances of young Johnny, a servant. Betty's social ambitions are modest and mirrored the hopes many real girls of her class must have felt:

> What tho' I am a Servant Maid,
> A Servant I will never Wed;
> For I a Shop-keeper will have,
> That will maintain me fine and brave.

Like those of the mercer's daughter, Betty's ambitions have fatal consequences. Johnny shoots himself in the heart rather than live without her.[133]

[132] 'The Two Unhappy Lovers', in H. E. Rollins (ed.), *The Pepys Ballads* (Cambridge, Mass., 1929), no. 137, iii. 224–5.

[133] 'The Faithful Lover's Farewell', in Rollins, *The Pepys Ballads*, vii. 291–3. This ballad was so successful that it inspired a sequel in which Betty repents, ibid., no. 499, vii. 295–6.

Exaggerated as the plots of these crude ballads are, they were often based on actual events. Similar stories were told in broadsides and newspapers. A 1684 broadside, for instance, reported that a Finchley man who had won the hand of a farmer's daughter sought after by many suitors became so distraught when she broke their engagement that he tried to murder her and then killed himself.[134] Men were as concerned about the prosperity and social standing of prospective spouses as women were. The ultimate marital catastrophe befell a tanner and a widow in 1760. Their courtship had been based on mutual duplicity; they had both lied about the fortunes that they could bring to the match. As soon as they were wed, they discovered that neither of them had any money, 'which, it is apprehended, drove them to a resolution to make away with themselves'. They formed a suicide pact and set out to drown themselves. She succeeded, but he panicked and ran, faithless to the last.[135] Men and women who fell in love with people of much higher or lower social rank could find themselves in a hopeless situation, and if they married, they sometimes could not endure their friends' disapproval or dispel the fear that their new spouses were gold-diggers. *Fog's Weekly Journal* reported a typical case of inappropriate passion in 1729, noting that a baker's apprentice had 'shot himself for Love of his Master's daughter'. His neighbour, the paper claimed, had attempted suicide 'in the like Case' before him and had survived.[136] Social inequities that reversed the usual roles of husband and wife quickly sabotaged a marriage that ended in suicide in 1684. A knight's widow who married Andrew Phillips, a clerk to a person of quality, quarrelled with her new husband over money, all of which was hers. The couple was briefly reconciled, but he walked out on the reunion celebration and she hanged herself.[137] In 1719 a similar incident was reported in the press: a gentlewoman who married her former servant hanged herself the day after her wedding.[138] A couple of months later a rich young gentleman who had married a taverner's daughter did exactly the same thing.[139]

Customarily, parents tried anxiously to make their love-struck children choose appropriate marital partners, and in spite of the gradual erosion of parental influence in the seventeenth and eighteenth centuries,

[134] *Strange and Bloody News of a Most Horrible Murder* (London, 1684).
[135] *Annual Register*, ii. (1760), 151.
[136] *Fog's Weekly Journal*, no. 17 (18 Jan. 1729). See also ibid., no. 130 (27 May 1721).
[137] *Sad and Dreadful News from Kings-Street in Westminster: A Most Lamentable Relation of the Untimely End of the Lady Phillips* (London, 1684).
[138] *Weekly Journal*, no. 23 (9 May 1719).
[139] *Original Weekly Journal* (18 July 1719), 1484.

their objections could be a decisive obstacle to marriage throughout the period. The events recalled in the many versions of the tragedy of James Bateman, for instance, epitomized the conflict between youthful sentiment and parental pragmatism. Having promised to marry James and broken a coin to seal the pledge, Isabella reneges on her promise when her parents persuade her to marry a rich old man named German.[140] This famous story had many counterparts; that is one reason why it was so popular and so enduring. Robert Norman, a man of thirty-two, fell in love in 1628 with a young woman whose parents refused to consent to their marriage. After he had drunk ratsbane in an unsuccessful attempt to kill himself, someone persuaded him to consult Napier, who recorded that he was still suicidal and threatened to leave home.[141] In 1692 a near kinswoman of Sir John Fenwick, perhaps his niece or even his daughter, 'hang[ed] herself at her lodging in Leicester fields upon account of love'. Her parents had prevented her from marrying a Hertfordshire gentleman who in turn shot himself a few months later.[142] Educated opinion sided increasingly with the children in such disputes, but some parents still longed to control as far as possible their sons' and daughters' marriages in the eighteenth century. James Hilton's father and uncle locked him in his room for ten weeks to prevent him from seeing a young woman he had intended to marry. Their cruelty succeeded in its aim: the romance died. He later wed another woman but never recovered from his misery and disappointment, and at last in 1768 he hanged himself.[143]

Writers sympathized with the victims of conflicts between love's commands and filial duty, and antagonism to mercenary marriages seems to have intensified in the later seventeenth and eighteenth centuries. Attacks on marriage for profit were a stock theme in eighteenth-century plays and novels: *Clarissa*, for instance, is a sustained protest against 'property marriage'.[144] Perhaps the most devastating satire on the pernicious effects of parental greed was Hogarth's *Marriage à-la-Mode*. The progress to catastrophe that follows the arranged marriage between

140 J. H. Marshburn, *Murder and Witchcraft in England, 1550–1640* (Norman, Okla., 1971), 88–9; W. Sampson, *Vow Breaker*, ed. H. Wallrath, Materialien zur Kunde des älteren Englischen Dramas, 42 (Louvain, 1914); K. Briggs, *Dictionary of Folk-Tales* (Bloomington, Ind., 1971), pt. B, i. 449–50; *Bateman's Tragedy* (London, n.d. [*c*. 1720?]).

141 Bodl., Ashmole MS 405, fo. 224$^r$ (Norman).

142 Luttrell, *Brief Historical Relation*, ii. 557, 604; A. Wood, *The Life and Times of Anthony Wood*, ed. A. Clark, Oxford Historical Society, xxvi (Oxford, 1894), iii. 401, 405.

143 Westminster Inquisitions, James Hilton (4 Apr. 1768).

144 W. A. Speck, *Society and Literature in England, 1700–60* (London, 1983), 104–11.

# THANK YOU
# Call Again

We appreciate your patronage and hope we may continue to merit it. If we please you, tell your friends. If we don't , tell us.
We strive to satisfy.

the son of a threadbare earl and the daughter of a rich burgher leads through adultery and murder to suicide. In the last plate in the series, the countess is seen dead in her father's house: an empty bottle of laudanum lies on the floor beside her, an apothecary admonishes an idiot servant for failing to prevent her death, and her miserly father is slipping her ring from her finger, lest it be forfeited to the crown.[145] Popular ballads also warned that parents who thwarted their children's passions in order to assure their fortunes risked driving them to their deaths. A characteristic piece published about 1690 told of parents who tricked their daughter into believing that her lover was already married. But instead of rejecting the suitor they disliked, the grief-stricken girl killed herself. The song ends with an unpoetical reiteration of its moral:

> Let her Mishap a Warning be
> To Friends of high and low Degree;
> Cross not your Children here in Love,
> Lest you their utter Ruine prove.[146]

The newspapers and magazines were usually on the side of lovers who had been thwarted by their parents. The *Loyal Impartial Mercury* alleged in 1682 that a young gentlewoman poisoned herself because her mother and father had 'put by her designed Marriage with a Gentleman to whom she was ingaged'.[147] Over a century later, in 1773, the *Annual Register* reported that a young lady had thrown herself into the sea from a cliff and drowned. 'This melancholy affair', remarked the author of the story, 'is said to have been occasioned by her father's refusing to let her see a young fellow a few hours before she died.'[148]

The most famous (and most ridiculed) martyr to parental obstinacy was Thomas Creech, the Oxford scholar. Frustrated in his passion for a local beauty called Philadelphia Playdell because of her parents' implacable opposition to their marriage, he hanged himself in his rooms in Oxford in 1700. The university bachelors reacted less kindly to Creech's death than most commentators on love-suicides. Oxford was a nest of

[145] For a full discussion of this picture, see R. L. S. Cowley, *Hogarth's Marriage a-la-mode* (Ithaca, 1983), 151–2. See also R. Paulson, *Hogarth: His Life, Art and Times*, abridged edn., ed. A. Wilde (New Haven, 1974), 202–19; D. Bindman, *Hogarth* (London, 1981), 108–17.

[146] Rollins, *Pepys Ballads*, no. 337, v. 320–1.

[147] Quoted ibid. v. 319. For other examples see ibid.

[148] *Annual Register*, xvi (1773), 123. For other examples, see also ibid., 68–9; *Fog's Weekly Journal*, no. 42 (12 July 1729), the story of a father so distraught at having caused his son's suicide by opposing his marriage that he took his own life in turn.

gossips with tongues as poisonous as wasps' stings, and the news of Creech's death attracted a swarm of nasty speculation. Some claimed, in the spirit of scholarly pettiness, that he had slain himself because of errors in the notes to his translation. At least two men were provoked by the real cause of Creech's death to publish their thoughts on the danger of loving women. The anonymous author of *A Step to Oxford* blamed Creech's suicide on the effects of love-madness, and his mocking was taken still further by the poetaster who wrote *Daphnis*, a satire that was not printed until 1709. This astonishing piece of bad verse and worse allegory places the blame for Creech's despair on Miss Playdell, not her parents. The beauteous Lalage (Miss Playdell) steals Daphnis's (Creech's) affection away from Alexis (a young colleague?) who helps to tend his flock of sheep (the students). And yet in spite of her conquest, she is proud and drives him mad by rejecting his love. The climax of the poem is the retributive death of the 'cruel Charmer', on to whom a statue of the god of love falls while she is in her bath washing away the polluting touch of Creech's corpse, which she has brushed with her gown. Her blood gushing forth, the 'ungrateful Nymph', dying declares:

> Lovers farewell, Revenge has reach'd my Scorn;
> Thus warn'd, be wise, and Love for Love return.[149]

Few young people really needed this advice. But love's pangs could be fatally sharp, even if their parents did not hinder their choice of suitors.[150]

## CONCLUSION

The motives that observers and suicides gave for self-killing are an index of what contemporaries were most afraid to lose. They demonstrate the importance of the nuclear family, the precariousness of economic life, and the importance of honour and shame. It is difficult to detect fundamental changes in suicide motives during the early modern period.

[149] *A Step to Oxford; or, a Mad Essay on the Reverend Mr. Thomas Creech's Hanging Himself, (As 'Tis Said) for Love* (London, 1700); *Daphnis; or, A Pastoral Elegy Upon the Unfortunate Death of Mr. Thomas Creech, With a Poem on The Despairing Lover and The Despairing Shepherd* (London, 1709).

[150] Many parents, of course, hoped above all else that their children would be happy. For the story of a Bristol man who hanged himself after his son was rejected by his sweetheart and fell raving mad, see *Fog's Weekly Journal*, no. 41 (5 July 1729).

The structure and emotional dynamics of the nuclear family remained much the same. Economic perils waxed and waned and changed in character, but the effect of sudden losses on individuals did not greatly alter. The behaviour that brought honour or shame may have shifted somewhat as more people moved to cities and adopted middle-class values. But the stress on respectability—honesty, probity, neighbourliness—does not seem to have lessened. The most conspicuous changes were in aristocratic mores. Greater emphasis on emotional satisfactions exposed young people of gentle birth to the dangers of romantic love. It may also have made the deaths of spouses and children harder to bear. The code of honour, although still expressed in terms of earlier ideals of chivalry and gentility, was manifestly debased by men who shot themselves or each other because of gambling losses. A martial and political élite had truly become a leisure class, many of whom were less concerned with leadership than with amusement. No wonder middle-class critics deplored the example that they set.

The apparently adamantine continuity of family life has led many historians to doubt that there were any significant changes in early modern society at all. Our examination of suicide motives would seem to add more stones to the edifice that they are building. But even at the most basic level, there were developments that have been swept aside too readily in the search for continuity. They are manifested in the details of explanations for suicide, although they did not affect their main social and psychological themes. John Gillis, for instance, has detected a shift from ritual to sentiment in courtship during the period, but he grants that the change was slowest among the lower orders of society and was a matter of the way in which feelings were understood and expressed, rather than a transition from calculating austerity to passion.[151] The evidence presented by witnesses and inquests and newspaper stories about love suicides is consistent with Gillis's thesis. Early in the period, stories about rejected suitors seem more often to have involved violations of the customs of courtship, such as Isabella's betrayal of her ritual vow to James Bateman, which Sampson made the title theme of the *Vow Breaker*. Newspaper accounts from the eighteenth century, in contrast, place more stress on emotional disappointment itself. They tended to reflect middle-class ideals of behaviour.

Among the poor, as Gillis suggests, customary usages seem to have had a longer run. Informal unions, cemented by ritual and regarded as

[151] Gillis, 'From Ritual to Romance'.

binding by couples and their neighbours, remained common in the later eighteenth century. Before he took his own life, a seaman named Jacob Miers, for example, wrote a letter to the coroner, explaining that his attack on Mary Taafe was prompted by her attempt to break up his 'marriage'. He had lived with a woman for seventeen years and fathered ten children with her. 'I naver cult persway har to be marid', he wrote, 'but salomly swore upon the bible under the Canapay of heven, so I always lookt apon har as my lawful wife.'[152] Another plebeian ritual, wife-selling, survived and prompted a suicide in 1766. 'In a fit of conjugal indifference at an alehouse', began a story reporting the incident, a carpenter called Higginson sold his wife to a brother workman. Wife sales were sometimes a form of customary divorce, and in this instance, the buyer and the wife were perfectly satisfied with the arrangement. A few days later, however, Higginson repented and begged his wife to come back to him. She refused and he hanged himself. It may well be that Higginson was really the injured party in this affair, talked into selling his wife against his real desires by her and her lover.[153] Such stories are suggestive because they point to shifts in courtship customs, in the expression and management of emotion, that historians have generally overlooked.

They also suggest that it would be unwise to place so much stress on the enduring similarities in suicide motives over the century that we neglect the shifting social conditions and customs that caused the specific crises that prompted men and women to take their lives. Instead of a stark dichotomy between continuity and change, we should think (much as Fernand Braudel long ago urged us to do) in terms of levels of change, strata of social and psychological life whose rhythms follow different tempos. People's understanding of what drove people to kill themselves included fundamental psychological needs that were linked with basic social institutions, specific social perils that arose out of economic fluctuations or cultural changes, and personal vices that were as variable as the pleasures and temptations that the changing world presented to them. The grammar of motives remained basically unchanged; the syntax of suicidal calamities expressed new perils as they arose; the diction of despair named every passing danger that took the lives of the foolish, the unwary, the wicked, and the unlucky.

[152] Westminster Inquisitions, Jacob Miers (2 Oct. 1772). For a similar example, see ibid., Elizabeth Kirkham (8 Feb. 1771).

[153] *Annual Register*, ix (1766), 75. See also, S. P. Menefee, *Wives for Sale: An Ethnographic Study of British Popular Divorce* (New York, 1981). For a much earlier incident involving the same custom, see Bodl., Ashmole MS 222, fo. 139$^{v}$ (Gray).

# 9

# *The Medium and The Message*

THE phenomenal growth of the periodical press and the continuing spread of literacy after 1700 transformed the hermeneutics of suicide, just as they affected almost every other aspect of social and cultural life. The proliferation of daily and weekly newspapers and monthly reviews created a new mode of communication. Oral tradition and communal rituals played a diminishing role in popular culture and reading became increasingly important. Pat Rogers rightly remarks that the rise of the periodical press 'affected the way in which people constructed the world around them'.[1] It greatly broadened the spatial and social horizons of its readers. It brought them news of events that occurred all over the country, particularly in London, and it publicized new attitudes and ideas far more effectively than pamphlets or the pulpit. It helped form political consciousness and exposed provincial readers of every social rank to the values and opinions current in London society.[2] It also carried news of suicides to a vast audience of readers and enabled them to form their own judgements about them. The rituals of judgement and burial were eclipsed as the chief means by which people learned of suicides and asssessed their significance. Moreover, the style and tone of newspaper stories about suicides promoted an increasingly secular and

[1] P. Rogers, *Literature and Popular Culture*, (Brighton, 1985), 22.

[2] G. A. Cranfield, *The Press and Society: From Caxton to Northcliffe* (London, 1978); id., *The Development of the Provincial Newspaper, 1700–1762* (Oxford, 1962); J. Frank, *The Beginnings of the English Newspaper, 1620–1660* (Cambridge, Mass., 1961); R. M. Wills, *Freshest Advices: Early Provincial Newspapers in England* ([Columbus, OH], 1965); J. R. Sutherland, *The Restoration Newspaper and its Development* (Oxford, 1986); J. M. Black, *The English Press in the Eighteenth Century* (London, 1987).

sympathetic attitude to self-killing. The papers persuaded the English that suicide was a frequent calamity that had social, economic, and psychological causes, rather than supernatural ones. Newspaper and magazine stories removed suicide from the realm of the supernatural and placed it firmly in the domain of the secular. They did this, we shall argue in this chapter, not because Grub Street's dunces were hack *philosophes*, promoting the Enlightenment assault on superstition, but because of the literary conventions and epistemological assumptions of the newspaper itself.

The press was a remarkably open medium. There were no professional reporters, and editors relied on friendly officials, self-appointed correspondents, plagiarism, and (notoriously) their own imaginations for the news that they printed. Newspapers reflected the views of their editors, who wrote or rewrote the stories in them and decided what to print. Nevertheless, almost anyone might contribute articles and comments to them, and the papers and magazines acted as a public forum for exchanging information and for debate. In 1722, for example, one R. Swann placed a notice in the *Stamford Mercury*, denying 'false, ill-grounded, scandalous and malicious' reports that he had 'violently, rashly, and unadvisedly destroyed himself'.[3] In a sense, then, the newspapers were a kind of collective popular literature. Their style and content were the product of many people's tastes and interests, not just those of their printers. Literary scholars have recently taught us to interpret works of art in terms of the cultural codes that they express and reflect upon. They have called for a 'cultural poetics' that regards literary texts as collective productions—manifestations of cultural practices and collective beliefs—rather than as the unique expression of their authors' individual imaginations.[4] No form of 'literature' lends itself to this approach more readily than the popular press.

At the same time, no form of 'literature' exercised a stronger influence over the consciousness of its readers. As a medium that transmitted cultural codes and shared knowledge newspapers and magazines have been lamentably undervalued. The periodical press grew rapidly, particularly after the Licensing Act lapsed in 1695, and the circulation figures soon achieved staggering totals. One historian has estimated that the circulation of each of the leading papers (most of which appeared

[3] Quoted in Cranfield, *Development of the Provincial Newspaper*, 220.

[4] For an exposition of these methodological principles and some brilliant examples of how they may be applied, see S. Greenblatt, *Renaissance Self-Fashioning: From More to Shakespeare* (Chicago, 1980); id., *Shakespearean Negotiations* (Berkeley, 1988); J. Bender, *Imagining the Penitentiary: Fiction and the Architecture of Mind in Eighteenth-Century England* (Chicago, 1987).

three times a week) in 1704 was around 15,000. Government taxation and the consequent efforts to evade it make estimates of circulation in later years guesswork, but it appears that a total of 7,400,000 papers were sold officially in 1753, and more than 15,000,000 in 1792.[5] These figures for papers sold measure only a fraction of their readership. Coffee-houses, pubs, and inns subscribed to newspapers and their patrons read and discussed them. The papers certainly reached more of the public than any other form of print, extending their audience beyond the boundary between literacy and illiteracy. To know what ordinary people knew and how they interpreted the events that they learned about, we should look first to the newspapers.

## SUICIDE AS NEWS

The press made suicide a much more public event than it had been before; the newspapers in particular became the principal means of learning about such deaths. Moreover, the audience of the new medium was different and much wider than the circle that had participated in the traditional rites of judgement and burial. All suicides played out their last acts on a stage that had a much larger audience than ever before.[6] Strangers could analyse the words and deeds of people who killed themselves. The ways in which suicide was depicted in the press helped to foster a more secular and tolerant view of the act. Long stories described in vivid and affecting detail the tragic circumstances of suicides. They made it more difficult for readers to regard self-murder as an intrinsically evil act, incomprehensible except in terms of diabolical instigation. The publication several times a week of brief stories and counts of suicides from the bills of mortality proved that suicide was not rare. At a time when the Establishment was becoming convinced that supernatural powers intervened less and less often in the world, it was unavoidably apparent that self-destruction, which must have seemed a rare and wonderful catastrophe in the sixteenth and seventeenth centuries, was actually a daily occurrence.

Some suicides had been reported in print before 1700. A character in Thomas Middleton's *The World Tost at Tennis* (1620) suggests that he could take up ballad-making for a living. A soldier commends his plan with this observation: 'Very well, sir, and I'll warrant thee thou shalt

[5] Cranfield, *Press and Society*, 32, 57, 139.

[6] Cf. E. L. Eisenstein, *The Printing Press as an Agent of Change* (Cambridge, 1980), 132.

never want subject to write of: one hangs himself today, another drowns himself tomorrow . . . fashions, fictions, felonies, fooleries:—a hundred havens has the balladmonger to traffic at, and new ones still daily discovered'.[7] But despite the soldier's optimistic assurances, before the Civil War very few suicides were widely publicized. We have already heard about most of them. There were examples of God's judgements, sectarian pamphlets, occasional broadsides and ballads reporting sensational deaths, and even Sampson's play about James Bateman. No doubt there were more suicides that were publicized of which we are unaware, but the list could not be lengthened very much beyond the handful of examples discussed in earlier chapters. Between 1640 and 1700 suicides were noted more often in print. The suicides of the traitors Miles Sindercome and the earl of Essex were, of course, very widely reported. Almanacs sometimes listed self-murders, and in the 1680s a series of ephemeral pieces reported the suicides of a number of otherwise unknown men and women. Their aim, as one of them declared, was to warn their readers against the evil suggestions of 'the Prince of Darkness, that implacable Enemy of Mankind'.[8]

After weekly and later daily newspapers began to appear, in the first couple of decades of the eighteenth century, the reporting of suicides increased rapidly. All of the students of the press are agreed that blood and politics were the staples of the domestic news. Eustace Budgell complained that the papers were full of 'Robberies, bloody Murders', and the like; Daniel Defoe said much the same: 'This Article call'd Home News is a new common Hunt, tho' upon a cold scent after Casualties.'[9] Suicides were noticed in the more sensational papers, often in the briefest of stories, sometimes in long and vivid accounts. It is impossible to give a sense of how frequently a reader might have encountered such items. Even a more or less systematic sample would be misleading. Typically,

[7] Quoted in L. J. Davis, *Factual Fictions: The Origins of the English Novel* (New York, 1983), 47.

[8] B. Capp, *Astrology and the Popular Press: English Almanacs, 1500–1800* (London, 1979), 80, 112, 129–30; *Sad and Dreadful News from Dukes-place near Aldgate; or, a True Account of a Barbarous and Unnatural Self-murther Committed by Dorcas Pinkney* (London, 1686), 1; *An Account of a Most Strange and Barbarous Action: How a Prisoner's Wife of Ludgate Threw Her Self from the Leeds into Black Fryers* (London, 1685); *A Sad and Dreadful Account of the Self-Murther of Robert Long, alias Baker* (London, 1685); *The Sad and Dreadful Relation of a Bloody and Cruel Murther Committed by Mr. Thomas Law, a Minister in Heart-Street, Covent-Garden, Upon his own Person* (London, 1684); *Sad and Dreadful News from Kings-street in Westminster, A Most Lamentable Relation of the Untimely End of the Lady Phillips* (London, 1684).

[9] Quoted in Cranfield, *Development of the Provincial Newspaper*, 71.

a paper that catered to the public taste for crime and violence would report suicides in every issue for a while and then notice them infrequently or not at all. *Fog's Weekly Journal*, for instance, published at least thirty-four reports of suicides in 1731, but only about half that many in the next year.[10] Still, the overall impression the papers created was that suicide was commonplace; often several notices of suicides appeared in a single week in the London papers, reporting deaths from all over the country. Provincial papers lifted good stories from the London papers and printed accounts of local suicides as well. The monthly periodicals and annual reviews reprinted and elaborated stories about suicides, and the volume of pamphlet literature also increased. The newspapers and the monthly magazines often complemented each other. The former permitted the immediate reporting of numerous suicides, but kept most of their stories very brief; the monthlies, of which the *Gentleman's Magazine* was the leader, afforded more space to discuss deaths and their implications.

The vast majority of suicides reported in the press were announced in reprints of the bills of mortality or in very slightly elaborated versions of them. The London bills listed the number of persons who died each week from illness and accident. Suicides were typically included in the 'Casualties' portion of the bill, together with others who died from various kinds of misfortune. The notices of their deaths were very short and formulaic, stating simply that one or more persons of a particular parish had killed themselves by hanging, drowning, cutting, or jumping. Brief elaborations on this formula might add (in the following order of frequency) the occupation of the dead, his address or the site of the death, his name, and the coroner's verdict. In the aftermath of the crash of South Sea stock, the *Weekly Journal* reprinted the casualties for the deadly week ending 21 January 1721, when there were half a dozen suicides: 'Hang'd themselves 6. One at Christ-Church in London, three (being distracted) at St. Giles in the Field, one (being Lunatick) at St. James Clerkenwell, and one at St. Martin in the Fields.'[11] The bills, with their lists of deaths by disease and accident, were printed to inform readers of the perils that attended life in the metropolis. They had a

[10] Two Norwich papers, the *Norwich Mercury* and *Norwich Gazette*, noticed suicides in the city pretty regularly in the 1730s, 1740s, and 1750s but for a while missed them all—printing occasional stories about suicides elsewhere in Norfolk and plagiarizing reports of suicides in London and the country from other papers. Someone connected with the coroners of Norwich who was supplying news must have stopped doing so.

[11] *Weekly Journal; or, Saturday's Post*, no. 112 (21 Jan. 1721), 669.

practical use, warning people of infectious illnesses so that they could flee or not journey into the danger zone, and reminding them of hazards to beware of, such as accidental drowning.[12] They also served a deeper psychological purpose, keeping readers aware of the fragility of life itself, and so affirming simultaneously their own good fortune and the uncertainty of its continuance.

More important for the understanding of suicide, the bills were a conspicuous feature of a bold epistemological assertion on the part of the newspapers. Lists of bankrupts, commodity prices, and vital statistics were the cornerstone of the press's claim to completeness and accuracy in reporting the news. As G. A. Cranfield has observed, provincial papers bragged about reprinting the bills of mortality. Together with basic economic data, for instance, the *Northampton Mercury* proudly announced that 'The Bill of Mortality, or Account of Christ'nings and Burials, shall also be inserted with precisest Exactness'. And the *Derby Mercury* claimed that its superiority over other 'Country Weekly Papers' lay in the accuracy and freshness of the information it supplied, notably 'the Diseases so particularly mention'd in the London Bill of Mortality, with an Account of the Ages of Persons dead, are what very few read over' [in the rival papers].[13] Reports of suicides taken from the bills of mortality served to shore up the press's claim to empirical veracity, which was constantly being undercut by discrepancies between what was printed and later intelligence.

Turning the perspective around, one can see that the lists of suicides in the bills reduced suicide to a purely secular phenomenon, a misfortune like other 'casualties'. The papers would hardly have gained credibility as vehicles of factual data had they treated the deaths in the bills as evidence of God's judgements or satanic influence, as the old broadsides had. The sheer frequency of suicide, as well as its presentation as a simple empirical fact, discouraged supernaturalistic interpretations of the deed. For this was an age when orthodox members of the upper and middle classes were increasingly inclined to deny that divine or diabolical powers intervened directly and often in human affairs. They derided sectarians and Methodists for claiming direct revelations from God and

[12] For some fascinating remarks on contemporary uses of the bills, see P. Slack, *The Impact of Plague in Tudor and Stuart England* (London, 1985), 239–45, 252–3.

[13] Cranfield, *Development of the Provincial Newspaper*, 95–6. The example of a bill that Cranfield reproduces omits the 'Casualties'; they were usually included. For the epistemological pretensions of the newspapers, see also Davis, *Factual Fictions*, chs. 3–4; M. McKeon, *The Origins of the English Novel, 1600–1740* (Baltimore, 1987), 46–50.

ridiculed the common people for clinging to superstitious beliefs in witchcraft and possession. Calvinists like Isaac Watts might still view suicide statistics from the bills of mortality as evidence that Satan stalked the streets of London. But such views were waning fast, and even Watts devoted most of his attention to the purely earthly causes of self-murder.[14] Inscribed in lists from the bills of mortality suicide was a social fact, not a supernatural sign.

## DEATH À L'ANGLAISE

The publication of the bills of mortality in newspapers all over England convinced foreigners and natives alike that self-slaughter was rampant. An anonymous blast against suicide and duelling proclaimed in 1728 that self-murders were more common in Protestant England than anywhere in Europe, and that there had been 'more again, within these few years last past, than ever were known before'.[15] The celebrated Dr George Cheyne explained in 1733 that he had been urged to write his famous book, *The English Malady*, by friends who were alarmed by 'the late Frequency and daily Encrease of wanton and uncommon self-murders'.[16] In the next decade, Robert Blair's political declamation, self-murder is 'Our Island's shame', was amplified by Edward Young in his *Night Thoughts*, one of the most revered poems of the mid-eighteenth century:

> O Britain, infamous for suicide!
> An island in thy manners! far disjoin'd
> From the whole world of rationals beside!
> In ambient waves plunge thy polluted head,
> Wash the dire strain nor shock the Continent.[17]

So frequent were reports of suicides that they were the subject of satire and black humour. Grumbling in 1754 that there was no news to report, Horace Walpole complained in a letter to Sir Horace Mann that Pope was dead, political opposition extinct, scandal exhausted, religious con-

[14] I. Watts, *Defence Against Self-Murder* (London, 1726).

[15] *Self-Murther and Duelling the Effects of Cowardice and Atheism* (London, 1728), 3.

[16] G. Cheyne, *The English Malady; or, A Treatise of Nervous Diseases of All Kinds*, 3rd edn. (London, 1734), p. iii.

[17] E. Young, *The Complete Works, Poetry and Prose*, ed. J. Nichols (1854, repr. Hildesheim, 1968), i. 77 (Night V: The Relapse, ll. 442–6). For Blair and others see, J. Sena, 'The English Malady: The Idea of Melancholy from 1700 to 1760', Ph.D. thesis (Princeton, 1967), 44.

troversy passé, 'and I think even self-murder is out of fashion'.[18] The view that suicide was actually all too fashionable was amplified in the works of moralists. Throughout the entire century, pamphleteers and sermonizers justified their jeremiads with the claim that suicide was increasing and more common in England than elsewhere.[19]

Foreigners helped propagate the myth that England was the most suicidal nation. The Prussian nobleman Baron de Pollnitz wrote to his friends from London in 1733: 'These Self-Murders are but too frequent here, and are committed by Persons of good Families, as well as by the Dregs of the People.'[20] A very influential letter by a 'Foreigner' to *Fog's Weekly Journal* in 1737 was reprinted in the *Gentleman's Magazine*. 'I could not', he marvelled, 'in several Weeks after my Arrival in this Metropolis of *England*, master the Astonishment it gave me, to hear of such frequent Self-Murders as happen here almost daily.'[21] The French, as might have been expected, were all too happy to validate the English's guilty conviction that they were prone to self-slaughter. Montesquieu, Voltaire and a host of *menus philosophes* indicted the English as gloomy self-killers, and so did mere tourists, men like Béat Louis de Muralt and Pierre Jean Grossly.[22] The French liked to exaggerate the nonchalance with which the English cast away their lives. The Romans, remarked Montesquieu, killed themselves on principle, but 'the English are apt to commit suicide most unaccountably; they destroy themselves even in the bosom of happiness'.[23] The wits called casual self-slaughter 'la mort à l'anglaise'.

[18] H. Walpole, *The Yale Edition of Horace Walpole's Correspondence*, ed. W. S. Lewis (New Haven, 1937–83), xix. 229.

[19] *A Discourse upon Self-Murder*, 2nd edn. (London, 1754), 4; *A Dissertation or Discourse on Suicide* (Northampton, 1785), 28; C. Fleming, *A Dissertation Upon the Unnatural Crime of Self-Murder* (London, 1773), 15, 16; G. Gregory, *Essays Historical and Moral* (London, 1785), 10–11; J. Herries, *An Address to the Public, On the Frequent and Enormous Crime of Suicide* (London, 1774), 6; J. Jortin, *Sermons on Different Subjects*, 3rd edn. (London, 1787), v. 145; J. Prince, *Self-Murder Asserted to be a Very Heinous Crime* (London, 1709), 7; *Self-Murther and Duelling the Effects of Cowardice and Atheism* (London, 1728), 3; *Two Dissertations: The First on the Supposed Suicide of Samson* (London, 1754), 43; Watts, *Defense Against Self-Murder*, pp. iii–iv, 100; T. Knaggs, *A Sermon Against Self-Murder* (london, 1708), 2; Z. Pearce, *A Sermon on Self-Murder* (London, 1736), 5.

[20] Sena, 'English Malady', 46.

[21] *Gentleman's Magazine*, vii (1737), 289–90.

[22] For discussions of foreign comments on the frequency of suicide (most by Frenchmen), see C. A. Moore, *Backgrounds of English Literature, 1700–1760* (Minneapolis, 1953), 204–7; R. Bartel, 'Suicide in Eighteenth-Century England: The Myth of a Reputation', *Huntington Library Quarterly*, xxiii (1959–60), 145–58; Sena, 'English Malady', 43–55; J. McManners, *Death and the Enlightenment* (Oxford, 1981), 427–30.

[23] C. L. de Secondat, Baron de Montesquieu, *The Spirit of the Laws*, trans. T. Nugent and J. V. Prichard, Great Books of the Western World, xxxviii (Chicago, 1952), 107.

There is in fact no evidence at all that suicide was more frequent in England than it was elsewhere. The rise of the periodical press, which reprinted the bills of mortality and reported sensational news with uninhibited gusto, was the main reason for the impression that the English were more suicidal than the inhabitants of other nations.[24] Voltaire admitted as much in 1739:

> These tragical stories which swarm in the English newspapers, have made the rest of Europe think that, in England, men kill themselves more willingly than elsewhere. However, I know not but there are as many madmen or heroes to be found in Paris as in London. Perhaps, if our newspapers kept an exact list of all who had been so infatuated as to seek their own destruction, and so lamentably courageous as to effect it, we should, in this particular, have the misfortune to rival the English.[25]

Few people realized that he was right—Voltaire himself could not resist repeating the myth when the mood struck him. The English press itself often complained of the frequency of suicide. *Mercurius Politicus* reckoned in 1720 that the total of suicides in Britain exceeded the number of such deaths in the rest of the world.[26] A more modest claim was made by the *London Journal* in 1725, which opened a report of recent casualties with the observation that 'there have happen'd more Accidents and more Self-murders this Week, than for many past'.[27] The satirical publication the *Connoisseur* complained in 1755 that suicide had become prevalent and grumbled that a foreigner reading the press would conclude England was the most lunatic nation on earth: 'Almost every day informs us, that the coroner's inquest has sat on the body of some miserable Suicide, and brought in their verdict, *Lunacy*.'[28] Also objecting to the tolerant ways of juries, *The Times* in 1786 declared: 'That self-murder is become a crime frequent among us is a truth too generally and too justly lamented.'[29]

The impression that suicide was excessively frequent was fortified by striking stories of the deaths of prominent people. In an age obsessed by rank and in which the middle class was striving to adopt the manners and tastes of their betters, the deaths of the nobility and of celebrities made a far greater impression than ordinary suicides. The suicide in 1702 of

24 This is the thesis of Bartel's excellent 'Suicide in Eighteenth-Century England'.
25 *The Works of Voltaire*, ed. T. Smollett *et al.* (New York, 1901), vii. 26.
26 Sena, 'The English Malady', 43.
27 *London Journal*, no. 311 (10 July 1725).
28 [G. Coleman and B. Thornton], *Connoisseur* (London, 1755), 296–7.
29 *The Times*, no. 588 (21 Nov. 1786), 2.

Francis Godolphin, a cousin of the Lord Treasurer, prompted John Evelyn to reflect 'Tis . . . sad to Consider how many of this Nation have murdered themselves of late years 15 or 16 in my remembrance'.[30] This was a theme to which he returned a few years later, as we have seen. Measured by the level of alarmed comment, the *annus mirabilis* of suicide was 1755, Cecil A. Moore has concluded. The poet Thomas Grey declared it epidemical that year. The number of such deaths reported in the bills was not, in fact, the highest recorded in the period, but a rash of suicides by men of rank and fashion created the impression that it was.[31] A prominent politician, Lord Montfort, shot himself on New Year's Day, for instance, and the fast-loving baronet, Sir John Bland, killed himself in September.[32] Suicides by politicians afforded the press with news on a regular basis. In 1783 Horace Walpole complained that John Powell had cut his throat just in time to convince a band of visiting French courtiers that suicide was a weekly occurrence.[33] Mary Dawes Blackett was moved to publish *Suicide: A Poem* (1798) by accounts of the deaths of five prominent persons, including Chatterton, which had persuaded her that suicide had been very frequent 'for a period of years'.[34]

Most of the explanations that were offered for the apparently high rate of suicide in England were moral and religious. The eighteenth century was still a decidedly pre-statistical age, and social thinkers tended to regard self-destruction in terms of their own anxieties and priorities. Their aims, in other words, were polemical. Deism, irreligion, and Methodist enthusiasm were routinely blamed for frequent suicide.[35] Isaac Watts, however, recognized that atheism was actually rare and suicides because of deistical principles still rarer. Some deaths, he remarked, were caused by the 'sceptical Humour' of the age, but more as a consequence of the neglect of religion than as a response to philosophical arguments.[36] This theme was the common cry of all the

[30] J. Evelyn, *The Diary of John Evelyn*, ed. E. S. de Beer (Oxford, 1955), v. 505–6. Godolphin's suicide was also reported in a broadsheet: *A Full and True Account, How Francis Godolphin, Esq., of Golden Square, Cut His Own Throat This Morning* (London, 1702).

[31] Moore, *Backgrounds*, 207.

[32] Walpole, *Correspondence*, xxxv. 201–3; R. Sedgwick, *The House of Commons, 1715–1754* (Oxford, 1970), i. 492; L. B. Namier and J. Brooke, *The House of Commons, 1754–1790* (London, 1964) i. 98. The wealthy ironmonger John Crowley killed himself in July, but his death seems to have been kept out of the papers: Walpole, *Correspondence*, xxxv. 236.

[33] Walpole, *Correspondence*, xxv. 407–8. Political suicides are discussed above, Chapter 8.

[34] M. D. Blackett, *Suicide: A Poem* (London, 1789), pp. iv–v, 1–12.

[35] *Two Dissertations*, 11–12.

[36] Watts, *Defense Against Self-Murther*, p. v.

moralists. It was developed by the Foreigner: 'People are to be restrain'd only by Religion, or by Dread of Death: And when both these Ties are become useless, what Crimes may we not expect to see reigning therein? Robberies, Rapes, Murders, &c. will become frequent. Ministers may tumble off the Perch in the Height of their Power; and even Princes on their Thrones will not be in Security. In what Detestation then ought we not to hold a crime which sets open a door to all Enormities?'[37] Neglect of religion, in other words, is tantamount to social disintegration; the proliferation of suicides is symptomatic of a general weakening of control over the disorderly rabble. This fear animated others as well. The author of a pious tract on suicide published in 1785 blamed the frequency of suicide on the fact that 'the cause of Liberty, both *Civil* and *Religious*, has been much pleaded of late'.[38]

Even writers who proclaimed that high rates of suicide were the consequence of religious laxity were disinclined in the eighteenth century to see so general a phenomenon as evidence of divine wrath or satanic temptations. A rare exception was Watts, who argued that the suicide rate was even higher than the bills of mortality indicated, and concluded that it revealed the presence of the Tempter. His combination of statistical criticism, philosophical argument, and religious traditionalism was unique.[39] Most eighteenth-century authors were reluctant to conjure with the name of Satan. Moreover, new, entirely secular explanations for the frequency of suicide appeared. Congreve had made the connection at the end of the seventeenth century: 'Is there in the World a Climate more uncertain than our own? And which is a natural Consequence, Is there any where a People more unsteady, more apt to discontent, more *saturnine, dark*, and *melancholick* than ourselves? Are we not of all People the most unfit to be alone, and most unsafe to be trusted with ourselves?'[40] His conclusions were endorsed by the medical writers of the Augustan age. The poetical physician Richard Blackmore asserted in 1725 that while the inhabitants of regions nearer the sun suffered from lunacy and wild imaginings, the English were typically overcome by spleen.[41] The celebrated Cheyne agreed: the variable climate led his list of geographical and social conditions that produced these atrocious

37 *Gentleman's Magazine*, vii (1737), 290.

38 *Dissertation on Suicide*, 28. The arch-priest of liberty, Tom Paine, took the blame in a couple of newspaper stories: see D. T. Andrew, 'Debate: The Secularization of Suicide in England, 1660–1800', *Past and Present*, no. 119 (1988), 160.

39 Watts, *Defence Against Self-Murther*, pp. iii–v.

40 W. Congreve, *The Complete Works*, ed. M. Summers (London: Nonesuch, 1923), iii. 206.

41 R. Blackmore, *A Treatise of the Spleen and Vapours* (London, 1725), pp. v–vi.

distempers of the mind to a pitch unknown elsewhere.[42] The myth that England's climate was deadly had an almost comical effect on the mood of some visitors to the country. Arriving London in 1727, Cesar de Saussure quickly grew despondent, a victim of its baleful weather. 'Had I been an Englishman', he declared, 'I should certainly have put myself out of my misery.'[43]

Montesquieu, the most famous and influential advocate of meteorological determinism, explained with pseudo-scientific precision the mechanism that made the English so susceptible to the murderous effects of bad weather. The effects of the dismal weather were fatal, he argued in the *Spirit of the Laws*, because of a constitutional malady, peculiar to the English, in which the ability of the bodily machine to filter nervous juices properly was impaired. Therefore while suicide among the Romans 'was the effect of education, being connected with their principles and customs; among the English it is the consequence of a distemper, being connected with the physical state of the machine, and independent of every other cause'.[44] Moralists were naturally inclined to disbelieve this theory. The *Connoisseur* pounced upon it with alacrity. He observed shrewdly that the climate was a lot worse in Russia, Sweden, and Greenland than it was in England, and yet these nations of perpetual winter darkness had low rates of suicide.[45] It was, however, generally accepted that there was a connection between gloomy weather and suicidal despair. Montesquieu's opinion was a commonplace among the *philosophes*, and many Englishmen believed it, too.

Then as now, most people thought that suicide peaked in the autumn and winter, when the weather was at its worst. November was supposed to be the deadliest month. Quoting the *Spectator*, Boswell facetiously proposed that the suicide epidemic could be stopped by using the 'New Freezing Discovery' to put Englishmen on ice during 'the gloomy month of November'. He hoped soon to see in every quarter of the metroplis signboards advertising, 'Cupping, Bathing, Bleeding, and FREEZING'.[46] In an altogether less witty mood, the mad-doctor William Rowley agreed that suicide was prevalent in November.[47] A few

42 Cheyne, *English Malady*, pp. i–ii.

43 Sena, 'English Malady', 48.

44 Montesquieu, *Spirity of the Laws*, 107.

45 [Coleman and Thornton], *Connoisseur*, 299.

46 J. Boswell, *The Hypochondriack*, ed. M. Bailey (Stanford, 1928), i. 107 [No. 47, Aug. 1781].

47 W. Rowley, *A Treatise on Female, Nervous, Hysterical, Hypochondriacal, Bilious, Convulsive Diseases, . . . With Thoughts on Madness, Suicide, etc.* (London, 1788), 344. See also *Weekly Miscellany*, no. 356 (20 Oct. 1739).

people, however, wondered if November deserved its reputation. Horace Walpole quipped in the hot summer of 1765 that sultry weather did not suit English heads: 'This last month puts even the month of November out of joint for self-murder.'[48] In 1789 a writer in *The Times* worried that April was becoming the cruelest month. For although suicides were formerly confined to November, they were beginning to encroach on the sprightly sunny season of sweet April; why not exclaim with the Moor that 'the Moon comes nearer to the earth than she was wont, and makes men MAD!' he asked.[49] He was, in fact, almost right. Just as the scientific explanations for the frequency of suicide fostered an unwarranted conclusion that suicide was more common in England than elsewhere, so they also encouraged the false belief that suicide was most frequent when the weather was worst. Ever since the sixteenth century, the peak months for suicide had always been in the spring and early summer; the lowest period of the year for self-destruction was late autumn and winter. (See Table 9.1.) But what matters is not that the

Table 9.1. *Seasonality of Suicide*

| Month | England 1485–1715 | | Norwich 1669–1799 | | London 1715–1799 | |
|---|---|---|---|---|---|---|
| | N | % | N | % | N | % |
| January | 938 | 7.6 | 21 | 7.8 | 139 | 8.7 |
| February | 889 | 7.2 | 27 | 10.0 | 92 | 5.8 |
| March | 1,111 | 9.0 | 16 | 5.9 | 118 | 7.5 |
| April | 1,282 | 10.4 | 21 | 7.8 | 152 | 9.6 |
| May | 1,501 | 12.2 | 35 | 13.0 | 149 | 9.4 |
| June | 1,360 | 11.0 | 28 | 10.4 | 179 | 11.3 |
| July | 1,255 | 10.2 | 21 | 7.8 | 155 | 9.8 |
| August | 903 | 7.3 | 22 | 8.1 | 134 | 8.4 |
| September | 771 | 6.2 | 19 | 7.0 | 112 | 7.1 |
| October | 809 | 6.6 | 17 | 6.3 | 117 | 7.4 |
| November | 743 | 6.0 | 22 | 8.1 | 118 | 7.5 |
| December | 786 | 6.3 | 21 | 7.8 | 118 | 7.5 |
| Totals | 12,348 | 100 | 270 | 100 | 1,583 | 100 |

*Sources*: PRO, KB 9, 10, 11, 140; PL 26; HCA 1; Norwich Inquisitions; Weekly London Bills of Mortality. The last source was used instead of the surviving inquests for London because they cover a longer time period and were published for contemporaries to read.

48 Walpole, *Correspondence*, x. 166–7.
49 *The Times*, no. 1148 (7 May 1789), 2.

'social scientists', reasoning was wrong but that suicide was widely believed to have been a very frequent occurrence with a physical explanation.

## JOURNALISTIC REALISM

Because the newspapers and periodicals were such an open forum, they often printed letters and essays from conservative readers, opposed to the trend toward tolerance. Alarmed and moralizing comment was certainly more prevalent in them than defences of self-killing or calls for leniency were. And occasionally, the papers themselves took the lead in calling for more stringent enforcement of the law. *The Times* went on a conservative offensive in the 1780s, for instance, praising the coroner of Middlesex for a rare display of rigour.[50] But the newspapers also printed thousands of stories describing actual suicides, and most of them were simply noticed or held up as objects of pity. *Fog's Weekly Journal*, for example, reported that 'horn'd despair' had driven Thomas Barrow, a Portsmouth merchant, to hang himself. 'He left a Wife and four Children in sorrow inexpressible. He is the Object of Pity and Grief to all that knew him; who in his Life and Conversation had been an example almost inimitable.'[51] Even when they were not so obviously eulogies, stories about suicides were often designed to evoke their readers' sympathy. To take an extreme example, the *London Evening Post* described the downfall and death of Patricia Green, 'the most noted Courtezan in the Southern part of the Town', in affecting terms, explaining that 'being grown old, miserably poor, neglected and despis'd, unable to bear the Frowns of her *quondam* Admirers', she had set fire to any empty house and flung herself into the flames. She was rescued before she smothered, but later 'expir'd in a most miserable Condition'.[52] *The Times*, in spite of its tough editorial stance, memorialized Mr Kennedy, 'if not an eminent . . . at least, a useful actor'. His face had been disfigured in a fire that had killed his wife. His career declined, and he was further reduced by a paralytic stroke. He was at last forced to depend on the generosity of a friend, but when his

[50] This point is effectively argued by D. T. Andrew, 'The Secularization of Suicide in England, 1660–1800: Comment', *Past and Present*, no. 119 (1988), 160–1.

[51] *Fogs Weekly Journal*, no. 160 (27 Nov. 1731).

[52] *London Evening Post*, no. 1950 (10–13 May 1740), 2. For the story of a young girl sold into prostitution that almost recapitulates the stock plot of *The Harlot's Progress*, see *The Times*, no. 461 (14 June 1786), 3.

benefactor died, the situation of 'poor Kennedy, who was a man of spirit and strict integrity, became insupportable, and he made his *last exit* with a razor in the 66th year of his age!'[53] Many similar tales could be cited.[54]

The newspapers promoted secular interpretations of suicide in more subtle ways than merely by describing many of its victims sympathetically. The literary problem that confronted newspaper writers and pressmen was how to make the deaths of strangers interesting and meaningful to their readers. They strove to present accounts of suicidal deaths that would be realistic and affecting, and like the novelists who pretended to be the editors of purely factual reports, they displayed considerable skill in deploying descriptive detail and in conveying the psychology of suicide. The style of their stories, particularly long narratives, enabled readers to identify with the victims of self-destruction. Michael McKeon has recently argued that during the late seventeenth and eighteenth centuries, popular literature encouraged people to think about social actions in secular, empirical terms. Writers such as Defoe presented their fictions as truth—as biographies or histories; they devised a literary style, exalting verisimilitude, that mirrored the triumph of empiricism in science and philosophy. McKeon's account of the emergence of literary realism and its relationship to epistemology is subtle and nuanced. He detects in a variety of fictional forms a dialectical tension between 'naïve empiricism' and 'romance idealism', which was subsequently complicated by an 'extreme scepticism' about achieving absolute veracity. Though this argument becomes complex, its essential point is not entirely new. Ian Watt stressed the same parallel between literary realism and philosophical empiricism in his classic *The Rise of the Novel.*[55] Neither McKeon nor Watt pay much attention to newspapers. And yet no other form of print was as committed to empiricist epistemology as the periodical press. As Lennard Davis has argued, there was a close affinity between journalism and novel-writing in the eighteenth century. Both were concerned above all to create the illusion of authenticity.[56]

Accounts of suicide longer than the lists purloined from the bills of mortality were generally based directly or indirectly on the evidence that was heard before coroners' inquests. Their details naturally varied

[53] *The Times*, no. 469 (23 June 1786), 2.

[54] A random selection of a few of the most striking might include, *Fog's Weekly Journal*, no. 160 (27 Nov. 1731); *The Times*, no. 461 (14 June 1786), 3; no. 469 (23 June 1786), 2.

[55] McKeon, *Origins of the English Novel*, 87. Cf. I. Watt, *The Rise of the Novel* (Berkeley, 1957), ch. 1.

[56] Davis, *Factual Fictions*, chs. 3–4.

greatly according to the editor or writer's sources. Often they simply reported the suicide like any other crime about which little was known. They focused above all on the circumstances of the death, and occasionally indicated the suicide's motive or his state of mind. When more information came their way, writers adopted many of the techniques of the contemporary novel to create 'what purports to be an authentic account of the actual experiences of individuals'.[57] They employed circumstantial detail and first-person narrative in so far as possible. Death scenes in long suicide reports are carefully, even obsessively described. Writers attempted to place their readers at the scene of the death, and invited them to reconstruct what had happened from the evidence before them. Suicide notes, real and fake, were reprinted in order to make the voice of the dead audible. Moral commentary was reduced to a minimum. The larger implications of the tale were conveyed instead by the narrative itself. The figure of Satan disappeared altogether.

Realism is as artificial a convention as allegory. To be convincing a narrative must satisfy our expectations of what a truthful account of an event includes. It must be able to be visualized, accurate in its circumstantial detail, and psychologically plausible. The newspaper is a poor medium for mimetic art. It affords little scope for creating narrative depth, for most newspaper stories are short, and serial publication makes it difficult to develop character. Wallace Martin denies that the newspapers are a realistic genre at all: 'No document is less "realistic" . . . than a newspaper, which records ordinary facts and sensational events simply because they happened, without any attempt to "motivate" them.'[58] This is partly true, but it also distorts the truth, at least the truth about eighteenth-century newspapers. For newspaper writers often strove to overcome as best they could the limitations of the genre. They noted circumstantial details and tried to make their stories conform to familiar plots. They used, in other words, techniques central to realistic

[57] Watt, *Rise of the Novel*, 27. The limitations of space and the journalistic need to appear as a plausible (and hence exterior) observer obviously greatly restricted the extent to which long newspaper stories could employ the conventions of literary realism. A much more sophisticated analysis would be necessary precisely to describe the balance of conventions, aesthetic and journalistic, that was possible.

[58] W. Martin, *Recent Theories of Narrative* (Ithaca, NY, 1986) 66 (and see 57–70 generally). The classic discussions of the conventions of realism are E. Auerbach, *Mimesis: The Representation of Reality in Western Literature*, trans. W. R. Trask (Princeton, 1968); W. Booth, *The Rhetoric of Fiction* (Chicago, 1967), chs. 1–2; Watt, *Rise of the Novel*, ch. 1. Also suggestive are E. D. Ermarth, *Realism and Consensus in the English Novel* (Princeton, 1983); J. Culler, *Structuralist Poetics* (Ithaca, NY, 1975), ch. 7; A. D. Nuttall, *A New Mimesis: Shakespeare and the Representation of Reality* (London, 1983), ch. 2.

fiction—they included material that established the 'reality' of the story, its origins in the physical and social world; they relied on conventional beliefs about behaviour and customs; they carefully structured their stories so that their own persona appeared in conventional ways. Long newspaper stories in the eighteenth century were, in fact, virtually indistinguishable from episodes in novels or in histories. Neither the novel nor the newspaper had achieved the pitch of generic distinctiveness, of conventionality, that it did in the nineteenth century. If it had, novels could not have masqueraded as journalism, as they routinely did before about 1800.

Newspaper writers were especially fond of circumstantial details and of suicide notes. The one allowed them to place the reader at the scene; the other enabled them to speak in the voice of the dead, to enter into the mind of the suicide himself. Precisely observed particulars could lend verisimilitude to the story, add temporal depth, suggest something of the suicide's state of mind, and even convey the moral significance of the death. Consider the accounts of Fanny Braddock's suicide. Descriptions of her body and the room in which she died were detailed and vivid. *Fogs Weekly Journal*, for example, found it important to stress that she had hanged herself with her golden girdle and to mention the position of certain objects in the room where she died, even though its account was relatively brief. For 'by the Position of her chair and a Book lying on the Table', it could be deduced that 'she had been reading just before she committed the violent Act itself'.[59] These particulars therefore allowed the paper to suggest that Braddock had been in a reflective mood before her death. Edward Cave's literary crew at the *Gentleman's Magazine* improved on the story by adding more significant detail. The magazine described the exact method that Braddock must have used to manage the door from which she had hanged herself and the chair on which she had stood, her bruised face and bitten tongue and the red girdle she had broken in an earlier attempt. It also pointed out that she had actually hanged herself with a noose made from two girdles that had been fastened together, one of them gold, the other silver. These precisely observed details lend verisimilitude to the scene; they also help to convey its moral implications. The girdles symbolize her fortune, which was amassed by joining together two £6,000 legacies, one inherited directly from her father, the other indirectly from her sister. She had gambled away her gold and silver, transforming her riches into the instrument of

[59] *Fog's Weekly Journal*, no. 150 (18 Sept. 1731).

death. The message that gaming was a vice that robbed its addicts of the accoutrements of fashion, the emblems of gentility, and deprived them ultimately of life itself would have been clear without any further comment. The magazine's writer closes, however, with an improbable scene. A gentleman present at the death scene, the author claims, spied a suicide note scratched in Fanny's window:

> O Death thou pleasing end to human Woe!
> Thou cure of Life! thou greatest Good below!
> Still mayst thou fly the Coward and the Slave,
> And thy soft Slumbers only bless the Brave.

Greatly affected by his discovery the gentleman broke into verse himself:

> O Dice! ye vain Diverters of our Woe!
> Ye Waste of Life! ye greatest Curse below!
> May ne'er good Sense again become your Slave
> Nor your false Charms allure & cheat the Brave.[60]

Although clumsier than many other such efforts, this ending is designed to sustain the illusion of reality established by the rest of the story. However dubious the gentleman's poetical expostulation may be, it is nevertheless placed in the mouth of a character on the scene, rather than interpolated as an editorial comment.

The story of Fanny Braddock's suicide is especially interesting because it shows how indeterminate the boundary between journalism and fiction was. The *Gentleman's Magazine* crew were not the last writers to improve it. Some years after Fanny's death, John Wood included an account of her death in his *Description of Bath*. Wood had been, according to his own testimony, Fanny's landlord during the last thirteen months of her life and knew her well. He supplied information about her background, the inheritance of her fortune, her habits, and her connections that had not been previously published. He also depicted her as the victim of slanderous rumours charging her with being sexually loose, but he added that she seemed to exercise a power over the desires of women stronger than her considerable attractiveness to men. Perhaps the oddest thing about Wood's highly charged and exceedingly circumstantial description of Fanny and her wretched death is the way in which he manipulates her identity. Taking a clue from a book called *New Court*

[60] *Gentleman's Magazine*, i (1731), 396–7.

*Tales; or, Modern Amours*, he changes her name to Sylvia, giving her own Christian name to a maid of dubious virtue, who attaches herself to Fanny. It was this fatal association of the dissolute lady with a corrupted maid that, in addition to her compulsive gambling, sealed Fanny's doom in Wood's account. His decision to change her name, however, casts considerable doubt on the veracity of his report. The whole narrative has a strongly fictionalized character.[61] Moreover, the practice of adding apparently true but actually fictionalized facts to the tale was carried still further by one of the leading authors of the age. Oliver Goldsmith, in his biography of Beau Nash, developed an even more poignant version of Fanny's story. He made her into the victim of an unscrupulous gentleman, whose dissipation causes her to waste her fortune. The bulk of the rest of his account, except for adding an initial 'S.' to Sylvia to stand for her surname, was more or less plagiarized from Wood. Goldsmith fleshes out the tale mainly with comment on Fanny's character, all of which must have been invented, for he does not seem to have had any idea even what her real name had been.[62] As the tale was retold, therefore, it became at once more vivid and more complex psychologically and morally; it also became at once more apparently accurate—since it purported to supply more authenticated facts—and more fictionalized—since especially in the case of Goldsmith, the facts were invented. Fiction and non-fiction had elided to the point where one wonders if Wood or Goldsmith were aware of such a distinction.

The literary models and techniques that were used by the press to depict suicide are perhaps best illustrated by a close examination of the reports about the double suicide of Richard and Bridget Smith. They were found hanged in their lodgings on 18 April 1732; their two-year-old child lay dead in its cradle near by, shot through the head. The three suicide notes that the Smiths had written to their landlord and a kinsman were not released to the press until a few days after their deaths had been reported in the papers. The first stories on the incident maintained that Smith had murdered his wife and child. A few concrete details were included to substantiate this version of events, and the protagonist was

[61] Wood, *Description of Bath*, 446–53. It is interesting to note that Wood seems to have stolen some of the details and language of his account of Fanny's religious views from reports of the Smiths' deistical suicide note. He notes that she 'lost no Opportunity of viewing the Moon with my Telescopes', and adds that 'a very eminent Surgeon assured me, that while Sylvia was thus amusing herself, he was not certain, but that she had consulted with him what Act of Suicide was the easiest, and attended with the least Pain': ibid., 448. See also Chapter 5 above and the paragraphs that follow.

[62] *Collected Works of Oliver Goldsmith*, ed. A. Friedman (Oxford, 1966), iii. 324–30.

provided with a suitable motive and mood. Smith, explained the *London Evening Post*, had been hounded by one of his wife's relatives, an old woman from whom he had borrowed money. Pushed beyond the breaking point, he 'got out of his bed in a great Passion, took his Wife out of Bed, and hang'd her to one of the Feet Bed Posts in her Shift; and afterwards with a Pistol shot his child . . . that lay in a Cradle by the Bed-side, and then hang'd himself to the other Feet Bed Post'. Grub Street's penniless hacks had an understandable sympathy for debtors, and many contemporaries agreed that the laws of debt were as much a social evil as improvidence. The mortal struggle round the marital bed was accordingly made to seem as much the fault of the meanness of Bridget's kinswoman as it was Smith's passion. The coroner's verdict was given incorrectly as lunacy.[63] This bloody tale of domestic homicide had many analogues in the popular literature of the day, where such murders epitomized unnatural crime, and the writers or their sources were probably fitting the few facts that they knew into a plot that was very familiar from chapbooks, ballads, broadsides, and other newspaper stories.

Within a week a kinsman of Richard Smith, acting on his posthumous instructions, released the notes that he and Bridget had written to the newspapers. Their publication caused a sensation. The newspapers quickly revised their accounts of the fatal events to accommodate a radically different and much more interesting set of facts.[64] They also changed their method of telling the story and drew on different literary models. The first of the Smiths' three notes asks their landlord to settle some affairs and to find homes for their dog and ancient cat. Money and goods were provided to compensate him for his trouble. The second, addressed to a relative named Brindley, attacks an unnamed person, probably a creditor, whose meddling, charges Smith, precipitated final downfall and left him penniless in debtors' prision. The third and most remarkable of the notes, also addressed to Brindley, offers a long philosophical defence of their actions, which we examined in Chapter 6.

Most newspapermen made the Smiths' notes the centrepiece of their accounts. The *Country Journal*, for instance, related the incident as a kind of epistolary short story, printing the notes with a minimum of other information: 'We chuse to give them genuine to the Reader, and leave

[63] *London Evening Post*, no. 685 (18–20 Apr. 1732); *Daily Post*, no. 3927 (18 Apr. 1732); no. 3930 (21 Apr. 1732); *Universal Spectator and Weekly Journal*, no. 185 (22 Apr. 1732).

[64] See e.g., *Fog's Weekly Journal*, no. 181 (22 Apr. 1732); *London Evening Post*, no. 686 (20–2 Apr. 1732).

him to make his Reflections on so shocking a Scene,' the paper's writer explains.[65] The notes were irresistible to the pressmen because of the vivid impression that they conveyed of the Smiths' personalities as well as the heterodox views that they propounded. They made the simple caricatures of the criminal story inadequate, and writers shaped their accounts to enhance their impact. Richard and Bridget Smith come alive as complex and contradictory human beings in their letters. They were industrious and honest but embittered against the system and people that had punished their industry with poverty and degradation. Capable of blowing their child's brains out, they showed a tender concern for their dog and cat. To heighten the verisimilitude and pathos of the tale that the notes told, the newspapers embellished it with significant details and anecdotes. They added new information about the death scene. The bodies of Smith and his wife were found hanging a yard apart with a curtain suspended between them. *Fog's Weekly Journal* remarked that the arrangement was 'suppos'd to prevent the Sight of each other when under the Agonies of Death'. Other weapons were at hand, a pistol beside him, a knife next to her, with which they could have killed themselves if they had been discovered prematurely.[66] Their careful preparations were thus at once touching and terrible. The papers also contrasted the horror of the death scene with reflections on the Smiths' good character. After vividly describing the crime and printing the notes, the *Historical Register* commented sympathetically on the Smiths and their dilemma. 'They were', the writer declares in a significantly phrased sentence, 'perhaps, the most loving Couple that is to be found within the Bills of Mortality.' Even writers who disapproved of the Smiths' views pointed out that everywhere they lived they were accounted honest, industrious, and loving by their neighbours.[67] The papers, in other words, strove both to enhance the visual clarity of the scene and to bring out the ironies and paradoxes implicit in the tale.

Several scholars have noticed a movement toward literary realism and an increasingly secular and even sympathetic attitude to criminals in popular literature about crime. Citing a late seventeenth-century fictional account of the divine revenge that befalls an adulteress, Maximillian Novak points to the clinically precise description of her disease's

[65] *Country Journal; or, the Craftsman*, no. 303 (22 Apr. 1732).

[66] *Fog's Weekly Journal*, no. 181 (22 Apr. 1732)

[67] *Historical Register*, no. 66 (1732), 151–4. For a less favourable reaction, see *Gentleman's Magazine*, ii (1732), 714–5, 722–3.

disfiguring effects. Not only is the realism starling here and in other sections, he remarks,

> but there is a new kind of fictional metaphysic at work. Instead of the continual reminder of God's presence and impending revenge, the author speculates on cause and effect as if the world were not entirely under God's control . . . . Just as the courts of law came to focus more and more on fact and evidence, so fiction came to function in a world of secondary causes and events'.[68]

John O. Lyons makes a very similar point comparing the criminal narratives of Richard Head with Defoe's fiction:

> Defoe's achievement depends on his seeing the world in which his characters exist as one divested of magic. For earlier writers the world is peopled with types through which a moral drama can be discerned . . . . Defoe reduced this moral element in his world, so his characters are what they are and what they seem to be.[69]

One consequence of this tendency toward a more secular and particularized account of events, motivations, and emotions was that the reader's response to characters could be both deeper and more ambivalent. Some authorities believe that the more realistic depiction of the characters' feelings and of the world in which they existed encouraged readers to identify with them, even with malefactors. John G. Richetti, for instance, claims that in eighteenth-century criminal biographies

> The criminal is a journalistically authentic and therefore partially attractive figure, who in so far as he is life-like acquires our sympathy, understanding, or hatred—what modern journalism might call 'human interest'. The reportage which deals in the concrete facts of his career tends to contradict the moral generalizations he is supposed to make us think on.[70]

Realistically depicted, criminals became, Richetti argues, the objects of admiration and sympathy as well as of horror. The same could be said of suicides. Realistically depicted, they became the objects of empathy and pity. In fact, suicides were perhaps more likely to invoke sympathy than other kinds of people who committed antisocial and violent deeds, since they were often otherwise faultless.

Lincoln Faller, on the other hand, has objected that Richetti overemphasizes the extent to which readers must have identified with criminals.

[68] M. Novak, *Realism, Myth, and History in Defoe's Fiction* (Lincoln, Nebr., 1983), 125.

[69] J. O. Lyons, *The Invention of the Self* (Carbondale, Ill., 1978), 82.

[70] J. G. Richetti, *Popular Fiction Before Richardson: Narrative Patterns, 1700–1739* (Oxford, 1969), 63–4.

He insists that contemporary narratives, especially accounts of 'familiar murders', were not meant to invoke any sympathy for malefactors and remained resolutely traditional depictions of God's providential design: 'Unable to deal as we would with the human depravity expressed in such crimes, the myth that attached to familiar murder strove to show how that depravity, inevitably, had been checked and overbalanced. At its simplest, . . . it counterpoised God's providence, His justice and mercy, against one of the most vicious—and vividest—expressions of human evil.'[71] Now it might be argued, extending Faller's views, that stories about suicide were supposed to be read in terms of a religious outlook so widely accepted that it did not need to be explicitly invoked. Readers would readily situate the bloody events they read about in the pattern of sin and judgement that still structured many longer accounts of crimes and criminal careers. William Bagshaw, a Nonconformist minister, appears to have been doing just that in about 1697, when he copied into his diary notes on the suicides of five people from all over England who had killed themselves among various 'Matters for mourning'.[72]

Other readers, however, seem to have regarded suicides they read about as objects of horror or pity but not examples of divine wrath or devilish wickedness. The famous parson Woodforde, after copying out a description of the suicide of 'Captain Bruce' just as explicit and gory as Defoe's account of the barber's butchery, concluded mildly, 'Such things are very dismal to read.' Although once, when he was 'so nervous', Woodforde referred to an attempted suicide as a 'bad and rash action', he had nothing but pity for suicides: Mr Baldwin hanged himself (1776)—'The Lord have mercy on his soul'; Alexander Paine made away with himself (1781)—'The poor Man, they say, had no vicious Ways whatever . . . . I am very sorry for the poor Fellow indeed'; 'Poor Love the Painter' (1791) cut his throat—'I am sorry for him'.[73] Horace Walpole remarked on dozens of suicides he read about in the paper or learned of from his correspondents. In spite of his caustic appraisal of their characters and motives, he nowhere condemned their deed as wrong in itself. He doubted that the real reason for printing stories about

[71] L. B. Faller, *Turned to Account: Forms and Functions of Criminal Biography in Late Seventeenth- and Early Eighteenth-Century England* (Cambridge, 1987), 71.

[72] Dr Williams's Library, London, MS 38.122, 53–5.

[73] J. Woodforde, *The Diary of a Country Parson*, ed. J. Beresford (Oxford, 1981), i. 195, 250, 338; ii. 324; iii. 291; v. 375. See also, 'The Diary of George Sloper, 1753–1810', in *Some Annals of the Borough of Devizes* (Devizes, 1925–6), ii. 248–82, *passim* (some entries refer to local cases and were probably not copied from newspapers).

suicides was to induce moral revulsion for the act, implying that simple sensationalism and gossip-mongering prompted the violation of the privacy of families: 'The pretence is, *in terrorem*, like the absurd stake and highway of our ancestors; as if these were a precautionary potion for madness, or the stigma of the newspaper were more dreadful than death.'[74]

It is not our purpose to adjudicate the quarrel among literary scholars. Much certainly depended, as Faller notes, on the crime that was being described. Much also depended on the type of publication in which it was described. The model proposed by Novak, Lyons, and Richetti accurately characterizes newspaper accounts of suicides, whether or not it works equally well for treatments of other violent offences. The only notable exception that we have discovered was John Wesley's *Arminian Magazine*, which tried to sustain older supernaturalist interpretations of many phenomena, including suicide. Descriptions of suicidal urges as diabolical temptations occur often in the spiritual autobiographies of Methodist laymen that Wesley printed in his magazine.[75] Actual suicides and suicide attempts were also occasionally described and interpreted much as they would have been in seventeenth-century broadsides.[76] Just how anachronistic and antipathetic to orthodox opinion Wesley's efforts to sustain beliefs in demonism, witchcraft, and divine interventions were is plain from the vicious assaults on them by Establishment writers. Such superstitions, complained M. J. Naylor in 1795, had been 'gradually yielding to the powerful progress of science, but of late [have] again been nourished and revived, in no considerable degree, by the many extra-ordinary relations, which the late Mr Wesley inserted in his Arminian Magazine'.[77]

## SUICIDE NOTES

The press made it possible for readers to analyse the words and deeds of people who killed themselves. Suicides, on the other hand, could for the

[74] Walpole, *Correspondence*, xxxi. 267; general index, s.v. 'suicide'.

[75] See e.g., *Arminian Magazine*, ii (1779), 147, 420–1; iii (1780), 209; vii (1784), 356; viii (1785), 413–14; xi (1788), 573; xiii (1790), 69; xiv (1791), 494–6; xv (1792), 478–9; xviii (1795), 6.

[76] See e.g., ibid. ii (1779), 147; xiv (1791), 494–6. But for a more sympathetic account of a suicide, see ibid. iv (1781), 25.

[77] M. J. Naylor, *The Inanity and Mischief of Vulgar Superstitions* (Cambridge, 1795), pp. iv–v. For other examples of attacks on Methodist enthusiasm, see M. MacDonald, 'Religion, Social Change and Psychological Healing in England, 1600–1800', in W. J. Sheils (ed.), *The Church and Healing*, Studies in Church History, xix (Oxford, 1982), 119–21 and, more broadly, A. M. Lyles, *Methodism Mocked* (London, 1960).

first time effectively influence the way that strangers responded to their deaths. Troubled men and women knew that their suicides might be described in the papers, and they sometimes arranged their deaths or composed notes to win attention and sympathy. They were not simply the passive subjects of the journalists' artistry; they were active participants in the hermeneutics of suicide. Increasing rates of literacy provided people of very humble social standing with the means to read about others' deaths and to write their own suicide notes. The main concern of most people who were about to take their lives was naturally with the response of their immediate circle of family, friends, and neighbours to their suicide. But that limited group was no longer the only one for whom their deaths might be meaningful. Suicide had become a performance mounted before a mixed crowd of intimates and unknowns, and suicides could choose which part of the house they played to. Suicide became a means of self-expression.

Suicide notes were the most effective means for people to influence the interpretation of their own death. Editors and writers were particularly fond of inventing them, if the clues that can be gathered are indicative. Often it is impossible to distinguish genuine notes printed in the newspapers from bogus ones. This is obviously a serious obstacle to reconstructing accurately the circumstances of a particular death. But it is of little consequence in studying the ways in which suicides represented their own deaths. For there was a continuum of conventions and of rhetoric between the suicide notes that were printed in the newspapers and those that exist only in manuscript. Men and women who were about to kill themselves borrowed the forms and language for their own suicide notes from the examples, genuine and fictional, that they read in the newspapers. Consider an extreme example: a barely literate woman called simply E. H. who drowned herself in 1783 after she had been turned out of the last place that she had to live. Homeless and indebted, she was an eighteenth-century bag lady. Her 'Last Will to the World' was discovered on her body. A disjointed and anguished letter, it leaps from thought to thought almost incoherently and ends at last with these words: 'I wish I Cold Live the [*sic*] and forgive the dradfull youengs [usings] I have been youesed with. I Hae no moore to say to the wol[r]d but dye a marted to money a[n]d Long suffurens I begg I may not be advetsed in the Noue in Regard to them that is Left be Hind. I have not Lade down in this 4 mounts my sufrine has [been] be yond the World['s] inmegen pray Let my dsyer be don for [I] Cold not dye on a bedd so a Doue to all the World the lost E. H.' This moving letter illustrates an awareness of one common form for suicide notes, the last will and testament. In the salutation, 'adieu to all the world, the lost E. H.', it employs the polite and literary language favoured by the authors of notes that were printed in the papers. Finally, E. H., unlettered as she was, had plainly read newspaper accounts of suicides and asked explicitly not to be included among them, lest her survivors be embarrassed.[78]

Indeed, as early as the 1770s the suicide note had become sufficiently well established as a literary subgenre to be used as a vehicle for satire. By far the most famous example was the second of Thomas Chatterton's fake suicide notes. It is an elaborate performance in three parts. It begins with a prose preface, alluding to some 'Enthusiastical Methodist' verses he has written, an in-joke apparently aimed at his employer, Burgum. It then proceeds to a poetical complaint about Burgum, who is presented as an uncouth miser. This elides into a mocking testament (a common satirical form), in which the young poet doles out his talents to his survivors. Much of the piece is an elaborate series of insults, settling scores with the men who have neglected him. Addressing the elders of Bristol the will proper begins:

> This is the last will and Testament of me Thomas Chatterton of the City of Bristol being sound in Body or it is the fault of my last Surgeon. The Soundness of my Mind the Coroner and Jury are to be judges of—desiring them to take notice that the most perfect Masters of Human Nature in Bristol, distinguish me by the Title of a Mad Genius therefore if I do a mad action it is conformable to every Action of my Life, which all savored of Insanity.

One passage that seems serious in light of Chatterton's later successful suicide is the inscription he commands for his monument, which he describes in detail: 'To the Memory of Thomas Chatterton. Reader—Judge not: if thou art a Christian, believe that he shall be judged by a Superior Power; to that Power only is he now answerable.' He closes with a threat to haunt the bailiff of Bristol as a ghostly spectre, if he does not discharge Chatterton's debts, and a reassurance to the young ladies of the city that he will never haunt them. A codicil demands that the proprietors of the local newspaper print his suicide note the first Saturday after his death.[79]

Chatterton's note was intended to provoke his master into releasing him from his apprenticeship, and it worked. Like the poet's fake, real

[78] Westminster Inquisitions, E. H. (10 Dec. 1783).

[79] T. Chatterton, *The Complete Works of Thomas Chatterton*, ed. D. S. Taylor and B. B. Hoover (Oxford, 1971), i. 501–5. This work is interestingly analysed by L. J. Kaplan, *The Family Romance of the Imposter-Poet, Thomas Chatterton* (New York, 1988), 138–40.

suicide notes were essays in persuasion. They aimed to influence their readers so that they acted and felt as their authors intended them to. Although they were generally even less talented than the writers who laboured for the press, men and women who wrote suicide notes confronted an urgent literary problem. At the moment of death, they had nothing left but language to put the world right. Suicides often addressed their attempts to justify their deaths to a specific person or group of people. But some suicide notes were composed with the expectation that they would also be read by strangers, either at the inquest or in the papers. A few people wrote expressly for the widest possible audience, using their deaths to gain attention so that they could air their grievances or to dramatize their ideas. A handful addressed themselves to philosophical and religious questions. Access to the papers and the capacity to write suicide notes thus enabled men and women to lend complex meanings to their own deaths.

Eighteenth-century suicides were aware of the potential for publicity that the papers offered, or threatened. Some of them exploited it, and some of them tried to avoid it. Richard Smith instructed his kinsman to publish the notes he and his wife had written. Thomas Davers ended his petulant poem complaining of the injuries that penury had inflicted on his pride with the demand, 'N. B., Advertise this'.[80] Other suicides, like E. H., dreaded the thought that their actions and last words might be publicized. Suicide notes had been very rare in the seventeenth century, but as literacy became more widespread many more people explained their deaths in writing. Most notes have not survived. We have assembled over seventy eighteenth-century notes from press reports and manuscript sources; the content of many others is evident from press reports that paraphrase or summarize them.[81] This sample is inevitably biased. The majority of both the printed and the manuscript notes were written by Londoners, mostly men and women of the middling classes. The style and content of the dozen manuscript notes closely resemble those that were printed in the papers. Like the newspaper notes, they employed the rhetoric of wills, of dying speeches, and of personal letters. Most are in prose, but several were written in verse.

Many notes had an instrumental purpose. They perpetuated the suicide's influence for at least a brief space after his death. Like the last wills and testaments that they often imitated, they settled the disposition

[80] *Annual Register*, x (1767), 59.

[81] More printed examples could undoubtedly have been located by an exhaustive search of contemporary newspapers.

of their property, bestowed blessings on their surviors, and even issued instructions for the burial of their bodies. Thomas Holman asked his best friend to bestow his possessions on his survivors and settle his affairs; he provided a list of his debts and detailed information about his finances.[82] Some suicides, knowing that their words would be read publicly at the coroner's inquest, sought to influence the coroner or the jurors. Jacob Miers, a German who cut his throat in 1772 after a bloody altercation with a woman he accused of inducing his common-law wife to leave him, granted that he was guilty of self-murder. 'It is custemery for the Corener in this Contery to sett on the body', he began; 'not to give you troble know I am in my sences and to senceble of the most horid Crime I am agoin to Comit to ofand my Just God.' Explaining his motives in the best possible light, he concludes: 'and as I wrote this on purpose not to give the gantleman coroner to much troble ife it is in your power to have my body burid as near as pasible by bethnal Green, this is my Last Request'. Miers's plea was apparently ineffectual: he was interred in Portugal Street, by the burial ground.[83]

Suicide inevitably afflicted surviors with shock, scandal, and shame, and most people who killed themselves tried to reduce the pain that their deaths inflicted on their loved ones. Occasionally, however, they used notes as a means of revenge. 'My Dear', John Stracy addressed his wife, 'This is to acquaint you that you are the fatal cause of this action; your behaviour to me has drove me distracted. We might have lived happily and in credit, had your conduct been like mine. I hope the man who has been the cause of it, will think of this sad catastrophe.'[84] E. H. asked that whoever found her dead body carry it to the house from which she had been expelled and told 'never to Return agne moor in this world'.[85] Sometimes it is difficult to tell if a note was meant sincerely to forgive an injury or pointedly to call attention to it. Thomas Holman assured his beloved that he wished her all the happiness the world could afford, but he declared that he had sacrificed his life for her and gave her one last admonition: 'I only give you this caution to love one man only.'[86] A

[82] Westminster Inquisitions, Thomas Holman (28 Aug. 1782). See also, London Inquisitions, George Davis (26 Jan. 1796) and the discussions above and in Chapter 8 of the notes of Richard and Bridget Smith. For other notes cast as wills, see *Gentleman's Magazine*, xxxiii (1763), 45; Westminster Inquisitions, E. H. (10 Dec. 1783).

[83] Westminster Inquisitions, Jacob Miers (2 Oct. 1772). See also, *Annual Register*, xxxiii (1791), ii. 34–5.

[84] *Gentleman's Magazine*, xx (1750), 473.

[85] Westminster Inquisitions, E. H. (10 Dec. 1783).

[86] Westminster Inquisitions, Thomas Holman (28 Aug. 1782).

London man who hanged himself in 1770 sent his wife a letter confessing his infidelity: 'The weight of my misfortunes, which I have brought upon myself by my criminal intercourse with Mrs. D. I am not able to bear any longer.'[87] Whether it was manipulated consciously or unconsciously, suicide was a weapon that could inflict great suffering on others, and the suicide note was its aiming device.

The overwhelming preoccupation in suicide notes, however, was with reputation. For the decline of the inquest and of ritual burial as a means of establishing the significance of a suicide meant that the final judgement about the legitimacy of a self-killer's actions was made informally by his family and friends and by people who read his death in the press. The suicide note was one last means for shaping the opinions of intimates and strangers. Most people who wrote suicide notes cast themselves as innocent victims of circumstances or penitent sinners, and they deployed all the rhetorical powers that they possessed to arouse the pity and sorrow of their readers. Lewis Kennedy implored the 'good Christians' who learned of his death, 'be not too censorious before you have thoroughly survey'd the Cause of my Misfortune: . . . look on my Condition with Compassion, and not Ridicule.' In a moving letter he explains that before he took up his present post as the duke of Bedford's gardener, he had suffered some sort of affliction that suddenly deprived him of his thought and reason. He had immediately resigned his job, apparently because of his shame and embarrassment, but now at Woburn Abbey he finds himself no better. He has become odious to himself and 'can expect no other than to be branded for a Fool'. He insists that his mismanagement of affairs at Woburn has been the consequence of his malady, not incompetence or dishonesty. Indeed, he presents his suicide note as a kind of letter of reference that describes his background and employment history, stressing his faithful service and orthodox piety. 'Farewell, all Friends', he closes, 'I am a Member of the Church of England, and in Peace with all but myself.'[88]

Some suicides followed the conventional models of dying speeches and presented their fate as a moral example to others. 'My Dear Friends', the coachman William Bold addressed those whom he expected to find

87 *Annual Register*, xiii (1770), 160–1. See also *Gentleman's Magazine*, xl (1770), 538; Westminster Inquisitions, Mary Banks (27 Feb. 1769); John Bawcutt (25 Mar. 1783); James Holt (23 Sept. 1782); BL, Lansdowne MS 99, no. 32, fos. 88$^{r}$–89$^{v}$.

88 *Gentleman's Magazine*, xiii (1743), 543–4. For other notes appealing to misfortunes and illnesses to extenuate their authors' suicides, see *Annual Register*, xxxviii (1796), 32; *Fog's Weekly Journal*, no. 34 (17 May 1729); *Gentleman's Magazine*, xiv (1744), 537; xlviii (1778), 329.

his note, 'I hope you will all take warning by me to see my shameful End, and I would advise you to leave off in the first place lewd women, and in the next to refrain drinking, and to live in the fear of God.'[89] Popular accounts of executions published by the Ordinary of Newgate made the conventions of repentance widely known. The Ordinary's pamphlets observed a strict formula that included a relation of the condemned prisoner's criminal career and a plea to the reader not to repeat his errors.[90] Penitent suicides followed much the same plan. Under arrest for felony in Suffolk, John Upson hanged himself rather than face execution in 1774. He left behind a poetical note that defied the world's opinon but nevertheless contained the usual warning to avoid his fate:

> Farewell, vain world, I have had enough of thee
> And now am careless what thou say'st of me:
> Thy smiles I court not, nor thy frowns I fear,
> What faults they find in me take care to shun,
> And look at home, enough is to be done.

He signed his dying doggerel, 'Poor John the Glover'.[91] A few suicides refused to plead for mercy or employ the rhetoric of repentance at all, just as a few prisoners defied the Ordinary's efforts to get them to speak and act correctly. 'Tis better to die than be exposed', an anonymous man drowned in 1719 had written on a slate discovered in his pocket.[92] A soldier who killed himself after refusing an order to mount the guard blamed his death on his sergeant.[93] Defiance was a risky course, for it invited the ignominy of a *felo de se* verdict, but at least that disgrace would not have to be endured while one was still alive.

As they stood poised, about to take their own lives, suicides naturally thought about their fate after death. Some addressed directly the question of whether or not they would be damned for their act. Few constructed so elaborate a philosophical justification for their hope of salvation as the Smiths, who remained confident that their creator would not repudiate them and argued that the desecration of their material remains was unimportant, although there may be an echo of their Epicureanism in the note of a gentleman who shot himself at Kew,

[89] Westminster Inquisitions, William Bold (4 Apr. 1765).

[90] P. Linebaugh, 'The Ordinary of Newgate and His *Account*', in J. S. Cockburn (ed.), *Crime in England, 1550–1800* (Princeton, 1975), 246–69.

[91] *Gentleman's Magazine*, xiv (1744), 329. For a more conventional example, see ibid., xxxii (1762), 91–2.

[92] *Weekly Journal*, no. 26 (8 Aug. 1719).

[93] Westminster Inquisitions, James Holt (23 Sept. 1782).

which ended with the declaration that he was returning his 'transmutable body to its primitive element'.[94] Frederick Pastroff, a surgeon and apothecary, may also have been influenced by contemporary justifications for suicide. He wrote two poetical notes before he shot himself in 1768. The first, in French, has deistical overtones, declaring that the Almighty, whose plan is executed by nature, does not cause pain and that his principles have prepared him for his death. The second, in English, is more equivocal. 'Oh! can the learned Prelate find / What future scenes await the mind!' he opens:

> And kindly prove, when life is o'er
> That Pains and Sorrows are no more.
> For doubtless dying is a course [*sic*],
> If Present Ills be changed for worse.[95]

The hopes that eighteenth-century suicides entertained seem commonly to have reflected the old popular conviction, denounced by generations of preachers, that a person who lived honestly would be treated fairly by God in return. A journeyman barber who cut his throat in Wandsworth in 1758 expressed this conviction but dared not to guess what God's judgement would be. 'I have wronged no man', he claimed, 'and I am now gone before God.'[96] Lewis Kennedy made the same declaration: 'I hope for Salvation, . . . for I have wronged no body.'[97] The foundation of some suicides' expectations is mystifying. A forger who stabbed himself in the New Prison in 1762 wrote to a relative of a lady he had cheated and driven to madness, concluding with his hopes that he would be in eternity soon and (impudently in the circumstances) soliciting a contribution toward burying his body decently.[98] A Mr Galliard, who stabbed himself at Guernsey, claimed that God would forgive him for slaying his rival for the affections of a young woman and killing himself because the 'Father of mercies' had implanted uncontrollable love in his soul in the first place. (He granted that his actions might seem to be

[94] *Gentleman's Magazine* xliv (1774), 537.

[95] Westminster Inquisitions, Frederick Pastroff (25 June 1768).

[96] *Annual Register*, i (1758), 99. The earlier examples are more complex. William Doddington's reasoning seems much like these examples, even though he was a Puritan: BL, Lansdowne 99, no. 32, fos. $88^r$–$89^v$. Sir Walter Ralegh made a nice discrimination between suicide committed out of despair (damnable) and to escape dishonour (pardonable): Wymer, *Suicide and Despair*, 20–1.

[97] *Gentleman's Magazine*, xiii (1743), 543–4. See also Westminster Inquisitions, Thomas Holman (28 Aug. 1782).

[98] *Gentleman's Magazine*, xxxii (1762), 91–2.

opposed to almighty providence.)[99] At the end of the century a London carpenter was less confident of his fate. 'I must be totily lost', he concluded, unless divine providence rescued him.[100] So was a man named Skelton, who lingered for hours after he cut his throat in 1775. He gestured at last for pen and ink and wrote: 'I am to let you know, that I was not right when I did this: take care to serve God as you ought.'[101]

The literary heights to which suicide notes could rise are best illustrated by the final letter written by a gentlewoman just before she cast herself into the sea at Deal in 1726. It was printed in the *London Journal*; it is an epistle worthy of *Clarissa*, which it anticipates by two decades. It describes her seduction and betrayal by a Mr L. The writer opens with an offer of forgiveness to all who have wronged her, even her lover, Mr L, 'the greatest enemy I ever met with'. She is, however, anxious to deny the false rumours he has spread about her character. He knows she is no whore: 'He cannot accuse me of any criminal Converse with any other than himself.' She provides her own version of her downfall. He took advantage of her weakness while her husband was away at sea, and having seduced her, 'He continued on his Knees, begging me to forgive him; promising all that Man could say.' The affair evidently continued. She lamely claims that she did not show her resentment of him, lest she destroy the long amity between her family and his. Her disgrace, she declares in an admonition, should be an *exemplum*: 'I wish my unhappy State may be a Warning to others, not to put too much Trust in faithless Man.' Her thoughts then turn to her family. She implores her parents to forgive her for the shame that she has brought upon them and begs her mother to care for her infant child. She is sure that her family would not want her to suffer, but she cannot face them. But even in her grief and shame, she cannot long forget Mr L. His hypocrisy arouses her to cynicism: 'Mr L. Should not read Mr *Locke's* Books so much and practise them so little; he inculcates the Necessity of doing as we would be done by, and of shunning a Lye, though to the saving of a Man's Life. Let him think on this when he thinks on me.' She nevertheless betrays her own ambivalence about him. He had promised to treat her as his wife, although it was not in his power to make her so: 'O that he had always kept his Word! then I should have been happy.' After again excusing herself because of her ignorance of the treacherous company of men and

99 Ibid. xlii (1762), 373–4.
100 London Inquisitions, George Davis (21 Jan. 1796).
101 *Annual Register*, xviii (1775), 150–1.

casting some final aspersions on Mr L.'s character, she returns to the sentiments appropriate to a dying speech. Even here, however, forgiveness and repentance are marred with bitterness: 'But I can still forgive him, and my own Fault. Let no one judge too rash, that does not know the cause I had for it.'[102]

This letter is an extraordinary achievement. The writer's oscillation between anger and grief, righteousness and shame, hate and love, creates an utterly realistic picture of a mind rent by powerful and conflicting emotions. Like a tragic heroine's last monologue, this letter captures the tension between the writer's recognition of the part that she played in her own downfall and her persistence in the delusion that ruined her. Contemporary tragedy is only one of the genres that provided the literary materials for this desperate work of art. Closer analogues may be found in contemporary fiction. Novels of seduction and betrayal were already popular fare before this letter was written. Eliza Haywood's labours in this genre won her a libellous reference in *The Dunciad.* There are echoes of the conventional dying speech in it as well. Books like Jeremy Taylor's *Holy Dying* instructed pious Anglicans how to speak and act in their last moments, and even the last orations of criminals were composed with parts of the standard formula in mind. The dying person had, as our writer does, to forgive others for their offences and also ask forgiveness for his own delicts. The writer of this final letter frames her tale with phrases of forgiveness and repentance and points to the moral of her story, much in the way that the narratives of condemned criminals did, although her bitterness towards Mr L. rather subverts the penitent mood.[103] Here, then, was a literary performance of considerable skill, rich in complexity and allusion, drawing on a wide range of models. Its aim—at which it is triumphantly successful—is to place before the reader a vivid and perfectly convincing portrayal of a wronged and tormented woman whose death is a tragedy.

Whatever rhetorical strategies they adopted, suicides tried in their notes to control the way in which others reacted to their deaths. Recall, in the examples recounted above, Lewis Kennedy's plea not to be censorious and William Bold's wish that his 'dear friends' would take

[102] *London Journal*, no. 359 (11 June 1726). For the first notice of the discovery of the author's body, see ibid., no. 358 (4 June 1726).

[103] M. A. Doody, *A Natural Passion: A Study of the Novels of Samuel Richardson* (Oxford, 1974), 18–19, 128–50; A. Pope, *The Dunciad*, in *The Poems of Alexander Pope*, ed. J. Butt (New Haven, 1963), Book II, ll. 157–60; P. Linebaugh, 'The Ordinary of Newgate'; J. A. Sharpe, '"Last Dying Speeches": Religion, Ideology and Public Execution in Seventeenth-Century England', *Past and Present*, no. 107 (1985), 144–67.

warning from his death. Kennedy and Bold were both forestalling censure: the one by anticipating it directly, the other by usurping the role of the moral judge and turning his suicide into an *exemplum*. Suicides attempted to influence the emotions that their deaths provoked and to determine what others who knew them or read their notes in the papers thought about their actions. They issued direct orders or made specific requests in an attempt to get survivors to act as they wanted them to. Their notes were, in effect, a means of perpetuating their identities beyond death, a literary substitute for speech and gesture, a last act of self-fashioning. Sometimes their efforts were undermined by the polysemous nature of language and by unintended irony. For instance, the care with which Richard and Bridget Smith provided for their pets and paid for the services of the landlord and a porter before they shot themselves and their child struck several contemporary observers as macabre.[104] Indeed, irony was the constant companion of self-destruction; pathos was always imperilled by the ridiculous. A schoolmaster who cut his throat after attempting to murder his landlord spent his last hours writing for his pupils 'full directions for the conduct of their life'.[105]

## CONCLUSION

The inaccuracies, inventions, and forgeries that abounded in newspaper accounts of suicides make it unwise to rely too confidently on the 'facts' they report. No one should cite evidence from the papers in the belief that it might not be contradicted elsewhere. We have tried here to use newspapers to illuminate attitudes and conventions, rather than subjects that depend on the strict accuracy of their reporting.[106] As a source of information about conventional ideas—what we have called folk psychology and sociology—they are invaluable. The stories that the papers recounted or embellished were shaped in terms of a common set of assumptions about the psychology of suicide. They both reflected and publicized popular notions about how suicides acted and why they killed

[104] See e.g., Voltaire, *Works*, vii. 25.

[105] *Annual Register*, viii (1765), Chronicle, 147.

[106] Thus although we cannot know whether the lady of Deal's letter is genuine and, if it is genuine, how much it has been tampered with, for our present purposes the question of authorship is beside the point. We have used such documents to illustrate the literary models and rhetorical conventions that suicide notes employed; even the fakes are relevant, for they helped teach those conventions. And the conventions are found in notes whose authenticity cannot be doubted.

themselves. They printed suicide notes whose conventions and rhetoric taught those who were about to die how to address the audience they were about to leave. These assumptions have been the focus of this chapter. They are far more significant than the facts of any single case, and on this level the press's insistent and contradictory blend of fiction with truth, of invention with claims of empirical fidelity, simply does not matter.

The newspaper did more, however, than merely reflect particular ideas, or symbols, or even convey an entire ideology. It was also an active agent of cultural change. It carried apparently factual information to a diverse and heterogeneous audience; accounts of events were read by people all over the country. The press fostered popular politics and eroded paternalism and localism. This much literary scholars and historians have taught us. But the press influenced popular culture more profoundly than we have grasped. The newspaper was a hermeneutical stage on which professional writers mounted their works and ordinary people played their parts. The rise of the press vastly enlarged the circle of people who interpreted specific events—the *corona populi*, one might say, echoing Sir Thomas Smith's characterization of coroners' inquests—and it increased the opportunities for individuals to communicate their thoughts and feelings to others. Readers' own creations sometimes appeared in the pages of the papers. Educated correspondents sent in articles and poems, many poems, for publication. Plebeian writers produced letters and notes that were incorporated into news stories. Advertisers hawked their goods on the back pages of the weekly journals.

The rhetoric of news reporting has been largely neglected, but it was crucial. By presenting realistic depictions of incidents and individuals, the papers made the lives of strangers significant. Readers could identify with the feelings and actions of men and women they had never met. They could evaluate their motives and even their thoughts and decide for themselves whether they deserved pity or scorn. Realism was the handmaiden of secularization. For the newspapers' attempts to achieve realism—partial though they may seem in comparison with histories and novels—placed the emphasis on the social and psychological significance of suicide. Abstractions and personifications were no longer relevant to the interpretation of self-murder. Press stories and the publication of suicide notes doubtless encouraged greater tolerance of suicide as well. Eighteenth-century traditionalists complained that juries always brought in *non compos mentis* verdicts when a suicide was a familiar member of their community. Sympathy for the victim and his survivors tended to overcome the horror of the crime. The publication of reports of suicide in the press made the victims members of the community of its readership. It was difficult to condemn people who suffered misfortunes that might befall anyone and felt the same extremes of love, and hate, and despair that the reader did. The very style of newspaper reporting thus fostered the secularization of attitudes to suicide.

At the same time, readers learned from the press the conventions of expression that made their experiences meaningful to others. The authors of suicide notes almost invariably drew attention to situations that everyone granted gave good reason to feel desperate: economic misfortune and destitution; frustrated love and infidelity; social ruin and dishonour; impulsive, irredeemable mistakes, and folly recognized too late. They created images of themselves in their notes that closely resembled the familiar figures of the penitent sinner, the contrite criminal, the wronged spouse, the honest debtor. The rhetoric of realism enlarged the roles that suicides could play. No longer simply depicted as the apostate victims of satanic temptations, they could present themselves as the casualties of life's common perils. They might also use their deaths to seize for the first time the attention and move the hearts of a multitude of strangers as well as of their families and friends. A suicide might be the vehicle for anything from simple exhibitionism to brutally specific revenge; one could die for a reason one chose for oneself. Others might reject or misunderstand his motives, but the suicide had gained the power to declare the meaning of his death.

Suicide notes were expressions of a new emphasis on individualism, and a new psychologized conception of the self. Many eminent scholars have argued that people in the eighteenth century sought personal satisfaction and gain as never before.[107] Among revisionist historians, this is an unfashionable idea. They retort that affective individualism had existed in peasant households for centuries; economic individualism had been practised in village markets for hundreds of years.[108] And yet these criticisms seem to us to ignore the obvious. Men and women had greater opportunities for self-expression in the eighteenth century than ever before. We have been misled by concentrating on specific values and

[107] See e.g., L. Stone, *The Family, Sex and Marriage in England, 1500–1800* (New York, 1977), ch. 6; Lyons, *Invention of the Self*; D. W. Sabean, *Power in the Blood* (Cambridge, 1984), 30–6, 205–13. See also, T. C. Heller *et al.*, *Reconstructing Individualism* (Stanford, 1986).

[108] The most powerful expressions of this point of view are A. Macfarlane, *The Origins of English Individualism* (Oxford, 1978); id., *Marriage and Love in England, 1300–1840* (Oxford, 1986).

neglecting the means of communication that were available to successive generations of ordinary people. Affective individualism was more than a set of attitudes; it was active participation in a literate culture that considered the feelings and actions of ordinary people to be worthy of realistic representation. The rise of the popular press and the common people's mastery of its rhetorical conventions changed forever the relationship between the individual and the society. All men and women were potentially makers of texts that might move the hearts and engage the minds of a multitude of others. They had gained access to a powerful new way to create images of themselves, even to make history.

# *Epilogue*

THE importance of the history of suicide in early modern England lies in what it reveals about the nature of cultural and social change. We have argued in this book that beliefs and the behaviour that expressed them were influenced by a very wide range of factors. Attitudes and responses to suicide were shaped by political events, religious reform and rivalries, shifts in philosophical fashion, changes in the relationship of local communities to the nation state, and the growth of the periodical press, which created a new mode of communication. The rise and fall of severity toward self-killers, which can be measured and timed in the pattern of suicide verdicts, was thus the product of developments that might seem at first to have had little to do with the treatment of suicides. One of the main aims of this book has been to bring out the complexity of cultural change and to stress its connections with social transformations and political events. But it is not enough to avoid reductionist explanations for historical phenomena; we must also try to show how the domains of culture, social action, and politics were related to each other.

In his book about popular culture in early modern Germany, *Power in the Blood*, David Sabean attempts to do just this, and his conceptual framework can be adapted to describe partially the forces that altered the history of suicide in England. Sabean's analysis turns on three key concepts: '*Herrschaft*', 'community', and 'person'.[1] As Sabean's inability to find a precise English equivalent hints, *Herrschaft* is the most elusive of his organizing ideas. It is a concept that expresses, he writes, 'institutional relationships of authority' and encompasses a range of kinds of power. Its forms are numerous and overlapping and change over time, but what they have in common, and what the term denotes, is that each of them is a 'domain of authority of a specific lord, whether that lord be

[1] D. W. Sabean, *Power in the Blood: Popular Culture and Village Discourse in Early Modern Germany* (Cambridge, 1984), 20–36.

a single person, such as a duke or a king, or a corporation, such as a monastery, a hospital, or a city council'.[2] Community is at once an easier and a more complicated term. It does not denote a bounded and united entity, the fictional village society of popular history, which existed neither in early modern Germany nor in early modern England. It suggests instead the networks of relationships that 'contain multiple links and are structured over time', the links between people that are established by exchanges of property, marriage, and participation in a common discourse or argument. Finally, like other historians mentioned in this book, Sabean insists that the person was 'constituted by his position within a matrix of relations'. The self, he argues, is not an immutable, biologically determined entity; it is instead the historically plastic product of changing cultural and social conditions. 'The positioning of the individual between spirit and flesh, God and the devil, friend and enemy, kin and neighbour is central to the way the person, his cognitive and motivational structures are grasped.'

It is not our intention to rewrite this book in Sabean's terms, but his organizing concepts can be used to highlight the implications of its arguments. The history of suicide was profoundly affected by changing relationships of authority. In the Middle Ages the coroner exercised the powers of his office in a manner that was strikingly independent of royal control. He was at once a representative of the crown (as his title proclaimed), and also a local official with a wide range of authority and duties. His main responsibility was to his country and its communities. The practice of applying the law of self-murder rarely and selectively was part of a style of rule that sought to accommodate the claims of the crown and the needs and values of local communities. In the sixteenth and early seventeenth centuries, the crown tried hard to achieve greater control over the administration of local affairs. The balance between royal power and local authorities in England was too complicated for this process to be described simply as the rise of an absolutist state. The absence of a royal bureaucracy and standing army, and the crown's

[2] The advantage of Sabean's term over the similar and far more fashionable Foucauldian '*pouvoir*' lies, if we understand him correctly, in its greater specificity. It implies that power is a function of relationships that are recognized and persistent (though changing). Though Foucault's insistence on the pervasiveness of dominance and submission is valuable, his notion of power seems to us to be too detached from institutional structures to be an adequately precise instrument for explaining social and cultural change and relating it to political change. For a very brief, incisive discussion of the elusiveness and expansiveness of Foucault's understanding of power, see A. Megill, *Prophets of Extremity: Nietsche, Heidegger, Foucault, Derrida* (Berkeley, 1985) 247–9.

consequent reliance on the aristocracy and gentry to staff the most important local offices, meant that legitimate power was always exercised by men whose authority derived both from their offices and also from their personal status. Nevertheless, incomplete though it may have been, the 'Tudor revolution in government' transformed the balance and nature of political power and altered the role of the coroner and his jury in local society. The claims of the crown and of manorial lords and corporations that shared its prerogative right to the goods of self-murderers became paramount.[3] These claims were legitimized and strengthened by the clergy's intensified emphasis on the diabolical causes of suicide and their acceptance of the popular rituals nullifying its supernatural consequences.

The revolutions of the mid-seventeenth century altered the relationship between central and local government again, changing the ways in which power was exercised once more. The abolition of the prerogative courts, the abandonment of close supervision of local institutions by the central government, and the exaltation of the property rights of individuals made it much more difficult to ensure compliance with the law against self-murder. Local officials, although they were servants of the crown, were left largely to their own devices after 1660. The privy council abandoned its attempt rigorously to supervise local government and directives from it to benches of justices grew scarcer and scarcer in the eighteenth century. Nor did the central courts try very hard to police the activity of royal officials in the shires.[4] Coroners and their juries escaped systematic surveillance in the later seventeenth century, and they were essentially placed under the direction of local benches of justices in 1751. The 'triumph of the gentry'—as Anthony Fletcher calls it—was articulated in terms of the rhetoric of liberties. Freedom and localism, resistance to apparently absolutist actions by the crown and resentment of royal interference, were inseparable. The constitutional conflicts of 1640 to 1660 and of 1688–9 weakened the crown's prerogative both in theory and in practice. In the long run these changes, ironically, made it impossible for lords to enforce their own rights to forfeited property.

Royal officials, including coroners, exercised their authority in the king's name, but in fact personal and political authority were more

[3] For overviews of the changing relationship between central and local governments, see P. Williams, *The Tudor Regime* (Oxford, 1979); A. Fletcher, *Reform in the Provinces* (New Haven, 1986); D. Hirst, *Authority and Conflict: England, 1603–1658* (London, 1986), esp. chs. 2, 12.

[4] Fletcher, *Reform in the Provinces*, 357–8; N. Landau, *The Justices of the Peace, 1679–1760* (Berkeley, 1984), 7–8.

intimately connected in the eighteenth century than they had been in the Tudor and Stuart period. This paradox can be clarified by a brief look back in time. The enforcement of the law of suicide in the eighteenth century resembled its use in the Middle Ages, but the resemblance is a deceptive one. To put the difference in Sabean's terms, the forms of *Herrschaft* were very different from what they had been three or four centuries earlier. Georgian coroners were part of a corps of gentry whose power emanated from the crown and at the same time was embodied in their persons, a nice balance of official power and paternalism. Authority was granted by the state and was wielded in its name; political power was justified in terms of an ideology that recognized both the prerogatives of the crown and the rights of the individual. The gentry, in other words, shared in state authority and appropriated it to run their counties more or less as they saw fit; they were not feudal magnates.

At the same time, authority was shared with a much wider range of people than it had been in medieval or Tudor and Stuart times. The emergence of village and corporation oligarchies of men of middling status, a phenomenon many English historians have remarked upon, lent local institutions—those that governed the affairs of communities—considerable autonomy. The law conferred upon them a degree of independence, and as we have seen, coroners' juries sometimes defied the wishes of the royal officials, the lords of franchises, and even the coroners themselves. Institutions such as coroners' juries appropriated royal authority just as the gentry did, using the power that the state permitted them to settle matters in ways that satisfied the social, economic, and cultural demands of local communities. In other words, as they became more polarized socially and culturally, local communities produced a new class of leaders, men of authority, who assumed positions as officials in local government. Social and economic change in local communities thus altered the forms of *Herrschaft* just as political and constitutional changes did.[5]

[5] Pioneering studies along these lines are K. Wrightson and D. Levine, *Poverty and Piety in an English Village: Terling, 1525–1700* (New York, 1979), chs. 6–7; K. Wrightson, *English Society, 1580–1680* (London, 1982), 222–8, esp. pp. 226–7; P. King, 'Decision-Makers and Decision-Making in the English Criminal Law', *Historical Journal*, xxvii (1984), 55–8; C. B. Herrup, *The Common Peace: Participation and the Criminal Law in Seventeenth-Century England* (Cambridge, 1987); Fletcher, *Reform in the Provinces*, 62–83. For similar arguments, see J. Innes and J. Styles, 'The Crime Wave: Recent Writing on Crime and Criminal Justice in Eighteenth-Century England', *Journal of British Studies*, xxv (1986), 404; M. Ingram, 'Ridings, Rough Music and the Reform of Popular Culture in Early Modern England', *Past and Present*, no. 105 (1984), 79–113.

Finally, these changes in relations of power between the state and local communities and between social classes were accompanied by changes that altered the conception of the person, people's understanding of themselves and the identities of others. We have argued in this book that throughout the whole period the family remained more important in defining personal identity than it is today. Profound as were the demographic and social changes that occurred between 1500 and 1800, they had not shaken the family from its position as the basic social institution. On the other hand, it is possible to detect noticeable signs of a change in attitudes toward personal happiness and misery. The rise of the popular press and the growth of literacy enabled suicides to use their deaths as expressions of their own failure to find personal satisfaction. The causes of suicide were located more in the quality of a person's social relationships and his success or failure in the market economy, and less insistently in his relationship with the spiritual forces of God and the devil. We take this shift in emphasis to be not just another stage in the secularization of the early modern world-view but also a step in the formation of a recognizably modern conception of the person.

Expressed so schematically, these arguments are bound to raise many objections. Other case-studies and wider surveys will be necessary to demonstrate that they are valid explanations of social and cultural change. Furthermore, the categories proposed by Sabean do not help to organize some of this book's most important themes. Sabean, for example, does not discuss the impact of political events on cultural change, and he recognizes, but does not attempt to explain, the emergence of a new set of values among the educated élite, a transformation from Reformation evangelism to Enlightenment rationalism. Moreover, although he stresses the importance of local officials as mediators between the agents of the central government and the village community, he has little to say about the implications of their emergence in the overall pattern of cultural change. This needs emphasis, however, because cultural historians of early modern Europe have tended to neglect groups that resist classification as élite or plebeian. We should therefore focus our attention briefly on the politics of cultural change and its social dynamics.

Recent trends in historiography have made it difficult to see the connections between political and religious events and social and cultural change. Our modern anatomists have worked over the English Revolution with minute attention to detail, and their busy scalpels have pared away everything except its political skeleton. The religious and constitutional conflicts that were the flesh and blood of the subject a generation ago have been reduced to historical offal. But much of the history of England in the century and a half after 1660 does not make sense unless the manifold influence that they had on the governing élite is recognized. In this instance, the strife that climaxed in the Puritan Revolution and the Revolution of 1688 fostered cultural and institutional changes that eroded traditional attitudes to suicide and punishments for self-murder. The governing classes' intense antipathy to radical religion and miracle-mongering sectarians and priests cast doubt on supernatural explanations for events and enhanced the appeal of philosophy and science. Ideas that few people can have fully understood became the shibboleths of a whole class, and views that had been anathema to an earlier age became badges of fashion. Although it would be a grotesque oversimplification to ascribe the eighteenth-century élite's disenchantment with supernaturalism entirely to the cataclysms of the previous century, it would be equally perverse to deny that they had profound consequences for upper-class culture.[6]

Thus even a phenomenon as apparently unrelated to politics as suicide was affected by religious controversy and political events. The history of suicide also suggests that the prevailing models of the relationship between social and cultural change are oversimplified. Many historians have observed that English society became increasingly polarized culturally as well as socially and economically in the seventeenth and eighteenth centuries. Students of popular culture have pointed to the élite's repudiation of beliefs and customs that had been the shared heritage of rich and poor alike.[7] E. P. Thompson and his followers have pursued this argument further than other historians and integrated it into a

[6] For similar arguments, see J. A. Sharpe, *Crime in Early Modern England, 1550–1750* (London, 1984), 154–6; R. Porter, 'The Rage of Party: A Glorious Revolution in English Psychiatry?', *Medical History*, xxvii (1983), 35–50; C. Hill, *The World Turned Upside Down* (Harmondsworth, 1975), 294–5, 355–6; id., *Some Intellectual Consequences of the English Revolution* (Madison, Wis., 1980); M. C. Jacob, *The Newtonians and the English Revolution* (Ithaca, 1976); id., *The Cultural Meaning of the Scientific Revolution* (Philadelphia, 1988), chs. 3–4; H. C. Payne, 'Elite Versus Popular Mentality in the Eighteenth Century', *Studies in Eighteenth-Century Culture*, 3 (Madison, Wis., 1979) 3–32.

[7] See e.g., Thomas, *Religion and Magic*, 666; id., *Man and the Natural World* (London, 1983), 80–1; P. Burke, *Popular Culture in Early Modern Europe* (New York, 1978), 270–86; Wrightson, *English Society, 1580–1680*, 220–1; D. Rollison, 'Property, Ideology and Popular Culture in a Gloucestershire Village, 1600–1740', *Past and Present*, no. 93 (Nov. 1981), 70–97; MacDonald, *Mystical Bedlam*, 10–1, 171–2; id., 'Religion, Social Change, and Psychological Healing in England, 1600–1800', in W. J. Sheils (ed.), *The Church and Healing*, Studies in Church History, xix (Oxford, 1982), 101–25; A. J. Fletcher and J. Stevenson (eds.), *Order and Disorder in Early Modern England* (Cambridge, 1985), 1–15.

compelling theory that explains the changing relationship between patrician society and plebeian culture.[8] Superficially, the transformation in attitudes and responses to suicide fits neatly into the scheme: the governing classes rejected plebeian beliefs and customs, and for much of the eighteenth century coroners' juries enforced the law against suicide in a manner that emphasized the privileges of rank. The traditional punishments for self-murder were transformed from communal rituals into instruments of social control. But as we have seen the changing pattern of enforcement did not simply reinforce ruling-class interests nor was it the consequence of the actions of men who were themselves members of the national élite. Resistance to forfeiture and the rise of the *non compos mentis* verdict eroded the rights of lords as well as of the king. It was coroners' juries whose decisions actually determined the legitimate response to suicide. To explain the secularization of suicide, therefore, one must introduce a third group into the model, the men of middling status who served as jurors.

Historians have recently begun to appreciate the part that substantial farmers and craftsmen played in local government. Constables, churchwardens, grand jurors, and trial jurors, all of whom were recruited from their ranks, acted as mediators between the state and local communities. Coroners' jurors came from the same background and behaved in the same way as these other local officials. They stood at the focal point between the national culture, which was dominated by the educated and the powerful, and local society, which had its own cultural traditions and moral concerns. They were not simply the passive instruments of ruling-class hegemony. They gradually accepted the tolerant and secular attitude to suicide propounded by philosophers and physicians and publicized in fashionable periodicals. But instead of abandoning the traditional punishments for self-murder altogether, they used them to reaffirm values that were dear to respectable villagers and townsfolk: sympathy for one's neighbour, distaste for departures from the normal customs of inheritance, regard for good reputation, and antagonism toward strangers, criminals, and deviants. Plebeian beliefs in the spiritual ramifications of self-murder were invoked in an increasingly narrow range of suicides until at last they were sanctioned only to justify

[8] E. P. Thompson, 'Patrician Society, Plebeian Culture', *Journal of Social History*, vii (1973–4), 382–405; R. W. Malcolmson, *Popular Recreations in English Society, 1700–1850* (Cambridge, 1973); D. Hay *et al.* (eds.) *Albion's Fatal Tree* (New York, 1975). Although they modify Thompson's model somewhat, the essays in J. Brewer and J. Styles (eds.), *An Ungovernable People* (London, 1980), also develop it persuasively.

punishing notorious malefactors. In tens of thousands of inquests, therefore, men of middling rank responded to cultural polarization by gradually giving the rites of desecration a new function that was at once consistent with élite opinion about suicide itself and responsive to the moral values of their communities. They thus avoided conflicts over the abandonment of traditional beliefs and practices and even satisfied popular notions of just punishment by resisting forfeiture and by prosecuting people who belonged to groups that were generally supposed to threaten the security of respectable men and women of every social rank. Until more work has been done to examine the part that the middling classes and local institutions played in early modern England, it would be premature to present the history of suicide as a typical example of the social dynamics of cultural change. Nevertheless, it suggests that mediation and compromise may have been as much a part of the cultural history of late seventeenth- and eighteenth-century England as hegemony and conflict.

A second inadequacy of the two-class model may be traced to the reformation. The legacy of the English Reformation was religious pluralism. The shifts in religious policy that characterized the decades following the break with Rome left an ineradicable Catholic minority and spawned diverse species of Protestantism. The English Revolution, which John Morrill has called (with only slight hyperbole) England's war of religion, made unification of the various kinds of Protestantism impossible.[9] The growing quietism of some of the denominations of 'old dissent', reinfusions of religious enthusiasm from abroad, and the emergence of Methodism further complicated the religious taxonomy of the country. As we have seen in this book, there were sharp differences in the degree to which different religious denominations accepted or rejected the secularization of suicide. Orthodox Anglicans were precocious in rejecting religious enthusiasm; evangelicals were keen to preserve popular beliefs in ways that made their theology more comprehensible and appealing. The result was to complicate the cultural divisions in England by creating communities of belief that cut across class lines. Upper-class evangelicals, such as William Cowper, and lower-class Methodists, such as John Valton, looked at the world in much the same way. Not every élite evangelical or plebeian Methodist shared the same set of beliefs and attitudes about the supernatural; but their similarities complicate any attempt to divide eighteenth-century England

[9] J. Morrill, 'The Religious Context of the English Civil War', *Transactions of the Royal Historical Society*, 5th ser., xxxiv (1984), 155–78.

simply into a scientistic upper class and a superstitious lower class. Moreover, there appear also to have been significant cultural variations between cities and rural towns and villages and among cities. Some of these seem pretty obviously to be connected with the religious complexion or economy of the locale, but others remain mysterious.[10] It is a weakness of this book that in a national study of suicide over three centuries we have been unable to do the sort of intensive local research that would allow us to be more precise about such social and ecological subtleties. But we have at least acknowledged some of the ways in which they complicate the study of cultural change.

## ENVOI

Perhaps the most perplexing feature of the decriminalization and secularization of suicide is its lingering incompleteness. Despite the fact that the law was almost never applied and that juries presumed that ordinary suicides were insane when they killed themselves, parliament did not abolish the religious penalties for self-murder until 1823 and the secular punishments until 1870. Why was reform so long in coming? No one has yet studied adequately the circumstances surrounding the nineteenth-century changes in the law. Some tentative suggestions may be made, however. Two issues seem to have been crucial: the relationship of the law of suicide to other criminal laws and anxiety over how to deter suicides. The aspect of the law that disturbed people most was, as we have seen, the forfeiture of self-murderers' property. Reformers, even those who were opposed to repealing the law, called for the abolition of forfeiture in the late eighteenth century. The great authority Charles Moore was one of these. 'If the pecuniary interests of the family', he argued, 'could be detached from the censure of the crime, it would be an important point gained; because it might give more frequent opportunities of executing the other part of the self-murderer's sentence.'[11] But

[10] Variations in cultural ecology are the central theme of D. Underdown, *Revel, Riot and Rebellion: Popular Politics and Culture in England, 1603–1660* (Oxford, 1985). Jonathan Barry has recently advanced interesting hypotheses about the extent to which provincial towns followed the cultural trends set by the metropolis; he will no doubt develop them in his forthcoming study of the cultural history of 18th-century Bristol (a haven for dissenters and Methodists, incidentally).

[11] Moore, *Full Inquiry into Suicide*, i. 339. See also, C. Fleming, *A Dissertation upon the Unnatural Crime of Self-Murder* (London, 1773), 17; R. Hey, *A Dissertation on Suicide* (Cambridge, 1785), 24–5, 82, 85.

forfeiture was also a penalty for other kinds of felony, including high treason. Members of Parliament seem to have felt that abolishing it for this single offence would weaken the law's ability to deter serious crime in general. Indeed, when Sir James Mackintosh urged the House of Commons in 1823 to repeal the penalties for suicide, he remarked that he had originally wanted to abolish forfeiture for other crimes as well, but that he knew that there would be insurmountable opposition to its repeal in the case of treason (and, one supposes, other felonies too).[12] When the forfeiture provisions were finally repealed, in 1870, they were removed by an omnibus bill that covered felonies of every kind. *Felo de se* is mentioned only once in the bill itself, and suicide was not discussed at all in the debates on it.[13]

The problem of deterrence preoccupied law-makers and social commentators. Some moralists proposed making the religious penalties for suicide even more severe, substituting dissection for burial in a highway. Others, including John Wesley, called for gibbeting the victims and leaving their corpses to rot.[14] But these proposals were to no avail. They were inconsistent with the general trend away from elaborations of capital punishment at the end of the eighteenth century, which was accelerated by the efforts of law reformers and, perhaps, by the popular resentment that the Murder Act of 1752 provoked.[15] When parliament finally did do something, it decided to repeal the custom of profane burial outright. The 1823 act accomplishing this was inconsistent with the advice that both the proponents and opponents of greater leniency had given. It left the fiscal punishments intact, which everyone believed were the greatest impediment to effective enforcement and hence to the use of the criminal law to deter suicide. The tale of the 1823 reform is intriguing. The first step was taken by Sir James Mackintosh, a leading figure in the law reform movement. In a speech to the House of Commons, Mackintosh criticized the way in which the law was enforced,

[12] *Hansard's Parliamentary Debates*, NS, ix, col. 414.

[13] *Hansard*, 3rd ser., cc, cols. 931–8; 3rd ser., cci, cols. 1688–91; 33 & 34 Vict., c. 23. For the circumstances that governed the pace of reform more generally, see L. Radzinowicz, *A History of English Criminal Law*, i (New York, 1948), esp. ch. 17; J. Beattie, *Crime and the Courts in England, 1660–1800* (Princeton, 1986), 623–36.

[14] *Gentleman's Magazine*, i (1731), 467–8; [B. Coleman and G. Thornton], *Connoisseur* (London, 1755), i. 298–9; Fleming, *Dissertation upon Self-Murder*, 16–7; Moore, *Full Inquiry into Suicide*, i. 339; J. Wesley, *The Works of John Wesley*, 4th edn. (1842; repr. Grand Rapids, Mich., n.d.), xiii. 481.

[15] P. Linebaugh, 'The Tyburn Riot against the Surgeons', in Hay *et al.*, *Albion's Fatal Tree*, 69–78; Beattie, *Crime and the Courts*, 525–38, 543–4, 630–3. R. Richardson, *Death, Dissection and the Destitute* (London, 1987), carries the story into the next century.

claiming that it was used against the poor but not the rich. This was, as we have seen, an exaggeration of the truth. He then proposed decriminalizing suicide altogether. He spoke in terms that might have been drawn directly from Beccaria, declaring passionately that punishing suicide was 'an act of brutal folly'. 'He would ask any gentleman', he reportedly said, 'whatever his opinions as to the moral turpitude of suicide, whether it was a crime that ought to be subject to human cognizance. The essence of it consisted in the withdrawing of the person from the power of human tribunals, and the law of England alone stretched itself to include an offence of this kind.'[16] Mackintosh's empathy for suicides and their families was prompted in part by personal experience. His great predecessor in the reform movement, Sir Samuel Romilly, had killed himself in 1818, a death that had shocked the nation.[17]

Just a year before Mackintosh's speech, the suicide of Viscount Castlereagh had caused even greater shock. It had entangled the problem of law reform in the brambles of partisan politics. As Barbara Gates has shown, Castlereagh's enemies protested at the lunacy verdict returned by the coroner's jury and howled when his body was interred in Westminster Abbey. Byron fulminated that 'if a poor radical ... had cut his throat, he would have been buried in a cross-road, with the usual appurtenances of the stake and mallet. But the minister was an elegant lunatic—a sentimental suicide—he merely cut the "carotid artery" ... and lo! the pageant, and the Abbey!'[18] Political hostility merged into moral outrage, and some protested anew against the lenient handling of suicide. And yet the controversy over Castlereagh's death notwithstanding, parliament would not be deterred. The House of Commons narrowly defeated Mackintosh's wide-ranging resolutions, but as soon as they had failed, T. B. Lennard introduced a separate bill, abolishing the ritual penalties for *felo de se* and substituting the milder sanction of night-time burial. He referred to the rites of desecration as an 'odious and disgusting ceremony' and rightly attributed them to popular

[16] *Hansard*, NS, ix. cols. 397–433; *The Times*, no. 11, 883 (22 May 1823), 3.

[17] *DNB*, s.v. 'Romilly, Sir Samuel'. Donna Andrew identifies the John McIntosh who killed himself in 1784 as Sir James's son, but the latter was only nineteen at the time. It is possible, however, that he was a near relation: D. T. Andrew, 'The Secularization of Suicide, 1660–1800: Comment', *Past and Present*, no. 119 (1988), 162 n. 13; *Annual Register*, xxviii (1784), 209; *DNB*, s.v. 'Mackintosh, Sir James'. Mackintosh may also have been the anonymous reviewer of Madame de Staël's *Reflexions sur le suicide* who turned his review into a qualified defence of self-killing: *Edinburgh Review* (1813), 424–32.

[18] B. T. Gates, *Victorian Suicide: Mad Crimes and Sad Histories* (Princeton, 1988), 3–5.

custom. He echoed the words of Mackintosh, who had referred to Lennard's bill in his speech on his own resolutions: 'the punishment inflicted in the case of suicide was rather an act of malignant and brutal folly. It was useless as regarded the dead, and only tortured the living. The honourable member for Ipswich had given notice of a bill regarding the disgusting course pursued in cases of suicide.'[19]

These remarks recalled the sentiments of the *philosophes* and their supporters, who detested the popular beliefs implicit in the rites of desecration as superstitious brutality. Lennard announced that he anticipated no opposition to the bill, but he was wrong. Lieutenant-General William Thornton attempted to amend it, substituting dissection for profane burial, but his motion failed. The only modification that was made in the bill during its passage through both houses was the addition of a paragraph making it clear that the repeal of desecration did not mean that ministers were required to perform the usual rites over the bodies of suicides. The services they provided were left to their own devising.[20] Some clergymen appear to have resisted pressure to read the burial service over suicides, and their right to do so remained controversial. Indeed, there is evidence that clerical conservatives were more vociferous between 1850 and 1880 than they had been when the 1832 act was passed. The controversy was, as Anderson has demonstrated, revivified by new challenges to the authority of the Anglican clergy. The scruples of ministers, however, neither overcame the lay élite's conviction that profane burial was 'revolting to every natural feeling' (as the *Annual Register* put it in 1823) nor arrested the trend toward greater leniency. That trend was promoted not only by the diffusion of Enlightenment sentiments but also by events that appeared to be unconnected to the interment of suicides. 'Thus between 1852 and 1880', Anderson concludes, 'as an unintended consequence of its concern with the quite unrelated issues of public health and Nonconformist citizenship, Parliament ensured that no suicide, even one adjudged *felo de se*, need be buried without religious rites of some kind.'[21] The Burial Act of 1880 and a short amendment to it two years later finally removed the last traces of ritual disgrace from the law.

[19] *Hansard*, NS, ix, col. 414.

[20] *Journal of the House of Commons*, lxxviii (4 Feb. 1823–25 Nov. 1823), 346, 351, 359, 373, 384, 393, 417, 425, 437, 455, 464; *Hansard*, NS, ix, col. 550; *The Times* (28 May 1823), 2; 4 Geo. IV, cp. 52.

[21] *Annual Register*, lxvii (1823), 88–9; O. Anderson, *Suicide in Victorian and Edwardian England*, (Oxford, 1987); Gates, *Victorian Suicide*, 152. For another prominent commendation of the 1823 Act, see *Gentleman's Magazine*, cxxxiv (1823), 549–50.

Why did parliament finally repeal the fiscal punishments for suicide? Partly the answer must lie in the belated success of the Enlightenment call for law reform; and partly it must also lie in the development of a new philosophy of punishment and deterrence, about which many historians have recently written. But the answer also lies in a slow shift in emphasis away from punishment and toward prevention. The most conspicuous sign of this change was the formation of the Humane Society in 1774. Originally founded to rescue drowning victims by reviving them with artificial respiration, the society quickly discovered that one of its main functions was hauling would-be suicides out of the water. In an anniversary sermon preached in 1797, George Gregory noted that the society's members had attempted to save over 500 atempted suicides since its foundation, and that they had succeeded in over 350 cases. He appended a collection of more than thirty remarkable instances to his text in its printed version to prove their effectiveness.[22] Undoubtedly more important than the Humane Society, however, was the gradual emergence of the common-law crime of attempted suicide. For most of the centuries that suicide had been a crime, it had not been against the law to try to kill oneself. During the eighteenth century, suicide attempters had been confined in madhouses, gaols, and workhouses to prevent them from succeeding in their self-murderous acts. But arrests for attempted suicide itself seem to have been rare.[23] In London, people began to be arrested for attempted suicide in increasing numbers after 1830, and the crime was recognized by the courts in 1850, if not before. By the later part of the century, authorities all over England arrested—and occasionally tried—people for suicide attempts.[24]

Anderson argues persuasively that the emergence of the crime of attempted suicide had its own dynamics, not directly generated by concern over the effectiveness of the laws against suicide itself. She points out that it was only after the development of the new police force that widespread arrests for attempted suicide were practicable, and she characterizes the new rigour toward attempters as one aspect of a crack-down on public disorder, which was the main preoccupation of

[22] G. Gregory, *A Sermon on Suicide, Preached ... At the Anniversary of the Royal Humane Society*, 2nd edn. (London, 1797). The annual reports of the Society are also illuminating; an incomplete set may be found in Bodl.

[23] Anna Clark informs us that she has seen 18th-century examples in London court records: Personal communication, Dec. 1987.

[24] Anderson, *Suicide in England*, 282–94; *R.* v. *Doody* (1854).

the force.[25] She is undoubtedly correct, but paradoxically the new severity was also a precondition for legal leniency. The criminalization of attempted suicide answered the persistent complaint of would-be reformers that the law of suicide punished the innocent and spared the guilty. After about 1850, the law could be seen to penalize those who might benefit from punishment, now conceived of as an instrument of rehabilitation. This may have extended its life—or, more accurately, protracted its death. As Anderson has shown, repeal of the remaining penalties met with some stiff opposition, and after 1882 conservatives called again on juries to abandon the temporary insanity verdict as a hypocrisy and convict self-slayers as *felones de se*. A few coroners' juries responded from time to time, but even in the year of greatest severity, 1909, only about one in twenty suicides was stigmatized.[26] The saga of the crime of self-killiing did not finally end until 1961, when parliament at last repealed the common-law felony of self-murder, relieving coroners and physicians from the burden of certifying that everyone who killed himself had done so when 'the balance of his mind was disturbed'.[27] The law was by then a mere fossil. It had become almost extinct over a century earlier, and efforts by conservatives to keep it alive had met with little success.

Even if Victorians were unwilling to resume the punishments that their ancestors had inflicted on suicides and their families, they still believed that self-killing was bad. The families of suicides shrank from the stigma such a death attached to them; they tried as hard as ever to conceal suicides whenever they could. Moralists and rural folk—at least in some parts of the country—continued to wish that there were acceptable ways to disgrace people who killed themselves and to deter those who were tempted to follow their example. The belief that self-murder was prompted by Satan survived in rural districts of England and in the Celtic highlands of Wales and Scotland: it is the central device in James Hogg's spellbinding *Private Memoirs and Confessions of a Justified Sinner*, which was first published in 1824.[28] Folklorists throughout the century

25 Anderson, *Suicide in England*, 282–4.

26 Ibid. 264–5.

27 Suicide Act, 1961, S.I.

28 Historians of suicide in 19th-century England have been unsure how much emphasis to place on evidence indicating the survival of folk beliefs in diabolical instigation and suicides' ghosts: compare, Anderson, *Suicide in England*, 234–4; Gates, *Victorian Suicide*, 6–8; J. Hogg, *The Private Memoirs and Confessions of a Justified Sinner*, ed. J. Wain (Harmondsworth, 1983). Hogg wrote a letter to *Blackwood's Magazine* in 1823, which purports to be a true account of the suicide recounted in the novel; it presumes the common folk believe in the devil's immanent reality: ibid., 230–4; D. Groves, 'James Hogg's *Confessions:* New Information', *The Review of English Studies*, xl (1989), 240–2.

reported that the burying-places of suicides were supposed to be haunted.[29] The practice of burying suicides who were *non compos mentis* on the north side of churchyards where unbaptized infants, excommunicates, and executed criminals lay seems in the nineteenth century to have satisfied a strong, lingering aversion to the legitimation of self-destruction. 'We are all aware', a Scottish correspondent wrote to *Notes and Queries* in 1852, 'of the popular repugnance to permitting the bodies of suicides to be interred within the "consecrated" or "hallowed" precincts of the churchyard.'[30]

It is very hard to gauge the force of such sentiments, particularly the power of folk beliefs in diabolical instigation and the ghosts of suicides. Flora Thompson, for instance, recalled that when she was a girl, in the 1880s, old fears of the supernatural still retained some of their potency:

> Ghost stories and stories of witchcraft lingered and were half believed. No one cared to go after dark to the cross roads where Dickie Bracknell, the suicide, was buried with a stake through his entrails, or to approach the barn out in the fields where he had hung himself some time at the beginning of the century. Bobbing lights were said to have been seen and gurgling sounds heard there.[31]

Olive Anderson quotes this passage, stressing the fact that the villagers of Lark Rise only 'half believed' in Dickie's ghost and arguing that talk of the devil driving people to kill themselves was merely a figure of speech. There is, she asserts, 'little evidence of taboo, unique dread, or primitive horror' of suicide.[32]

Anderson is right to be dissatisfied with the assertions of early anthropologists and historians who dwelt on the 'primitive horror' suicide inspired among uncivilized peoples and ignorant rustics. But the evidence suggests, in fact, that the fears that had been deepened in the Tudor and Stuart centuries wore themselves out very slowly.

[29] *Notes and Queries*, 1st ser., iv (1851), 212, 329–30; 9th ser., v (1900), 288. See also, D. Jones-Baker, *The Folklore of Hertfordshire* (London, 1977), 83; K. Palmer, *The Folklore of Somerset* (London, 1976), 45; R. L. Tongue, *Somerset Folklore*, ed. K. M. Briggs (London, 1965), 104; W. W. Sikes, *British Goblins* (Boston, 1881), 146–7; J. C. Atkinson, *Forty Years in a Moorland Parish* (London, 1891), 216–17. For literary examples of suicides' ghosts, see Gates, *Victorian Suicide*, 9, 11, 109–17.

[30] *Notes and Queries*, 1st. ser., v (1852), 272. See also, Brand, *Observations on Popular Antiquities*, ii. 290–9; G. L. Gomme (ed.), *The Gentleman's Magazine Library: Popular Superstitions* (London, 1884), 205–6. It should be stressed that the placement of the bodies of suicides judged *non compos mentis* was highly various. Some were consigned to the north side; others were interred in family vaults or other favoured locations.

[31] F. Thompson, *Lark Rise to Candleford* (Harmondsworth, 1973), 266.

[32] Anderson, *Suicide in England*, 233–7.

Thompson's recollection is significant. After at least sixty years, the people of her village still recalled Dickie Bracknell's name, where he had been buried, and how and where he had killed himself.[33] Even if they only 'half believed' tales about his ghost, they had obviously preserved the memory of his death and burial longer than the recollection of most or all of his contemporaries. Suicide remained a singular way to die; it still aroused in the common people, at least in some rural areas and in some cases, a sense of danger, a sense that it was not like other sins, not like other ways of dying.

The conviction that suicide was supernaturally evil and dangerous had, as we have seen, a very long and complex history. It was never simply a 'primitive horror' or an irrational superstition. It was instead the result of a concatenation of secular and religious change, of the conjunction of theology and folklore, and of the convergence of élite and popular beliefs. Moreover, it illustrates the ways in which both the ruling élite and the plebeian classes appropriated cultural practices and ideals. The clergy reinterpreted and accepted popular beliefs and rituals about the supernatural causes and consequences of self-murder; the common people embraced the clerical notion that suicide was a diabolical crime without abandoning their conviction that supernatural forces that God was not using for his purposes might provoke it. The very gradual decline of the early modern conception of suicide was every bit as complicated as its rise. That the country folk eventually abandoned the last vestiges of earlier convictions, no one doubts. But they remained meaningful for centuries after they had arisen, and if we can understand why certain sorts of people in certain places continued to 'half believe' in them even in the nineteenth century, we shall understand more about the disenchantment of the world, the sociology and geography of secularization. We have in this book tried to start that task by tracing the history of suicide through the centuries in which it was by turns criminalized and decriminalized, mystified and demystified.

[33] A still more vivid ghost story is recounted by Atkinson, *Forty Years in a Moorland Parish*, 216–7. Atkinson remarks, and Anderson stresses, that suicides were buried in remote places because their ghosts were restless and not because of any 'intended scorn, or horror, or abhorrence'. It is not precisely clear what Atkinson meant, but we think that his distinction refers to the aplomb (or even offhandedness) that people who believe in supernatural forces and practise rituals to placate them often seem to display. This is an implicit theme in many anthropological accounts of belief and ritual, and it has been noted by historians as well. See e.g., Richardson, *Death, Dissection and the Destitute*, ch. 1, esp. p. 17; Sabean, *Power in the Blood*, ch. 6.

# APPENDICES

# APPENDIX 1

## *Sources*

THIS book is based on a very wide range of sources, printed and manuscript. Most of the actual cases of suicide we located (around 20,000 in all) were recorded in coroners' inquisitions and newspapers; information about attitudes and responses to suicides were widely scattered in almost every conceivable kind of document. The vast number of suicides recorded in inquisitions obliged us to treat that data statistically, and we discuss the methods we used and problems we encountered in Appendix 2. Two kinds of records that we did not use systematically were parish registers and ecclesiastical court cases. Both contain potentially interesting information, but both proved too difficult to exploit for this study. Embarrassingly, there were also sets of records that fell within the scope of our research that we simply missed.

As part of a pilot study, we surveyed all of the parish registers for the period published by the Yorkshire Archaeological Society. We found that very few of the Yorkshire suicides recorded in the inquisition data were noticed in the relevant registers, and the total number of suicides that were mentioned in them was very small. Moreover, the burials that were recorded with any explanatory comment at all were rather often distinguished by acts of leniency.[1] Because Yorkshire offered the best opportunities for supplementing inquisition data with parish register data, this disappointing experience persuaded us that it would have been a luxury to spend the time and money required to read a much larger sample of the surviving registers.

The difficulties presented by parish register evidence are especially regrettable because they complicate the attempt to demonstrate conclusively that profane burial was the norm in the Tudor and Stuart periods. There are, however, several good reasons for believing that lenient treatment was exceptional. First, coroners were supposed to issue certificates, ordering the interment of self-murderers in

[1] It would be desirable to be able to quantify this impression, but because the numbers involved are so small and are drawn from registers whose keepers adopted very different and incompatible habits of record-keeping (a very few were chatty; many laconic in the extreme) the numbers would not be meaningful.

a public highway.[2] Second, an Elizabethan bishop's licence to allow a suicide to be buried in a churchyard survives, which suggests that episcopal intervention was necessary to avoid profane burial.[3] Third, the very rare instances of payments for profane burial record the same fees, which suggests that there may have been a customary level of payment for the ritual.[4] Finally, when Tudor and Stuart commentators wrote about profane burial, they implied that the practice was usual. John Weever, for instance, remarked 'we use to bury such as lay violent hands upon themselves, in or neare to the highwayes, with a stake thrust through their bodies'. Now obsolete in the present tense, this construction of 'to use' meant 'we are wont to' or 'it is customary to' in seventeenth-century English.[5] If all of these admittedly weak bits of evidence do not satisfactorily account for the absence of most suicides from the appropriate registers, at least they should shift the burden of proof to those who wish to maintain that the small number of burials that are described in the registers were typical.

Ecclesiastical court records are a less obvious and more difficult source. There is no doubt that some actions concerning the burial of suicides and probate of their wills found their way into the church courts. But very few of those records have been printed, and they lie buried in vast and mostly unindexed repositories scattered around Britain. Even the leading cases mostly remain in manuscript. Finally, we found the history of the ecclesiastical law of suicide extremely baffling. The main points are easy enough to discover; but the evolution of the law and its application proved impossible to unriddle in detail with confidence. Neither our own efforts, nor the advice of experts in the field got us very far. The subject will best be tackled by scholars well versed in ecclesiastical law and records who discover the relevant cases in the course of their research into broader topics.[6]

As if all this special pleading were not enough, we have also to confess that we simply overlooked some potentially important sets of records. In 1982, Michael MacDonald wrote to over forty record offices listed in *Record Repositories*

2 Unfortunately, very few early examples survive, since these orders were directed to the churchwardens of the parish in which the death occurred. For a printed paraphrase of a 1590 order, see T. R. Forbes, *Chronicle from Aldgate* (New Haven, 1971), 164–5. These orders were more commonly saved by punctilious coroners in the 18th cent. They may be found bundled with *felo de se* inquisitions in the Westminster Inquisitions and London Inquisitions, for example.

3 Moore, *Full Inquiry into Suicide*, i. 308.

4 Compare, for example, PRO, KB9/769/3, m. 227; KB 9/772/1, m. 181.

5 J. Weever, *Ancient Funerall Monuments* (London, 1631), 22; *Oxford English Dictionary*, 1st edn., s.v. 'use.' Note also William Samson's declaration that burial with a stake through the body was 'the custom of the Country': *The Vow Breaker*, ed. H. Wallrath, Materialien zur Kunde des älteren Englischen Dramas, no. 42 (Louvain, 1942), II. iv. 123–6.

6 G. R. Elton admonishes: 'Only young scholars, still enthusiastic, physically strong, and possessed of a sound digestion, are advised to tackle these materials.' After a brief foray into them, we decided he is right, and neither of us any longer meets all of the requirements: G. R. Elton, *England: 1200–1640* (Ithaca, 1969), 105.

*in Great Britain*, enquiring whether they possessed inquisitions or other documents pertinent to the study of suicide. The archives to which he wrote were selected because their printed guides hinted at the existence of such records, because allusions to them could be found in printed sources, or simply because the place in question seemed promising because of the range of documents that survive. Between September 1982 and May 1983, he visited two dozen archives whose responses indicated that they had continuous runs of inquisition records. He also travelled to some archives that had not replied or had replied discouragingly, because he had reason to suspect that there might nevertheless be important documents to examine. We later learned of sets of records, almost all of them in municipal archives of variouis kinds, that he had not found. These are now displayed fully and in precise detail in J. Gibson and C. Rogers, *Coroner's Records in England and Wales*, Federation of Family History Societies (Birmingham, 1989), which appeared after this book had been submitted for publication. Gibson and Rogers's splendid guide should be the starting-point for all future students of suicide, accidents, and other sorts of sudden death in England, including those who wish to develop or refute the arguments of this book.[7] We trust that the range of inquisitions we have examined provides a firm foundation for this study, but there are several sets we should have liked to have been able to see in time to add them to our data base.

[7] Gibson and Rogers located several good sets of inquisitions in record offices to which we wrote and that MacDonald visited without learning of them or even suspecting that they existed.

# APPENDIX 2

## *Statistical Problems and Summaries*

SEVERAL intractable problems confront historians who try to analyse statistically the data contained in early modern coroners' inquisitions, some of which have been discussed in Chapter 7. The largest difficulties are posed by the uneven pattern of record survival, itself a consequence of several factors: jurisdictional anomalies, the variable diligence of coroners, the rise and decline of reporting to the central government, and shifts in legal and customary practice in the eighteenth century. The largest cache of inquisitions is filed among the Ancient Indictments of King's Bench; others may be found filed separately in the records of the Palatinates of Lancaster and Cheshire. The King's Bench inquisitions are more or less complete for the period 1485 to about 1714; many that have not survived in the indictment files are noted in the court's controlment rolls (KB 29).[1] Because there are so many inquisitions in the King's Bench series, and they are cross-referenced in the controlment rolls, it should be possible in theory to reconstruct an accurate yearly count of the suicides reported to the central government. Indeed, several historians seem to have believed that such a count would yield a virtually complete record of suicide in Tudor and Stuart England.[2]

But of course the ambit of King's Bench's jurisdiction did not extend over the whole kingdom. Coroners in many cities and towns, such as London, Norwich, and Bristol, were not required to return their inquisitions to the court, and they did not normally do so. Moreover, Admiralty and the palatinates, whose separate collections of inquisitions are far from continuous, were not the only liberties that fell outside the court's jurisdiction. There was, for instance, a coroner of the Verge, a nominal geographical space surrounding the king's court, who could hold inquests in the jurisdictions of other coroners. No records of this office survive. More seriously, there were many smaller liberties that apparently did not have to return verdicts, or at least did not choose to do so and got away with it. How many or where they were, the present authors do not know. Traces of

[1] Easily the best discussion of the surviving records of King's Bench, how they were produced, what their weaknesses are, and the factors that affect their accuracy is S. J. Stevenson, 'The Rise of Suicide Verdicts in South-East England, 1530–1590: The Legal Process', *Continuity and Change*, ii (1987), 37–75.

[2] For instance, M. Zell, 'Suicide in Pre-Industrial England', *Social History*, xi (1986), 303–17.

only a few emerge from time to time. To determine correctly the geographical coverage of the surviving King's Bench records, it would therefore be necessary to do detailed local research to locate as precisely as possible jurisdictions whose records are missing.

These geographical faults in the most complete series of surviving inquisitions have had serious consequences for this study. In the first place, as we explained in Chapter 7, they contributed to our belief that it was futile to try to reconstruct an accurate *national* suicide rate. We carried the attempt to do this as far as we could before we put it aside. Using Murphy's notes, MacDonald correlated a large number of inquisitions with entries in the controlment rolls, attempting to discover patterns of missing records. Unfortunately, this laborious process was complicated by mistaken entries in the controlment rolls, and while it soon became apparent that the totals for individual years could be corrected by this method, the corrections did not greatly alter the pattern of the suicide rate based on either the surviving inquisitions or the entries in the controlment rolls. It is easy to see why when one compares graphs of surviving inquisitions and entries. (See Figures A2.1 and A2.2.) We therefore decided to set aside the task of matching the 27,000 inquisitions and entries and to correlate the two sets of records only for years that seemed particularly interesting, either because of

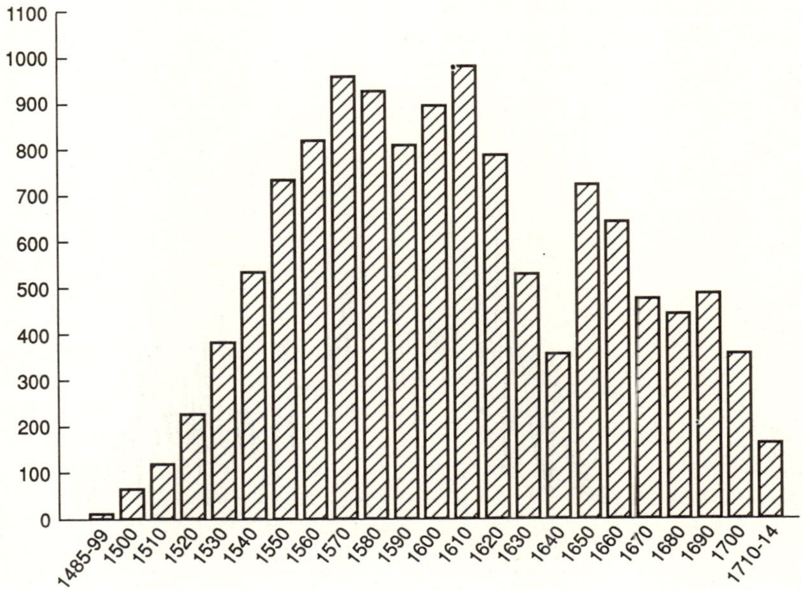


FIG. A2.1. Reported suicides, 1485–1714

*Source*: PRO, KB 9, 10, 11, 140; PL 26; HCA 1.

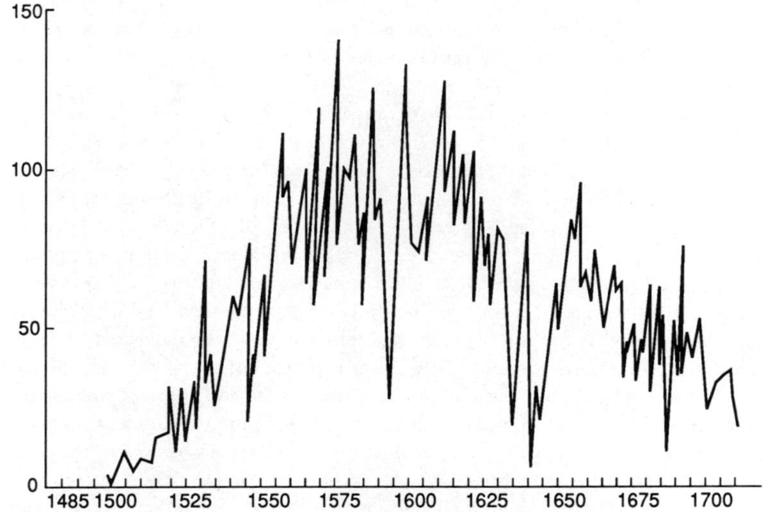


FIG. A.2.2. Surviving suicide inquisitions, 1485–1714
*Source*: PRO, KB 9, 10, 11, 140; PL 26; HCA 1.

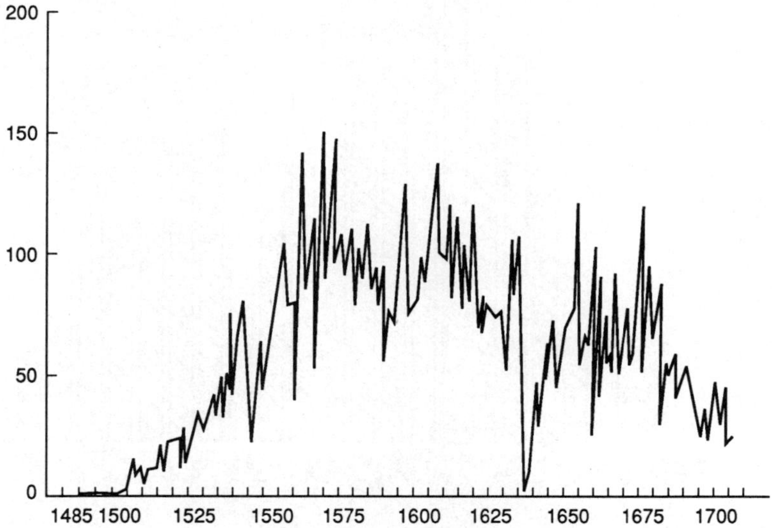


FIG. A2.3. Enrolled suicide verdicts, 1485–1714
*Source*: PRO, KB 29.

unusual (e.g. high or low) patterns in the documents or because of notable events (e.g. abnormally high prices) that might be somehow connected with the incidence of suicide.

But it was not just the computation of an overall suicide rate that proved too difficult and unrewarding to justify the effort. We also failed to find meaningful variations in the pattern of suicide by region, type of settlement, and social group. The reasons for our failure in the last instance are set out in the Introduction and Chapter 7. The most obvious geographical comparisons we wished to make were between rural and urban settings and between regions with differing economies and social structures. The rural/urban comparison was unilluminating for two simple reasons. First, up until about 1750, the evidence is overwhelmingly rural. Only a few towns of secondary importance, such as York and Southampton, returned inquisitions to King's Bench. (And even they may not have returned them all.) Second, when for the eighteenth century sets of rural and urban inquisitions do both become available, there appear to be few notable differences between them. A few mysterious anomalies aside, we could find none of the dramatic differences of the kind Anderson was able to discover for the Victorian period. No doubt it would be possible to pursue this topic further and to identify subtle differences we did not detect. We concluded that the task would be best left to students who conducted intensive research on a particular county or region, so that suicides could be traced and fine comparisons made. For this task, coroners' bills, preserved in local record offices in Quarter Sessions records, would be an indispensable eighteenth-century source.

Perhaps even more regrettably, we were unable, given the limitations of the King's Bench data, to construct comparative suicide rates for different economic and social settings. In a pioneering article, using sophisticated methodology and based on exhaustive research, S. J. Stevenson has found that there were some differences in the pattern of suicide in wood pastoral and mixed farming regions in East Anglia. This is exciting, because it hints at fundamental contrasts in cultural and social life (and death) in those different ecologies. The statistical differences were not great, however, and they were age-specific: 'For the most part . . . there is no conclusive evidence to demonstrate any polarity between agrarian regions, save that the "wood-pasture" region appears to have implied a greater suicide risk among the youngest.'[3] We attempted to replicate Stevenson's work on a national basis, but our findings were not statistically significant nor did they support his findings. This does not mean that he is wrong; in fact, we think that the contrasts may be even greater and more varied than he was able to discover in the East Anglia data. Two problems prevented us from performing a really adequate test of his hypothesis. First, our data are coded by county, but regions crossed county boundaries. Second, ages were recorded systematically only by East Anglian (especially Essex) coroners. Except for the Norwich

[3] S. J. Stevenson, 'Social and Economic Contributions to the Pattern of 'Suicide' in South-East England, 1530–1590', *Continuity and Change*, ii (1987), 247.

Table A2.1. *Summary of Inquisition Data, 1485–1714*

| Years | *Felo de se* | *Non compos mentis* | Mixed | Ambiguous | Total |
|---|---|---|---|---|---|
| 1485–99 | 6 | | | | 6 |
| 1500–9 | 61 | 1 | | | 62 |
| 1510–9 | 108 | 1 | 5 | | 114 |
| 1520–9 | 216 | 10 | 1 | | 227 |
| 1530–9 | 343 | 18 | 11 | 11 | 383 |
| 1540–9 | 499 | 15 | 14 | 5 | 533 |
| 1550–9 | 714 | 7 | 10 | 1 | 732 |
| 1560–9 | 798 | 14 | 4 | 1 | 817 |
| 1570–9 | 940 | 15 | 4 | | 959 |
| 1580–9 | 909 | 5 | 8 | 1 | 923 |
| 1590–9 | 797 | 5 | 9 | | 811 |
| 1600–9 | 873 | 7 | 14 | | 894 |
| 1610–19 | 967 | 1 | 8 | | 976 |
| 1620–9 | 751 | 17 | 12 | | 780 |
| 1630–9 | 503 | 12 | 9 | | 524 |
| 1640–9 | 328 | 22 | 6 | | 356 |
| 1650–9 | 654 | 6 | 60 | | 720 |
| 1660–9 | 573 | 54 | 12 | 1 | 640 |
| 1670–9 | 409 | 51 | 9 | 1 | 470 |
| 1680–9 | 363 | 70 | 5 | 5 | 443 |
| 1690–9 | 337 | 135 | 14 | | 486 |
| 1700–9 | 202 | 149 | | | 351 |
| 1710–14 | 93 | 63 | | | 156 |
| TOTALS | 11,444 | 678 | 215 | 26 | 12,363 |

*Note*: Inquisitions that could not have been dated have been omitted.

*Sources*: PRO, KB 9, 10, 11, 140, PL 26, HCA 1.

data, the evidence about ages of suicides elsewhere seems to be too random to be useful for a nation-wide study.

Once again, the best way to proceed seems to us to be try to replicate Stevenson's work in selected regions or counties, trying where possible to learn about the circumstances of individual cases. In sum, the solutions to many of the problems we confronted in our statistical exercises lie in more intensive local research and subsequent comparative analysis and not, we think, in attempting either to refine the national data set or improve upon the crude statistical techniques we have employed to analyse it. The data have to be improved before they can be subjected to more refined and more fruitful manipulations. J. A. Sharpe is doing just this, using inquisitions from one or more northern counties,

Table A2.2. *Summary of Inquest Data, 1660–1799*

| | 1660–9 | 1670–9 | 1680–9 | 1690–9 | 1700–9 | 1710–19 | 1720–9 | 1730–9 | 1740–9 | 1750–9 | 1760–9 | 1770–9 | 1780-9 | 1790–9 | Totals |
|---|---|---|---|---|---|---|---|---|---|---|---|---|---|---|---|
| King's Bench (England) | | | | | | | | | | | | | | | |
| *Felo de se* | 573 | 409 | 363 | 337 | 202 | 93 | 0 | 0 | 0 | 0 | 0 | 0 | 0 | 0 | 1,977 |
| *Non compos mentis* | 54 | 51 | 70 | 135 | 149 | 63 | 0 | 0 | 0 | 0 | 0 | 0 | 0 | 0 | 522 |
| TOTAL | 627 | 460 | 433 | 472 | 351 | 156 | 0 | 0 | 0 | 0 | 0 | 0 | 0 | 0 | 2,499 |
| North-west counties | | | | | | | | | | | | | | | |
| *Felo de se* | 2 | 0 | 0 | 3 | 2 | 6 | 6 | 6 | 6 | 1 | 0 | 1 | 0 | 1 | 34 |
| *Non compos mentis* | 0 | 0 | 0 | 1 | 1 | 1 | 10 | 3 | 2 | 9 | 39 | 49 | 72 | 15 | 202 |
| TOTAL | 2 | 0 | 0 | 4 | 3 | 7 | 16 | 9 | 8 | 10 | 39 | 50 | 72 | 16 | 236 |
| Western counties | | | | | | | | | | | | | | | |
| *Felo de se* | 0 | 0 | 0 | 0 | 0 | 0 | 0 | 2 | 11 | 13 | 26 | 9 | 13 | 4 | 78 |
| *Non compos mentis* | 0 | 0 | 0 | 0 | 0 | 0 | 1 | 2 | 20 | 68 | 81 | 80 | 72 | 48 | 372 |
| TOTAL | 0 | 0 | 0 | 0 | 0 | 0 | 1 | 4 | 31 | 81 | 107 | 89 | 85 | 52 | 450 |
| Greater London | | | | | | | | | | | | | | | |
| *Felo de se* | 0 | 0 | 0 | 0 | 0 | 0 | 0 | 0 | 0 | 0 | 4 | 1 | 2 | 7 | 14 |
| *Non compos mentis* | 0 | 0 | 0 | 0 | 0 | 0 | 0 | 0 | 0 | 0 | 146 | 188 | 358 | 379 | 1,071 |
| TOTAL | 0 | 0 | 0 | 0 | 0 | 0 | 0 | 0 | 0 | 0 | 150 | 189 | 360 | 286 | 1,085 |
| Norwich | | | | | | | | | | | | | | | |
| *Felo de se* | 0 | 0 | 0 | 0 | 0 | 1 | 1 | 8 | 13 | 16 | 2 | 0 | 0 | 0 | 41 |
| *Non compos mentis* | 0 | 0 | 0 | 0 | 0 | 17 | 10 | 26 | 25 | 40 | 32 | 27 | 11 | 5 | 193 |
| TOTAL | 0 | 0 | 0 | 0 | 0 | 18 | 11 | 34 | 38 | 56 | 34 | 27 | 11 | 5 | 234 |
| Grand totals | | | | | | | | | | | | | | | |
| *Felo de se* | 575 | 409 | 363 | 340 | 204 | 100 | 7 | 16 | 30 | 30 | 32 | 11 | 15 | 12 | 2,144 |
| *Non compos mentis* | 54 | 51 | 70 | 136 | 150 | 81 | 21 | 31 | 47 | 117 | 298 | 344 | 513 | 447 | 2,360 |
| TOTAL | 629 | 460 | 433 | 476 | 354 | 181 | 28 | 47 | 77 | 147 | 330 | 355 | 528 | 459 | 4,504 |

*Note*: A few inquisitions from scattered locations outside these regions have been omitted from this table.

*Sources*: For England 1660–1714, PRO, KB 9, 10, 11; PL 26; HCA 1; for North-west Counties 1700–99, Cumbria Record Office [Carlisle], D/Lec/CR I; Q/11 (Cumberland); PRO, CHES 18/1–6 (Palatinate of Chester); PL 26/289–94 (Palatinate of Lancaster); for Western Counties 1729–99, PRO, KB 13 (Various South-western counties, Salisbury); *Wiltshire Coroners' Bills, 1752–1796*, ed. R. F. Hunnisett, Wiltshire Record Society, xxxvi (Devizes, 1981); Somerset Record Office, D/B/bw 1917; for Greater London 1760–99, Corporation of London Records Office, Coroners' Inquests for London and Southwark, 1788–99; Westminster Abbey Muniment Room and Library, Westminster Coroners' Records; Greater London Record Office, MJ/SPC.W; MJ/SPC.E (Middlesex); for Norwich 1670–1799, Norfolk and Norwich Record Office, Coroners' Inquests, Cases 6a–c.

and others at an earlier stage in their research are also undertaking more sophisticated statistically based studies of suicide and related phenomena on the local level.[4]

Finally, to provide a concise summary of the inquisition data we examined for this book, we have constructed Tables A2.1 and A2.2 and Figures A.1 and A.2 to show the pattern of returns from various regions over the whole period of the study. Table A.1 summarizes the inquisition data returned to King's Bench between 1485 and 1714. It includes mixed and ambiguous verdicts. It will be noted that those returns, as well as *non compos mentis* verdicts, began to be a little more common in the 1620s and 1630s than they were earlier. It is possible to speculate about the significance of this development, but the numbers are too small and the other evidence too ambiguous to make such speculations worth very much.

Table A2.2 summarizes the inquest data for the difficult period after 1660. It does not include mixed and ambiguous verdicts, since those verdicts are rarely or never found in later runs of inquisitions. The table has been arranged by region to give an indication of the geographical distributions of the various sets of coroners' records we were able to locate. It should be noticed that the number of inquisitions we found for the 1720s and 1730s was very small, and that in the later eighteenth century, much of the evidence comes from London, which is unrepresented in the earlier series. For these reasons the percentages of *non compos mentis* verdicts given in Table A2.2 ought to be taken as indicative of trends, rather than exact measures of the proportion of such verdicts that juries were returning. The tilt of the evidence toward London is offset partially by the good series of inquisitions available for Cumberland and Norwich in the later eighteenth century.

[4] Sharpe described his research to a meeting of the Social History Society at Oxford in 1987; for a summary, see *Social History Society Newsletter*, xii (1987), 6–7.

# BIBLIOGRAPHY

## *Manuscripts and Periodicals*

The list that follows includes the manuscripts consulted and the periodicals cited in the text. After some reflection, we decided not to include modern editions of documents, primary printed material (other than periodicals), and modern scholarship. This is because so little of the vast quantity of relevant primary sources contains more than a few notices of suicides or a passage or two devoted to the subject; the exceptions are almost all concerned with the religious and philosophical issues raised by suicide. For tracts related to that subject the reader may turn to Richard Greaves, *Religion and Society in Elizabethan England* (Minneapolis, 1981), Wymer, *Suicide and Despair*, and S. E. Sprott, *The English Debate on Suicide* (La Salle, Ill., 1961).

### MANUSCRIPTS

#### LONDON

*Public Record Office*

King's Bench, Ancient Indictments, Coroners' Inquisitions (KB 9, 10, 11)
King's Bench, Coroners' Inquisitions (KB 13, 14, 140)
King's Bench, Controlment Rolls (KB 29)
King's Bench, Precedent Books (KB 15/40, 45; KB 33/12, 25)
Palatinate of Lancaster, Coroners' Inquisitions (PL 26)
Palatinate of Chester, Coroners' Inquisitions (CHES 18)
High Court of Admiralty, Coroners' Inquisitions (HCA 1)
Star Chamber, Almoners' Suits (STAC 2–8)
Requests, Suits over Suicides' Goods (REQ 2)

*British Library*

Ralph Thoresby's extracts from Diary of Dr Henry Sampson (Add. MS 4460)
William Cole to Horace Walpole on the Suicide of John Damer (Add. MS 5824)
Sir John Harington, 'Whether It Be Dampnation for a Man to Kill Hym Self' (Add. MS 27632)

Roger North, 'On Self-Homicide' (Add. MS 32526)
Memorandum on Disposal of Suicides' Goods (Cotton MS Vesp. C. XIV)
Records Relating to the Coroner of the City of London (Hargrave 142)
Notes on Law of Suicide (Hargrave 146)
Sir Geoffrey Gilbert, 'A Discourse on Personal Property' (Hargrave 265)
Notes on the Death of the Earl of Essex (Harleian MS 1221; Sloane MS 78)
Suicide note of William Doddington (Lansdowne MS 99, No. 32)
Request to Bury a Suicide in the Churchyard (Lansdowne MS 825)
Nehemiah Wallington, 'Gods Judgement of Sabbath Breakers' (Sloane MS 1457)
Isaac Brereton to Edward Cave on the Suicide of Thomas Beach (Stowe MS 748)

*Dr Williams's Library*

John Jones, Letters on Enthusiasm (MS 39. B 24)
Diary of William Bagshaw (MS 38. 122)

*Guildhall Library*

Nehemiah Wallington, 'A Record of the Mercies of God: or a Thankfull Remembrance' (Guildhall MSS 204, 205)

*Corporation of London Record Office*

Coroners' Inquisitions for the City of London and Southwark, 1785–99

*Greater London Record Office*

Coroners' Inquisitions for Middlesex, 1780–1800 (MJ/SPC.W; MJ/SPC.E)

*Westminster Abbey Library and Muniments Room*

Coroners' Inquisitions for Westminster, 1760–99

AYLESBURY

*Buckinghamshire Record Office*

Earl of Buckinghamshire's List of Notable Suicides, 1798 (D/MH, Private Papers A 14)

BRISTOL

*Avon Central Reference Library*

Diary of William Dyer (MSS 20095–6)

CARLISLE

*Cumbria Record Office*

Records of the Liberties of Cockermouth and Egremont, Coroners' Inquisitions, 1610–1799 (D/Lec/CR I)

Quarter Sessions Petitions, Coroners' Bills, 1759–90 (Q 11)
Quarter Sessions Minute Book, Morland v. Lowthian (Q/1/2, p. 429)
Gosforth Parish Register (PX/37/1)

CHELMSFORD

*Essex Record Office*

Records of the Liberty of Writtle, Coroners' Inquisitions (D/DP/M 607/1, 12)
Records of the Borough of Maldon, Coroners' Inquisitions (D/B 3/3.79)
Records of the Borough of Sokens, Coroners' Inquisitions (Cr/S1)
Records of the Borough of Chipping Waldon, Coroners' Inquisitions (D/DAd 20)
Records of the Borough of Witham, Coroners' Inquisitions (D/P 30/28/9)
Parish Register of Great Hallingbury (D/P. 27/2, 9)
Inquisition on Hannah Baldwin (D/DHt/T140/100)

DORCHESTER

*Dorset Record Office*

Miscellaneous Coroners' Inquisitions, 1698–1753 (D/131/X8)

EXETER

*Devon Record Office*

Miscellaneous Coroners' Inquisitions

MAIDSTONE

*Kent Archives Office*

Folkstone Coroners' Inquisitions (Radnor MSS, U20/04/1–3)
New Romney Borough Records, Coroners' Inquisitions (NR/J/JC)

MANCHESTER

*John Rylands Library*

Methodist Archives, MS Autobiographies and Diaries of Susanna Designe, John Hardy, Samuel Hodgson, William Holder, Thomas Rankin, Richard Rodda, Hester Ann Rogers, James Rogers, John Valton, and Zachariah Yewdall

MATLOCK

*Derbyshire Record Office*

Records of the Honour of Tutbury: Coroners' Inquisitions, 1665–1713

OXFORD

*Bodleian Library*

Medical Practice of Richard Napier (Ashmole MSS: 60 vols. Full listing in MacDonald, *Mystical Bedlam*, 300–2)
Anonymous Notes on *Biathanatos* (Rawlinson MS C. 522)

NORWICH

*Norfolk and Norwich Record Office*

Norwich Coroners' Inquisitions, 1669–1799 (Cases 6a–c)

PRESTON

*Lancashire Record Office*

Petition to Move the Body of Elizabeth Seed, *felo de se* (QSP 1248/5)

ST ALBANS

*Hertfordshire Record Office*

Diary of Lady Sara Cowper (Pensanger MS D/EP/F29)

TAUNTON

*Somerset Record Office*

Records of the Borough of Bridgwater, Coroners' Inquisitions

SAN MARINO, CALIFORNIA

*Huntington Library*

William Hudson's Treatise on Star Chamber (MS EL 7921)

## CONTEMPORARY PERIODICALS

*Annual Register*
*Arminian Magazine*
*Connoisseur*
*Country Journal; or, The Craftsman*
*Flying Post*
*Free-Thinker*
*Fog's Weekly Journal*
*Gentleman's Magazine*
*Historical Register*

*Humourist*
*London Evening Post*
*London Journal*
*London Review*
*Mist's Weekly Journal*
*Monthly Review*
*Norwich Gazette*
*Norwich Mercury*
*Original Weekly Journal*
*Spectator*
*Tatler*
*The Times*
*Universal Spectator and Weekly Journal*
*Weekly Journal; or, Saturday's Post*
*Whitehall Evening-Post*
*World*
Weekly Bills of Mortality, London, 1715–99
Yearly Bills of Mortality, London, 1660–1799

# Index